Acclaim for Marie Etienne's

STORKBITES

Storkbites

MARIE ETIENNE

Alluvium Books
Walnut Creek • California

For information contact:
Alluvium Books
3335 Freeman Road
Walnut Creek, California 94595
(925) 947-1282
FAX (925) 274-0733

ISBN 978-0-9748474-0-5
(Previously published by Donald S. Ellis and distributed
by Creative Arts Book Company, ISBN 0-88739-508-2)
Library of Congress Catalog Number 2003105237
Printed in the United States of America

Acknowledgments

Every Tuesday and Thursday evening for a year, I scribbled away on reams of lined white paper at Walnut Creek's Barnes & Noble while my ex-husband watched our young boys. In those twelve months, I produced two thousand handwritten pages—the first draft of *Storkbites*.

Thank you T.S. for your support.

My gratitude to the following people who zealously edited this book: Shelley Singer, Tom Jenks, Adair Lara, Cathy Luchetti, Lynn Parks, and Sally Gambrill.

A huge hug to my writing partners: Kathleen Goldin, Bibby Gignilliat, Holly Rose, Joanne Prewitt, Catherine Shepard-Haier, Lyssa Friedman, Barbara Snow, Terry Leach, and especially, Peggy Vincent.

Heartfelt appreciation to my sisters and their families who have allowed me to tell this story.

Eternal love and gratitude to my sons. There is nothing more wonderful than those eager smiles you offer me when finally I shut off the computer and run outside to ride bikes with you.

To Jerry and Steven

Storkbites

There was an old woman who lived in a shoe,
She had so many children she didn't know what to do;
She gave them some broth without any bread;
She whipped them all soundly and put them to bed.
—Mother Goose

1 ～ Louisiana, 1966

The house was quiet. Every so often, a rumble of laughter from the television in my father's study made its way to our bedroom. I brushed my doll's hair and listened for Daddy's footsteps. My sister Claire, older by two years, which made her six, hummed "This Old Man" as she looked at the pictures in her book.

Finally, the sound of heavy feet. My father cleared his throat. A door opened down the hall.

"Good night, Junebug. 'Night, Butterbean." The door shut before my sisters finished saying, "I love you, Daddy." He walked a little farther.

Another door opened. "Good night. Don't study too late."

His pace quickened. I tossed my doll and her hairbrush into the wicker basket near my bed. Claire set the book on her nightstand. We jumped into bed, just as the door opened. Daddy stood there, a smile spread across his Clark Kent face. My sister and I lay flat like soldiers in our matching blue nightgowns, waiting. With three long strides he stood at my bedside, pulling the covers up to my chin and tightly tucking the edges under my arms and legs.

"Good night, Daddy," I said, feeling as if I had been stuffed and sewn between the sheets like the feathers in my quilt. His smile broadened, and he bent down farther to touch his lips to my forehead. The smells of cologne, cigarettes, and whiskey tickled my nose.

"Good night, Sweetheartsabean."

He turned to tuck in Claire. "'Night, Ugaboo," he said, hemming her into her bed sheets.

I watched him head to the door. As he reached for the light switch, my sister and I said, just like always, together, "I love you, Daddy."

"I love you too, darlings." He paused for a moment to flash us another smile. His teeth were stained the color of old newspaper, but still I thought my father was the handsomest man in the world. "Sleep tight and don't let the bedbugs bite." He pushed the frames of his glasses up against his eyebrows. Just before his suit disappeared behind the closed door, he switched off the light. The paneled, windowless room turned black as licorice.

We called it The Darkroom. A room no one else wanted.

Momma had found out she was pregnant with me, number seven, just as they got the final drawings for our maze-like brick house on Canterbury Street in Lafayette. The architect squeezed in a seventh bedroom by pushing out the walls of a hall closet, stealing a few feet from an adjacent bedroom. As the two youngest at the time, Claire and I got The Darkroom. With the births of my little sister and baby brother, we numbered nine children, two boys and seven girls. We came along roughly every two years, except for a gap of six years between Yvette and Chess. After Chess followed Aimee, Penny, Nanette, Claire, me, Anne, and finally, Nickey.

Soon after Daddy left, I fell asleep. My body had just become heavy when the lights flicked on again. The bright yellow light burned my eyes. I squinted at Momma, swaying in the doorway, breathing hard, dressed in her pink nylon nightgown.

"Get out of bed now!" she slurred, closing the door and stumbling toward us.

I struggled against the tight bedspread. It wasn't good to keep Momma waiting. I looked over at Claire, her face buried in her pillowcase, her mess of straight brown hair going off in a thousand directions. I wanted to scream, "Get up, Claire! Don't make Momma madder!" But I didn't make a sound.

Momma stormed over to me, ripped off the covers, and yanked me out of bed. Then she grabbed Claire and dragged her to her feet. She stumbled, still half asleep. We took our places, silent, side by side, in the middle of the room. Towering over us, in a low, hard voice, Momma muttered, "Pull your panties down."

Quickly, gathering our gowns up to our chests with one hand, we slid our cotton underwear down to our ankles with the other. We watched to see who Momma would choose first. When she grabbed Claire's arm, I looked straight ahead. On the wall I could see Momma's shadow, her hand swinging across Claire's skinny shadow. Blinking away the shadows that kept trying to make me cry, I shivered. In my mind I climbed up on the painted horse in the backyard and pushed on the rubber handles till I was swinging back and forth, back and forth. Every time I heard the stinging slap on Claire's behind, my body grew stiffer and stiffer. What had we done to make Momma so angry?

When it was my turn, I squeezed my bunched-up gown tighter and secretly hoped that Momma was tired, worn out from hitting Claire. She never was. She always managed to save enough anger to give me my fair share. As she held me in place and struck my bottom, I stood as still as I could, the tears rolling down my face, trying not to jerk away.

Every time she cocked her arm, she nearly fell over, pulling me down with her. When she stumbled, I dug my toes deeper into the carpeting. I was scared that she'd fall down on top of me and I'd never get out from under.

I prayed Daddy would come. But he didn't. He never did.

Momma finished and then gave me a hard push. Her words smelled like vodka. "Get back into bed and go to sleep. I don't want to hear a word out of you."

We reached down and pulled up our panties, the elastic scratching against our tender bottoms until it snapped into place. Panting and nodding, looking happier than she had when she came in, Momma turned away and flicked off the light as we climbed into our beds and pulled up the covers. When my sister and I were alone again, I let out my breath. I heard Nanette's door open and shut. Yelling. I grabbed my pillow and climbed into bed with Claire. We held each other tight, lying on our sides. We took turns softly rubbing circles on each other's backs.

Snot and tears ran down my face. I rubbed my nose in my pillowcase, sniffling. Why didn't Daddy stop her? I pictured him sitting in the dark leather chair in his study, a cigarette burning in the owl ashtray full of butts and ashes, his eyes glued to the ten o'clock news while he sipped his Jack Daniel's and Coke.

Nanette's bedroom door opened and shut again. My older brother and sisters were next. Claire's hand stopped moving. Her fingertips pressed into my shoulder blades.

"Rise and shine, sleepyheads." We blinked. Momma was standing at the doorway, her dark brown hair pulled neatly back and twisted into a bun. Steady on her feet, bathed and dressed in her yellow knit slacks and pressed blouse, Momma held out two mugs of warm coffee-milk.

"Time to get up," she said.

Claire and I yawned and carefully pulled ourselves to a sitting position, crossing our legs under us like Indians. I lifted my face as Momma bent down. Quickly I touched my lips to her soft cheek and then pulled away. My kiss of silence. My kiss of pretend.

"Good morning, Momma," I said, taking one of the mugs she held out. Then, Claire surrendered a peck and took the offered cup.

"After you drink your coffee, help your little sister get dressed, and then come to breakfast," she told Claire, firm but sweet-like.

She was all smiles as she left, the saintliest mother in the world. I took a big sip of the sugary, creamy coffee. Vodka amnesia?

I turned to look at Claire. Her left pinkie automatically rose to her mouth. She chewed on her finger as ferociously as she did her crayons, straws, and pencils. We drank our coffee-milk with our gowns stretched taut over our knobby knees and listened to the others make their way to the kitchen. Of the three big meals Momma prepared every day, breakfast was the quickest, often just grits, bacon, and toast. Soon we'd be free to play in the backyard.

Morning dew sprinkled my bare ankles as I skipped past the new merry-go-round and swing set that Daddy had purchased from the company installing play equipment in the oil-center park. I tore a honeysuckle flower from the vines creeping along the chain-link fence that separated our backyard from the neighbors and their gang of kids. The fence sat on the edge of the coulee where we collected tadpoles in spring. But it was early June and already the ditch stood dry, cracked, and full of weeds.

After licking the drop of nectar, I yelled, "I want to get on!" Sitting next to each other on their ponies, humming to the music of the carousel, Nanette and Claire pretended not to hear or see me. "Stop, I want on. I'm gonna go tell Momma," I warned, hoping they hadn't heard her station wagon drive off just moments earlier. My mother and all the other housewives, white women we knew who didn't work, were heading down to the Winn Dixie, it seemed, to exchange pleasantries with their butchers for an extra nice cut of meat, to trade gossip for laughs. Strange accents from other parts of the country filled our local stores and schools as families poured into South Louisiana so the men could find jobs at the big oil companies.

That threat worked nearly every time. Nanette slid off her horse and walked over to the switch to turn it off. I stood next to the carousel, waiting for the horses to slow down enough so I could jump on.

"You're a baby," Nanette taunted.

"No, I'm not." I grabbed a cold, damp metal bar. Nanette flipped the switch back on and the carousel jerked forward.

"Baby, baby..." Claire joined in. Eleven months apart, they looked like twins with their matching brown eyes and long hair. Even Grandma couldn't keep their names straight half the time.

"I am not a baby. I'm four," I spat. "Anne is a baby, and you're stupid."

"Sticks and stones may break my bones but words..." Nanette yelled.

"I hate you!"

"We hate you too," they yelled back, even though none of us meant it. After Daddy, I loved Nanette and Claire best in the world.

"Wanna go swing?" Nanette asked Claire. They dismounted and jumped down, leaving me to figure out how to get off the moving carousel.

I could get off the horse by myself, but someone had always turned off the merry-go-round before I jumped to the ground. Thinking about the jump, making myself scared, I rode that horse for a long time before I gathered the courage to climb down and go to the edge of the carousel. I looked over at my sisters, swinging, not looking back at me. They absolutely were not going to help, and I was not a baby. I took a deep breath and jumped down, falling and skinning my knee.

I blew on the red scrape. It hurt but I didn't cry. I lived in the only house on the block that had a merry-go-round, and I could get down by myself, no matter what.

2 ∼ California, 1989

"Nickey, is that you? We all thought you were dead. I saw them bury you."

My brother stood perfectly still, his brown eyes jumping from me to the place in the kitchen were Momma always fixed dinner. I climbed off the stool and ran toward him.

"We've missed you," I said, grabbing his shoulders. I drew his lanky body into mine. It was Nickey all right. He smelled like a stinkbug in June, kind of sweaty and dirty but sweet after playing outside for hours.

I grabbed his hands. "Come on, Momma and Daddy are at the Duhons'. I can't wait to catch the look on their faces when they see you."

I led him out of the gate and screamed, "Race you."

Just as we started to cross West Bayou Parkway, a car came out of nowhere, honking, tires squealing. I jumped onto the driveway but Nickey froze. The driver couldn't stop. From just a couple of feet away, I watched the car ram into him, sending him flying to the side of the road. The only sound was the thud as he hit the grass.

"Nickey! Nickey!" Running. Running. Running until I reached him. He lay there, covered in blood. "No. You can't die again. It's not fair. Why'd you send him back just to take him away?"

I sat up in bed. Looking around the dim room, I saw my cosmetics scattered about the antique vanity, the empty wine bottle, and the overturned glass on my pink chair. Some of my textbooks had spilled off the bed onto the carpet. The red light on the answering machine blinked—phones messages I had ignored the night before.

I clutched my knees, rocking back and forth. Three years had passed since Nickey's suicide. While working full time, I'd enrolled in an evening MBA program at University of San Francisco, opened a card store that failed shortly after the '89 earthquake, and bought a structurally unsound condo in downtown San Francisco.

Closing my eyes, I tried to resurrect Nickey. I dreamed of him often. But he had vanished once again.

Sobbing, choking for air, my head ached. My throat felt as if I'd gargled Liquid Plumber. Why couldn't it be Saturday? Why couldn't we have another earthquake, no casualties, just one strong enough to decommission my office for a day or two? Like the no-school days of my childhood during hurricane season.

Looking at the clock, I knew it would be too early to call anyone in Louisiana. Claire and Nanette would be cranky if I woke them and their babies. And Penny would be out jogging, trying to run off her own hangover.

The ache invading my body told me I definitely had the flu. Perhaps a flu shot would help foil the virus. I pulled my address book from the nightstand and telephoned Dr. Schmidt's service. Then I dragged myself into the shower. A few hours later, at work, the doctor returned my call. We agreed to meet at his office at 7 P.M. after his hospital rounds. Even though he was my gynecologist, he'd become my de facto primary care physician. He was the only doctor I knew in San Francisco.

Rather than leave me in his deserted reception area, Dr. Schmidt invited me to wait in his office as he made a few quick phone calls. He scratched his graying mustache as he rifled through a stack of messages. I rolled and unrolled the strap to my leather handbag, praying I wouldn't have a coughing fit.

After his last phone call, he arched his back and yawned. "It's been a long day."

I smiled, trying to appear sympathetic. A hint of cologne wafted through the air as I followed him into the examining room.

"Take your shirt off."

"Can't you listen through my blouse?" I shivered to provide an excuse rather than admit I felt awkward. Usually his nurse stood beside him.

"No, too much noise from the fabric." The lines above his brow deepened as he glanced at his black sports watch. I reached for my top button and looked past his head of curly hair to the diplomas hanging on the wall. He and his wife had both attended medical school in France even though he was obviously from Brooklyn. I read her certificate and wondered why anyone would choose to specialize in ears, noses, and throats. Ear wax and boogers. Venereal diseases, though, that could be yucky, too. But at least Dr. Schmidt got to deliver babies. They both, undoubtedly, had their fill of neurotic patients like me, who called in a panic, mistaking stomach ulcers for cancer. I climbed onto the examining table and crossed my ankles.

He slid the stethoscope down my chest and ordered me to take a deep breath. Then he ran the cold metal disk along the center of my back. The hair on my arms stood upright as a chill advanced toward my neck. I felt foolish. Could he hear my heart racing?

"Your lungs sound fine. Get dressed. I'll write you a prescription for antibiotics for your throat and get you some nose spray."

He stood waiting for me in the reception area. "Here you are. Don't use the spray longer than four days."

I thanked him and headed for the door. He drummed his fingers on the desk and asked, "Hey, how were your holidays?"

A vision of my parents sloshing sherry at breakfast popped into my head. I shrugged. "I visited my family in Louisiana."

"How are you doing with the stress? Did you ever talk to a psychiatrist?"

"No. I felt better for a while, especially after the Zantac."

He glanced at the mail on the counter. I looked down at the scuffed tips of my pumps as he cleared his throat. "I'm starved. You want to grab some Chinese food? We can talk about it while we eat."

I felt my face flush. "All right. But I don't want to impose."

He shook his head and asked me to drive. I agreed, trying to remember the state of my Honda.

Why was he offering to listen to me? At my last annual exam he had offered, but I declined out of shame. I didn't want pity, but now I needed someone's advice and comfort.

"Hang on a minute." I opened the passenger door. Leaning inside, I grabbed handfuls of old Wall Street Journals, crumpled napkins, and accounting ledgers and threw them onto the backseat with the other junk. "I wasn't expecting company," I said, brushing the crumbs off the stained black upholstery.

We went to a Hunan restaurant on Clement. Six tables crammed into a narrow space filled with steam from the open kitchen. During dinner, straining what was left of my voice, I told him that I'd depleted my savings with my failed card store venture and that my debt was mounting. I was in a dead-end job that required lying on behalf of my boss to creditors, tenants, and his family. I was depressed because I hadn't dated in the two years since I'd begun graduate school at night. I wanted to start going out again, but I felt too fat. I didn't mention I frequently drank alone until I passed out. Or how I ate like a fiend, going from a size eight to a fourteen.

I whispered to him about my childhood. Nickey's suicide. He shook his head when I chronicled Momma's hospital visits. His reactions seemed nonjudgmental, so I continued on until I realized he was waving his credit card in the air to get the waitress's attention. Just like Daddy did when he'd had enough. Ashamed, I stared down at the plate of food I'd barely touched. I figured he was anxious to say good night, vowing never to invite a whiney patient with ulcers out for dinner again.

I pulled up in front of his office. Before he opened his car door, he looked at me and said, "If you're not too tired, we could have tea inside and talk some more."

He wasn't gritting his teeth waiting to get away from me? Why did he care so much? Tea sounded good, even if I wasn't sure I could squeak out another word.

Rather than entering his office again, he unlocked the door to the right. My face must have betrayed my confusion because he explained that this hall led upstairs to his house, where he and his family lived. A few minutes later, with a tray in hand, he motioned for me to follow him to a set of cream-colored sofas. He patted the cushion next to him. But that seemed too close, too awkward. I pretended not to notice his gesture and chose the opposite couch.

"We're not going to wake your family?" I nodded toward the stairs.

"They're not here." He cocked his chin to one side and smirked. "They're in France visiting my in-laws."

He poured the tea. I looked at a photograph of a dark woman with four sunburnt children. I felt like an intruder in these kids' house. "Your wife is beautiful." This somehow sounded like the right thing to say.

"She used to be. She let herself go since the children."

"Oh." I sucked in my stomach as I reached for my tea.

"So you were saying earlier that your other brother was murdered. What's that all about?" he asked, raising his *I Love Papa* mug to his lips.

I told him how Chess was drugged and dumped in a ditch. How my parents had stored some of his body parts in our deep freeze before shipping them off to a friend in Houston for an independent autopsy.

"Wait. You're telling me they put your brother's body in your freezer?" He set his cup down and moved to sit beside me.

"Well, no, not the whole body. Samples or something. That's what we were told. There was police tape all over the freezer. Then after the funeral the tape and whatever was in there disappeared," I said, feeling my legs and arms begin to tremble. I always shook when I talked about my brothers. "I'm really not sure if it was his body or his organs or what. But it was pretty creepy at the time."

"That's absurd. There's no way a hospital would release someone's body parts to a family to take home, especially if the death was under investigation." He shuddered. I turned up my hands.

"I don't know," I said, fiddling with my shirtsleeve buttons. "Maybe they do things a little different in Louisiana."

He stared at me as if I had concocted it. "It must have been a very difficult time for you and your family. How'd your parents cope with losing two sons?"

"We're survivors. Sort of, anyway. My parents drink to blot out the memories, and they don't talk about the bad stuff. I used to be terrified of seeing my brother Chess after he died. I thought he'd come back to get me."

"What do you mean *get you?*"

"I'm not sure." My voice kept breaking up. I took a sip of tea and continued. "Just that when I was doing something bad, like having sex or drinking a lot, I thought he'd show up at the foot of the stairs and grab me, maybe tell me to stop screwing up my life. But I've always been scared of ghosts. Even now I still don't sleep on my stomach because I'm scared someone will hurt me if my back is exposed and I can't see all around to protect myself."

I had his attention—I could tell by the way he leaned toward me and chewed on his lower lip as I spoke. So I talked on. I told him about a dream I had where a woman in white lay next to me in bed and I thought she was an angel to take me to heaven.

Even the warm tea didn't extinguish the chill that ran through my veins. I knew I shouldn't be talking about scary stuff so late at night, especially since I was going home to sleep by myself.

"How bizarre." Dr. Schmidt fingered his mustache. "You know, when I was in medical school I once had a similar dream. A woman appeared in my window and slowly drifted toward me. She lay down on me in a sensual yet virginal way. She felt so real. Her skin was warm and soft. Our bodies melded and we became one. I felt so, oh, I don't know, so aroused. I actually had an orgasm. I woke up in a sweat. My sheets were soaked with semen."

He looked dreamy, like he was remembering his first true love. How in the world had we detoured to this?

"I'm sorry. Have I made you uncomfortable?"

"Oh, no, it's okay." Is this why he listened to my sob story so that I'd listen to his wet dreams? I reached down and picked up my mug of tea. I had missed the warning signals. I wasn't naïve after all. I'd been tricked and seduced by other married men. But whether I was in a fog of ill health or whether I allowed my low self-esteem to convince myself that no successful Jewish doctor would have the slightest interest in me, an overweight, stressed-out Gentile, the signals flew right by.

"You know, my wife and I," he said, pausing to sigh.

I watched his fingers run along the creases of his slacks.

"Sex is so important to me, but she doesn't want it much anymore…" Here it came, man's timeless complaint. "She's not even willing to be creative, you know? Hell, if she'd lose weight, she'd probably feel like a new person." Why does he keep talking about her weight?

"Maybe." I shrugged, trying to look at my watch without his noticing. He brought my eyes back up with his fixed stare. Suddenly, he stood, reached down and took my hands. What was he thinking? He'd made it clear that he didn't even find his own wife attractive. So if he wasn't going to seduce me, he hadn't even tried to kiss me, then what.

"Follow me," he said and pulled me up from the sofa.

Don't panic. Maybe you're overreacting.

Curious, I let him steer me down the hall until we came to a dark room in the back of the house. Without turning on the lights, he guided me through the doorway and then paused. I stood perfectly still, listening to his even, deep breaths. When I felt his hands on my waist I knew I had walked right into a trap. It was too late to run. I drew in a tiny gasp of air as he eased me onto a sofa or a bed.

"Lie here," he whispered.

He climbed on top of me. You could protest or scream, I told myself. But my body didn't budge. I felt the warmth from his nostrils on my face and closed my eyes. It was simply *too* late. Like a traitor, my body had responded. He pressed his lips to mine.

"You feel so good," he whispered. His mustache tickled my ear.

His hands slowly moved from my neck to my breast and then down between my legs. Of all his patients, why me? He kissed me, pressing his lips down hard on mine. Moaning, he hurriedly unbuttoned my blouse while rubbing his hard penis on my legs. Throw him off, Marie. You must have given him the wrong kind of signal. But it felt kind of good to have someone wanting me. It had been so long.

"Stand up," he ordered.

I swung my legs and found my footing. He took off my blouse and unbuttoned my skirt, pulling it down my unshaven legs. I stepped back so he could pick it up. As my eyes adjusted to the darkness I could see the floral patterns on the daybed cover and chairs, the modest size of the room. A guestroom or possibly an au pair's room, I figured. Standing there shaking in my bra, underwear, pantyhose, and shoes, I waited while he folded my clothes and draped them over the armrest of a chair. He turned back to me, locked eyes for a moment, and then unhooked my bra. He was so quiet, so methodical. I felt like a little girl being undressed by her father and readied for bed. I swallowed hard as he removed my underwear and added it to the other garments. I listened but didn't watch as he undressed. His steady hands cupped my shoulders. He lowered me back down onto the bed and climbed on top of me. His body felt clammy and hairy. His eagerness was obvious.

"Does this feel good?" he asked, his fingers exploring between my legs.

"Yes, I guess." I felt fairly numb. What did he expect?

"You tell me what you like," he whispered. "I want to make you feel good. This is so nice." His warm breath pelted my neck.

"Relax. I'm not going to hurt you."

"Okay." I hadn't considered the possibility that he would hurt me. I tried to breathe evenly. I didn't want to appear tense and make him angry.

With one hand he rubbed between my legs, and with the other he squeezed my breasts. I wasn't sure if I was supposed to touch him, so I just lay there with my hands clutching the pillows. He kissed my mouth, harder this time. My tongue moved with his as if summoned to a primal dance. He sat up and inched down along my body, nudging my thighs with his stubble chin. "Loosen up." His mustache brushed my inner thigh and I jumped.

"Are you all right?"

"It tickles," I said, nervous.

He laughed. I tried to concentrate on what he was doing and enjoy myself. To reverse the rigor mortis that seemed to have invaded my body. But his efforts to please me were futile. When he couldn't wait any longer, he pulled away, and thrust his penis inside me. Three pumps—he stiffened and cried out in pleasure. His body collapsed on top of mine.

When he caught his breath, he whispered in my ear. "You know, I could lose my license if anyone found out about this. This has to be our little secret. Are you going to be my special girl?"

I coughed. My throat ached. "I won't tell anyone," I squeaked out.

"Good. That was really nice. Did you see how excited you got me?"

He leaned on his elbow next to me and grinned like the Cheshire Cat. The lines around his eyes deepened as he stared at me.

I didn't know what to say or what to do. I just lay there while he waited for a response. Raising my head up to his, I kissed him, assuredly, on his lips. My kiss of silence. My kiss of collusion.

His hand reached toward my face and I startled. He smiled, brushing aside a strand of blond hair caught in my eyelashes. "You *are* going to be my special girl, I can tell."

3 ~ Louisiana, 1966

I was four the first time Momma tried to kill herself. I imagine now that whatever I was doing that day was interrupted by the worried sound of Daddy saying, "Esther! Esther, wake up!" I'd poke my head out of The Darkroom to find Daddy lugging Momma down the hall. Her arms hanging limply, her eyes closed, just like my baby sister, Anne, when the maid carried her to her crib at night.

Daddy would have laid Momma across the backseat and slammed the door. I'd watch the Eldorado peel out of the driveway and then I'd run to the backyard to find my sisters and brother. We'd find a note left bedside by Momma, a note written in red crayon.

Many years later, sitting in an ICU waiting room after Momma had once again landed herself in the hospital, Aimee told me those scraggly red letters spelled: Mom, I'm sorry I was such a disappointment. I love you and Pops. She was writing to her parents, who lived 20 miles away in New Iberia, the small town where she and Daddy were both raised.

Fearing gossip, Daddy told everyone, including us, that Momma was away at a "hotel," resting. This I remember. He promised she'd return soon. Mrs. Credeur, a nanny, arrived to take care of our family. She was a lumpy, gray-haired woman with a flowered bag full of frumpy dresses. She pinched her lips as if they held invisible sewing pins. Silver and beaded chains hung like swags on a Christmas tree from her cat-eyed glasses.

"What are you cooking?" I peered over the pink Formica counter, staring at the black strings around her neck. The musty-smelling ladies in the front row at Our Lady of Fatima Church also wore those strange little squares of cloth. But Mrs. Credeur's religious thingamajigs had been swallowed up by her enormous breasts.

She moved her wooden spoon around a cast-iron pot. "Chicken and dumplings. Do you like that?" The loose skin under her right arm jiggled like Jell-O as she stirred.

"I think so. Can I watch?" Momma hated it when we hovered in her kitchen.

"Certainly, sit down at the counter and I'll show you how to make a roux." I climbed up on a stool and looked over the top of the pot. "See? Flour and oil. You mix them till it looks just right." She stirred the mixture until it formed a honey-colored paste and then tossed in a heaping bowl of chopped onions and green peppers. The vegetables sizzled and popped, lending the kitchen its strong smell.

"My mommy makes her roux dark like dirt," I said, slipping off the stool. "Daddy won't like it unless it tastes just like hers."

Mrs. Credeur smiled and turned toward the sink. Much later, in high school, I would unknowingly befriend the granddaughter of Mrs. Credeur. She'd say that her Nanna used to come and stay with us periodically. How much more did her grandmother tell her? I would wonder, reddening with shame.

One evening just as Mrs. Credeur began pouring eight glasses of milk for supper, Daddy shuffled through the house, mumbling hello, carrying a drill and a screwdriver and a paper bag tucked under his arm. Nanette and Claire glanced at each other over the sudden silence at the table. I wolfed down my dinner so I could run out and see what Daddy was drilling.

"Maybe he's putting those locks up to keep Momma out of our rooms at night," Claire whispered as we watched Daddy put pencil marks on each bedroom door. So far he'd installed gold chains on the outside of Nanette's door and The Darkroom door. Penny's door was next.

"What are the locks for, Daddy?" Nanette asked, chewing on her hair.

He pulled another screw from his coat pocket. "Darling, to keep you and the other young ones from wandering the halls after bedtime. I don't want y'all bothering your mother when she returns." When he was finished with our doors, he patted Claire, Nanette, and then me on our heads as if we were pets. We sat in the hallway, staring at those locks long after he left to go fix himself a drink. The first night after Momma returned and I heard the lock on The Darkroom door slide into place, I panicked. What if I have go pee during the night? Or have a bad dream? How do I get out if there's a fire? In my mind, I saw Claire and me throwing our bodies against the door and busting through like Popeye on television.

One night while Momma was away, my older brother, Chess, and his best friend, Bill, showed off their flips, gainers, and diving board cut-aways. Chess roared with laughter when Bill sprang from the water with a red, stinging belly. Nanette, Penny, and Aimee, all strong swimmers by then, took turns competing for the farthest and prettiest swan dive. Claire and I floated around miserably in the roped-off shallow end of our pool in our orange life vests. When Bill tired of the diving board, he dared Chess to climb to the roof of the dressing room and dive over the cement patio. Holding my breath, I watched my brother barely skim past the pink-tiled edge of the pool and break the surface of the glistening water. His slick head popped up from the wake of his splash. Like a dog, he shook out his hair, pelting his buddy with droplets, grinning, reaching above the water to share a high-five.

Chess was the epitome of cool, often banging away at his sparkly maroon drum set, his thick brown hair flopping, his brown eyes glittering as he and his friends played their music and sang along to the spinning albums. Bill and he had a band for awhile, and even played on local tel-evision once. They and their friends were going to be the next Beatles.

"You girls wanna hear some scary stories?" Chess asked my sisters and me after they'd exhausted themselves in the pool. Of course we did! We jumped out of the pool and followed them into the narrow, humid dress-ing room. Skirted in damp towels, Penny and Aimee sat together, as always, on one bench with Chess and Bill. Claire, Nanette and I scoot-ed together on the smaller bench.

"Not so long ago," Chess began as he leaned into the huddle, "there lived this evil, jealous man. He did yard work for a family who lived in a big fancy brick house in Abbeville."

"Where's Abbeville?" Claire asked.

"Hush!" Chess shot Claire his silly, demented look and then contin-ued. "Now Clarence, that was the gardener's name, hated this family because they were so rich. He and his Mama lived in a dilapidated ol' shotgun house that was overrun with roaches."

Nanette chewed on the ends of her hair as Chess told how the man was trimming the hedge one afternoon. He stumbled over a tricycle one of the children had left in the yard and fell, cutting off his hand with the hedge clippers. Chess grabbed his right wrist and pretended he was Clarence. He waved his severed hand around while we cringed and squeezed closer.

"The mother of the house came out to have a look, and when she saw the bloody hand, she shrieked and ran back in to call an ambulance. The old man couldn't believe she'd just leave him there by the hedge, bleeding to death, so he cursed the house and everyone in it."

Chess and Bill exchanged a glance, each trying not to smile, and then my brother told how the ambulance came too late. A week after the man died, late at night, the children heard the sound of something crawling through the flowers and rustling the leaves. It stopped right under their window. The little girl opened the blinds and looked out. There was the gardener's cut-off hand, gray, wrinkled, covered with dried blood, tendons and bone sticking through the wrist, clutching the sill and clawing at the glass. They ran to tell their parents, but when the daddy went to look there was nothing there. He told them to lock their window and go back to sleep.

Every night, the hand came to the window, scratching, clawing its way up. Every night, the children locked the window and the hand couldn't get in.

But one night they forgot to lock the window. The hand climbed up to the sill, pushing and clawing at the glass—and the window opened. It crawled under the blinds and dropped down to the floor, running on its bloody fingers to the little girl's bed, climbing up the blankets, leaping to her throat, and strangling her before she could cry out. Then it leaped across to the other bed and strangled her sister. In the morning, the parents found their children dead, and on the carpet, spots of blood and pieces of rotting flesh.

Squeezing my trembling thigh, Claire screamed first and then we all joined in until Chess and Bill doubled over laughing.

"Tell us another one," Nanette begged.

And so they did. We shivered as we listened to tales of horrible deaths.

Later when we moved into the new house on West Bayou Parkway and I finally got to sleep in a room with windows, I always kept the shutters closed. I was afraid I'd see that bloody, severed hand or hear its dirty nails scratching at the windowpane.

Just as Daddy promised, Momma returned before he had to pick his way through a fourth dinner prepared by Mrs. Credeur. The shock treatments I'd later learn about had left my mother looking like she'd been whirled around in a spin-cycle. Her hands trembled each time she lit a cigarette. She acted strange, forgetting to sugar my father's iced tea and setting out the "big" napkins at all our dinner places rather than just at the grownups'.

Daddy moved his feather pillow into Nanette's room and bunked in her extra twin bed because, he said, he didn't want to disturb my mother with his snoring. Claire and I giggled at the sight of his hairy white ankles and his size thirteen feet hanging off the edge of the mattress. Every night after he tucked us in and kissed us good night, we heard the locks slide into place.

Mrs. Credeur stayed on for a week to help out. The night before we hugged her good-bye, she stayed late so that Momma and Daddy could steal off to dinner by themselves. I awoke to the sound of laughter and whispers in the hallway. The next morning after breakfast, if anyone would have dared to peer over her shoulders to see what our mother scribbled into her new spiral notebook, we would have read the notes she kept for her psychiatrist: *Sexual relations improving…you can be the next Godfather.* And just like that my father moved his feather pillow back to their bed. Before summer's end he stopped bothering with the locks that had seemed so magical. They had kept, I believed, our mother from our rooms.

A commotion in the hallway yanked me from sleep. "Look at you," she yelled at Chess, "you're drunk." My heart pounded. When she couldn't goad my father into a fight, she went after his namesake. "I won't have you coming home drunk like this night after night. Your teachers have called me twice now."

"Fuck you! Get your stinkin' hands off me."

It was getting to be a routine between her and Chess. Scrambling across the room, steps ahead of Claire, I peeked out the door. Chess ducked just as Momma's hand came around.

"You missed me," he taunted, combing back his greasy brown bangs. His face was swollen with purple and red pimples.

"You little bastard!" She swung drunkenly, missing his shoulder and catching the wood paneling with her knuckles. "Goddammit," she panted.

"Look at you…" Chess pointed at her protruding belly. The veins above his turtleneck bulged. "All that fat…you're so slow. You're the last person in the world who should be having another baby. You can't even take care of the ones you've got." His hand struck the wall so hard that Daddy's boat painting rattled and fell, landing cockeyed.

How could he talk to her like that? I flinched as Momma lunged for him. Maybe he was still mad about the other night. Edna, the maid, called him into the bathroom as she bathed Claire. I heard her say, "Look at this child's bottom. Black and blue like I ain't never seen before. That mother of yours, she sure has it in for these poor girls." After that Chess ran to his bedroom. It sounded as if a gorilla was pounding on the walls.

Chess's hands caught Momma's shoulders. He shoved her backwards. Her body slammed into the door jam, and I felt Claire's fingernails dig into my arms. Across the hall, Nanette stared wide-eyed, sucking on a ribbon of hair and clutching her crotch so as not to pee in her panties.

"Stay away, willya?" Chess yelled. "I want to go to sleep."

Momma came at Chess, swinging both arms. He lifted his boot, planting his foot right in the middle of her big, pregnant belly. She flew backwards, hitting the wall with a thud, then slid down to the carpet. Her nightgown flew up to reveal her cotton underwear. I cringed at the thought of the tiny baby being crushed inside her.

Suddenly Aimee ran past our door. "Momma!"

"Leave me alone," she said, pushing Aimee away and scowling at Chess. He laughed and turned toward his room. That was when he saw us.

"Close your door and go to sleep," he snapped, blinking back tears. After Chess's door slammed shut, I heard Daddy's footsteps. Claire and I stepped back from our door and listened.

He sighed deep. "Esther, are you all right?"

"I'm fine." She sniffled. "Help me up, goddammit."

"Run along, Aimee. It's late," he said. Claire and I ran to our beds and pretended to be asleep in case he came to check on us. In the dark room, I wished Momma would go away for another rest.

Nickey, my new baby brother, arrived in December. "Finally, another son," my father told everyone who stopped by the house for a drink. He had Daddy's round pug nose. We all did, to some degree. But the family was divided among brunettes and blondes. Anne's and Penny's eyes sparkled sky-blue, and their hair was as white as the cases of Kleenex Daddy brought home from his wholesale pharmaceutical business, Etienne Drug Company. Aimee and I had dirty-blonde hair and green eyes. The others took after Momma and Daddy, with brown eyes and muddy hair. By the time Momma had Nickey, Yvette was twenty and had long since left for college.

I have a photograph of Yvette, home from college, standing in the driveway wearing a full-leg cast and leaning on wooden crutches. She drove her new car off a bridge, landing right in the Mississippi River. She managed to swim to shore with a broken leg. Not long after, she was diagnosed as having schizophrenia. With her dark hair, teased and turned out at her shoulders, she looked like Jacqueline Kennedy.

During my childhood I don't remember Yvette being around. She seemed like a distant aunt. In my adolescence I resented her for abandoning us, for not seeming to care. But now I know that sometimes it's all one can do just to take care of oneself.

An odd thing happened to Momma's face after Nickey was born. She sprouted lots of fuzzy blond hair. Every couple of weeks she summoned Nanette, Claire, Anne, and me to her bedroom to trim her beard and mustache. We took turns leaning toward her with sharp, bird-like scissors, careful to cut close to the skin without nicking her. I'd gather a clump of fine hair between two fingers and hold my breath as I brought the scissors to her face. Every sudden movement on the mattress—Anne trying to corral Nickey so he wouldn't roll off—caused me panic. It scared me being so close to Momma, especially with pointed scissors.

One night Momma told us that she had taken medicine to help her conceive Anne and Nickey. She'd lost two babies between Claire and me. "Why do you want to have so many children?" I asked.

She shrugged and reached for a cigarette. "Your father enjoys it when I'm pregnant. He's more attentive when I'm carrying a baby."

"Oh," I said, feeling disappointed but not understanding why at the time. I handed the scissors to Nanette—she had the steadiest hands.

All my life people have said, "Wow, nine children. You guys must be Catholic." I smile and nod. But I knew, even as a kid, it had nothing to do with religious convictions or my mother really liking us. A baby in her tummy was simply a way of getting love from our father.

4 ~ California, 1989

A month went by with no call from my gynecologist. Some days I hated Dr. Schmidt for what he had done—seducing me when I was sick and had sought his help and advice. But other days I downplayed his misdeed and actually fantasized about seeing him again under different circumstances. Perhaps he'd fall in love with me. Marry me, even. (I hadn't worked out the details of what he'd do with his current wife.) But with his thriving practice, he could surely pay off my debts, buy me a nice Victorian house, and father my children. One night after polishing off a bottle of wine I decided to have him paged.

"Why'd you call?" he asked in a low voice.

"I wanted to talk to you."

"Well, I'm home with the kids. My wife is out of town. How are you?"

"Pretty good. Busy with school and work. I never heard from you after, you know, and I thought maybe we should discuss it."

"I can't just leave the kids right now. But let's talk for a little bit. Hold on." I could hear his children playing in the background. Then a door closed. "Are you alone?" he whispered.

"Yes," I whispered back sarcastically.

"Is the line safe?"

"Safe from what?"

"Never mind. Where are you?"

"My apartment?"

"Where in your apartment?"

"I'm sitting on the kitchen counter. Where are you?"

"I'm in my bedroom. What are you wearing?"

"Sweats, why?"

"I want you to touch yourself," he said in an authoritative voice. My smile froze.

"Huh?"

"Rub yourself. Pretend it's me."

Oh, how romantic. "No way! This is too embarrassing."

"Come on. You know what I'm doing right now?"

"What?"

"I'm stroking my penis very slowly. I'm thinking about how soft you feel inside."

I pictured him sitting on the edge of his and his wife's king-size bed, his meticulously pressed khaki slacks puddled at his feet to reveal his hairy legs and the stiff object of his desire.

"I can't believe you're doing this. What about your kids?"

"Come on now."

Grabbing my salad fork from dinner, I began scrapping black mildew spots off the grout around the sink while I waited. He began to groan, and I stabbed the fork into a nearby tomato. Jabbing at the flesh, I listened and shook my head. By the time the doctor had finished his deed, all that remained of the tormented tomato was a disgusting mess.

"Are you there?" he asked when his breathing slowed down.

"Yeah."

"How did you like that?"

"Oh, just wonderful." You sick-o! "Hey, you better go check on your kids. They might be setting the house on fire."

"Call me again."

Right!

The fork took flight across the kitchen as I slammed down the receiver. Bits of pink pulp stuck to the cabinets. If you have an ounce of self-respect or want to have any, I told myself, don't you dare call or see him again. I ran to my bed and threw myself on the comforter. What a stupid, stupid, slut. Simon Schmidt wasn't going to leave his wife. He wasn't going to bail me out of my financial troubles. Who in the fuck names their kid Simon anyway? Mother of some pervert, that's who. "Simon, come here Simon," I screeched to no one but the television. I was nothing more than a teething ring the good doctor sucked and chewed on to cut new teeth. I could have been anyone and everyone. It didn't matter to him or others like him. I cried until my nose was so congested that I could hardly breathe. But as I listened to the traffic outside, cars speeding by, honking their horns, I wondered, How can I expect someone to love me, respect me, my body, if I first don't love and respect myself?

5 ~ Louisiana, 1967

The Canterbury Street house, as it turned out, wasn't built right from the start. The kitchen faced the backyard instead of the street. The contractor had somehow read the drawings backward. When Daddy discovered the swimming pool was slowly sliding toward the coulee, he said enough and took our neighbor, the contractor, to court. The year I turned five he won the lawsuit. He used the large settlement and dividends from the thriving wholesale business he'd inherited from his father to build a bigger red-brick house a few streets over on West Bayou Parkway.

One afternoon, sitting amid stacks of moving boxes in the old playroom, Claire worked on a jigsaw puzzle of a white kitten like our own Fluffy. Each time she leaned over to grab a puzzle piece, I saw the black bruise peeking out of her underwear. Proof of Momma's late-night trips to The Darkroom. I walked over to where Claire's favorite doll sat in its red chair, picked it up, and started to swing it around in a dance. How it happened I'm not sure, but the next thing I knew, I'd broken off one of its arms. Claire heard the doll hit the floor and turned around. Her face immediately changed when she saw the amputated arm.

Pursing her lips like an old lady, she got up and grabbed my shoulders, shoving me against the brick wall. I stared into her crazy face as she slammed my head into the hard wall, again and again. Crying, I begged her to stop. She looked right past me and kept banging me against the bricks. When she finally let me go, I ran to Momma.

Momma continued pressing her biscuit cutter into the white dough, saying, "If you can't play together nicely, then go play separately." I hated Claire and her. I ran back to my bedroom and curled up on my bed, swearing that I'd get even, no matter what.

That night, as Claire snored and mumbled in her sleep, I heard

Momma in the hallway. I knew if I made noise, Momma would think one of us was still awake and she'd be angry. She usually went for Claire first, so I felt around the cluttered surface of the nightstand for something that would make a loud bang. I grabbed a wooden puzzle, my heart beating like a metronome turned up full speed. I threw the puzzle across the room and it hit the wall with a crash, the pieces scattering on the carpet. Claire said, "Huh?" and threw back her blanket. I quickly slid under the covers and pulled them to my chin. Trembling, I squeezed my eyes shut and tried not to move one tiny bit. Momma stormed in and turned on the light.

"What in the hell is going on in here?"

I held my breath and squinted, ever so slightly, to see Claire sitting up. Momma headed straight to her bed, and my heart galloped.

"You goddamn children are so bad. Why can't you just give me some peace for a change? You're gonna drive me crazy. Is that what you want— you want to send me back to the hospital?"

She spanked my sister for a long time. Claire just mumbled over and over, "I'm sorry, Momma. I'm sorry for whatever I did."

The pleasure I got from that trick disappeared instantly. Hearing Claire whimper each time Momma's hand hit her made me feel like the meanest person alive. When Momma left the room, I lay there listening to Claire cry. I wanted to go rub her back, but I was too scared. What if she figured out what I had done? She never mentioned that evening, but I often wished she had.

The next morning, as always, Momma brought in our coffee milk. After we kissed her freshly powdered cheek and took our mugs, she smiled at Claire. "I thought we'd go buy you some new sandals today."

Claire nodded, nearly spilling her drink. Turning to leave, Momma kicked aside a piece of my puzzle and said, "Marie, clean up this mess."

"Yes, Ma'am." I didn't dare look at Claire.

As moving day approached, Momma's mood darkened like the sky before a hurricane. Her daily life normally revolved around groceries, errands, cooking, and entertaining, but now she and Edna packed cabinet after cabinet of Daddy's family china and crystal, volumes of dusty books, and endless toys. To be near her was to tremble like branches in a storm. Each evening, by the time Daddy and a parade of family and friends made their way to our house for cocktails, I found myself jerked into the bathroom for a spanking or given a stern warning to stay out of the kitchen.

One morning when Grandma, Momma's mother, dropped by to super-
vise the pre-moving activity, Momma complained that Daddy was no
help, that he was like having a tenth child to wait on and clean up after.
I ate my oatmeal one small blob at a time so that I could listen to the
grownup talk.

Grandma sat on the stool at the pink Formica counter and just
clucked her tongue. "What'd you expect, Esther?" Her head shook so that
the loose white skin under her chin flapped. Her forehead still had the
fresh scar from her cancer operation that gave me the creeps to look at.
"You married a man who has had servants always doin' for him. Even his
Aunt Mim had everything done for her. Didn't know the first thing
about raising a child. And that Chester Sr. He sure didn't set a fine example about either family life or family responsibilities." Momma sighed as
her mother warned her simply to smile and look happy when Chester
walked through the door at five o'clock.

And that's exactly what my mother did. She lay in her bed of thistles
and squirmed ever so slightly. As Daddy dropped the afternoon mail on
the table and tossed each of us little ones in the air a few times to hear
us squeal, Momma smiled and reached for another silver goblet to wrap
in newspaper.

"Cocktail time, Bump?" Daddy asked.

"Sure," said Momma, sighing. Sitting at the kitchen counter, I
watched her scrub the black smudges from her shaky hands. The frown
on her face faded with each step she took toward the bar.

The bar was mysterious—Momma's personal laboratory and the place
where she concocted potions that made people laugh, sing, and sometimes yell or cry. I watched her measure out the clear and dark liquids and
then fill the glasses. Just as Momma had, I memorized who drank what.
Bloody Mary for Aunt Lilia and Mrs. Dooley, gin martini with olives for
Uncle Joel, Gibson with onions for Mr. Dooley, white wine for Grandma
and Pop, Schlitz for the Duhons, Jack Daniel's and Coke for Daddy, and
Sanka or Jim Beam for Dr. Guree.

"Marie, will you ask Edna to bring me some more tall glasses."

I nodded and skipped away. As I checked room after room, I thought
about what Mrs. Dooley had said earlier in the day as Momma changed
Anne's diaper.

"Esther, what are all those little marks on the baby's bottom?"

She sighed and said she was afraid that Edna was burning the baby
with her cigarettes.

When I heard her say that I wanted to shout, "Liar, liar, pants on fire! Edna wouldn't ever do that. You're the one who's mean." But of course I kept my mouth shut. Mrs. Dooley shook her head, saying "My word. Lordy be."

Edna was usually sweet as a Tootsie Roll. Oh, once she spanked Claire with a hairbrush because she let the boys next door see her panties. But that was just a spanking, and I don't remember anything worse. Besides, she didn't smoke. Eventually, she said the new house was too much for her, and she quit.

All around, it seemed, a strong code of silence existed, especially among the grownups. No one wanted to tattle and find themselves cast outside the circle.

On moving day I stood in the carport watching the sweaty black men load into the moving van our swing set, slide, and seesaws that they had dug up from our backyard. Nickey toddled over to my father, who had come out to retrieve the newspaper, and pointed, saying, "Merry-go-round?" My father scooped up my little brother.

"Sorry Little Fellow, we're leaving it here."

"But Daddy," I whined, "we've got to take it with us."

"It's too hard to move, Sweetheartsabean." Daddy tapped my head with the rolled paper. "You can come back to visit and play on it."

I jerked my head away. I thought of how I had hugged and kissed Bullwinkle, our first basset hound, before he went for his overnight at the vet. I waited for days for Daddy to pick him up again. Finally I asked, "When's Bullwinkle coming home?" only to find out that he was never coming back. The vet gave him a magic pill to help him get to heaven because he was also too hard to move—too old and too much trouble.

The notion of other kids riding up and down on our ponies, listening to the music under the twinkling lights, made me steaming mad. I kicked a pebble to the far corner of the carport and sniffled as the rock pinged against a can of turpentine. If my parents could give away our merry-go-round or kill a dog that craps too often, why wouldn't a troublesome kid simply be dropped off in the country somewhere?

6 ~ California, 1986

Of all the American cities, Houston, Austin, Los Angeles, Phoenix, I had not given San Francisco much consideration. Wasn't the place swarming with gay men? With all the talk about AIDS, I feared I'd bump into some guy on the street and end up dead. But it wasn't so scary once I got there. People were friendly, the bars and the financial district were filled with straight men, and the city was so exciting. And I knew two girls there from my family's last Caribbean cruise. On my fourth day I telephoned Daddy from the Hilton.

"Hey Sweetheartsabean, how's my world traveler?"

"Busy taking in all of San Francisco. I love it here."

"Great. Where're you driving to next?"

"I think I'm going to look for an apartment here." I felt my shoulders rise as I waited out the long pause. Finally Daddy sighed.

"San Francisco, Sweetheart? That city is full of fruitcakes. What about Austin or Dallas?"

"But I really like it here."

Silence.

"I'm sorry, Daddy."

"Well, I wish you'd reconsider. Love you, darling. Here's your mother."

I felt like my new wings had just been sprayed with lead.

By the end of the week I was settled into a new apartment in Cole Valley, not far from the Haight. My friend Suzy assured me that $650 a month was a good deal, even for a third-story apartment with a tiny kitchen and no elevator, laundry facility, or parking.

Of course Daddy wasn't pleased. He kept spewing off gloomy statistics about what a bad choice San Francisco was: the exorbitant cost of living, the violent crimes, the earthquakes, the homosexuals, and the crazy people. He claimed it was too far for him travel. He talked like he was 80 instead 58. But the more he tried to break my confidence, the greater my resolve.

For two weeks I sat on the floor in my empty apartment, bending over my typewriter answering newspaper ads. The longer I spent on the floor with an aching butt and stiff neck, the more flexible my goals became. Bank teller, financial manager, secretary, entry-level bookkeeper, temporary data entry clerk, anything would do. When I wasn't hovering over my typewriter, I was dressed in one of my new suits, briefcase in hand, going from bank to bank on California Street and Montgomery Street downtown, reviewing job listings, and leaving resumes with the receptionists.

When I finally received a call for an interview, I was ecstatic. But it turned out to be only a screening interview by an employment agency. I sat in a cubicle while some bored woman red-inked my resume, circling nearly a dozen typos and grammatical errors. "Did you finish college in 1885 or 1985?" she asked. I wanted to disappear as she marked up my beautiful work. She drew a big red 'X' over the hobby section of my resume. Don't you dare start bawling, I told myself. She advised me to start again (as if I had a choice) and to delete some of my restaurant work, emphasizing my accounting experience. She sent me away with a handout entitled "How to Make Yourself Irresistible to Employers."

After I got over my initial anger, I realized she was right. So I rewrote the resume, had Suzy edit it for me, and sent it out again. I set up interviews with more agencies for the following week. Satisfied I was now on the right track, I headed out for dinner to celebrate.

Clutching my purse close, I walked up Cole toward Haight. Scraggly men and women sat in doorways, drinking or spaced out.

"Got a cigarette, Miss?" an old man asked. I pulled the pack of cigarettes from my pocket and handed it to him, hoping he wouldn't accidentally brush against me. "Thank you!" he said, revealing the gaps in his mouth. "Thank you."

I hurried to off to a Mexican restaurant I'd spotted earlier. It was 6:30, and there was only one other customer, a worrisome sign when you consider food turnover. After dinner I stopped at a liquor store to buy cigarettes and more beer. I placed the six-pack on the counter and started to point to the Virginia Slims, then stopped. Why not quit? I hated my nagging cough, the winded feeling. I didn't want people in San Francisco wondering if my coughing was AIDS-related. And besides, Suzy and her friends didn't smoke. I decided right then to quit.

The retro rotary black phone I'd just bought was ringing as I entered my apartment.

"Marie, it's Nanette. I've got some terrible news. Nickey shot himself and he's in the hospital."

The hours between Nanette's first call and getting in the taxi to go to the airport felt endless. Sitting on a plastic lawn chair Suzy had loaned me, I stared out the window, watching women come and go from the popular dyke bar on the corner. I thought about a trip to Arkansas my friend Mignon and I had taken in college. Nickey tagged along. My Honda had stalled at the top of a steep hill. Mignon and I designated Nickey to stand behind the car and push as I revved the engine. We were so lucky I didn't run him over.

I closed my eyes and cried, letting the sounds from below—MUNI buses taking off and screeching to a halt, jazz from another apartment, and drunks passing under my window—commingle with my thoughts.

When I landed in Lafayette, Nanette and Anne and Lynn, her new girlfriend, were waiting for me. They looked awful, probably just how I looked. Red, puffy eyes and wrinkled clothes.

"Is he still alive?"

Anne shook her head, and I dropped my bags. We threw our arms around each other, sobbing.

"When?"

"They disconnected him at eight," Nanette said. "They saved his organs for donation."

In the car Anne told me the story. She and Lynn had been babysitting Aimee's son, Michael, left behind when she ran off with some creep to Tennessee.

"The patio door opened and Nickey ran by. Lynn hid in the bathroom because she's scared of him. I chased after him but tripped on the stairs, and he took off. Somehow I knew I shouldn't follow him upstairs. I ran outside to see if his friends knew why he'd come over. When I came back, Lynn told me she called 911 because she heard a shot."

Anne's voice cracked. Nanette rubbed her shoulder until she could continue. "He was lying on the floor, bleeding, when I found him in Momma and Daddy's room. Daddy's gun was next to him. His heart was still beating. I called Momma and Daddy in Gulf Shores while we waited for the ambulance. You should have heard her. She went crazy, screaming and crying."

When I walked into the house, Momma met me in the den, calling out, "Marie, Nickey's dead. Your brother is dead." We embraced, each crying on the other. She was looped and nearly toppled me. From the open foyer door I noticed a young black woman kneeling at the banister with a rag. Ellen, Momma's new maid. She glanced at us and then away. She'd have an earful to tell her friends later.

I hurried to the study, where Daddy swept me into an embrace. It felt so nice to have his strong arms around me, holding me close. Everyone except Aimee gathered in the dark-paneled study. No one knew where in Tennessee Aimee and her new husband lived.

"Oh, Sweetheartsabean," Daddy said, pulling apart, "the Little Fellow is dead. It's such a shame. I'm so glad you're home." Tears rolled down his face as his shoulders rose and fell. He looked so defeated. Both of his sons were dead. I held his hands and everyone around the room bowed their heads as he sobbed. I thought about how right before I'd hightailed it out of Lafayette I heard Daddy warn Nickey that if he couldn't visit quietly he wouldn't be invited back to the house. "Peace and quiet!" That's what my father had wanted. He was getting his wish.

Throughout that next week I stayed close to home, visiting my family, attending Nickey's wakes and then the funeral. I met his girlfriend, the one he'd been so giddy about, and saw one of the kids from Nickey's last stay in rehab. I drove to New Iberia to see my grandmother for the last time before she died—clipped her nails as I'd once done for my mother after Nickey was born. I said hello and then good-bye again to all my friends and family.

Momma drove me to the airport. This would start a tradition with us. Every flight home she'd sit with me at the gate and wait until I boarded the plane.

"I feel really bad that I'm leaving y'all."

"You've got to follow your heart, Sweetheart. We'll miss you, but I want you to be happy. Your father—well, he'll accept it." She seemed sincere. I didn't detect a trace of resentment.

"Do you think you'll ever come visit me?"

"We'll see," she said smiling, taking my hand into hers. I knew that meant never.

As she turned to glare at a squealing toddler, I thought about my thirteen-year-old nephew, Michael. Living with my parents seemed to be no better than when we were kids. He said how Momma pounded on his bedroom door at night, blitzed out of her mind, yelling about his stereo or the mess. I hoped she wouldn't hurt him. He said that Daddy just ignored him, even at the dinner table, pretending he wasn't there. Michael's dog took advantage of the first time he found the gate left open and ran away, bolted just like I was doing. But for some reason, Prissy, his cat, adopted Momma as her new owner.

We sat there, my mother and I, holding hands, all talked out from the past week, and I wondered, how can this woman, who can be so sweet and harmless by day, turn into such an ogre at night? Is it just the alcohol? Had it occurred to her yet that both Nickey and Chess died at age 19? Was it a coincidence? My sisters and I didn't think so.

Two days after I returned to San Francisco, I interviewed with a shopping center management office at Fisherman's Wharf. By Friday I was the new bookkeeper/office manager. My starting salary: $22,000. I was thrilled. Even though I had really wanted to work for a large company downtown, where all the handsome professional men worked, I grabbed the first offer and called my friends and family to tell them the good news. Suzy said we could have lunch often because she worked nearby in North Beach. Daddy said he was surprised someone was willing to pay me that much money. Penny teased that my boss sounded really cute and she looked forward to meeting him. Nanette said, "See? I knew you could do it." And Nickey began visiting me in my dreams.

7 ~ Louisiana, 1968

Anne and I raced down the stairs of our new house on West Bayou and flung open the foyer doors. They banged against the wood paneling. We winced as Daddy jerked around.

Seated at the long kitchen table, his scowl quickly faded. "What have you got there, sweethearts?"

My four-year-old sister held out her basket and yelled, "The Easter Bunny came." Momma looked over from the sink and smiled. She was already dressed for church.

We took turns kissing Daddy as he bent over in his rumpled pajamas. Next to his newspaper sat a pile of small presents wrapped in bright yellow paper.

"What are those?" I asked.

Daddy handed a box to each of us, and we ripped open the packages to find identical silver bracelets with tiny tulip-shaped bells.

Anne and I spun around, waving our wrists and giggling at the sound of the bells. Momma brought Daddy another cup of coffee and rested her hands on his shoulders, chuckling. Soon the floor was littered with baskets, and all six girls jingle-jangled their way through breakfast until it was time for church.

The novelty of the bells ended when one of the church ladies turned around in her pew and scowled at Momma. Just outside the Cathedral, my mother spat, "Take those goddamn bells off right now." She shifted Nickey higher on her hip and glared at Daddy as if he purposely set out to humiliate her. Chess slid his hands in his trouser pockets and smirked. I prayed my new bracelet wouldn't be thrown in the trash like other gifts that turned out to be a nuisance to my parents.

"Sorry, Esther," Daddy said, following Momma.

We piled into the station wagon. Crammed in between Claire and

Nanette, I sat perfectly still and watched Daddy fold his tall frame behind the steering wheel. After he shut his door, he waited. On cue, Momma whipped around and began yelling at us. "That was absolutely humiliating. People were staring at us as if we were a bunch of idiots." I tried to paste a sorry look on my face. Chess, seated between my parents, didn't turn around.

Momma finished shouting and pulled a fresh pack of Virginia Slims from her purse. She ripped off the whole left corner of the package, leaving a ragged hole. My father reached into his coat pocket and pulled out his Winstons. He tapped the pack on the steering wheel twice, and a cigarette emerged from the neat, square foil opening. Daddy pushed in the lighter and started the car. When the silver button popped out, he brought the glowing red rings to his cigarette. I loved the sizzle of the paper and tobacco.

We drove past the ice factory that also sold fresh crawfish when in season and headed to the country club. We were having Easter lunch there because Momma hadn't unpacked the dining room yet.

Yvette was waiting for us in the lobby at the club. She waved and took a long drag off her cigarette. Smoke streamed out of her nose and mouth as she leaned on her crutches. The gray cloud hovered around her bouffant, slowly dispersing into the cold air.

"Happy Easter, darling." Momma kissed her forehead, leaving red lipstick there. "You still need those without your cast?"

"Yeah. Another week. Hey, Daddy."

"Hello, Sweet Pea." He removed his hat and then pecked Yvette on the forehead. Reaching in his pocket he pulled out the last of the presents. "Happy Easter. Open it later, though. Okay?"

Momma didn't notice the exchange. She was busy yanking on Nickey's britches to keep him from climbing all over the lobby furniture.

"Shall we?" Daddy pointed to the maitre d'.

Three chandeliers sparkled above the dining room tables. In the parking lot, we watched the leaves on the trees quiver as a departing airplane from the nearby airport roared by. Tilting my head, I imagined myself jumping up and hanging from the golden branches, swinging from fixture to fixture like Tarzana of the jungle, brushing my arms against the glistening crystals, the translucent leaves. I could crash through the window, invincible like Superman, and then swim through the air to another place. In my imagination anything was possible.

"Mrs. Etienne, you have such a lovely family." The host held out Momma's starched napkin. "I've never seen so many beautiful girls at one table." She thanked him and smiled at Daddy.

"Yes, I've got my own little harem," my father boasted. Yvette's eyes rolled, and Momma's smile vanished. Daddy grinned unaware.

An old black waiter carrying a bottle of champagne appeared. "Yes, please," Momma said, even before he had spoken.

"You'll have some, won't you?" Momma asked Yvette.

She nodded. The man walked around the table.

"Chess, would you like a glass?"

"Sure," he answered my mother, grinning at Aimee. Even though Chess was only fifteen, Momma let him have a little wine or beer occasionally. Which didn't make sense since half their late-night arguments were about him coming home drunk.

"And will you bring Shirley Temples, please, for the children?"

Momma always made sure everyone had a drink. At restaurants, several times during a meal she lifted an index finger in the air or waved and nodded at a waiter standing on the other side of the room or pointed down at her or Daddy's highball. I couldn't wait until I got to be a grownup so I could make a sparkly glass of wine appear simply by sticking my finger up.

We went to the buffet line and heads turned to watch our eleven-member procession. I tried to ignore the onlookers. It was bad enough to have Momma and Daddy always watching over us to make sure we behaved properly and used good manners. But a roomful of strangers eyeing us, waiting for a reason to laugh or whisper always frightened me.

With our plates loaded down with smothered green beans, dirty rice, cornbread muffins, and roast beef, we went back to our table. Momma started talking to a skinny woman seated at the next table. "Thank you, they *are* good children," my mother said, flashing us a look of approval.

Once in the grocery store I'd asked her why she was so nice in front of other people. She pushed the cart ahead, ignoring me, but later dragged me to the kitchen bathroom to wash my mouth with Lava soap. I learned not to ask her such stupid questions.

My parents sipped glass after glass of champagne, smiled at all of us, and nodded when we asked if we could get dessert. Over coffee, Chess and Daddy sketched plans for an elaborate two-story playhouse they would build for us. Momma frowned at the stack of scribbled-on cocktail napkins, suggesting they keep it simple. As we pulled out of the parking lot, she yawned and proposed a nap before the egg hunt. The car filled with a chorus of whiny no's, and she relented. It was Easter, after all, Daddy argued. Momma drew in a deep breath and stared out the window. Did she console herself with the idea of beating us later? Was it ever as premeditated as that?

That evening my father invited Aunt Lilia and Uncle Joel and their children, along with the Duhons, over for baked snapper. The rain fell in sheets, in waves. I imagined God and all the angels standing knee-deep in a wide river, refilling and pouring bucket after bucket of water down from heaven. Thunder and lightening filled the sky as laughter erupted from the study. The power faltered before shutting off. By candlelight, we sat in the kitchen and feasted. Baked fish, green beans wrapped in salty bacon, French bread, Momma's famous salad with hearts of palm, and Aunt Lilia's blueberry cheesecake.

After dinner, while the grownups drained the liquor bottles on the patio, my brothers, sisters, cousins, and I played our favorite game—smash-each-other's-fingers-with-the-pool-table-balls. On the count of three everyone rolled a ball fast across the table and then reached for one rocketing past. The object was to smash as many opponents' fingers as possible. With delirious smiles and malicious intent, we sent balls back and forth, cheering when we made a direct hit. The clacking sounds of balls colliding, screams, and cheers filled the room. The game ended when Anne got creamed by two balls at once and ran crying to Daddy.

Chess and our cousin Brent stole a few beers out of the study refrigerator. We all went out to the front porch and sat on the cold cement, partially hidden by the holly bushes.

"Go! Go! Go!" we yelled over the downpour. My sisters and I rooted for Chess. My cousins cheered for their brother.

Around ten the lights flickered back on. Daddy and Uncle Joel came into the living room and announced the party was ending.

"No, not yet, Daddy," I screamed, and Anne copied me.

"Come on, Babushka. It's late." Daddy scooped my little sister up off the sofa and tossed her in the air. His red cheeks glowed as Anne squealed.

"Do it again, please," she begged.

"Once more." He threw her up and her blonde hair brushed against the ceiling tiles just as the other grownups entered the living room.

Swaying slightly, Momma squinted around the brightly lit room. "All right, kids. Upstairs with your father."

"Chester," Mrs. Duhon called out, "how about giving me a toss in the air like that?"

Momma nudged her friend. "You keep your hands off my husband, Jigger *dear*." She flashed a pretend smile, but her voice had an edge to it. Daddy was Momma's, that was clear. We even got a mean look if we accidentally missed Daddy's cheek and kissed his lips.

Daddy lowered Anne to the floor, swatting her playfully on the bottom. "Okay, kids, you heard your mother. March." We yelled our goodbyes and ran to the foyer.

"Do we have to brush our teeth?" I asked Daddy as he led us to our room.

"No, Sweetheartsabean. Just climb in. It's late." He suddenly sounded very tired.

Daddy tucked Anne and me snuggly into the bed we now shared, as Claire and Nanette had called dibs on the room across the hall before we moved in. Planting a gentle kiss on our foreheads, my father mumbled, "Good night, my sweethearts."

"Good night, Daddy. I love you," we both called out as he left our bedside.

"Sleep tight." He turned out the lights and closed the door. The room was dark except for the fragments of the street light that shone through the shutters.

Our bedroom sat above the carport. I could hear Momma and the other grownups laughing in the driveway. Soon the car engines started, and the back door slammed. I shifted slightly to face my bedroom door.

I heard someone come up the stairs. Momma's cough. Heavy footsteps that grew fainter. She wasn't coming to our room. More, quicker footsteps coming up the steps, but not Daddy's. I clutched my blankets.

"What do you want?" Chess yelled, in that tone Momma called his sassy-pants voice.

I turned toward Anne. Asleep. Already asleep. I heard Penny's slippers padding down the hall toward my father's study. She always ran for safety.

Soon I joined Anne in sleep despite the sound of Momma and Chess at the other end of the hall. Their argument was like television without the picture, TV voices traveling from room to room.

Hours later the light switched on. Momma staggered toward me in her nightgown. "Wake up. Get out of that bed right now." She swished the words from behind tight lips. Before I had a chance, she ripped off my bedspread. Anne lay dead to the world, snoring like she had been clubbed.

Digging her nails into my arm, Momma yanked me out of bed. Without waiting to be told, I pulled down my underwear and lifted my gown. My panties fell to the floor as Momma swung me around to face the bed. I stared at Anne for a moment. But when the first whack came, I squeezed my eyes shut.

"You children are so bad," she said as she hit me. "Damn Chess, he doesn't even listen to me. No one listens. I give and give and give, but what do *I* get in return?" Faster and faster, her hand struck. A couple of times her hand missed my behind and she hit my thighs. I swayed with draining tiredness as I listened to her pant. Soon she'd be done, and then I could fall back to sleep.

Finally she stumbled away from me, but before closing my door, she slammed her fist into the light switch as if to teach it a lesson, too. In the darkness, I heard Nanette and Claire's door open. In seconds they would be torn from their dreams. I felt wide-awake now. I needed to listen, to make sure Momma left my sisters' room after their spankings. I knelt in bed, running my fingertips over the raised flesh on my thigh, and I looked at my three-year-old sister. I wanted to shake her awake. Why doesn't Momma get you? How come you get to sleep? As far as I could remember, she'd grabbed her only once, one afternoon in the kitchen bathroom. When it suddenly dawned on Anne that Momma meant to spank her, my little sister jerked herself loose and ran. Momma chased her around the center-island and past the noisy icemaker, screaming at her to stop. Finally Anne turned and headed to the den. Momma stopped dead in her tracks because Daddy was home. She never went after Anne again. Just like she rarely, if ever, went after Penny. Were there unspoken agreements between my parents—Daddy would ignore, as often as he could, Momma's warped discipline as long as she stayed away from his favorite girls?

I heard Nanette's door open and close again. Momma coughed and headed down the hall toward her own room, past Aimee and Penny's door. I slipped under the covers and stared at Anne. Her mouth was open slightly. Her face looked so innocent and calm. How come you run? What do you say to Daddy when you throw yourself in his arms? (She can't spank me. That's just not fair. You won't let her, will you?)

Did she and Penny have stronger survival instincts than the rest of us? Did I believe I was bad? Early on my mother must have taught me that if I dared tattle to my father, the next spanking would be worse.

8 ～

Two days before Father's Day, Claire and I decided to make a special card. Claire let me, six at the time, direct the project because my artwork usually pried loose a smile from Daddy when he seemed sad or angry. He'd been in a foul mood since he came home from work and showed Momma a black and white picture of a gray-haired lady. Years later, I'd find this photograph with a letter from a hospital in St. Louis, an insane asylum. The letter said, "We wish we'd received your request earlier, for Mrs. Etienne was very upset about having her picture taken without her front teeth." Mrs. Etienne was his mother, a woman we were told was dead.

Claire and I sat down on the carpet to tear assorted sheets of construction paper into tiny pieces. I smelled a burning cigarette and looked up.

"Whatareyoudoing?" Momma muttered, leaning on the doorjamb.

"Making a card for Daddy," Claire replied, sitting up straight and drawing her hands into her lap as Momma stepped toward us.

Momma cocked her head and stared down at our mess. Her cigarette hung loosely between her fingers. Speckles of gray ashes peppered the lace collar of her nightgown. "What kind of card?" she asked, blinking.

"Um, a collage," I stammered.

Her eyes were red and puffy as they were more and more often on Wednesdays, the day we drove to New Iberia to visit Grandma and Pops. As Grandma began nursing my newly bed-bound grandfather, she took greater pleasure in finding fault with her daughter's parenting or marital relations. One castigating remark, and either Daddy or we felt our mother's shame. "We're going to glue all these—"

"Esther," Daddy's voice called from the hall. Momma turned as Daddy appeared at the door. His gold tie hung loosely around his neck. "What are you doing up here?"

Momma opened her mouth but Daddy interrupted her. "Why don't you just leave the girls alone?"

I was shocked—he never said anything like that to her—but not as surprised as Momma looked. She just stared at him for a minute. Perhaps she knew it wasn't really concern for his daughters that stirred him from his study. Perhaps the picture of his mother had ignited his anger, sent him upstairs to goad my mother into a fight.

Momma spat, "I'm not doing anything. I only came to see what they were doing."

Daddy cast a skeptical glance at Claire and me. Even though he was here now, I knew he wouldn't be later when she came to yank us out of bed. I looked away from him to find Momma's eyes fixed on us.

"She wasn't doing anything, Daddy," Claire said meekly, tucking her hair behind her newly pierced ears. Momma had taken us all to one of her lush doctor friends to have our ears pierced. We were lucky he was having a good day. He hit our ear lobes on the first try unlike the dentist who often pricked our tongues and lips.

Momma laughed and took a drag off her cigarette, waving her other hand dismissively. "Why don't you get out of here, Chester?"

Daddy shook his head. "They don't want you in here," he muttered. He left Momma there, but she wasn't interested in talking to us anymore. She turned and followed his footsteps down the hall to their bedroom.

"Why'd you even take up with me in the first place?" she shouted, launching into her If-I-hadn't-married-you tirade. "I could have finished college or married that attorney fellow from New Orleans."

"Oh, hell, Esther, I wish you would have. He'd have saved me the disappointment of finding out there's not a damn thing going on inside that head of yours. You think I haven't wanted to kick myself a million times for pulling your drunken ass off the floor at Deare's and asking you to dance."

"You spineless bastard," Momma screamed. "Come back here!" Her footsteps pounded down the hall after his.

Claire and I didn't want to work on the collage anymore. We stuffed the torn pieces of paper into the trash can, gathered the Elmer's glue, the scissors, and the unused paper, stashing them in my desk drawer. Claire ran to her room. I flipped off the light and jumped into bed, pulling the covers up. Momma screamed, "I hate you too. You're the crazy one, just like your mother."

My bedroom door sprang open—Momma? No. Anne darted in while Daddy yelled, "I'm warning you, Bump, you better settle down, or else."

Momma laughed even though he'd used his mean voice to emphasize "or else."

"You bastard, what are you going to do?"

"Go back. Close the door," I told Anne.

She twisted around, squirrel-like, and banged it shut, then leapt onto my bed in her filthy shorts and T-shirt. "They're fighting in the hallway."

"No, really?" I asked, letting go of the covers so she could climb in. "Do you know why Daddy's so mad?"

Anne shrugged and turned toward the window. She never talked about the scary stuff the way Claire and I often did when we shared a room. Momma let out a shrill scream. Something banged into the wall.

"Let go of me!" She sounded like a cat coughing up a fur ball. There was a silence and then a moan. "I can't…"

Anne turned back and we both sat up. Momma was crying.

"You bitch, I should kill you."

Kill Momma? I ran to the door and opened it. Anne scrambled behind. Claire and Nanette were already in their open doorway. I looked past them to Daddy. He had Momma's head pinned against the wall; one hand gripped her jaw and the other hand held her right arm back. Her free hand kept trying to hit his face. But she couldn't reach.

"Stop it, Esther! So help me, I'll break your fucking skull."

Aimee opened her door. She stood there in her nightgown, nervously crossing and uncrossing her arm, and then motioning us to go back inside our rooms.

"All I want is some peace and quiet. Just peace and quiet," Daddy pleaded. Momma glared back, clenching her fist and striking out at him again. Daddy's knuckles got whiter as he squeezed her jaw.

"Go to hell," she said, trying to pull her head out of his grasp. Daddy yanked her forward and slammed her back into the wall.

"Do you give up? Will you let me be?"

Momma blinked a couple of times and then raked her fingernails over his shirtsleeve, raising little spots of blood through the cloth.

"You goddamn bitch."

Momma twisted and pulled, but Daddy shoved her again. I squeezed my hands tight as I watched Momma struggle to free herself.

Tears rolled down her face, and then Nanette screamed, "Daddy, stop it. You're hurting Momma!"

His hair fell forward as he slammed Momma against the wall again. I wondered if he could hear anything.

"Daddy!" Claire and I screamed.

He finally turned, looked at the four us, then Aimee. Grabbing a handful of Momma's hair, he swung her around and led her to the stairs. She tried to pull away, but he yanked harder. She looked like she was thinking the same thing I was: Was Daddy going to throw her down the stairs?

The closer they got to the first step, the harder Momma fought. Her eyes bulged with fear. But instead of throwing her off the edge, he began slamming her head into the wall with each step he took. Every time Momma's head struck the wall, the oil painting of the sailboat above the staircase shook.

What if Daddy kills her? Would the police come and take *him* away the way they did on television? Who'd take care of us? Yvette wouldn't move back home because she hardly ever came to visit. Chess was only sixteen and always out with his friends, and Aimee and Penny weren't even allowed to baby-sit us yet. Running to the top of the stairs, I screamed, "Stop it, Daddy. Please don't kill Momma."

He reached the last step and released her. She landed with a thud at the foot of the stairs. Hugging her knees, she moaned. He stepped over her, and she kicked at his leg. Shaking his head, he mumbled, "I can't take this anymore. Why are you doing this to me?" His shoulders trembled as he walked into the kitchen. I heard the back door slam.

What's going to happen now? Has he left us with her?

Aimee called out, "Momma, do you want me to call someone for you?" Momma gasped out Dr. Guree's name, and my sister ran to her bedroom.

I watched my mother and waited for Aimee to come back. If Momma sat up, I'd run to my room and get in bed. A few minutes later, Aimee reappeared. She had thrown on clothes. Penny trailed behind her. Claire and I scooted over to let Penny have a space along the banister. Hadn't she heard all the commotion? Why didn't she come out until now? Was she gabbing again on the phone with one of her middle school friends? She smelled of Noxzema and nail polish remover. Her nails were perfectly filed but her hands were trembling.

Aimee slowly walked down the stairs. Standing back from Momma, she said softly, "He's coming right over." Momma didn't budge. She whimpered like a baby, her arms covering her face. Aimee clutched the railing. She looked up at us and shrugged.

Penny turned around, and said, "Y'all better go to bed."

"But what about Momma?" Nanette whispered.

Yanking a loose thread from her blue nightgown, she sighed. "Dr. Guree will be here soon. She'll be fine." Her voice was so calm. Did she really not care?

She disappeared inside her room, and Anne and I followed Nanette and Claire into their room. Huddled together on the carpet with the door open a little bit, we waited for the doorbell.

It wasn't long before the chimes sounded. I listened for Daddy's footsteps but all I heard was Aimee, and then Dr. Guree's familiar, raspy voice in the foyer. "Hello. Oh, Esther dear. Don't move. Let me see if anything is broken. That must have been some nasty fall."

I listened for her to tell my father's former classmate what Daddy had done. But Momma just sobbed. We weren't the kind of family that told on each other.

"Everything looks fine. Nothing is broken. I'm going to carry you up now and put you in bed. I've got something that will help you sleep."

Aimee said, "Here. Let me carry your bag for you."

"Fine. You lead the way."

We opened the door wider. Four pairs of eyes followed Aimee and the doctor down the hall. Dr. Guree cradled Momma in his arms. He shuffled slowly toward her bedroom, panting under Momma's weight.

Sniffling with her face buried in his sweater, Momma said, "I wish you could take me away from here. I could marry you."

The following evening my father returned from work, tossing his gray hat on top of the kitchen stereo. He kissed Momma's forehead and pretended not to notice she was wearing her hair down. She usually pinned her thick brown hair up in a bun. But surely with all the bumps and bruises on the back of her head, she wasn't going to stick bobby pins anywhere near her scalp. She offered him a drink. Everything was going to be okay. They'd just had a fight, like my sisters and I often did, but now they were happy again, or so I thought.

Days later my sisters and I were in the kitchen cleaning up after dinner and Momma, plastered, wobbled down dressed in her robe and slippers for her nightly inspection. She opened the dishwasher and then closed it, glanced at the steaming cast iron pot Penny held out to Aimee to dry. As Claire and Nanette wiped down the table and counter tops, their hands cupped to collect crumbs, I walked around our restaurant-size kitchen balancing a stack of four smelly ashtrays in my arms.

"Give me one," Momma said, taking one off the top. She went to the bar and returned with a drink. As I wiped black smudges out of the other trays, Momma sat down at the table and lit a cigarette.

Earlier she'd complained to my father about the demands of the big house and all the kids. When he said, "Bump, can't you be thankful that you've got help, and that we don't have the financial worries of some of our friends," she nodded and turned away. It must have seemed to her that no one was listening.

Momma tossed her match into an ashtray as Penny and the others went to the den to watch television. Elbows on the table, Momma pressed her palms to her forehead and nearly singed her hair with the burning cigarette. I wanted to tiptoe up to her, kiss the sleeve of her robe, and whisper, "I love you, Momma," but I knew she'd swat me away.

She sat in the kitchen crying, while my sisters and Nickey and I watched *Bewitched.* From the next room her soft sobs accompanied the swishing and humming of the dishwasher. Sometime before the evening news, Daddy shooed us off to bed. A few minutes later the doorbell rang. I heard Dr. Guree's scratchy voice saying that he'd carry her up. In my mind I saw his slightly hunched back following as Daddy led them toward my parents' room. I fell asleep before the doctor left.

During the night, my mother woke and swallowed what she must have hoped would be a permanently numbing amount of sleeping pills.

In the morning I awoke and saw Evelyn, our newest maid, standing in front of my window flinging open the shutters. She looked like a black angel in her starched white uniform with the glow of the morning light surrounding her.

"Girls, get out of bed now so I can strip the sheets," she told Anne and me. "I'll be down in a minute to fix you some breakfast."

"Where's my mother?" asked Anne immediately. Momma was the only person who cooked in her kitchen unless she and Daddy were away on business.

Evelyn ignored my sister. I ran downstairs to find only Momma's purse sitting on the counter. The strong smell of coffee was absent. The ashtrays I'd cleaned the night before sat around the gas and electric stoves unused.

I hurried back upstairs to see if perhaps Momma was still sleeping. I crept along the gold carpeting, dubbed by us kids the Yellow Brick Road, to her bedroom door. I peeked inside. Their bed was empty. The covers had been pulled back and spilled over onto the floor. Daddy's long pillow, the one he partitioned their bed with, sat dimpled under the weight of the telephone. Momma wasn't in the bathroom, either. The door was closed; the space underneath it dark. I turned and ran.

Despite the craziness at night, by morning Momma always managed to pull herself together. Once again, nothing seemed dependable.

At breakfast, Chess announced that he and Bill were taking us swimming at the country club. We returned at dinner time to find Mrs. Credeur standing at the kitchen table trying to shoo Bernard away. The hound's brown and white tail slapped furiously on the bricks as he barked at her.

"Why are you here again?" asked Claire. Mrs. Credeur had baby-sat us for a week recently when my parents went to New York for the annual wholesale pharmaceutical convention.

She smiled as she set out forks and knives on the paper napkins she'd neatly folded into triangles. Nickey toddled past her to hug the dog, and she ran her spotted hand over his fluffy brown wisps. "Your mother is not feeling well. I'll be staying here a few days."

"Is she upstairs?" I asked.

She straightened Aimee's place setting. "I'm sure your father will talk to you when he gets home tonight. Run now and dry your hair."

When I came down for dinner, I hoped to see Momma standing at the stove. I thought that maybe she'd gone to the beauty parlor, gotten a new hairdo, and was now ready to come home to serve us dinner. Instead, there stood Mrs. Credeur in her purple- and pink-striped housedress, ladling red sauce over spaghetti.

Daddy sat at the head of the table, his eyelids looking as if cotton had been tucked beneath the splotchy skin. He leaned over his plate of noodles and sighed.

Seated in his booster seat, Nickey stared at the gray-haired Mrs. Credeur in Momma's chair and asked, "Where Mommy?" Daddy heaped grated cheese over his spaghetti and then reached for the salt shaker.

Nickey's nostrils flared and his lips puckered. "I want Mommy!"

My own fear bubbled to the surface and my chin wobbled. Daddy looked up from his plate. Heads turned in his direction. He wiped his face and cleared his throat. "Your mother has gone to a hotel for a few days to get some rest. She'll be home soon."

Chess and Aimee exchanged a glance. That's what he'd said the last time she went away. Daddy addressed Mrs. Credeur, "I've hired a second maid for the evenings and weekends. Her name is Ruby. She'll come by tomorrow at three, so please introduce her to Evelyn and show her around. I'll leave a check on the table for groceries. Esther's car keys are in her purse. Chess can take the young ones swimming at the club during the day. Call me at the office if there are any problems. But kids, you listen to Mrs. Credeur. Y'all hear me?"

We nodded. I felt safer than I had all day. Daddy was back in charge.

For much of my life, my father amazed me with his ability, most of the time anyway, to keep his head on straight. He was the fulcrum of our family, balancing and turning so that things never got too loose. At work, after a night of fighting with Momma or hard drinking with friends, he could still think clearly and make good business decisions to grow the struggling company he'd inherited into a multi-million dollar business. Other business leaders and his friends sought his advice, elected him to their bank board and to clubs, and overlooked his personal failings.

Ruby arrived the next day just as Daddy said she would. A skinny black woman with a shiny gold tooth, she didn't have a shy bone in her body. When Nickey toddled up to her, she crept her fingers under his armpits and tickled him until his diaper nearly fell off. Even though she looked a little scary with her gold tooth and dark skin and leathery hands, I felt drawn to her. Evenings while Daddy sat in his study, staring at the television and drinking Jack Daniel's and Coke, Claire, Anne, Nanette, Nickey, and I surrounded Ruby on the sofa like a litter of kittens, seeking the warmth of their mother as we watched our favorite programs.

She kept Dentyne in the pocket of her uniform, and if we swore not to swallow it—she said that gum took seven years to digest—she'd let us each have a stick. Unlike Evelyn, Ruby wasn't scared of Bernard. She brushed her wrinkled toes against the dog's smooth brown fur while he slept on the floor under the coffee table.

And Ruby was a storyteller, just like Chess. She told us how as a young girl she often skipped school to go crabbing with her older brothers. How once at Spanish Lake she out-swam a water moccasin. Some of her stories were sad. Once she ran her dark fingers through Anne's fine hair and told us about her daughter who loved to wear her hair in plaits with colorful barrettes. When we asked if she'd bring the girl with her so

we could play together, her eyes darkened, and she said that her baby was
with sweet Jesus. When we asked what happened, she shook her head
and said the girl had died before she even learned to tie her own
shoelaces.

Some stories she made up to tease us. Like how her husband came
home once stinking of whiskey and walloped her on the head with a broken chair leg because she wouldn't get out of bed to fix him some fried
eggs. Sometimes, she said, she set the deadbolt on the back door and
went to bed with a rifle hugged to her chest. One night she woke up to
find him standing at the bedroom door holding a crowbar and with the
look of the devil in his eyes. Before he reached the bed, she shot him
twice. But she was so gentle with us I knew she was lying. With all the
cruelty I had witnessed, I wanted more than anything then to believe in
the innocence of this loving woman.

"Ruby, what does your hair feel like?" I asked as she lathered her black
kinky hair over the bathroom sink.

"Ain't you ever touched a black person's hair before?" she teased.

"No. That's neat how it makes those ringlets."

"Here, put your hand right there and get you a feel but watch out!" I
jumped back and she laughed. "Oh, girl, it's not gonna bite you. I was just
foolin' with you."

"That feels neat. It's really soft. Can you make it straight if you want
like I've seen on some other black people?"

"Yeah, I can iron it but it's too much work. I don't have the time for
all that. Now move aside, girl, so I can rinse it out." She bent over and
ran the hot water over her curly mop. She squeezed the hair between her
fingers into dry frizzes. Drying it with a towel, she took out a hair pick
from the drawer where she kept her things.

Ruby and Evelyn shared the bathroom off the laundry room. This was
the only one they were supposed to use. Momma didn't want them using
our toilets or sinks. And when they ate their lunch in the laundry room,
they stood in front of the dryer looking out the window at our big oak
tree where later they'd sit on brown paper bags (so as not to stain their
white uniforms), commiserating and gossiping with other maids until the
city bus came screeching up to their corner. I felt embarrassed for our
maids when I walked in to grab an ice cream sandwich from the deep
freeze and found them standing to eat their meals.

"Is your boyfriend picking you up tonight?" I teased as she rung out her wet curly ringlets. The bathroom smelled like Palmolive—the dish soap she shampooed with.

"No, girl, I ain't got no boyfriend. Had me a husband, but I told you I shot him good when I found him with a lady."

"You said you shot him 'cause he had a crowbar," I said. "You're lying!"

She just shrugged. "Run along, girl, and get yourself ready for bed." I started out of the bathroom but then turned and gave her a big hug.

"What's that for?"

"I don't know. Bye."

She smiled at me, flashing her gold tooth. There was love in her smile. That's what I'd remember most about her, later, after my mother fired her.

Not long after Momma swallowed too many of her own pills, I made an amazing discovery. It was the next best thing to candy, and I loved anything sweet. Daddy asked me to run upstairs and get a bottle of aspirin from the armoire next to his bed. I went up to my parent's bedroom and pulled open the heavy mirrored door of the antique closet.

And there it all was. Besides the usual medicines like cough syrup, adult aspirin, and blue jars of vapor cream, I uncovered a stash of bottles of orange aspirin. I grabbed Daddy's aspirin and paused. Penny had been busy singing along to her record player when I passed her room. The others were either in their bedrooms or downstairs watching television. No one would see me.

Even though it was aspirin and taking too much could make my stomach bleed as Momma always warned, I figured I'd take my chances. I shook four orange pills into my palm, tossed them into my mouth, and squished them to a sweet fruity paste between my tongue and the roof of my mouth. Not quite satisfied, I ate a few more and returned the bottle to the shelf. Next I snatched a box of cherry cough drops, tore open the package, then dug out three. I slid the candy into the side pocket of my shorts, putting the box back in its exact spot. Closing the heavy door, I looked around the room.

It wasn't often we kids got to really spend any time alone there, except for Nickey. Whenever I got scared during the night and shuffled into their room, I found myself pointed back toward the door. But Nickey's crib, and later his twin bed, stood opposite my parent's own king-size bed. Their mattress dipped slightly in the two spots where they lay at night, back to back with the long pillow vertically separating them.

Popping a cough drop into my mouth, I headed to Momma's closet to pet her mink coat. I ran my hands up and down the soft, cool fur. I buried my face in it, pretending it was alive and warm as I inhaled the traces of Momma's perfume and hair spray.

Now standing before my father's recliner, I smiled falsely. "Here Daddy, your aspirin."

He took the bottle. A few minutes later Claire, Nanette, and I put Bernard, our dachshund, on the pool table and enticed him with a cookie to jump. Daddy walked through with his ice bucket and didn't even turn to yell at us when the dog hit the floor and yelped in pain. It seemed we were invisible.

I managed to keep my armoire discovery a secret, even from Claire and Nanette. After the first few visits, I had eaten more than half the aspirin in the first bottle. I began taking a few out of a different bottle every time, so no one would notice.

Momma's stay at Our Lady of Lourdes Hospital was interrupted by her escape. While my siblings and I were at school, Momma showed up dressed like a cowboy—blue jeans, a plaid shirt, a big belt with a round silver buckle, and boots. I can imagine the shocked look on Daddy's face when he opened the front door and saw Momma standing on the stoop in her getup.

"Bump, what are you doing here?"

"I'm back!" she announced, looking as if she'd just returned from a splendid vacation.

9 ~ California, 1991

Robert, one of the 50 respondents to my Bay Guardian personal ad, and I agreed to meet for coffee—one o'clock, Saturday afternoon, Zuni Café. I walked from my condo up Van Ness toward Market Street, my palms damp and itchy. Garbage swept along the sidewalk as a MUNI bus roared by and I rehearsed all the things I'd tell Robert about myself: I'd just completed my MBA at USF. I'd just been hired as senior project accountant for an architecture firm. And I really wanted to start playing tennis again. Then I'd ask about his sailing, noting that I'd sailed a sunfish once and loved it. Twenty feet from the Café, I saw him sitting at a corner table under the blue awning, staring at a golden retriever tethered to a nearby parking meter.

He was as cute as his photograph. Wavy brown hair. Nice build. Chiseled chin. What's he going to think when he sees me? There's still time to turn back and forget the whole thing, I told myself. I could go home and never answer my phone again. No, just get it over with. What can it hurt to meet him?

He turned away from the dog just as I approached his table. Nonchalantly, I wiped my moist hands on my blue jeans one last time.

"Robert?"

"Marie? Hi."

We shook hands, his brown eyes running the length of my over-dyed blond hair to my clogs. No amount of sucking-in would hide my potbelly.

He smiled and looked around as I sat down. God, is he embarrassed to be seen with me? Why did I buy these goofy designer brown and orange glasses? I forced a smile. "Beautiful weekend, isn't it? I guess you don't sail much in the winter."

"No. Besides, that boat in the picture belongs to a friend. I'm actually remodeling my flat, and I've been spending most of my weekends working on it."

"What are you doing to it?"

"Everything. Right now the bathroom's torn up. It's funny because that's sort of how I came to answer your ad. I had a girlfriend living with me for the past couple of years, but after I tore out the john and told her she'd have to pee in the shower until I replaced the floor and toilet, she left. I guess she'd had enough. So now I have to wait until I get to the office to take a dump or find a restaurant and borrow their facilities."

I waited for him to chuckle, to say he was joking, but he didn't. Trying not to reveal my disgust, all I could manage was, "Oh, I see." Get out of there, Marie, a faint voice whispered.

"So, you said you're an accountant?"

"Yeah, I work at, uh, Bank of America," I lied. "It's pretty boring stuff. Well, you know what, I was going to call you last night but it was too late. You see, this is going to sound pretty strange and all, but I just got back together with my boyfriend. Just yesterday. So I'm sorry you came all the way out here for nothing, but I'm not really, uh, available anymore. It was nice meeting you."

"Likewise."

"Have a nice weekend and good luck with your bathroom." I left the table, praying he wouldn't follow me home.

Since the prospect of ever finding anyone seemed daunting and remote, I immersed myself in work. I worked until eight or nine in the evenings. Weekends I trudged in to sort through the mess of paperwork I had inherited from the woman before me. In December I sold my Honda because, short of begging, borrowing, or stealing, or even worse, asking Daddy for another loan, I knew I'd never come up with the money for my property taxes. When Penny came out for another one of her biannual visits shortly before Christmas, I told her I was actually much better off without a car—taking the bus forced me to walk more and I saved money on gas and insurance. Graciously, she didn't mention the noticeable lack of accessories around my once overcrowded condo or my diminished jewelry collection. I'd sold many of my furnishings at the Sausalito Flea Market and my rings and bracelets at filthy pawnshops off Market Street to keep my homeowners' association from placing a lien on my condo for delinquent dues.

As the New Year approached, I drew up a list of resolutions. Besides making a serious dent into my debt, I decided to quit drinking. The reason: loneliness. I'd never sustain a relationship if I continued to drink. More than one guy remarked on my blackouts, my inability to remember

conversations and events. Besides, drinking contributed other stresses—
I constantly charged liquor on my credit cards even though they were
nearly at their limits. I wasted years of Saturdays and Sundays incapaci-
tated from hangovers. I behaved so obnoxiously when drunk that I was
often too embarrassed to see friends again. And the severe munchies I got
when I drank made me fat.

I knew I could do it. I'd already solved my chronic lateness to work.

I was always late. Fifteen, thirty, sometimes forty-five minutes. Every
time I walked by the secretary's desk, nervous, self-conscious, I swore I'd
get up earlier the next morning. I started getting paranoid. Did everyone
know I got drunk the night before? Did they all know I had to sell my
car? I felt out of sync with my coworkers—as if something important had
occurred while I was still on my way to work. I always blamed my tardi-
ness on the lousy MUNI buses, my fickle alarm clock, or the stupid taxi
driver who never showed up. One morning as I threw myself down in my
chair, panting from having run all the way from the Embarcadero, a
notion struck me. Decide right now to wake up at seven o'clock, no matter what, and you'll never have to think of another excuse for being late.
The dirty looks, imagined or real, the paranoia, the lying on my
timesheets, would be a thing of the past.

I resolved to be punctual. And it worked. If I could stop one behavior, change my life overnight, then I could make other huge changes. It
was as obvious and simple as that. I hoped. And that was the catalyst for
me to quit drinking.

Now the only problem: facing my family. Daddy's words always stuck
in my mind: What's worse than a renounced whore? A renounced
drinker! Ha. Ha. He treated Yvette with contempt ever since she quit
drinking and started blabbing family secrets at her AA meetings.
Grandma, before she died, always badgered Aimee about her decision to
go on the wagon, "Oh, come on now. What's *wrong* with you anyway?
There's no harm in one little beer."

I didn't dare claim to be an alcoholic or any of that nonsense. If asked,
I simply said I wanted to see what it was like not to drink. No elabora-
tion. Let my friends and family think it was just another passing whim.
That way I'd be less of a target for ridicule.

Ironically, my friends and coworkers seemed unfazed by my decision.
I began noticing that a lot of people in San Francisco didn't drink and
people didn't treat them like outcasts.

10 ~ Louisiana, 1968

Family lore says that Momma rang the front door while Daddy was home napping after lunch before returning to the office. He found her standing there, grinning from ear to ear in her blue jeans and plaid shirt. Somehow she'd made her way from the hospital to Bell's Sporting Goods in the Oil Center, charged a new outfit to Daddy's account, and then home. She sashayed past, the heels of her boots clicking against the brick floor.

It wasn't long before an ambulance announced its approach with siren and flashing lights. Two men in blue uniforms barreled up the sidewalk to the front door. One of them had something white tucked under his arm.

"She's back there," Daddy said in a low voice, tipping his head toward the den. He swept the dachshund up into his arms and threw him into the piano room, closing the door. "She doesn't know you're coming. She's going to be pretty upset." The guys nodded and followed him.

Suddenly there was a high-pitched scream and Momma cried, "NO! NO!" A chair leg screeched across the brick floor. Bernard began barking loudly again. "No, goddammit!" Her fancy cowboy boots shuffled against the floor.

"Esther, calm down," Daddy called out.

"Get away from me. Ow! Let go."

"Mrs. Etienne, we don't want to hurt you. Please. It'll be easier if you don't fight us," one of the men pleaded.

Something made of metal—probably a TV tray—hit the floor. Another scream. Bernard scratched at the piano room door, growling and barking.

"Hold her still," one of the men yelled.

"Please, Chester, I don't want to go back there. Please. I'll be good."

"Damn, she bit me!"

"Hang on, hang on—there, I've almost got it."

"Esther, it's for your own good. Just till you get—"

"Take this damn thing off of me," Momma sobbed. "I can't go back there."

"Got it. Come on."

Daddy darted into the foyer and ran to open the front door. The men held Momma, her arms bound to her body in the white jacket. Even bundled up, she kicked at the men's shins and jerked her body to try to free herself, crying, "Please! I don't want to go back!" They yanked her toward the door while Daddy stared at the floor.

"You fucking bastards better get your hands off me! You're trying to kill me! Chester, you coward, you spineless bastard."

Dr. Guree came to visit my father that evening. By then my older sisters had heard from the maid abut Momma's surprise visit and her cowboy outfit. From there the story trickled down to me. I crept over to the patio door, not far from the backside of my father's recliner, and listened to them talk in the study. Dr. Guree told my father to give her some time, that she was pretty angry at being restrained. The doctors had drugged her to calm her down. He mumbled something about giving her more shock treatments and apologized for not seeing sooner that she needed more help than he could offer. Daddy's head dropped, and he sobbed. His tears sent chills through me.

We didn't dare ask Daddy directly about Momma or mention her name. There were established rules in our family. We didn't ask grownups direct questions that would make them get upset, and since it was not clear which questions were safe and unsafe, we found it best not to ask too many at all. Instead, in our rooms at night, Nanette, Claire, and I whispered about all the possibilities.

"What if they kill her in that hospital?" I said. "You think Daddy would marry Mrs. Credeur so she could take care of us?"

"I hope not," Claire said. "She's too old and her boobs hang all the way down to her underwear." We all laughed remembering how we had spied on her during her last stay.

At night I lay in bed, wondering if Momma was lonely and scared. Images of her lying in a bed like a zombie, tied down with straps, of her being electrocuted, smoke shooting out of her ears and mouth and her eyes bulging the way Chess described it, haunted my dreams. Had she really waltzed into Bell's Sporting Goods wearing only slippers and a hospital gown and slapped a size 14 jeans, belts and boots on the counter with the instructions, "Charge it to Chester Etienne"? I imagined the snickers of the sales clerks when she strolled out in her tight blue jeans and matted brown hair.

I felt guilty about not really missing her. It was nice without her. We got cakes from her friends Mrs. Duhon and Mrs. Dooley, and Aunt Lilia showed up one day with ice cream and made Coke floats for us. Mrs. Credeur never spanked us—she just twisted our arms if we didn't listen to her. If we stayed out of the study at night, Daddy didn't make us go to sleep at eight. The yelling had stopped. And most of all, no one came into my room at night. I could sleep. I no longer had to be so vigilant.

But at the country club pool I was sure that all the swimmers knew my mother had been locked away for weeks now. Certain they knew that Momma hated her children and her life *so much* that she kept trying to kill herself to get away from us. Did my friends' parents tell their daughters to watch out because that Etienne girl's mother is crazy? I told myself perhaps other families were just as crazy. But somehow I didn't think so.

On weekends my brothers, sisters, and I paddled around in our swimming pool in the new hard plastic lifeboats Daddy bought for us, while he lounged by the pool, smoking his Winstons, his eyes hidden behind dark sunglasses. He took us out in the Gulf of Mexico on his fishing boat, to the movies, to baseball games, and on long, quiet car rides. His favorite destination: the farmland he owned in the country. He parked his Eldorado at the white picket fence where sugarcane stood tall on the flat land and seemed to stretch from one parish to another. We crunched on the sweet, celery-like grass, brandished our stalks like swords in play battle, and then pretended to make crank calls with the new black rotary telephone that my father had installed in his car as he hummed to the radio and stared out into the endless fields.

Chess and my father began framing in our two-story playhouse that would sit in the shade of an old oak tree. They drank beer to cool themselves as they worked silently, side by side. They'd spend hours, it seemed, exchanging only nods or smiles, ignoring the rest of us buzzing about. This project seemed to be their joint refuge.

Daddy brought home a furry white Samoyed puppy. He named her Bubbalinka. Bernard had to be put to sleep because he had disk problems. We had played too rough with him, forced him to jump once too often from the pool table. Sadly, the cruelties we inflicted on our pets were overlooked, just like the cruelties inflicted on us.

My father took us to his business, the Wholesale, where the thick concrete walls kept the building bone-numbing cold. Nickey always headed straight to the gun case display—Daddy's vast collection of pearl, ivory, and wormwood handled pistols—and pressed his tiny hands to the glass. His eyes traced the longer barrels, the short barrels, and then jumped from silver bullet to gold-tipped bullet. While Nickey gaped, Daddy unlocked his desk drawer. He handed the keys to the candy and Coke machines to Nanette, at nine, the oldest child present.

"Stay out of trouble." Daddy's voice echoed through the quiet building as we took off running.

Nanette opened up the room and headed to the candy machine. Encircling her, we pushed and shoved our way closer to the dispenser while she unlatched the machine. Immediately we ransacked the rows of potato chips, chewing gum, and chocolate bars. She unlocked the Coke machine and handed us each a bottle.

After the break room, we headed to the warehouse.

Rows and rows of wobbly metal shelving lined the enormous space. Nanette flipped on the overhead fluorescent lights that hummed as we tore through the dusty-smelling place, running in and out of the rows chasing each other, screaming in surprise when one of us suddenly darted out from around the corner. We ran carelessly. When we bumped boxes off the shelves we stood around pointing fingers at each other until Claire or Anne gave in, replaced some of the boxes, and kicked the rest under the shelves. Then we were off again.

When we tired of chasing each other, we snooped around at the bottles and boxes of pills, diapers, toaster ovens, Kleenex, toilet paper, toothbrushes, douche bags, Band-Aids, and needles—some of them really big.

"Look at her butt," Anne teased, holding up a bottle of Coppertone lotion that pictured a dog ripping off a girl's bathing suit bottom.

Nanette ran by with Claire chasing behind and I called out, "Look at these chocolates." Nanette snatched the box from my hands.

"EXLAX. Chocolate flavored. This is to help you take a dump. Gross, Marie!" She threw the box back at me and rolled her eyes.

And on the Fourth of July my father took us to a parade on Jefferson Street. I watched his eyes mist with patriotism when the marching band went by in their green and white uniforms playing the "Star Spangled Banner."

That night Daddy came into the den carrying a scuffed black case.

"Hey, kids. Watch this," he said, setting the case on the coffee table. He grinned, producing a shiny gold trumpet from the box that was lined in rich blue velvet. I'd never seen it before. It was beautiful. Bubbalinka stood on her hind legs to sniff inside the case.

"I played this horn in college."

He cleared his throat, pressed the mouthpiece against his lips, and then blew. Bubbalinka reared back and barked at the horn as though the metal had come alive. Daddy's cheeks puffed out like a blowfish; his whiskers were the spines. He started and stopped a few times, laughed at himself, and wiped his lips, and then played until the jerky notes finally came together to form a recognizable song. My father's long, smooth fingers moved up and down on the buttons. He played "When The Saints Go Marching In," the song we knew well from the Mardi Gras parades, and my sisters and I bounced on the sofa cushions and clapped our hands. After a while, despite our pleas to continue, he packed it away and shoved it back on the top shelf in his study closet. Over the years we begged him to take his horn down, but it wouldn't be until Penny was asked to be a royal maid in a Mardi Gras ball that he played another note.

With Momma away, it was safe to leave our rooms at night as long as we didn't wake Daddy. I often climbed in bed with Claire and Nanette. Lying side by side, we drew words and pictures on each other's back with our fingers. Nanette and I giggled, taking turns tickling Claire. As Claire squirmed and begged us to stop, Anne crept into Aimee and Penny's room and crawled under their sheets.

During the two months Momma was gone, I made many trips to my parents' bedroom to steal orange aspirin and cherry cough drops. I rummaged through Momma's dressing room, sniffing her face powder and hairbrush, spraying my wrists with her perfume. I drew tiny hearts in the fine beige dust that covered the bottom of the drawer that she always left open when she dabbed the round powder puff on her fuzzy cheeks.

In a warped way, it was a very good summer despite its beginnings, despite an increasing number of arguments between Daddy and Chess over speeding tickets and mysterious scrapes and dents that speckled his second-hand Ford and despite the knowledge that one day my mother would return.

Pale and thin, Momma finally returned in early August. Dr. Guree told Daddy her depression had lifted and she was no longer a danger to herself.

She stood at the wrought iron gate wearing a pretty new dress. Holding

Daddy's hand, Momma squinted in the sun and smiled. I dropped the oar that Claire and I were fighting over and swam to the steps.

Nickey reached her first, leaving a trail of tiny footprints on the cement. Water dripped from his life jacket and his body as he threw his arms around Momma's legs.

"Hold on there, Little Fellow, let's get you dried off," Daddy said, grabbing a beach towel from a nearby chair. He peeled Nickey's hands off Momma and removed the vest. While the rest of us fought over towels, Daddy started to dry my brother, but Momma didn't seem to care about her dress getting wet; she reached down and picked him up. I draped myself in a towel and waited my turn to say hello.

That day by the pool, Momma hugged me tighter than I can ever remember. I wanted her to hold me forever. Her brown eyes sparkled with tears as she looked down at each of us and said, "I've missed you, darling. I love you."

"I love you, too," I remember whispering nervously, afraid I might do something to send her back to the hospital. Daddy had warned us to take it easy on her. Now that she was back, I never wanted her to be taken away again.

Daddy enrolled us in the neighborhood schools so that Momma wouldn't have to drive us back and forth to the Catholic school. Claire and I walked the three blocks to Woodvale Elementary. Nanette's and Penny's school, L. J. Alleman Middle School, was only a block away. Chess drove himself and Aimee to Lafayette High School, where she was a freshman and he a junior. Yvette made the long drive from New Orleans every Saturday for lunch.

After Momma's return, Daddy brought her little gifts more often. Once it was a pearl bracelet; another time it was a hand-painted porcelain bouquet of flowers. For their wedding anniversary Daddy bought her a fancy diamond necklace. Aimee whispered that their anniversary had mysteriously changed from May to December, exactly three months after Yvette's birthday.

One day some men delivered a huge plastic box with rounded corners, lots of dials, and a door. Daddy called it a portable steam bath. He wore the biggest smile when he came downstairs in his swim shorts and led Momma over to it so he could demonstrate to her how to operate the new present. We all watched Daddy set the metal knobs on "medium" and "ten," open the door, and climb into the strange box. When he pulled the door shut, he looked as if a gray monster had swallowed him whole, leaving only his head poking out of the mouth. As steam escaped from the narrow opening around Daddy's neck, Momma's jaw dropped and she shook her head.

"Oh, but Esther, you've got to try it," said Daddy, watching her back away from the hissing monster. "It feels wonderful."

My mother's head shook harder. She warned, "Chester, there's no way you're getting me in that contraption." She and Chess exchanged a little nervous laugh before she returned to the living room to continue reading her paperback romance novel.

The steam box sat on the porch for months untouched. Momma never went near it except to show it to Mrs. Duhon and Aunt Lilia, who also shook their heads and laughed at the absurdity of the gift in light of her recent confinement at the hospital with its own hissing monsters. Finally Daddy asked the colored men who mowed our lawns if they wanted to take it home. Listening to Daddy explain the dials, the sweaty men approached the steam box cautiously as they did the flowerbeds by the porch window when Bubbalinka pressed her nose against the glass and barked at them. The next morning they showed up with a bunch of their friends and carried the contraption out to their truck. I imagined passing a row of dilapidated shotgun houses on the way to the country club and spotting Daddy's steam bath on someone's front porch.

For weeks after Momma came home, I slept on my back facing the door just in case. The creaking sound of the floorboards and the feeling of someone approaching my bed awakened me frequently during those weeks. But always when I opened my eyes, no one was there. For the longest time, she didn't come to our bedroom to spank us, and there was no fighting in the hallway. When we misbehaved, she simply asked us to stop. When we taunted Nickey, she told us to quit. She didn't pull us into the kitchen bathroom. She cleaned up endless piles of dog shit, never once kicking Bubbalinka or smearing her nose in it.

When she caught me in her bedroom shaking orange aspirin into my palm, all she did was warn me to stay out of the armoire or I'd give myself a bleeding stomach. It seemed that no matter what we did—even traipse through the kitchen in our wet swimsuits, dripping water over the freshly mopped floor—she wouldn't yell. Instead she just sucked in a deep breath and smoothed down her blouse with her shaky hands.

I knew it wouldn't last forever. And in a strange way I wished the change would come sooner rather than later. The anticipation seemed scarier than the actual punishment.

11 ~

Momma set the mugs of coffee-milk on my nightstand and then scowled at the sunflower seeds scattered on my bedroom floor.

"I didn't do that," I stammered, "Nickey was playing there and—"

"Shut up! Get out of bed this instant."

Anne sat up, scooting away from me as if I had cooties.

Yanking me into the bathroom, Momma grabbed the closest hairbrush. "I've told you kids a thousand times."

Nodding and trembling, I gathered my nightgown and pulled down my underwear. The first strike sent me crashing into the white cabinets, and I gasped.

"Hold still, goddamn you," she said, panting.

The stiff bristles bit into my behind and my legs buckled. I pictured myself standing on the edge of the high board at the country club. Eyes squeezed shut and toes pressed against the gritty surface of my imagination, I envisioned myself stepping forward, knowing that in moments my body would smack against the water.

When I felt her hand finally slacken its grip, I squinted to see if she was done. She caught me looking at her marble-like brown eyes in the mirror. Her hand came around, and I flinched. The brush struck the glass, and I ducked at the sound of the crash, expecting the mirror to shatter.

Sucking in a huge breath of air, Momma exhaled with a satisfied sigh. "Now go clean up that mess and then get dressed for school." It was the first day of third grade. Ten brand-new dresses hung in my closet.

When my bathroom door closed behind her, I fell onto the cold tile floor. Sobbing, with my panties draped around my ankles, I turned as Nanette's adjoining door creaked open.

"You all right?" She tiptoed toward me. "Why was she mad?"

"Sunflower seeds." I choked on my tears. "I hate Nickey."

"What'd he do?" Nanette sat beside me.

"He kicks over my trashcan and I get spanked. He's her favorite. Goddamn little brat. I hate him. I hate her. I wish they were both dead."

"Don't say that." Nanette reached back and tapped her knuckles three times on the door to ward off bad luck. Then she gently rubbed circles on my back until I finished crying.

Shame started its hurried ascent as we passed others in the hall. My eyes were still puffy from crying, and worse, my mother looked as if she'd swallowed a 50-pound turkey, bones and all. Since her return from the hospital she'd quickly plumped herself back up. Her sweater barely stretched over her enormous stomach, and she cared not a bit that her polyester pants didn't even reach her loafers. Hand and hand, just like regular mothers and daughters, we walked into my new classroom. I waved to my best friend, Robin, who stood near the teacher. Robin's mother, looking as if she just stepped out of a Sears catalog, waited behind the crowd of moms. Why couldn't Momma be skinny and pretty and nice like Robin's?

Seeing the line ahead, Momma glanced at her gold watch.

"You don't have to wait," I mumbled, "the teacher looks kind of busy."

Momma nodded and leaned over to receive a kiss. I surrendered a peck hoping no one would notice.

Throughout school I worked hard at being popular. I wanted to be well-liked and admired like the pretty, sought-after girls. Though my looks weren't extraordinary, no one ever compared my face to an orangutan's butt. My sandy blond hair didn't flip up in funny ways. My nose turned up slightly at the end but wasn't too wide or pointed like some kids' beaks.

I didn't really dislike the unpopular girls, but I avoided getting dumped into their group. My friends and I swapped cruel insults about them. We drew cartoons of the smart girls naked, giving them humongous boobs like our mothers. I feared the other girls' differentness. I feared being teased or talked about behind my back the way my parents talked about their friends. I didn't want conversations to screech to a halt when I nudged my way into a group. I didn't want people to stare at me, to point, to giggle at my clothes or the way I walked or smelled, so I learned how to fit in. Being the last person called for Red Rover was worse than getting caught with your finger up your nose.

I jumped rope faster and longer than the reigning champ. I stole money from my parents to buy candy for my friends. I became the silly one. The brave one. The clever one. *See what I can do. Hey, watch this. Don't look at her—look at me.*

I pretended that my friends saw only what I wanted them to see. I convinced myself that no one knew Momma had been locked up in a hospital for crazy people. No one noticed, I told myself, the way my parents and their friends stumbled into furniture, garbled their words, and argued in loud voices as they poured drink after drink. Some days, protecting my popularity felt like struggling to climb to the top of a flagpole only to find gravity pulling me back down.

"I can't wait till Friday. Can you?" Robin asked, hugging me hello.

I smiled and shook my head. By age eight, I was finally old enough for overnights. Robin was having the first slumber party of the year. For weeks we'd been talking about all the games we'd play and the girls she'd invite.

Ten minutes into Robin's party, playing a game of Monster where I was *it*, I twisted my leg jumping off her playhouse roof. Nothing could have been worse, I thought, than having to leave my best friend's party early and having to disrupt my mother during her cocktail hour, especially on a night she and my father had plans to go out with their friends for dinner.

Standing at the kitchen door, holding me in his arms, Daddy asked, "Shall I take her upstairs?"

My leg throbbed as he waited for my mother to take the last three gulps of her cocktail. He shifted my weight, and I moaned in pain, staring at the damp napkin stuck to her glass. Finally the ice clinked and Momma lowered her drink. "No. Put her on the sofa. That way I won't have to go up and down those damn stairs all evening to check on her."

He set me down on the scratchy gold cushions. "Are you comfortable?"

"I'm okay." I squeezed my eyes shut, waiting for the wave of pain to pass. Momma had insisted on bringing me home rather than taking me to the emergency room. Even though I hurt a lot, I didn't beg them to take me to the hospital because I feared my making my mother angrier.

"Can I watch TV?"

"Sure, Sweetheartsabean." He turned the television on and disappeared into his study before the picture came into focus. I was left watch-

ing the six o'clock news with the weird newslady who was always changing her hair color—from vanilla ice cream to chocolate pudding to black
licorice to carrots.

I sat on the sofa for a long time trying not to move my leg, staring at
the television. Claire, Anne, Nanette, and Nickey came downstairs
briefly to hear my story of jumping off Robin's playhouse. But the sound
of Momma banging pots and dishes in the kitchen sent them upstairs, out
of her way. Chess, Aimee, and Penny stopped by for a minute before
heading to a high school football game.

"I was hoping for something a little more impressive. Like a bone poking through your skin," Chess teased as he slid on his blue jeans jacket
and waved good-bye.

Momma heated up Campbell's chicken noodle soup and fixed tuna
fish sandwiches for my father and me. The others had eaten burgers from
McDonald's earlier. Just as the ten o'clock news came on, the back door
opened and Penny and Aimee came in.

"Is she pretty looped?" Aimee asked me, pulling off her purple fake fur
coat and glancing toward the study where my parents were watching TV.

I nodded. At least a half dozen times that evening I had looked out
the French doors to see Momma standing at the patio bar with a cigarette
dangling from her mouth, tossing her used ice into the metal sink and
scooping out fresh cubes.

Aimee sucked in a deep breath. She and Penny trudged into the study
to let them know they were home.

Momma said something I couldn't make out. Penny responded, "He
dropped us off. He said to tell you he was going out with his friends for
awhile." I figured she was talking about Chess.

After Aimee and Penny went upstairs to bed, Momma brought me my
blue nightgown. She threw it on the sofa.

"Sit up so I can take your pants off."

Her hands clumsily tugged at my pants zipper. I bit my lip. I didn't
think I could take any more pain.

"Stop pulling away from me." She leaned over me breathing into my
face. The stinking alcohol made my stomach queasy. I was terrified I'd
throw up.

"You've got to straighten your legs for me or else I'll never get these
damn pants off." She yanked them out from under me and I let out a
scream so loud that even she looked startled.

"Please, Momma, please don't!" While I took short, quick breaths, she tugged on my belt loops until she got the pants down to my knees. I pressed my hands harder against the cushions to keep my butt up to help her. My arms and shoulders shook violently. "It hurts, Momma. I'm not pretending."

"Shut up. If you didn't act like such a fool, I wouldn't be dressing you like a baby."

She dropped the nightgown into my lap. "Now take your shirt off and put this on. You can sleep down here tonight if it hurts that much."

She left and came back with my sleeping bag and a pillow. "Good night." She planted a cold, firm kiss on my forehead. I watched her big butt cross the room and disappear into the foyer. Evil thoughts scurried through my head.

Chess came home around eleven, and Daddy went about his nightly routine. He checked and locked all the doors, turned off all the lights, and fixed himself a tall glass of ice water.

"Sweetheartsabean, you'll be all right down here tonight, won't you?" Daddy asked, tucking the sleeping bag under my chin.

I nodded and he smiled wearily as he bent down to kiss me.

Abandoned. Trapped. I waited for my eyes to adjust to the darkness.

I heard a tapping in the kitchen and turned my head, holding my breath until I could make out the shape of our new gray puppy, Penelope, lumbering toward me. I wished for sleep so I could escape my terror. But just like on Christmas Eve, when you pray for the night to pass quickly, it seemed the harder I wished for sleep, the longer it took to arrive.

The house came alive with odd sounds. I tried identifying the noises to tame them, to crush their power. On the patio it was trapped crickets calling their friends for help. Over there, fresh ice falling from the ice-maker. The air conditioner clicking on and off. The sofa springs squeaking as I tried to find a comfortable position. Just a twig tapping at the window. Not a severed hand, I prayed.

How could Daddy leave me down here by myself? I couldn't even move. No one had bothered to ask me if I needed to go to the bathroom —and I did.

A vision of Bubbalinka, our Samoyed puppy, smeared with her own blood and lying in the neighbor's yard, popped into my head. We'd accidentally left the gate open. The dog ran straight to the street. And just like Daddy had warned, she was struck by a car. Nanette, Claire, and I had stood next to him, sobbing as he pointed the gun and told us to look away. I wondered if it might not be better to be dead than in pain. I began crying again until I finally fell asleep.

I woke up when I sensed someone standing over me. Daddy pried my fingers off the sleeping bag. A chill ran through my body as he pulled the cover off.

"Marie, it's Daddy."

"What? What's wrong?"

"Shu, sweetheart, don't make a sound," he whispered. "I'm going to take you to the hospital."

I felt drugged and exhausted as he slipped his hands around me. Penelope sniffed at Daddy's slacks.

"Go away, mutt." He kicked the puppy away.

As he lifted me I felt the familiar pain shoot through my leg. "Is it morning already?"

"No, it's one o'clock. Be quiet now. We don't want to wake your mother. Hold on tight." He carried me out of the house into the muggy dark night.

After setting me down in the front seat of his Eldorado, he slid behind the steering wheel. "Are you all right?"

"I'm fine, Daddy." I smiled at him as the car engine revved. I watched him light a cigarette, and then I rolled my window down an inch. The sound of crickets kept us company as we stole away in his car.

"It's broken here at the tibia," the doctor said, pointing with his stubby fingers to the x-ray. The bone in my right leg had split into two nearly equal pieces that overlapped each other.

"The break looks clean," he assured Daddy.

I smiled proudly as if that were a good thing. Now Momma would know I wasn't pretending.

The doctor stepped away from the x-ray. "She'll need a cast. May I speak to you for a minute outside?"

Daddy nodded. Before leaving me alone, he bent over to kiss my forehead, brushing his sharp whiskers against my skin. "I love you, darling."

"I love you too, Daddy."

A nurse came in, and shortly after, my father returned. "It looks like you get to stay here for a few days," he said, taking my hands into his shaky grasp.

The sound of metal clanging on metal woke me in the morning. The greasy smell of scrambled eggs filled the room. For a moment I'd forgotten what happened the night before.

"I'll just leave this tray here for when she wakes up and come back later to bathe her," said a nurse, unaware of my eyes struggling to open.

Momma sat next to my bed. Was she going to be angry with me? Her head turned toward me.

"Look who's awake," she said.

She didn't look mad. Her eyes narrowed and a gentle smile formed as she reached over the bed railing to kiss me.

"Where's Daddy?"

"He went home to shower," she answered, stroking my arm. "He'll be back later. Can I adjust your bed for you? You must be hungry."

I nodded. Momma examined the controls on the side of my bed and then chose a button.

"This is cool." I grinned as the back of the bed lifted forward. The thin blanket sank into a ravine between my legs. My right leg in its cast looked huge as a tree trunk compared to the left one.

"Wanna see my cast?" I yanked back the sheet.

Momma gasped when she saw the bumpy white plaster extending from the very top of my thigh to the end of my toes. "Oh, Lord!" Her eyes glistened with tears as she jerked her head away and sucked in a deep breath. When she turned back toward me, her eyes searched mine for forgiveness.

"You can be the first to sign it."

She wiped her eyes, shook her head no, and reached over to squeeze my hand.

"I brought you something." She bent down. From the rustling of a paper bag she produced a teddy bear.

I took the bear and hugged him to my chest. I don't think I realized then the courage it took for my mother to come to my hospital room that day.

I stayed at Our Lady of Lourdes Hospital for a whole week. They had had to reset the bone, and my leg still ached. Also, Daddy said the doctor wanted to ensure that I didn't move around too much and was properly looked after.

Every morning Momma visited me with a gift. And every evening after work Daddy stopped by. He brought me candy bars from the office. Together we watched the five o'clock news. After the business report, he kissed my forehead and wished me a good night. Of the kids, only Chess, Aimee, and Penny were old enough to visit. They came by twice as a group, once sneaking Nanette past the nurses' station.

Two nights before the doctor sent me home, I was lying in bed looking around for a stick or a fork to shove down into my cast—I had a terrible itch—when suddenly the door opened. Peeking around the corner, Chess whispered, "Can I come in?"

"Sure." I whacked at the hard cast as if that would somehow help.

My brother crossed the room with his hands folded across his chest. His face looked pale against his dark green turtleneck.

"I've got an itch that's killing me," I announced, raising my bed. "What are you doing here so late?"

He combed his fingers through his oily brown hair. "I'm meeting some friends later and decided to stop by for a quick visit. How's it going here?"

"All right, I guess. The doctor said I have to wear the cast for four to five months."

"Wow, bummer for you. This room looks like a damn toy store." He surveyed the stuffed animals and dolls, the unopened board games, the huge Playskool parking garage and cars, and the vases of limp flowers lining the window. "You've sure got Momma going on a heavy duty guilt trip, haven't you?"

"She just brings the presents. I didn't ask for them." I suddenly felt ashamed. To shift his attention, I asked, "Where do you and your friends go at night?"

"Shoot pool. Drink some beer." He glanced at the stacks of gifts again. "Hey, you want to play a game of checkers?"

"Sure. I'm not very good, though."

He walked over and removed the checkers box from underneath the Operation game, and on his way back he grabbed my new Barbie by her blond ponytail. Her tiny pink pumps dangled from her toes as he carried her over. Setting the game on the edge of my bed, he took hold of Barbie's skirt. The green stone in his new senior class ring glittered as he lifted the sheer fabric.

"What are you doing?" I asked.

"I've always wanted to know if she's anatomically correct."

I nodded, pretending as if I understood him, as I dumped out the checkers.

He chuckled, setting the doll face down on the night table. Her skirt was still up and her butt stuck out. "Too bad for Ken. Black or red?"

"Red."

I watched him as he set up his pieces. His happy-go-lucky smile faded away.

"You go first," Chess said when he caught me staring at him.

"Will you tell me a story?"

I moved and then he advanced one of his black checkers. "How about the mayonnaise one?"

"No way, that's too scary and gross. Something funny."

"All right, I've got one. Once there was a little girl, who was lost in the forest. Hungry and scared, she searched the brush looking for berries or nuts when all of a sudden she saw a pair of shiny, red shoes." He rushed the story like I did with my piano pieces just to say I'd practiced them.

Chess jumped my checker.

"Aw, that's not fair."

He shrugged and continued telling me how the little girl slipped on the shoes and soon found her way out of the forest. She ran home to her mother to show her the beautiful red shoes. The cruel mother accused her daughter of stealing the shoes. She demanded to know where she got them. Even though the little girl swore that she'd found them, the mother didn't believe her. She forbade the girl to wear the shoes outside the house. But every day, when the mother went into town to collect mending work, the little girl slipped on the beautiful red shoes and danced.

I tried to envision the little girl and her red shoes gliding across the rough wood floor. Waving his hand in front of my face, Chess said, "Your move."

I pushed a checker forward and my brother shook his head. He jumped two of my men and added them to his pile.

"So, where was I…oh…so one day the mother returned home early and found the girl dancing in her shoes on the front porch. The mother tore the shoes from her daughter's feet and stashed them on a closet shelf.

"Then the old lady fell deathly ill. As she lay in bed dying, the girl got the shoes. She slipped them on and admired them. Suddenly her feet began dancing all on their own. She danced right past her mother's bedroom as the hag took her last breath."

Chess crowned one of his black checkers. Then he told how me the little girl danced through the streets. Night came and her feet still tapped and swirled even when she tried to stop for a rest. The girl became frightened. She wanted the shoes to stop but they refused. They danced even faster. The wind howled and the weary child began crying. She tried to yank the shoes off, but she couldn't.

At sunrise she danced by a small farm and saw a man outside chopping wood. She danced over to the man. "Will you cut off these shoes?"

she begged him, dancing in circles around him. He cut the straps but she still couldn't get the shoes off. They kept on dancing. "Will you cut off my feet?" the girl pleaded. The man was horrified and said no. "Please, please." She begged and cried until he finally gave in, lifted his ax and aimed it at her ankles. Whap! Blood spurted all over the beautiful red shoes as her feet fell off and danced away without her. The little girl spent the rest of her life sitting in a rickety old wheelchair, begging in the Town Square for food and pennies.

"That's disgusting," I told my brother as he finished off my red checkers. "Why would she tell the man to chop off her feet?"

He swept the board with his hand. "Because she was trapped and wanted to stop dancing. She wanted to rest."

"Well, that's stupid. Don't you think so?" I looked at his sullen face and wondered if he missed his girlfriend. Daddy had called the girl and cussed her out when he learned she'd dumped Chess.

He asked, "Another game?"

12 ~ California, 1991

I seemed to have the uncanny knack for finding work environments that mirrored the dynamics of my family. My boss put me in charge of breaking in the endless stream of accounting temps who shuffled through our corporate office. Usually the unsuspecting recruits quit in exasperation or were fired for not being able to untangle the mess our systems had become.

One sunny February morning, chatting in the coffee room, I heard my name announced over the loud speaker.

"Hope this one's better than the rest," the secretary teased as I picked up my mug of tea.

Beneath a wall of windows in the lobby sat a young man, fresh out of college it appeared, wearing a ill-fitting navy suit. Straight ginger-blond hair fell neatly to his timid blue eyes.

"Kyle Jones," he said in a high-pitched voice as we shook hands. The residue of cigarette smoke permeated his suit and fair skin. A smoker, too bad, I thought, leading him to my office and willing my behind not to jiggle through my wool dress.

I pointed him to the chair. My new inductee set his briefcase on the edge of the cluttered desk. His hands trembled slightly as they fiddled with the lock. He pulled out a yellow-lined tablet.

"Well, let me just give you an overview of what we're hoping you can accomplish," I began, "and then I'll show you where the bathroom and coffee machine are located."

All week my coworkers and I bounced Kyle from one project to another, commandeering him out from under each other. He was quick and smart. A spreadsheet wizard. "Do you think he's gay or straight?" we whispered in staff meetings. It wasn't until the fixed-asset accountant overheard a telephone call that she announced he was straight and apparently just ending a turbulent affair with a married woman. On Friday I asked him to put in some overtime during the weekend so we could get ready for an upcoming audit. He agreed and suggested we have lunch. I was thrilled. Unfortunately, Saturday morning, the phone woke me.

"Ma-ree, it's Daddy," he said in a wobbly voice. "Sweetheartsabean, Claire's little Emma died this morning."

"What? How?" On my nightstand sat a recent photograph of Claire's two children: Emma, nine months old, bald but precious; Tommy, two, the spitting image of his mother with dark brown hair and brown eyes.

"They're not sure. Probably crib death. She was napping and Claire couldn't wake her. Your sister is devastated."

"But Daddy," I said, starting to cry, "I can't afford to fly out. Could you help me with the airfare?" I had sworn to myself never to ask him for money again.

"Sure, darling. Call Wayfarer Travel and have them arrange it."

I shuffled into work to tell Kyle and the others I had to fly back to Louisiana for my niece's funeral. One of my coworkers asked if I had enough money for the flight (she knew my financial situation), and I told her I'd asked my father. Kyle said if he still owned a car that he would have driven me to the airport. I thanked him and said I had that covered as well. I didn't tell anyone I had stuffed a few more pieces of jewelry into my purse, and before I caught a cab I'd stop by my favorite pawnshop.

My parents and I drove to the funeral home. When I parked, straddling Daddy's Eldorado across two spaces the way he always did to avoid nicks, I turned to my father and said, "I know we can't talk about this right now, but I wanted to let you know I'm thinking about moving home. If the sale of the Wholesale falls through, perhaps you could train me to take over."

"Let's discuss it later in my study, sweetheart," he said, blinking back tears.

Momma squeezed my hand as we walked into the familiar room where now my baby niece's body lay in a tiny mahogany coffin under dimmed lights.

"Claire." I tapped her on the shoulder. Nanette had warned me that she hadn't lost much weight since Emma's birth. Claire's face looked swollen. If I didn't know better I'd have thought she was in her third trimester.

We just moaned, hugging and rocking in each other's arms. I felt I understood a little better the losses Momma had suffered.

A black woman, Emma's daycare provider, walked into the room and let out a wail. Claire looked up and she covered her mouth. The woman hurried over, and I moved aside for her.

I knelt beside Emma at the casket. She looked like a beautiful porcelain doll dressed in her white eyelet dress. Her thin brown hair curled just above her ears. What an adorable face, perfect little rose-colored lips, smooth cheeks pink with blush, and a blue tint on her eyelids.

When Uncle Joel and Aunt Lilia showed up, I overheard Momma tell them their new condo in Gulf Shores was already pretty much booked up for the summer. That if they wanted a week or two, they'd better put in their requests soon. I shook my head at her timing.

Penny arrived in an expensive suit, went to the casket briefly, and then approached Claire. After she said hello to everyone, she came and sat down next to Nanette and me.

"Boy, Emma was sure a beautiful baby," Penny whispered.

"Haven't you ever seen her before?"

"No, today was the first time I've really spoken with Claire since we got into that big fight last Christmas. I never went to see Emma after she was born." Penny looked genuinely sad. She could be so cold; I hoped she felt guilty.

The next morning I went over to pick up Nanette. From the porch where I stood, I could hear her boys, Chris and Jack. When Nanette's husband, Sam, answered the door, he said the kids were upset they couldn't go with us to Aunt Claire's house.

As I pulled out of her driveway, Nanette rubbed her red, swollen eyes. "They've been asking Sam and me nonstop about death and heaven. Wanting to know if Emma was going to be all alone up there. Does it hurt to die and can they go visit her? I feel so bad. I want to yell, 'Leave me alone!' when I know they're just scared. This morning Jack asked if there were toys in heaven. I nearly lost it. I locked myself in our bedroom and screamed into the pillow."

"It's got to be tough. But at least they can ask you about it. We couldn't even do that much when Chess died." Nanette nodded and sighed.

We arrived at Claire's townhouse. The fabric of her warm-up suit swished as she led us through the hallway. In the living room, the glass coffee table was surrounded by dozens of assorted floral arrangements.

"I thought we'd start by putting the nicer flowers in these vases." Claire pointed to eight crystal vases lined up on a nearby end table.

Nanette grabbed a horseshoe-shaped arrangement consisting of red and white carnations. "So, what exactly do you want me to do with this?"

Claire frowned. "For Christ's sakes, just toss that. You'd think we won a damn horse derby. Toss all the carnations, I hate those," Claire ordered. "And those tall, funeral looking flowers, too."

"You mean these?" Nanette held up a gladiolus. Claire nodded. Nanette snapped the stem and stuffed it into a waiting garbage bag. I kept wondering if and when Claire was going to start talking about Emma.

Plucking and pruning red, pink, and yellow roses, pink and white lilies, irises, daffodils, and calla lilies, we worked quietly arranging the flowers.

"Don't these smell sweet like Fruit Loops cereal?" I held a stem of freesia to Claire's nose.

"Yuck, toss those too; they're too strong."

"O-kay." I looked at Nanette, and we giggled nervously.

When Ronnie, Claire's husband, returned from the gym he found the three of us on the sofa encircled by arrangements and garbage bags filled with plucked-over baskets.

"What are y'all doing?"

Without turning around to look at him, Claire replied, "Making table arrangements. What else am I supposed to do with all these flowers?"

"Hell if I know, perhaps give them away to a hospital or something. I'm gonna go by the office if you're okay here. I'll get Tommy on the way home."

When the back door slammed, Claire said, "You know, I just don't feel like being a wife or a mother right now. I know Tommy is upset, but when he comes to hug me or starts crying, I just want to tell him and Ronnie to get the hell away from me."

She started crying and Nanette scooted closer to her. "It's okay. You can't imagine the feelings I've been having toward Sam and the kids the last couple of days. It's hard to be the perfect mother and wife when you're upset like this. Don't beat yourself up about it. It's normal. Okay?"

Claire nodded. I was happy Nanette was there to comfort her. All this mothering and wife stuff was completely foreign to me.

"What do y'all think about this?" The tall vase Claire held up appeared to swallow the bunch of flowers.

"I think the proportions are somehow wrong." I tried not to laugh.

"Ah shit, you know what, I don't want any of these damn flowers.

This was a stupid idea. It still looks like a damn funeral parlor in here."
Claire grabbed the flowers from the vase, twisting and crumbling them
until they were destroyed. She let out a huge sigh and reached for more.
Laughing and sniffling, we crammed every last flower, every basket, every
florist vase and pot into the garbage bags until only two potted plants
remained.

"You want those?" Claire asked Nanette.

"Sure." She grabbed them before Claire could change her mind.
"Boy, I feel better now."

In the kitchen Claire said, "You know, if it wasn't for Tommy, I don't
think I could live. It's not fair." Her shoulders began shaking. She set the
tea pitcher down. "Why me, why us for Christ's sake? Here I've gone and
had my tubes tied, and I can't have anymore children. What kind of God
takes your baby from you? I keep hoping I'm gonna wake up and it will
just be a bad dream. But it's not. Is it?"

"No, sweetie, it's not a dream." Nanette pulled her into a hug. "Let it
out, come on, just let it out."

I joined in their embrace and the tears streamed down our faces.

"We're a fine mess," Claire said after a few minutes. "Let's go for a walk."

Claire lived on a cul-de-sac that used to be a chicken farm. The
Hebert's place. A renovated one hundred-year-old A-frame house was all
that remained of the original structures. The rest of the property had
been subdivided in half-acre lots and expensive brick, New Orleans-style
townhouses planted side by side.

"It's nice they at least kept these old oaks." I pointed to a couple of
sprawling trees at the end of the street. "They must be fifty years old."

"Or more," Nanette replied. "So I hear you offered to move back and
run the business."

Word spread fast in our family. Daddy told me there was a good
chance the buyer's financing might fall apart.

"Are you moving home?" Claire asked. "Please, please move back."

"Hang on. I'm just thinking about it." A wave of regret rushed
through me.

"Oh, come on, Marie. Think about how much fun it'd be. The three
of us just ten minutes away from each other."

"The sale still could happen. But Daddy said if I'm serious, he won't
let the buyers have another delay. It's either come up with the money in

two weeks or they're out. But you know who called me this morning to say that now she's interested in taking over the business?"

"Are you serious?" Claire was dumbfounded, knowing I meant Penny. "No way. I thought she was desperate to move away. That's all she's been talking about for years."

"Yep. Daddy told Penny that I had talked to him. So suddenly she wants the job. She calls me saying that maybe I could be the Controller since I'm the bean counter and she'd be the president. 'Wouldn't it be fun going to all the conventions together?'" I said, mocking Penny's bubbly voice. "Yeah, right. Last thing I want is to be taking orders from her. Flying around the country getting drunk and picking up men together. I've had enough of all that."

"Good for you," Nanette said, patting me on the back. "So what did Daddy say about Penny?"

"Well, he hadn't heard about her interest until I mentioned it to him and Momma this morning. You won't believe what Momma said."

"What?" they both asked.

Putting my hands on my hips like Momma had that morning, I mimicked her. "She said, 'That *bitch*, there's no way she's going to run the company. No one would want to work for her. She's so damn grumpy and undependable. You should hear half the crap she tells your father. She's always yelling at him about something her goddamn therapist has gotten her all riled up about. And besides, after six months of being in charge, the novelty would wear off and she'd be ready to quit.'"

"Did she really call Penny a bitch?" Nanette asked, smiling.

"Yes. But Daddy said I'd be the one to take over, not her."

"Well, if he doesn't pick you, then I'd rather see it sold than go to Penny," Claire said.

"Yeah, she'd just run it into the ground." Shaking her head, Nanette kicked a loose pebble into the gutter. "What a shame too. Ninety-one years in the our family, and the business might not make it to its one-hundredth year."

We were near Claire's house when Anne's black truck came barreling up the street. From a distance she looked like a boy with her short hair. She pulled over and asked, "Hey, can I come for a walk with you guys?"

"Sure, go park and we'll wait for you here," Claire told her.

We watched as Anne ran toward us.

"That Arkansas police academy must be keeping you in shape," Nanette teased.

"They sure are."

"Hey, I really like your friend Pamela." I was referring to Anne's latest girlfriend. She'd brought her to the funeral.

"Yeah, she's probably too nice. I don't know how long she'll put up with me."

As we walked, I told Anne about my conversation with Daddy and how Penny had had a change of heart.

"Wouldn't that be a hoot if you came in and fired her!" Anne said. "Or maybe you could transfer her to the warehouse." We all laughed at that idea. It was a shame that Penny always set herself apart from the family by her greed. Sometimes she could be so generous. Just the year before she'd loaned me three thousand dollars and told me to take my time paying her back. But even more than the rest of us, she always seemed to want what everyone else had.

"Are you sure you really want to move back here?" Nanette asked. "You seem so happy in San Francisco."

That was the Marie my family saw: busy, successful, and happy. Ironically, Penny was the only sister who I felt wouldn't be shocked or disappointed to hear the truth.

"I know. I miss y'all and it makes me sad that I can't see my nephews grow up. They won't even know me. Plus I started getting a little bummed out a few days ago because I may never be able to climb that stupid corporate ladder. It's so damn political out there. So I thought, here's a perfect opportunity."

"Sounds good to me," Anne said. "That's what I hate most of all about being in the police academy. Being a woman and having to put up with all the male ego shit. They didn't even want to let me try out for the motorcycle patrol because they say women aren't strong enough to handle a bike. But I showed them. I worked out until I could pick up the bike, and then they had to let me into the program."

"So you really quit drinking?" Nanette asked me.

I laughed at her directness. "Yeah."

"I never knew you drank a lot," Claire said.

"I did. I felt like it was holding me back from doing the things I really wanted to do."

"Like what?" she asked.

Claire had enough to think about without taking on my worries. I decided just to gloss over my situation. "Oh, just sewing, dating, seeing friends, reading, exercising."

"I've got to go check on the boys," Nanette said.

"Aw," I whined. I wished Nanette wouldn't constantly worry over her children. She never let them out of her sight for more than a couple of hours. I couldn't believe I was so jealous over the attention she gave to a couple of toddlers.

I returned to San Francisco figuring I'd just coast until I heard whether Daddy sold the business. Staring at my computer screen, feeling depressed about having said good-bye to my sisters, I turned when I heard a knock at my office door.

"Hey, you're back." Kyle greeted me with a big smile. "We're walking to Chinatown for lunch today. You want to join us?"

"Sure," I said, my mood lifting. "Noon?" Momma had given me one hundred dollars at the airport the day before. Kyle nodded, turning to leave. I called, "Wait, heard you're leaving us already. You know, I'm going to have to be the one to break in the next rookie, you turkey!" I tried not to sound disappointed but I was. On the flight home from Dallas I'd fantasized about Kyle and the beautiful blond-haired, blue-eyed children I could have with him. But it seemed a remote possibility now.

13 ～ Louisiana, 1970

I'd had my cast for almost four months, and we were going on our annual Christmas Eve drive to see the lights and decorations. Penny climbed into the front while Daddy set me on the back seat of his Eldorado. My graffiti-covered cast left barely enough room for Anne and Nickey. The others were stuck riding with Momma.

I pressed my fingers against the damp crotch of my underwear. I knew I was dying. For weeks my urethra had burned. I felt a constant pressure on my bladder. Yet when I went to the bathroom, nothing came out.

Momma would pace the white-tiled floor. "Are you finished yet?" She'd glance at me, blowing smoke from her cigarette.

Even if I failed to produce a drop and my stomach still burned, I nodded like a coward.

"Look at Santa Claus," Anne screamed, wiping the window with the sleeve of her sweater. A man dressed as Santa rocked on his front porch, waving a furry red crawfish at the traffic. Daddy honked his horn and pretended to be neighborly while mumbling "Idiot" to Penny. She giggled, of course. Daddy's Golden Rule applied to everyone but himself. Santa waved back as he reached down to grab a long-neck bottle of beer.

For blocks we crept along and I squeezed my thighs together, shuddering with burning pain as a trickle of pee escaped. Please God, I pleaded silently, at least let me live to unwrap my Christmas gifts. I just have to bake one cake in my new See-and-Bake oven. I won't tell any more lies or fight Momma about piano lessons or catechism.

Nickey sat on the carpet next to Anne's feet, searching for treasures while we looked at the lights. I thought about how Momma had thanked my principal over and over for taking me to the school Christmas party. It was the first time since I'd broken my leg that I'd gone anywhere other than the doctor's office. A rare occasion during the past four months that I had worn something besides Grandma's get-well nightgowns.

My friends and classmates had encircled me to admire my cast, propped up on an overturned, dented trashcan. I heard a hundred times how lucky I was that I didn't have to go to school. I smiled, enjoying the attention. I didn't tell them that I spent most of my time alone. That often I waited, sometimes for hours, until Momma came home from the grocery store or finished making lunch or drank coffee with her friends or ate dinner with the others, for her to ask if I needed to go to the bathroom. How she slammed down the phone if I interrupted her cocktail hour and then sighed loudly when I couldn't produce a single drop. How all my brothers and sisters wanted to do when they came home from school was play outside where I couldn't go. How I sat shivering on the bathroom floor on the days my mother stripped me down to nothing and scrubbed at my naked body with a wash rag and soap, raking her hard nails into my scalp for what she called my nigger-baths. How embarrassed I felt to have my mother rub a soapy washcloth between my legs as if I were a baby instead of eight years old.

I didn't mention to the admiring kids how some nights I sat on the sofa listening to my parents argue as they made trip after trip to the bar. How I waited for Momma to carry me up to bed and feared she'd drop me and snap my healing leg in half. I didn't tell a soul how I wished my whole family, even Nanette and Claire, would just vanish or die. How I told myself I could survive without all of them on boiled corn and hot dogs. How loneliness and anger percolated in me like the black liquid in Momma's coffeepot. How I felt bitter and discarded like the damp, clingy coffee grains that Evelyn washed down the drain every morning. How I missed Ruby, whom my mother had fired after deciding she could manage with only one maid. How I hated myself for hating everyone around me.

"Here we are," Daddy announced. Every year he saved White Subdivision for the finale.

Nickey popped up and pressed his nose against the window as we crept along behind a stream of red brake lights. I looked back and saw Aimee, Claire, and Nanette in the other car leaning over the front seat between Momma's and Chess's heads.

Huge candy canes outlined the front sidewalk leading to Dr. Guree's house. A mechanical Santa Claus waved from a sea of white lights on the roof. Swags of colorful lights wove through the enormous branches of the oak and magnolia trees in the front yard. Red candles illuminated every window of the doctor's two-story white house.

Daddy rolled down the car windows. Tiny drops of water slid down the polished leather interior. I stared at the life-size plastic carolers standing on the front lawn, their toothless mouths painted permanently open as they sang "We Wish You a Merry Christmas."

On the left side of the yard stood a large barn. Statues of Mary and Joseph in faded gray robes knelt beside a wooden crib. Three Wise Men, who looked like Mardi Gras kings in their fancy fur-trimmed mantles and jeweled crowns, each held out a golden box. Bright spotlights shone down on the baby Jesus. Dr. Guree had called Daddy a few days earlier to say another baby Jesus had been swiped. Since Momma's return from the hospital, Dr. Guree had visited just once, briefly, for a cup of coffee.

Daddy pulled a pack of Winstons from his coat pocket and tapped it on the steering wheel. "Shall we go?" Without waiting for an answer he waved to Momma to let her know we were leaving.

As he pulled away from the curb, I looked out the rear window, hoping to spot a red light moving across the dark sky. I didn't believe the lie that Nanette and Claire kept forcing on me—that Momma and Daddy were really Santa Claus. I needed to believe that the world, indeed, held some magic. That evening as I lay in bed listening to Anne snore, I heard footsteps on the stairs and paper crinkling. I imagined Santa turning to read the glitter names decorating each of the eleven furry stockings that Momma tied to the banister every year with red velvet ribbon. Even though the whispers and the coughs sounded a little like my parents'.

In the morning I awoke to the sound of Claire yelling, "Wake up! Wake up! It's Christmas." Anne sprang from the bed, and I lay there for a moment wondering if anyone would remember about me.

Soon Daddy stood at my door in his rumpled pajamas, rubbing his eyes. "Good morning, Sweetheartsabean. Merry Christmas."

"Merry Christmas, Daddy."

He lifted me up and carried me to the top of the stairs where Momma and the others waited. Chess leaned against the wall frowning in his torn undershirt. Aimee laughed as Momma's hand gripped the back of Nickey's shirt to keep him from bolting down the stairs. He danced around as if red ants were stinging his butt.

"Ready, get set." Daddy paused to survey the eager faces. "GO!"

Nickey led the race down the stairs, past the bulging stockings. His bare feet slapped the brick floor, and he scrambled to the foyer doors.

Desperate to unwrap my presents, I wanted to jump from my father's arms. Finally we entered the living room and I gasped. Like every other Christmas morning, assorted boxes—wrapped and unwrapped—covered the furniture and room.

My heart pounded when I spotted my See-and-Bake oven supporting a two-story dollhouse. Pushing aside a pile of gifts, Daddy set me down.

Momma watched us open a few boxes before she retrieved Daddy's gifts from under the tree. The sounds of paper tearing and crumpling accompanied the high-pitched squeals and cries of *Ooh, Cool! Hey look at this! Thank you! Whoa! All right! Neat-o!* My father laughed at the spectacle of empty cardboard boxes hitting the floor. He took tremendous pleasure in seeing the excitement in his children's faces at the absurd amount of gifts. Often his laughter turned to tears as he told us how he hated being an only child and that he'd decided early on to surround himself with a large family.

In the middle of all the commotion, Yvette shuffled into the house in gray sweatpants and bulky shirt. She kissed Momma and Daddy and then turned to me.

"Oh, hey, how's the leg?" Without waiting for a response, she headed toward the stockings hanging by the stairs. The boxes of sweaters, nightgowns and slippers could wait. She wanted the white envelope that Daddy tucked in the older kids' stockings.

As I spilled the packets of cake mixes onto my lap, I heard a thump and looked up. Red faced and lips pouting, Nickey gripped the crotch of his pajamas, which meant he was either angry or excited. His other hand curled into a fist as he cocked back his right leg. I waited for him to kick the box with the picture of the riding fire truck.

Daddy called out, "Let me help you with that, Little Fellow." He studied the box for a moment. "Hang on, I'll get some scissors."

While Nickey waited for Daddy to return, he bounced up and down on his toes, squeezing his penis. He'd had an imaginary friend named Charley for a while, but he gave him up when his pecker became his new buddy.

"Pecker Head, why don't you just go to the bathroom," I taunted. He could, after all, just go whenever he needed to.

His hand dropped to his side. "I don't need to go."

"I'm going to tell Momma that you were holding yourself again." Grandma had driven over for a visit earlier in the week. She nearly dropped her iced tea when she saw Nickey playing with his penis on the sofa while watching television. Anne and I almost died laughing when she warned him that if he were her son, she'd take a razor blade and cut that *nasty* thing right off. Ever since Momma became vigilant about slapping Nickey's hand if she caught him touching himself.

"No, you won't. I'll tell her you called me a bad name." He bounced over to grab another gift from his pile.

Daddy returned with Momma's kitchen scissors. Nickey yanked a red and blue fireman uniform from another box and held it up to his skinny chest. "Cool!"

"Look in here, Little Fellow." Daddy handed Nickey another box.

He ripped open that package and pulled out a silver badge, a gun and holster, shiny knee boots, handcuffs, and a plastic whistle.

Nickey pointed his play gun at Daddy's face, screaming, "Pow, pow! You're dead." We all laughed at the gun-slinging fireman as Daddy grabbed his chest, and scrunched up his face.

"Ready to try your fire engine out?" Daddy asked.

Nickey threw down his gun and hopped on, grabbing the steering wheel. The motor whined as he stepped on the gas and lurched forward, straight for the rocker.

"Stop!" Daddy called out.

My little brother giggled and pressed down harder. Daddy ran over and grabbed the truck by both ends. The back wheels spun around in the air as my father turned Nickey and the engine around, kicking away wrapping paper and boxes with his slipper to clear a path.

"Turn it!" Anne screamed when he headed for her new record player.

Momma came in with a second load of coffee mugs, and Daddy asked, "Esther, will you slip his uniform on while I run and get my camera?"

I decided I better nab her before she got involved in dressing their adorable little boy and taking endless pictures of him.

"Momma, could you take me to the bathroom, please?"

She hesitated for just the tiniest second before she slid her cold hands around my back and under my legs and carried me to the closest bathroom. I squeezed my eyes shut as the burning pee poured out.

Momma sniffed. "What is that rank smell?"

My urine had stunk for days. She asked if it hurt and I nodded feeling ashamed. "It's probably a bladder infection, darling. I'll take you to see Dr. Guree after the holidays."

14 ~

My father's boyish enthusiasm infected us all, and we skipped along in its wake. Even Momma, try as she might, couldn't help but smile as Daddy called out, "Hold on!"

Tugging on his captain's hat, Daddy flashed Momma a smile, and then pushed the throttle forward. Momma clutched Nickey against her lap, her knuckles turning white as she gripped the railing.

The tip of his newest boat, the *Unkabee*, shot out of the murky gray water. As we crashed against the wake of a smaller fishing boat, I wiped the spray of water off my thighs and compared my legs. In January the doctor had sawed off the cast, leaving my left leg skinnier and weaker than my right. Finally six months later my legs looked like a matched set.

I held one of the cleats, bumping up and down against the fiberglass at the front of the boat as the warm ocean sprayed my sisters and me. We were heading out toward the Gulf of Mexico. The camps around Cypermort Point grew smaller until they looked like specks on the water's edge. Penny, Chess, and Aimee leaned into each other, whispering and laughing together at the rear.

Daddy's tanned face grinned into the wind. He was always at his best on the water, with a cold beer and a full tank of gas, waving hello to the other boaters. He tilted his head back to pour a steady stream of beer down his throat, wiped his mouth with the back of his wrist, and then crumpled the can like an accordion. Tossing the can overboard, he nodded to Momma to get another Schlitz from the ice chest.

"Can I have one too?" Chess hollered as my mother bent over the Igloo.

She nodded, tossed him one, and extracted two more before making her way back to her seat. In unison, my parents yanked off the tabs, and flung the shiny metal into the Gulf. Before long we reached the Trash

Pile, a fishing reef where barges had dumped old washing machines, cars, and other household appliances to create a shallow area that would eventually be covered with barnacles. Once the barnacles multiplied, fish and crabs turned out to feed. Daddy dropped the anchor, and we stood in line to get our fishing poles.

Daddy baited our hooks with shrimp, and Momma took out a container full of raw chicken necks. The ice chest creaked under her increasing weight as she sat down to slice off long pieces of string. Tying one end of the string to the railing and the other end to the slimy bones, she dropped the crab bait into the water. *Plop. Plop.* One after another the skinny necks disappeared.

We had the entire Gulf to ourselves. The rhythmic sound of the water lapping against the boat, the occasional call of a bird overhead, and the splashing of jumping fish filled the quietness. I waited for my first tug.

"I've got one!" Claire shrieked. The tip of her pole bent toward the water. "Help, Daddy! What do I do?"

"I'm coming," he said, flicking his cigarette overboard.

Daddy pointed the pole down over the side of the boat, saying, "Now, watch this," before pulling back on it. The pole bent even more, until it looked like it would snap.

"Esther, I think she's really got one here. Bring me the net."

Momma grabbed both the net and the fish clamps and passed them to him. Daddy dipped the net below the water. Trapped in the dripping net, a large gray fish flapped angrily. Claire clapped her hands.

Daddy looked at the fish and frowned. It had whiskers. "Looks like you caught yourself a hardhead. Sorry, but we're going to have to throw this one back in."

"Aw, can't we eat it?"

"No, catfish are just trash." Daddy gripped the fish with the clamps and yanked the hook out of its mouth.

Claire looked so sad when Daddy handed her pole back. A piece of fish skin dangled from the hook. Daddy cocked his arm back and slammed the fish against the side of the boat.

"You killed it!" I screamed as he flung the creature into the water.

"No, Sweetheart, I just stunned it. That'll keep him away from our bait."

The dazed catfish floated away. What a bummer to wake up later with a pounding headache and find half your mouth missing.

The sun moved overhead as the cooler filled with red snapper and yellow bass. Daddy announced that he was hungry. Momma nodded, stealing one more glance at her romance novel before dog-earing the page. I reeled in my line and tossed the soggy shrimp as far out as I could, hoping that pathetic catfish would find it.

Claire and I sat together on the engine cover, unfolding the waxed paper with our names scribbled across with a black Marks-A-Lot pen. Without our having to remind her, Momma knew exactly how each of us liked our sandwiches. I peeled back the white bread smeared with yellow mustard and put potato chips on top of the baloney and cheese.

Aimee and Penny finished their lunches first and, glistening with baby oil lay out in the front of the boat to bake in the sun. They nudged each other and laughed privately, as usual. They rarely told us younger kids what they were whispering about. Everything we did was babyish. Everything they did was mature. Especially Penny. She spent half her time in front of the mirror rolling her long blond hair on empty orange juice containers and singing "You're So Beautiful" while we stood at the doorway, snickering at her vanity.

"Hey, y'all want to go swimming?" Nanette asked.

"Sure!" I drank down the rest of my Coke and let out a loud burp.

"Marie, where are your manners?" Momma snapped as I stood up and dusted the crumbs from my legs.

"Daddy does it."

With a mouthful of bread and ham, my father replied, "Well, Sweetheartsabean, young ladies shouldn't."

Claire, Nanette, and I raced to the cabin and pulled out three faded, musty-smelling orange vests from underneath the seats. We jumped on the count of three, and instantly our heads popped up to the surface like Ping-Pong balls.

"Hey, watch this," Chess called out, trying to balance himself on the edge of the rocking boat. His body wiggled as he reached up and threw himself backward into a flip. But he didn't rotate fast enough and landed on his stomach. Everyone laughed.

Daddy tossed Anne and Nickey overboard. Nanette and I competed to see who could do the most consecutive somersaults. We were having a great time until I noticed Momma check a crab line. She pulled the string up, inch by inch. Before the chicken neck emerged from the water, she reached over with the net to scoop up two blue crabs. Suddenly, a notion struck me. What if a crab or a fish mistook my dangling toes for bait and decided to bite me? I furiously paddled away from my sisters and called for Daddy to pull me in.

When I was safe on the boat, I yelled to my brothers and sisters to watch out that their toes didn't get pinched off by crabs. My warning caused a stampede of swimmers rushing toward the boat.

"That's not funny," Momma snapped as I sat on my towel and snickered at the sight of Nickey flailing his scrawny arms and kicking yet failing to make any progress against the waves.

He began to bawl and I laughed harder. Momma slid her sunglasses down her nose and shot me a warning glare. I knew the look. "Just keep it up and you'll find yourself yanked out of bed tonight." I turned away and ignored her. Where her precious Nickey was concerned, she had absolutely no sense of humor. And besides, even when I behaved like a perfect angel, I still got spanked.

Once the others were back on board, Claire and I offered to take over the crab lines. Part of our job, as we saw it, included opening the ice chest every five seconds to terrorize our prisoners. We played with the crabs until Daddy pulled up anchor.

From the pier, Claire, Nanette, and I raced each other across the broken white shells, squeezing the rubber straps between our toes to hold onto our flip-flops. Reaching the car first, Nanette proclaimed herself the winner. Claire and I argued over second place. As armies of crickets in a nearby ditch chirped and buzzed in the fading afternoon sun, I looked over at the boat launch. With his arms around my mother's waist, Daddy leaned in to kiss her right on the lips. I'd never seen him kiss her any place other than the top of her forehead. When they separated, Momma pushed up her sunglasses and then gave my father a sly smile. She looked at Aimee, who was leaning against a nearby gas pump, and said something that made my sister quickly turn away.

We divided up into the two cars and headed back down the old highway toward Lafayette. Other drivers crossed over the yellow line and sped past, sometimes flipping my father the bird; I checked the odometer, wishing for once that he'd at least drive the speed limit. I also wished for, hoped for, a million days like these. To skip along happily in Daddy's wake. Even Momma seemed happy.

15 ~

At sixteen, Aimee began dating a boy name Percy, her first real boyfriend. Momma and Daddy didn't like him. It wasn't just the pimples covering his face or the greasy black hair hanging over his shirt collar or the fact that he'd probably end up roughnecking on an offshore oilrig like his father. They disliked him because Momma thought he was "having his way" with my sister.

One school night Aimee went out for an ice cream cone with Percy. Momma warned her that if she wasn't home promptly at nine, she'd be in *big* trouble. Anne and Nickey and I sat in the study eating red pistachios and watching television. Every commercial break, Momma checked her watch and then went out to the patio to fix Daddy and herself another drink.

My father's feet rotated in circles like parallel second hands on a watch—something he did when he was upset. His ankles creaked like my grandmother's floorboards. At nine-thirty, we heard a car pull up outside. Momma gave Daddy a "come-with-me" jerk of her chin.

Minutes later, Aimee ran through the den yelling, "Chess! Come quick! They're trying to kill Percy."

Anne and I beat Nickey to the hallway door. Tears streaming down her face, my sister pounded on Chess's door. He appeared from a haze of smoke in his cutoff shorts. "What is it?" With bloodshot eyes and disheveled hair, he looked as if he'd just awakened from a nap. At age nine I didn't know anything about marijuana.

"Help me. Percy and I were talking in the car. Momma yanked me by my hair, and Daddy grabbed Percy and started punching him in the face."

I looked at Anne and bit my lip to stop my nervous laughter.

Sniffling, Aimee said, "We weren't even doing anything. But Momma said if I didn't go inside the house she'd let me have it right there for all the neighbors to see. You've got to help. They've gone nuts."

"Shit, Aimee," Chess said, sighing loudly. "What the fuck do you expect me to do? Get the crap beaten out of me? Percy's gonna have to take care of himself. You just better get your ass upstairs."

"But Chess, please," Aimee begged, tugging on his shirt. He shook his head. She whined, "It's not fair. They always pick on me."

"Aimee!" Momma yelled from the kitchen. "Where are you, goddammit?"

I jumped, wondering if I should hide. Anne grabbed my arm. Nickey ducked behind Anne. Chess mumbled, "You're in for it now. I'm wasted. I can't help you tonight."

"Let's go," I whispered to my little brother and sister. We ran to the den and saw Momma stomping up the stairs. I spun around. The three of us collided. Nothing seemed funny anymore. "Over there." I pointed to the pool table. We crouched behind one of the pockets.

Aimee ran past us toward the stairs. I couldn't believe she was going upstairs to face Momma. The back door opened. My father's heavy feet padded across the kitchen and then stopped. Nickey called out, "Daddy."

I shook my head, but Nickey shot up and left our hiding place. Anne bounded after him, so I followed. When Daddy saw the three of us running his way, he yelled, "Go to bed this instant!"

The soles of our shoes skidded to a halt. Daddy's hand trembled as he pointed to the foyer.

"Yes, sir," we mumbled in unison.

We crept up the first flight of stairs. I heard Aimee screaming, "Please, Momma, you're hurting me. I swear."

A loud crash. Our legs froze mid-step. I knew Anne and Nickey were creating images in their heads to match our sister's cries. I took shorter and shorter breaths until the air in my lungs wouldn't fill a thimble.

"You want to get pregnant and ruin your life? Is that what you want, you little slut? You're just a goddamn tramp."

We tiptoed to the top of the stairs. I flinched as Aimee begged for somebody to come help her. What could I possibly do to help? No door creaked open. Aimee was on her own. I heard the dull sound of a fist landing. As I got to the top, I saw Aimee's skinny body crash into her door. She slid to the floor, moaning and sobbing.

Anne and I ran to our room, and Nickey turned toward our parents' bedroom. He was still sleeping in a twin bed in there. I ripped away the bedspread and scooted in next to Anne. I thought about Nickey, nearly five years old and still having to sleep in the same room as Momma. It would scare me to death. Why didn't they move him to another room? I wouldn't have traded places with him for anything. Or with Aimee.

The bathroom door squeaked open. My heart pounded as a figure moved into the doorway, but then I heard Nanette whisper, "Good night."

"Good night," I whispered back. The door shut quickly. I heard her feet tap against the floor, her door open and close. I looked over at Anne. Her breathing had slowed down. Her eyes were shut. She was asleep. I felt so alone, lying there, trembling, waiting for the flick of the light and the *boing* of the door hitting the doorstop. Lucky for me Momma didn't come to my bedroom that night. She wore herself out on Aimee.

I awoke to the repeated buzz of the telephone, squinted at the morning sun, and reached for the receiver. Long gone were the days when Momma greeted us with a warm cup of coffee-milk to jump-start us.

"Marie, you and your sister get up and dress for school. Breakfast is ready," she said. Her tone warned me it wasn't a good day to go back to sleep until a follow-up call.

I pulled a baby blue dress down from the closet and thought about the battle the night before. Why did Momma pick on Aimee so often? Was it because she was so timid? Shaking and jumping at the slightest noise, she was like the pet hamster we'd had for a while. All Momma had to do was tap on the glass to send it into an eye-blinking, head-bobbing tizzy. I couldn't recall Aimee ever provoking a fight or failing to come to Momma's aid when she needed help. But I figured that didn't count for much in my mother's book. Earlier in the week Momma had decided to forbid Aimee from charging clothes and shoes on Daddy's accounts anymore. She announced at dinner that she and Daddy had decided to give Aimee $35 a month to take care of all her purchases. Aimee argued that singling her out for no reason wasn't fair, especially since Penny had a locked closet crammed full of clothes and shoes. I wondered if they'd ration her food next. Perhaps make her pay room and board. Would we be next? Momma's rules were so arbitrary. So spiteful.

Entering the bathroom, I found Claire staring zombie-like into the mirror and biting on her thumbnail. "I guess you heard them last night, huh?" I said, squeezing Crest onto the flattened bristles of my toothbrush. I wondered how she tolerated the pain of chewing her nails so far down they bled.

She rolled her eyes and yawned. "No, I slept through the all the crying and screaming and door banging."

Aimee's chair stood empty that morning. A fog of smoky bacon grease hung in the air. Daddy gulped down a glass of ice water. Rubbing his temples, he mumbled, "Good morning," as Claire, Nanette, and I slid into our chairs. Momma had burned the cinnamon toast and bacon.

The foyer door opened. I looked over and gasped.

"Good morning," Daddy mumbled without looking up.

"Morning," Aimee replied. Her hugely swollen left eye protruded in shades of black and purple and blue. Only her right eye blinked, nervously and rapidly.

Daddy's eyes remained fixed on the pile of assorted pills before him. He reached for the largest first, an evil-looking brown vitamin, placed it on his tongue, and swallowed. Next he grabbed the round orange tablet and then worked his way down through the collection of pills by size, leaving the tiniest white ones for last.

"Marie," said Claire, nudging my arm with the edge of the serving platter. We exchanged horrified looks as I grabbed some charred bacon.

"Who wants grits?" Momma asked, carrying a steaming pot over to the table. Standing in her bathrobe, Momma waited for an answer. "Well?" she asked.

"I'll have some," Aimee said. Sitting perfectly erect, she reached over and removed a napkin from the holder. "Just a little, please."

Momma nodded. She ladled a heaping blob onto Aimee's plate. She went around to serve my father next.

Daddy shoveled bite after bite of the grits into his mouth. He'd eaten about half when he finally looked at Aimee. His mouth closed. He glanced at his plate and then pushed away from the table.

"Thank you, Esther. That was delicious." He stole another peek at my sister before heading to the study. My father didn't have the stomach for ugliness. Even the ugliness he and my mother created.

The kitchen was quiet as everyone ate breakfast and avoided looking at the black eye. Birds chirped. The refrigerator hummed. A couple of times, I glanced at Aimee. Instead of hanging her head as she normally did, she held her chin up as if daring us to look at her. But mostly we studied the tines on our forks or read the plaques hanging around the room, like Daddy's favorite: Well Done Is Better Than Well Said. Ella, our newest maid, shuffled into the house, bidding everyone good morning.

When she glanced at Aimee's bruised face, her eyes widened. How long would she last?

I wondered what it would be like to live in Mayberry or on Gilligan's Island. I thought about the raft I had recently tried to build with scraps of rotting lumber from the pile that sat in the backyard after Chess deserted Daddy and his elaborate playhouse project. I hammered countless nails into the thick redwood, trying to bind the pieces together. But the nails bent and popped out of the wood. I was crying and pounding my fists on the boards when Daddy shuffled by after work and asked what I was doing.

"I'm building a raft," I answered, sniffling. "I'm going to run away just like Huckleberry and Tom. Momma's so mean. I hate her and I hate living here."

"That's nice, Sweetheartsabean. Just remember to put my hammer and saw back when you've finished."

He doesn't even care, I thought at the time. Now I realize he just figured I'd never be able to construct a seaworthy raft, and then drag it across town to launch it on the Vermillion River. Maybe he told himself just to let her comfort herself for a little bit by thinking she can float down the river to freedom.

A week later Nanette came home with a brochure for Camp Windywood up in Pollack, Louisiana. Aimee's eye had faded to a golden yellow. Momma and Daddy agreed to let Nanette, Claire, and me go away to camp right after the Fourth of July. But two days before Daddy planned to drive us to camp, Momma and Chess had a big fight. Momma's voice woke me from a flying dream, one where I was doing the breaststroke between the treetops to escape hands threatening to pull me down.

"I told you to be home by midnight," Momma yelled in the hallway.

I looked at the light shining under my bedroom door and thought about the lake and the horses waiting for us at Camp Windywood.

"I'm nineteen years old. I can do whatever I damn well please."

On Monday morning we'd throw our new trunks into Daddy's car and wave good-bye to Momma and the others.

"Are you drunk again?"

They had arts and crafts, according to the brochure. Maybe we'd make square candles that look like Swiss cheese or tie-dye T-shirts like Penny came home with a couple of years ago.

"Go to hell, woman."

"You know what, you little bastard? You go to hell. I hate you and I wish you were dead."

And kayaking. Penny said they even had races. Heck, I already know how to paddle.

"Esther, come back to bed," hollered Daddy in a deep, groggy voice.

"Why? So I can hug my side and not dare touch you or the pillows you put between us to keep me away? Do I have to get pregnant again just so you'll want to—"

"For Christ's sake. You two deserve each other." It sounded like Chess was snickering.

I thought about the little white "Marie" tags Momma had sewn into my new camp clothes. My eyes squeezed shut, I could see the way she carefully printed "Etienne" across the top of the twin sheets with her black permanent marker.

"Come back here, you little prick!"

Footsteps tramped along the hallway and disappeared down the stairs. I folded my pillow over my ears and wondered what kind of mother tells her own son she hates him and wishes him dead.

The next morning, I went downstairs to tell Daddy that I wanted to go fishing with him. Momma stood at the sink puffing on a cigarette and said he'd already left.

Chess shuffled in. His greasy brown hair stuck out in every direction. "Momma, will you fix me a sandwich? I'm starved." His idea of breakfast was a roast beef sandwich slathered in mayonnaise and mustard.

"Sorry, but I'm in a big hurry. You'll have to make your own this morning."

I sat down with a carton of milk and a box of Fruit Loops. Chess went to the study and returned with a can of sardines. He snapped the key off the bottom and rolled back the metal top.

"Did you take those from Daddy's refrigerator?"

He nodded.

"He's not going to like that." The Cokes and snacks in the study were off-limits to us. My father threw a fit if he opened his refrigerator and found we'd drunk his last soda or eaten all his special olives, Vienna sausages, chocolate-covered macadamia nuts, fruit cocktail, cashews, or sardines.

Anne came in and saw Chess pinching a fish by its tail and dropping it into his mouth. "Yum, can I have some?"

Chess licked the oil off his fingers and nodded. She reached into the can and pulled out a slender fish.

"You two are so disgusting," I said. "Those things stink worse than tuna."

"Have you even tried one?" Chess asked, dangling an oily, iridescent fish over my cereal.

He smiled and winked at Anne. I watched them devour both layers of sardines. They reminded me of two cats bent over a bowl. As Chess licked his paw, I wanted to ask him what it felt like to hear Momma say she wished he were dead. But I was afraid to.

Late that afternoon I sat on the den floor next to Claire. She set a red Lifesaver in the center of the nine-square grid I had drawn on a scrap of paper. I placed my marker, a cherry-flavored Starburst, in the lower left corner. We were playing tic-tac-toe, winner eats all. Momma lounged on the sofa reading a novel, laughing quietly to herself every few pages. Occasionally she touched her stiff new curls. A thick red line stretched across her forehead where the perm solution had leaked out and burned her fair skin.

Claire grinned as she set a green Lifesaver down and called out, "I won! Three in a row." She scooped up all the candy.

The telephone rang. Momma picked up a postcard from Yvette, tucked it between the pages to mark her spot, and set it aside. The top of a pyramid stuck out of her book. Yvette was in Mexico City, working with the Catholic Diocese of New Orleans on some mission. She rarely called but sent home postcards every couple of weeks. Momma reached over to the end table and grabbed the phone.

"Is he all right? I'll be right there. No, he's on his boat…in New Iberia…the *Unkabee*…he's got a radio." She stood up. "Chess is at Charity Hospital. Tell your father, if he calls, to meet us there."

I watched Momma run from the room. Then I turned to Claire, who was picking at a big scab. She had such patience. With fingernails chewed to the quick, she still managed to loosen the flaky parts until all that was left was the bumpy brown scab. Finally, I saw her wince. A dark drop appeared. A minute later that drop disappeared into the red brick floor. I felt around my legs for something to pick at.

My parents didn't come home for dinner. They didn't come home to go to bed. We didn't see them until after breakfast, when Daddy went straight to his study and Momma went straight upstairs. They didn't say a word to us.

16 ~ California, 1991

Our family's business did sell. Two weeks after Emma's funeral, Daddy received word that the financing had gone through. There would be no ugly family fight over the presidency of Etienne Drug Co.

Even though obviously sad—a family legacy had ended—Daddy seemed relieved. No more living in limbo. At sixty-three, he could retire without financial worries. They sold the big house off West Bayou Parkway and bought a brand new three-bedroom house near St. Mary's Church. They no longer slept in the bedroom where Nickey shot himself.

I still had my burdens, however. Daddy said we wouldn't receive our distribution checks for at least six months. Given my debt of nearly $18,000, I began painting my condo to put it on the market.

Kyle, the accounting temp, and I kept in touch. He usually called after I'd finished dinner. He'd be drinking beer. I'd sit on the kitchen counter with a glass of ice water and a decorating magazine to flip through. One night he said he was so depressed he'd be better off dead. He wanted advice. He had no idea how screwed up my own life was. A couple of months later he and his married girlfriend broke up for good. Not long after that, he finally had enough money to buy a used car, which he drove to pick me up for dinner.

Our first date in May lasted three days. He kissed me on Friday evening and grinned when he discovered I wasn't wearing a bra. That first night he said we were going to be together forever. I wanted to believe him. We talked about quilting, drugs, sailing, and past loves. We both loved the water. He wanted to build his own house just like his father had and write children's books. When I admitted I didn't know who Jane Austen was, he insisted we rent "Pride and Prejudice." He promised to show me Greece, Paris, and Rome, as well as his favorite burrito spot in Berkeley.

On Monday morning he headed across the Bay to work, and I felt relieved. Exhausted by his constant attention but relieved. I had found a tennis partner, friend, and lover, all rolled into one.

In June I flew to San Diego to meet his stepmother. Once we cleared that hurdle, we made plans for a trip to Louisiana.

I felt nervous about Kyle's meeting my parents. Their drunken behavior embarrassed me. But so did Kyle's. Plus, he was liberal compared to most of the guys in the South. I was scared he'd blurt that we were sleeping together or that he smoked pot.

"Hey, Daddy," I said, entering the study, "this is Kyle."

My father rose from his recliner. He and Kyle stood about the same height.

Daddy's eyes traveled from Kyle's California blond hair to his loose fitting, faded jeans down to the new tennis shoes we'd run out to buy before the trip. They shook hands and then Daddy introduced Buzz and Jigger Duhon, seated across from him on the sofa where I'd lost my virginity.

Mr. Duhon shook his hands, saying, "You've sure got some white hair." Kyle nodded, shifting his weight.

Daddy continued to inspect Kyle as Jigger stuck out her knobby hand.

"I hope you don't mind a little rain," she said. "It was raining nigger babies last night." I cringed as Kyle smiled.

"Can I get you a drink?" Momma asked, coming up from behind us. Her generous smile in the kitchen had told me all I needed to know: he passed her first inspection. But when he refused, she dismissed him with a shrug, walking to the bar to fix another round for the others. So much for future favorite son-in-law status.

"You sure picked some foul weather for your visit," said Buzz, puffing on his cigar. "The sugar cane farmers are crossing their fingers, hoping it'll stop before everything is—"

"—Ma-ree, you've got to take him out for some crawfish," Jigger interrupted.

I nodded, saying we were having dinner with some of my friends from high school.

"Be sure to charge it to me, Sweetheartsabean."

"It's okay," I told Daddy, "we've got money."

"So Kyle, what kind of work do you do?" Buzz asked. Daddy sipped his drink and waited for his response.

"I just started with APL, American Presidential Lines. I'm programming their new accounting system."

"What industry is it?"

"Transportation. Shipping," Kyle answered.

Daddy didn't say anything for a minute, just stared at his feet, rubbing his chest. He let out one of his little belches and looked mortified, covering his mouth with his hand. "Pardon me." He glanced at Kyle and then shook his head. "I don't really follow that industry."

"Well, just be glad you're not in the oil business," Buzz remarked. The South, or Buzz Duhon, still had not recovered fully from the '80s oil recession.

Next visit on our list: Claire's house. Claire and Kyle hit it off immediately. He kept her laughing with his puns and the sarcasm that tended to grate on my nerves. When he excused himself to go to the bathroom, she grabbed her son, Tommy, Mister Wiggles and Squeals, into her lap and whispered, "Marie, he's adorable. You've got a good catch there."

I grinned, having known beforehand that she and Nanette would like him. I just hadn't solidified the relationship in my mind yet. His beer at breakfast habit on weekends still bothered me.

We spent two days in Lafayette. Kyle received a quick tour of my hometown, including dinner with my old friend Suzanne and her husband, and a stop by the wholesale to show him off to Mr. Delahoussaye, my former boss.

When we drove up to the old building, it was reassuring to see the sign still read Etienne Drug Company. I was nervous about seeing my former coworkers. Did they feel betrayed when Daddy announced he had sold the business?

Kyle and I pushed open the tall blue door. Making our way through to the back offices, I waved to the women seated at the front desks.

I tapped on the door and peeked in. Mr. Delahoussaye's hands came together in a loud clap. "Ma-ree, is that you, girl?"

We embraced, and then I introduced him to Kyle.

"Little lady, you look wonderful." I was finally starting to lose some weight. "How long are you in for?"

"We're going to Gulf Shores tomorrow. My parents were supposed to come with us, but they cancelled at the last minute," I said, rolling my eyes.

"Well, that's a mighty fine place your parents have there. I'm sure they're thrilled to see you. Have you met the new owner, Mr. Schiller?"

Mr. Delahoussaye knocked at Daddy's old office and told the man sitting at my father's desk, Mr. Schiller, that he had another Etienne girl he wanted to introduce him to. The gray-haired man rose from his desk and walked toward us. Mr. Delahoussaye started telling him that I used to work in the accounting department and that I was now in California and had recently finished my MBA. The man couldn't have been less interested as he kept glancing down at his unopened mail. He had nothing to lose by showing his indifference to the former owner's daughter. Cutting Mr. Delahoussaye off, he said, "Wonderful for you. Hope you have a nice visit, and be sure to stop by again soon."

Following Mr. Delahoussaye to Penny's office, I wondered how long it would be before Mr. D got canned. It hadn't taken long for Mr. Schiller to convert Yvette's office in the warehouse to extra storage space and eliminate her position. She was one of the first casualties of the buyout. Soon Penny and then Nanette's husband, Sam, would be shown the door.

We visited with Penny for a few minutes and agreed to pick her up the next morning to drive to Gulf Shores. Since my parents had bailed, they were sending my sister, their van, and their credit card along in their place.

"Are you okay?" Kyle asked as we walked to Momma's car. "You look a little sad."

I hadn't realized how angry and upset I'd be to see someone else sitting at Daddy's desk. His gun collection, the pictures of us as children, the knickknacks we gave him each Father's Day, the black and white photographs of three generations of Etienne men sitting at their desks: all of these things were gone. In their place were a fresh coat of white paint, some pictures of people who had nothing to do with us whatsoever, a fancy gold pen and pencil set, and a man with cold eyes and an icy smile.

I sighed and told Kyle how Penny had called me the day after the sale was finalized. She said upon Mr. Schiller's arrival, he held a meeting with Daddy to introduce himself and to assure everyone their jobs were secure. But then he threw Daddy out of his own office, telling him he could use one of the front desks to answer his mail. Daddy had agreed to stay on as a paid consultant. Penny said Daddy sat there, at the same desk he let us use when we were kids, and started sobbing. Right in the middle of all the order takers. In plain view he buried his face in his hands, his shoulders shaking, until finally Mr. Delahoussaye escorted him outside. After that day Daddy never went back.

"I hate that man," I told Kyle, using his cruelty toward my father as an excuse. But the truth was, Mr. Schiller made me doubt the sincerity and kindness of all my father's employees over the years. Had Mr. Delahoussaye treated me so kindly because I was the owner's daughter? Did he ever want to yell at us girls, "You spoiled brats, I only put up with your insane family because I've got a wife and a mortgage"? But I had pulled my weight, most of the time, I thought, trying to reassure myself as we drove away.

The second night of our stay in Lafayette, Kyle and I lay awake in the sofa bed at Claire's house. He said he couldn't understand why I had depicted my parents as being so awful. So they drink a little too much and they were set in their old ways, look at how generous they were. He just couldn't believe they had ever been as mean or as screwed up as I had described.

I drove Daddy's van over to Penny's townhouse to pick her up. She yelled from the bedroom window that she was running late, for us to come in.

"That one used to be mine," I said, pointing to a unit several doors down. "Now my dad just rents it out. Mr. Delahoussaye says he's holding on to it in case I ever decide to move back."

We entered Penny's house and exchanged wide eyes at the cobalt blue and pumpkin orange walls. "Looks like someone has gone a little berserk with the paint."

Kyle grinned and ran his hands through his hair.

"Okay, I'm ready," Penny called, descending the stairs. She grabbed a thick novel and her sunglasses from the dining room table and then put out her hand. "I'll drive."

I dutifully handed her the keys to Daddy's van.

Driving toward Baton Rouge, blue August skies above us, Penny interrogated Kyle. "What'd you think about Lafayette, the crawfish, our parents, Mr. Delahoussaye, and Nanette and Sam's filthy housekeeping habits?" He did a pretty good job of remaining neutral. The most she got from him was that he thought everyone was so friendly, and even in the grocery stores checkers knew all the customers' names. He thought the Cajun accents the warehouse workers spoke with were really funny to listen to, even though he didn't understand a word that girl Elvena said to him. He said it was unheard of in California for a gas station attendant to wash your windows, empty out your ashtrays, and vacuum your car while you had the tank filled. He thought the South had some of the prettiest woman he had ever seen. And crawfish, well, they looked pretty disgusting at first, but after he tasted one, he rather enjoyed them. Just thought it was a lot of messy work to fill your stomach.

He finished, and she turned up the radio, ignoring us for the rest of the drive. When we saw the sign welcoming us to Gulf Shores, she said, "Just a couple of miles on the right, and we'll be there."

We drove along a two-lane road, sandy dunes on the left, ocean and beach on the right. Jutting out from the sand stood hotels and condominiums. The security guard opened the gate and waved as we pulled away.

"This is nice," I said, surveying the parking lot full of Jaguars, BMWs, Cadillacs, mini-vans, and Volvos. We grabbed our bags and followed Penny. Looking around the lavish lobby, I couldn't believe my parents owned a unit here.

The condo was on the thirteenth floor, Daddy's lucky number. Walking along the open breezeway, the warm dampness stuck to our skin.

"Here we are," Penny announced.

It was huge. Right off the entry was an enormous kitchen and then a dining area with a table that sat ten. A model of a ship took up half the table. The living room just beyond the dining room had pink- and crème-colored sofas and chairs, much nicer than what Momma and Daddy had back home.

"Is this real?" I asked, tapping on the surface of the square stone coffee table.

Penny offered us the master bedroom and went to her own room for a nap.

I headed to the sliding glass door to check out the view. "Kyle, come see this."

I slid the door back, and a rush of hot air hit us. "This is unbelievable. Look at that beach."

Kyle slipped his arms around my waist. "It's beautiful, just like you. Want to check out the bed?"

"I want to go swimming," I whined, breaking free. "We've got all weekend for that." Instantly the smile left his face, and a familiar look of hurt settled in his eyes. "Okay. But I want to get to the beach while the sun is still strong. Make it quick."

"You're so romantic."

I hadn't expected to feel this way, but now that I had a boyfriend, sex was a nuisance. I just wanted someone to talk to, hang out with.

Sitting on our rented beach chairs later, we looked over and saw

Penny approaching. The left side of her fluffy blond hair lay flattened against her pink scalp. "Hey, how was your nap?" Kyle asked.

"Good, I feel a million times better now. I brought some paddles and a ball. Anyone up for a game?"

Kyle said he'd play. Stripping down to her tiny bikini, she picked up the paddles and threw one to Kyle. I have to hand it to the guy; he tried really hard not to stare at her augmented boobs. He looked everywhere but at her while she drew the boundary lines in the sand with her paddle.

"Fifteen to ten, my game," she yelled. "I won, I beat you!" I rolled my eyes behind my sunglasses as she began her victory dance in the sand. When she finally stopped wiggling her ass, she asked Kyle if he wanted to play again.

"No, I need to go sit in the shade for awhile, but thanks anyway."

"I'll play you." I grabbed the paddle from Kyle, hoping to cream her. Three games in a row she beat me, the last one nearly a shutout. Satisfied she had proven herself to be the supreme paddle champion of our trio, she quit and went swimming.

For dinner, we headed to a seafood restaurant right up the beach. The waitress asked if we wanted a drink to start off with. Penny ordered an old-fashioned, and Kyle ordered a Budweiser. When the waitress left the table, Penny looked at Kyle. "Thank God one of you drinks." We hadn't ever talked about my decision to stop drinking. Maybe that was why she'd also started to back out of this trip as well, citing a last-minute work crunch.

While we waited for our food, Kyle and I listened as Penny delivered the family gossip—Momma and Daddy's drinking was worse than ever. Sherry in the morning, cocktails from noon on, wine with dinner. By 6:30 every evening, our parents were unconscious. She told me that Yvette had asked Daddy for her inheritance early because she didn't want to have to work anymore. Daddy said no and told Yvette that at age forty-seven, she was too young to be thinking about retirement. Michael, Aimee's boy, who was in high school and still living with my parents, was cutting school, stealing money from Momma and Daddy, drinking, and doing drugs. In fact, he'd sold the Apple computer Daddy bought him to buy drugs. And most recently he took Momma's car with a bunch of his friends and totaled it, abandoning it at the Cajun Dome. She said that Momma heard from Aimee occasionally. Just recently, in fact, Aimee had called from a hospital in Nashville. The gorilla she married had broken a few of her ribs and temporarily reconfigured her face. Aimee needed money and wanted to know if she was welcome to come back home.

Momma wired her some money but hadn't heard from her since. Momma thinks she either changed her mind about leaving Trevis or is buried in some trailer park in Tennessee. And Penny confirmed what I already suspected, that Claire was going to undergo surgery to have her tubes untied. She and Ronnie wanted to try for another baby.

That Penny can go from normal to slut in just under sixty minutes, with only a few drinks, was a painful reminder of who I'd been. After dinner we went to the Flora-Bama Bar the waiter recommended. From the road it just looked like a dilapidated, wood-shingled shack. From the inside, it didn't look much better. But it had great music and was packed with vacationers. There were bars within the bar, separate rooms, each staffed by surfer-looking bartenders who shouted over the noise of the band. Outside a huge deck and bar overlooked the ocean. Kyle and I lost Penny as we headed for a table in the fresh evening air.

"Are you okay? You seem a little agitated," Kyle asked, rubbing my hand. He always watched me, like Daddy did with Momma, vigilantly guarding against downward shifts in my moods. His watchfulness unnerved me. Was he looking for a reason not to love me? He complained often about my choice of clothes, my goofy glasses, and my weight.

"I'm fine, I guess. It's just that Penny acts like such a tramp when she gets drunk. I don't have as much patience with her as I did when I was drinking, too."

"Well, if you behaved anything like that, I'm glad you don't drink anymore. I love you." He kissed me. All I tasted was stale cigarettes.

"I love you," I repeated but wondered what love was.

The band started playing Jimmy Buffet's "Margaritaville." Everyone on the deck joined in, belting out the lyrics.

"Looks like she's snared a couple of hot prospects," I shouted to Kyle.

"What?" he shouted back.

I pointed to the bar, where Penny sat surrounded by two guys.

"She's just having a good time."

I sat back in my chair and listened to the band. I was perfectly content at the moment. Good music. A warm night with a slight breeze to keep the hair from sticking to the back of my neck. A beautiful half-full moon reflected in the black ocean. Waves lapping up on the beach.

As the band played the last song and the waitress came around for the last call, Penny trudged over to our table.

"I'll have a Manhattan," she told the waitress.

"So what happened to the guys you were talking to?" Kyle asked.

"Those bastards. Hell, I was just about to go back to the hotel with one of them when his friend accidentally blurted out something about a wife. I'm not getting involved with any more married men." She slurred her words and rubbed her red eyes.

"Penny, he's not worth getting upset over," Kyle said.

"But he was so cute. I really wanted to get a little action tonight," she whined.

"Gross me out, Penny. Let's go."

When we got to the van, I tried to grab the keys but she jerked away. "I'm driving."

"I can drive," Penny said, stumbling over a rock.

"Give me the damn keys."

"You better be careful with Daddy's van," she said, throwing the keys at me. "He'll be pissed if you wreck it."

"I'm not the one who's drunk." I went around to the driver's side and crammed the key into the lock.

"Slow down, Marie," Penny warned, as I pulled out of the parking lot.

"I know how to drive." I didn't even look over at Kyle because I knew he'd be giving me that pitiful scared look he puts on when he's sure I'm about to lose my temper.

The whole way home Penny kept warning me to drive more slowly, watch out for the car stopped up ahead, stay in the right lane. When we got to the parking lot of our condominium, I started to pull into a tight space. She screamed, "Stop, you're gonna hit that other car. You can't make it."

"Would you just shut up and let me drive!" I backed up and straightened out the van. Kyle sat silent as I crept up to the spot, looking right and left to see how much room I had.

"Back up. You're *too* close," Penny said.

I slammed my foot on the brake and shoved the gear shift into park. "Goddammit, just shut up. You hear me? I've been driving since I was fifteen fucking years old. I've had enough of your shit for one night."

Kyle reached across and said, "Calm down, Marie."

"You shut up, too. Penny's been acting like the world's biggest slut all evening, embarrassing me in front of you, whining about some jerk she just met in a bar, and now she's trying to tell me how to drive, like I'm stupid." I turned to Penny and yelled, "You're so fucked-up!" She snickered and blew cigarette smoke in my direction.

"You park the car then." I opened my door and climbed out of the van. "I'm going to bed."

Penny rolled down her window as I stormed away and screamed, "You're such a baby, Marie. You're calling me fucked up. You're the one with the major problems. You're the one who thinks that you can have whatever you want, no matter what the costs. Daddy's always bailing you out."

I turned around and exploded. The truth was painful to hear, especially from her. At the top of my lungs, I yelled, "I hate you, you stupid bitch. God, you're so mean. Why'd you even come on this trip? Just to embarrass me in front of Kyle? I hope you go straight to hell." I ran to the elevator and pounded my fist on the button until the doors opened.

When Kyle came up to bed, I buried my face in his chest, apologizing for going berserk.

"It's okay. Come on now, don't cry. Everything will be fine in the morning. Your sister probably won't remember a thing."

Well, I'd say that was an overestimation on his part. When I woke up, I found Kyle in the kitchen opening and closing every cabinet.

"What are you doing?" I walked up to the kitchen counter and sat down on a stool.

"I'm looking for something to eat. Is there cereal or something?"

"Nope, my parents have the housekeeper throw out everything, including condiments, after each visitor. Everything except coffee and sugar. Want some chips?"

"No, thanks." He picked up his mug of coffee and joined me at the counter. "Penny left a little while ago. She said we could call a shuttle for the airport. Oh, she also said to give you these." Kyle slid a bag of Biscotti d'Suzy across the counter. It had become a tradition—I'd bring home bags of handmade Italian cookies my friend Suzy sold throughout the Bay Area.

"That bitch, she always has to get the last word in." I looked down because I was about to start crying and I didn't want to make another scene. "I hope I never see her again."

"You don't mean that, Marie. Maybe just give her some time to diffuse her anger."

"If you're thinking I'm going to eventually call her to apologize, you're crazy. I shouldn't have started yelling like that, but everything I said was true. I really don't know why she came."

"She said her therapist told her it wasn't a good time for her to take a trip."

"It's always her fucking therapist. She's been seeing that woman for years, and it doesn't seem to be helping. She probably doesn't even know how much Penny drinks. What a joke."

Kyle shrugged. That gesture meant, Enough Marie, I don't want to hear anymore.

When we returned to San Francisco, there were several messages on my machine. One was from Claire, who had called to tell me that Daddy was in the hospital. He had fallen on his way to bed and broken his hip. They'd operate in the morning and he'd be laid up for awhile. I felt guilty for thinking he deserved to be punished for standing Kyle and me up at the beach and leaving us alone with Penny.

17 ~ Louisiana, 1971

It was so hot outside it felt as if crayons would melt on the driveway. Evelyn, our maid, had opened the front door and shooed us from the house.

The five of us—Nickey, Claire, Anne, Nanette, and I—stood under the shade of the sprawling oak tree, not saying a word about Chess or my parents' odd behavior.

"Y'all want to play freeze-tag?" asked Nanette.

"I'll be *it* first," I said.

Everyone scattered as I counted to ten. We took turns chasing each other around the trees and back and forth on the lawn. When Claire was it, she slapped Nickey's back so hard that he stumbled and fell onto the sidewalk.

Nickey shot up rubbing his wrists. Tears streamed down his cheeks. He flailed his fists at Claire, screaming, "You're a meanie! I hate you!" She grabbed his bony shoulders and laughed as he tried to hit her.

"What in the world are you kids doing?" Evelyn yelled. We turned and saw her standing on the front step under the gas lamp. Nickey kicked at Claire's shins. "Stop that!" She ran over and grabbed his arms.

"What's wrong with you children? Your parents are upset enough about Chess being dead. You want them to have to come out here and fuss at you?"

Did she say…dead? Evelyn's black eyes narrowed as she met my stare. I looked down at my tennis shoes and kicked the grass. Tee-ninecy dislodged bugs swarmed above the uneven green blades.

"Chess's dead?" asked Nanette. "What do you mean? How?"

Evelyn looked back at the house and then said in a softer tone, "Yes, he's dead. But don't be asking me a bunch of questions. Just behave out here or else I'll come back and whip you kids good."

She released Nickey's arms. He rubbed the red marks her fingers left. When the front door closed behind her, we exchanged glances.

The silence frightened me. I forced my lips to curl up in a stiff smile and sang, "Chess's dead. Chess's dead. La, la, la, la, la."

For a minute, they stared at me. But then Nanette and Claire started singing, too. We all held hands and sang, "Chess's dead, Chess's dead, the old man is dead." We danced around in circles on our front lawn and laughed shrilly. Nanette chanted, "He's dead. Just like Bubbalinka and Penelope and Pops. Doo da, doo da."

It wasn't just the shock of hearing words we never expected to be spoken. It wasn't simply sadness we didn't know how to express. It was fear. Fear of who-knew-what, but a putrid, tangy-tasting fear. People driving by smiled at us probably thinking we were celebrating the Fourth of July.

"Ain't you got no sense, girl?" Evelyn asked that afternoon as I stood in the laundry room.

I looked again at the freezer and the yellow tape zigzagging all over it.

"Get away from there right now!"

In big black letters, the tape shouted, "DO NOT ENTER...DO NOT ENTER...DO NOT ENTER." Big strips of gray tape sealed the door, with its dented metal handle, shut.

Before she had a chance to swat my behind, I turned, begging her with my eyes to tell me what had happened to our upright freezer, the same freezer where Momma stored our ice cream sandwiches, Drumsticks, Popsicles, and TV dinners. The same freezer Momma filled with plastic containers full of raw shrimp that the shrimp man in the old ice cream truck delivered to our house.

"Skedaddle!" She brushed her hand across my shorts, and I ran back out to the front yard to tell the others about the freezer.

Nanette looked at the house. "You think it has something to do with Chess dying? Is that why Evelyn made us go with her on a long drive right after lunch today?"

A station wagon pulled into the driveway and stopped. Penny climbed out.

"Thanks for letting me sleep over!" she yelled, slamming the car door. She lifted her bag and started toward the house. But then she noticed us and drifted over.

"Hey, what are y'all doing out here?" she asked, shielding her eyes from the bright sun.

I studied her cheerful face and realized that she didn't know. It was one of the rare times in our lives that we knew something before she did. Feeling cocky, I blurted out, "Chess's dead, and there's police tape all over the ice cream freezer. Just like on Hawaii-Five-O!"

The corners of her mouth fell straight down. "Ha, ha. Y'all are real funny. You better not let Momma or Daddy hear you saying something mean like that."

Nanette captured Penny's blue eyes and said, "She's not lying."

"What are you talking about?" she asked, looking over at the front door as if she expected to see a huge banner. "When?"

"Some time yesterday," Nanette answered. "Dr. Guree just stopped by a few minutes ago. He carried in his black alligator bag, so I think he came to see Momma."

"Well, I'm going to find out what happened." Penny ran to the front door.

Letting their clover flower chains fall to the matted grass, Claire and Nanette followed her. The rest of us trailed along behind. In the enormous mirror that hung in the foyer, I watched the reflection of the six of us, ranging in age from fourteen down to five, running past. From oldest to youngest, tallest to shortest, we traced Penny's steps to the locked hall door that led to the study. Penny tapped lightly and waited. My father opened the door a crack.

"What do you want?"

"Is Chess really dead?"

"Yes, Junebug, he is. Now go on."

The door began to close, and Penny put her hand out to hold it open. "But Daddy, how?"

His face crumpled. "I don't know, darling." He covered his mouth and the door shut. Nickey looked up at Penny with his pouty lips and huge brown eyes. We stood there listening to Daddy sob as his footsteps moved away. We followed Penny upstairs. She headed straight for her room and closed the door, leaving us in the hallway. She would go through the adjoining bathroom to Aimee's room to find out what she knew. And we weren't welcome.

"Y'all want to go see the freezer?" I whispered, listening for Evelyn. Nickey's head nodded first. We crept downstairs and huddled at the laundry door to stare at the yellow tape.

Nanette chewed on her hair, mumbling, "What's in there?"

We stood there gaping as if a UFO had landed right in our very own house. My heart beat like mad as I reread the words, Do Not Enter. I half expected the freezer door to fly open and a Jack-in-the-box clown to spring out and scream, "Rah!" Maybe Chess would throw open the door and shout, "Fooled you! I'm not dead, after all."

"What are you kids doing?" Daddy called out.

Claire grabbed my arm, and we swung around to face him. Nickey stepped on my foot, but I didn't dare hit him.

Daddy blew his nose into a handkerchief and approached us carrying the ice bucket. "Get away from there right now. You hear me? Go! Get out of here!"

We scampered like roaches when the light comes on.

That evening we used any excuse to steal another look at the freezer and its yellow tape. At least a dozen times I wandered into the kitchen to pour myself milk.

The morning of Chess's funeral, Momma was back in her place behind the stove. She issued orders as we entered the kitchen. "Eat and then go upstairs to put on one of your Sunday dresses." Aimee shuffled in, her eyes like swollen lips from two days of crying over Chess. She looked worse than when Momma gave her the black eye. She walked over and kissed Momma good morning, her lips trembling as Momma hugged her.

"Marie, will you run to the study and get a can of fruit cocktail for me?" Momma asked.

I nodded and left the kitchen. Skipping past the pool table, I noticed one of Barbie's pink pumps lying under a nearby table lamp. As I turned to walk to the study, a blue shape caught my eyes. Slowly I turned to look into my brother's bedroom. In the open doorway, only partly visible, a shoulder, an arm, and a leg stuck out. The muscles in my neck tightened, and my breath caught in my throat.

My eyes traveled from the familiar broad shoulders down the length of the still arm. I swallowed deeply. Though I couldn't see his face and didn't recognize the light blue suit, I knew him by the knotty knuckles, the senior ring with the green stone and the gold lettering, and the chewed-off nails. It was my brother.

"Chess?"

He didn't reply or move. Nor did he vanish. The coat sleeve hung perfectly still at his wrist. My arms and my legs began shaking. Why didn't he step out from behind the doorway? I twisted my nightgown in my sweaty hands.

"Momma!" I screamed, running toward the kitchen. My mother set her coffee mug down and looked at me as I dashed in. "I saw Chess!"

"What are you talking about?"

I threw my arms around her. "He's alive. I just saw him at his door. He was wearing his class ring."

"That's impossible." She pushed me away. "Your brother is dead." Her eyes narrowed.

"But I swear, Momma, I saw him. I did. And he scared me. I thought he was going to get me."

"What do you mean, 'Get you?'"

I stared up at her. "Like he was playing hide and seek and he was going to get me." Her quick sigh said she didn't believe me, so I added, "I didn't want him to take me back with him to heaven or somewhere."

"Let's go see."

"No, Momma, I'm scared," I whined as she led me on toward Chess' room.

Her slippers slapped at the brick floor. When we reached the back hallway, her head moved left and then right. She tugged on my wrist. I pulled back.

"Come on, goddammit." But I shook my head. She jerked me forward, digging in her nails. I stumbled across the threshold. Her eyes scanned Chess's room: the bed, the drum set, the closet doors, and the bookshelves with all his mysteries. I looked back and forth between my mother and the room. I couldn't decide which was worse, for Chess to appear and prove I wasn't lying, or for him not to appear, making me a liar and confirming his death. Glancing down at me, Momma headed to the study. I went along obediently, now sensing that what Momma was looking for she wasn't going to find.

After she checked my father's study and found nothing, she walked over to her recliner and sat on the armrest. The chair creaked as she looked straight into my eyes and murmured, "See, it was just your imagination." She sounded disappointed, and her eyes begged me to protest. She sat there for a moment, her chin quivering, then shook her head, stood up, and walked to the small refrigerator to remove a can of fruit cocktail.

After breakfast, Daddy took Nickey shopping for a dark suit and some dress shoes. Nanette, Claire, and I crept into Aimee's room.

Standing at her sink in her bra and bikini underwear, her long brown hair reaching halfway down her back, she leaned toward the bathroom mirror and rubbed beige foundation under her swollen eyes.

"Aimee," Nanette said, "no one's telling us about Chess."

She looked at us in the mirror and nodded for Claire to shut the door. "I heard Daddy talking to Mr. Duhon." She sat on the edge of the tub, and we surrounded her. "They found Chess in a ditch off old Highway 49 and brought him to Charity Hospital. He was unconscious, so they didn't know who he was at first because he didn't have a wallet. When he came to, they asked his name. That's when the police called Momma. Soon after Momma got there, he went crazy, running from the paramedics. He had a heart attack and died."

"Why would he be in a ditch off a highway?" Nanette asked.

"The police think someone slipped some drugs in his drink. Then threw him in the ditch when he passed out. There's going to be an investigation."

"Why's the freezer got tape all over it?" asked Claire.

Aimee shrugged. "Don't know for sure. Daddy told Mr. Duhon that he has an old classmate from New Iberia who works at NASA in Houston. This doctor friend is going to perform an independent autopsy because Daddy didn't believe the hospital. They couldn't find anything in Chess's body but alcohol, and he doesn't think Chess would have gone berserk like he did and have a heart attack just from drinking."

"Gross, you think there's part of Chess in our freezer?" Nanette asked.

I knew I'd be having nightmares for certain. It was as if one of Chess's creepy stories had come to life.

18 ~

The gaunt funeral director took my mother's arm and nodded a greeting to my father. "We'll go to the Gardenia Room." We followed, passing the Azalea Room and the Camellia Room.

"The viewing will be held in here." The *viewing* of what? I wondered, until I noticed the mahogany coffin sitting on a platform with a light shining down on it. Part of the top was open. Red roses covered the other half. The casket looked so huge, compared to the little sofas and folding chairs.

Momma clutched a rosary and approached the coffin. Daddy whispered for us to wait with him. I shivered. The Gardenia Room felt colder than the ice cream section at the A & P.

My mother's behind shook slightly beneath her black dress as she made the sign of the cross. She leaned over the coffin to kiss Chess. Then she just stood there, staring at him, crying, shaking her head.

Daddy closed his eyes while the rest of us began crying. His head drooped down toward the worn carpet like forgotten fruit on a thin branch. He sighed. One inhale, followed by a deep, yearning exhale. When it was his turn to go to the casket, he peeked at Chess and turned his head away so quickly I expected to hear a snap. I lowered my eyes when Daddy's shoulders began shaking.

One at a time, beginning with Aimee—Yvette was still in Mexico and no one had been able to reach her—and working our way down by age to Nickey, we said our good-byes. By the time it was my turn, visitors had begun filling the room.

Chess lay in a bed of white puffy fabric. Momma's rosary rested in his hands. He wore the same light blue suit and white cotton shirt I had seen him in earlier. My legs trembled, as I knew then that what I had seen was real—no matter what Momma said.

My eyes fixed on my brother's senior class ring. The same emerald green stone he'd worn standing in the doorway of his bedroom. The ring he used to tap on his steering wheel as he kept time with the music. The same ring he rapped on our heads when he first came home with it.

I stared at Chess's buttoned jacket, half expecting to see it rise and fall as if he were only sleeping. Someone had trimmed his long bangs and combed them back away from his temples. The red pimples that usually decorated his face had disappeared. He looked so much like Daddy. Why had he returned and shown himself to me? I prayed that if he came back again, it would be someone else's turn to see him.

Silently, I thanked him for visiting me in the hospital when I'd broken my leg.

I joined the family on one of the two small sofas that faced the casket. Aunt Lilia and Uncle Joel entered the viewing room with our cousins. Momma and her younger sister's eyes linked, drawing their bodies together in an embrace.

Aunt Lilia sobbed with my mother. Daddy and Uncle Joel looked down at the cuffs on their slacks. "Damn shame," Uncle Joel mumbled. "Damn shame."

Momma pulled away and said, "I was with him when he started turning blue. He died while I sat right there next to him. I couldn't do a thing to help him." My mother let out a little snort as her shoulders caved in and she covered her mouth.

Aunt Lilia drew her sister to her chest. "There, there, Esther," she whispered, patting the back of Momma's black collar just below the tiny specks of dandruff. My slender aunt managed to sway and lean in time with my mother without snapping under her enormous weight.

Aunt Lilia squeezed in next to Aimee on the small sofa. They exchanged a kiss, and then she gave Aimee's arm a couple of pats before turning back to Momma.

"Chester said something on the phone about Chess being found in a ditch. What happened?" Aunt Lilia asked.

"I don't know," Momma said, blowing her nose into a tissue. "When I arrived at Charity Hospital, he was conscious. He said he wanted to go home, but he could barely stand up. His eyes were huge. When the paramedics tried to transfer him to Lafayette General, he went crazy—he started yelling and running. They practically had to tackle him and carry him to the ambulance." Momma opened her mouth but for a moment nothing came out. "Then he just died. One minute he was running around, the next his heart stopped. By the time Chester arrived he was dead. The policeman told us he felt certain Chess was on drugs."

Aunt Lilia glanced at her oldest son, Brent. Was she thanking God it wasn't him lying there in the shiny brown box?

Momma kept talking. "He asked me to make him a sandwich that morning for breakfast, but I was having my hair done so I told him no. I said no!" She let out a shrill cry and buried her face in her hands. "Maybe if I had fixed him a sandwich he'd still be alive."

"Oh, no, Esther. A sandwich wouldn't have made any difference."

Momma reached down to pull a clean tissue from her purse. Did she remember telling Chess that she wished he were dead?

From the wake we drove in long black cars to the church for a mass. And then on to Calvary Cemetery. It seemed like a movie, a very long movie we'd all been hired to star in for the day.

The driver opened our door. Gravel crunched under my black patent leather shoes as I followed my family to where the priest stood wiping sweat from his brow. Car doors slammed. Daddy and the other pallbearers gathered behind the hearse and waited for Mr. Blanchard to open the rear doors.

Momma chose a folding chair right in front of the coffin. I sat beside her and looked at her face. In the course of the day she had managed to uncover her pores by wiping off all the beige powder from her nose and chin. Her naked face looked like the rind of an orange.

My slip clung to me like Saran Wrap as I listened to the car doors slam and feet hurry along the gravel walk toward the burial site. Whispering voices buzzed behind me. Periodically I turned to see who had arrived. I overheard Mr. Duhon tell Mr. Joubert that he and my father were on the *Unkabee* when the call came in over the radio. He said he was surprised they weren't burying three bodies that afternoon because as soon as Chester cut away the anchor, he hightailed it back to the port, ignoring the "No Wake" signs and then drove like a madman down the highway.

Glistening faces and squinting eyes turned toward the late afternoon sun as my father and the other men carried the coffin toward us.

Daddy sat beside Penny. The priest raised his silver scepter and mumbled a prayer as he sprinkled holy water over the coffin. I tilted my chin toward the blue sky to see if I could catch a glimpse of my brother's soul ascending to heaven. I saw nothing but a small bird flying off in the distance.

"I'd like to read a prayer before we depart today," the priest said. "It's entitled 'Safely Home.'" He slipped his fingers inside the pages where a yellow ribbon marked his place. His deep voice rose above the chirping birds and crickets.

I am home in heaven, dear ones; Oh so happy and so bright! There is perfect joy and beauty in this everlasting light. All the pain and grief is over; every restless tossing passed...

I felt Momma's arm begin to shake. She coughed and snorted, releasing my hand.

After the prayers, Mr. Blanchard escorted my family over to a towering pine tree. He pointed to a freshly dug rectangular hole inside a patch of grass. "This is where the coffin will be buried after everyone leaves today. The other three plots you purchased are right here."

Mr. Blanchard's long white fingers tapped the air once, twice, and a third time under the shadow of the tree. Daddy nodded. His weary eyes stared at the soil piled at the side of the hole. My fingers froze on a lock of hair I had twisted into a corkscrew.

Had I heard correctly? Four plots. Four? Why four? Why not one? Or eleven?

My father turned his head and looked at me. I panicked. Had I spoken aloud rather than just silently to myself?

Daddy's eyes rested on mine for just a second and then drifted away. Behind his gaze I saw depths and places I couldn't go.

Four plots?

"Are you ready to go, Chester?" my mother asked. Daddy pushed his glasses up his nose and quickly scanned the surrounding headstones as if he were memorizing the spot.

There wasn't any sort of after-funeral gathering at our house. Momma set her purse on the counter and headed straight upstairs. My father went to his study. The others went upstairs to change out of their Sunday clothes. Nanette, Claire, and I loitered in the kitchen, peeking under neatly folded foil covers—lumpy casseroles, homemade pies, baked meats friends and neighbors had dropped off—until the coast was clear. Then we ran to the laundry room. As mysteriously as the yellow Do Not Enter tape had appeared, it had disappeared. The humming white box had been stripped of its decorations. Claire stood at the doorway keeping guard while Nanette and I exchanged nervous glances and then yanked on the metal handle.

We stared at the shelves for a minute.

I pointed to the gaping space in the middle shelf. Some of the bulging

white containers of bait had been moved to share the shelf below with
the TV dinners.

"They couldn't have stored anything very big in here."

Nanette shrugged nervously and reached for the ice cream sandwiches. "You want one?" She took three from the box. We closed the door
before anyone caught us snooping. Then we sat outside on the Ping-Pong
table and ate the ice cream without saying a word.

For dinner that night, Momma carved up the honey-baked ham and
roast beef and fixed sandwiches for everyone. Nickey was the last to shuf-
fle into the kitchen. He approached the table with his BB gun tucked
under the fraying sleeve of his Joe Namath football jersey.

"Little Fellow, what are you doing with your new gun?" Daddy asked
as Nickey slid the rifle under his chair and sat down.

"If any bad guys try to get us, I'm gonna shoot and kill them."

Momma didn't even look up from her potato salad.

For weeks following the funeral, Nickey asked, "When will Chess be
home? Does being dead hurt? Is Chess coming with us when we go to
Disney World?" No matter how many different ways we explained that
Chess was dead and that we wouldn't see him again, it didn't penetrate
Nickey's five-year-old brain. In the middle of dinner, he'd blurt out, "I
miss Chess. Can we go visit him in heaven?" Daddy tried ignoring him
or shooting him a warning look. If Momma heard Chess's name mentioned, she bolted from the room in tears. I've often wondered if she ever
woke in the night, listening for my brother and preparing for a fight
when she'd hear him whisper, "I'm home" at her bedroom door only to
realize that Chess was dead.

Though I didn't ask my parents questions about Chess's death, I gathered stray bits of information. Hovering near the piano room where
Daddy and Mr. Duhon now went to whisper, I'd swoop down to pick up
a feather. Often Daddy would sense me flittering nearby and he'd pause,
telling whoever was at the door to fly away. I heard my father say that he
knew who killed his son. He couldn't prove it, but he knew which boy
had done it. He even knew the odd nickname of the killer's fiancée. How
frustrating it must have been for him to know the killer, to see him driving around Lafayette, free as a kite.

I pulled strings and twigs from any willing source. My nest grew bigger
but there were always gaping holes. Evelyn offered tidbits of gossip from her

neighborhood to pad my roost. The police had questioned a black woman who cleaned a house down the street from us. They showed up one day at her work and wanted to know if she'd been at the Holiday Inn Bar on July 3. The woman said yes, and she remembered seeing Chess drinking with some other white men that afternoon. She suddenly disappeared.

Aimee held out thorny branches that I reluctantly added to my nest. She said that the pieces of Chess had gone to a NASA lab in Houston. The police report stated that "through the grapevine the coroner had heard that Chess was planning to do something big." A big drug deal? Later the story would change, and we would believe for awhile that our brother's organs had been frozen in our house awaiting donation. We were young. We believed and feared what we were told.

Whatever the results were from the Houston lab, they weren't shared with us. That was something Daddy and Momma sat on and never hatched.

They didn't share his possessions with us, either. Momma packed my brother's clothes and shoes into fifteen or so brown grocery bags, stuffed them in the trunk of her Fleetwood, and drove off to the Salvation Army. She sent his drums and stereo home with the gardener, despite our pleas to keep them. We rode our bicycles in circles around the carport while a tow truck hooked up Chess's dented-up car. The only traces of my brother she left in the house were an oil portrait in the piano room, a framed high school photograph that sat on her nightstand (the same picture they used in the newspaper obituary), two shelves of paperback novels, and the half-finished playhouse he and my father had begun building.

For years I scanned the television, the crowded streets during Mardi Gras parades, and the faces of strangers in cities when we traveled, looking for my brother. I thought that maybe he was really alive, just hiding somewhere, afraid to come home. Or that he'd returned from heaven, maybe hell, in a different body, and if I looked hard enough, I'd see a trace of familiar sadness in a foreigner's eyes and recognize my brother. Though I longed to see him, to ask him what really happened, I was afraid, too. The mystery surrounding it all terrified me. He became the silent ghost lurking behind doorways, the sad eyes in red flames that spooked me at my window once, and always, the chunks-of-flesh-cut-out-and-sent-to-Houston body lurking at the bottom of the stairs.

The police never arrested anyone for Chess's death. Years later, when Anne became a police officer, she looked for his records but found the files had vanished. They had been tossed out with other unsolved cases and old records over the years.

Hannah Bantry, in the pantry,
Gnawing at a mutton bone;
How she gnawed it,
How she clawed it,
When she found herself alone.
—Mother Goose

19 ~

After Chess' funeral, Yvette returned from Mexico. Daddy laid down four new rules: (1) No one was allowed to drive outside of Lafayette without his permission. (2) We were not to use the new private line he had installed in his workshop. (He had offered a $10,000 reward for information leading to Chess's murderer.) (3) We were to tell our mother before we left the house. (4) And no pitching a tent in the backyard. ("No, Sweetheartsabean, there are a lot of mosquitoes outside at night. They may carry you away.") His house, his love, his fear became our prison.

Toward the end of the summer, Nanette, Claire, and I were drying the dishes after dinner when the doorbell rang. "Who could that be?" Momma asked, ripping off a sheet of aluminum foil to cover a plate of food for Daddy.

We followed her to the front door. Through the sheers I could see it was already dark outside. Momma unlatched the chain and opened the door. A tall, skinny man in a black sweater and blue jeans stood there.

"Can I help you?"

"My car just broke down," the man said. "I was wondering if I could use your telephone."

I peeked to see if his car was smoking, but Momma's hand yanked me back. "Go inside, darling," she said, trying to sound sweet. She told the man, "I'll phone the police and they can help you."

He opened his mouth but Momma interrupted him. "Oh, I insist. I'll be right back." She smiled and shut the door. She slid the chain back into place and set the deadbolt.

"Get away from there," she warned Claire, who had pulled aside the beige curtain to look at the stranger.

In the kitchen Momma dialed the operator and asked for the police. Her hand shook as she waited and lit a cigarette.

"Hello, this is Esther Etienne," Momma began. "There's a man at my door. He says his car is stalled. I was wondering if you could send someone out to see about him because I'm all alone here with seven young children." She listened for a moment, sucking hard on her cigarette. Then, as she recited our address, a stream of smoke escaped her mouth and nose.

"Momma," Claire shrieked as Momma replaced the receiver. "The man just drove away."

"What? Are you sure?" Momma asked, running toward the foyer with us right behind. Four sets of eyes peered past the curtain to the empty curb.

Momma stepped away from the window, cleared her throat, and said, "The police will be here soon. Let's just wait."

She sat on the edge of the sofa, smoking cigarette after cigarette. Nickey wandered in and must have sensed our fear. He ran into the kitchen and came back with his BB gun. Sitting on the coffee table, he held his gun across his lap. The responsibility of protecting his family, as Nickey saw it, now rested on his scrawny shoulders.

The police finally arrived. They searched the front yard, the back yard, the side yard, the carport, and the pool equipment room. Nickey showed them his BB gun. They smiled and asked us to describe the man and his car. They wanted to know if we noticed the license plate. As we shook our heads, Nickey grabbed one officer's gun handle and asked, "Can I hold your gun?" He pushed my brother's hand away. So, instead, Nickey circled him, counting the bullets on his belt. Claire insisted the man wore a black shirt while Nanette argued it was blue. Momma described the car as gray and old, I said it looked green. As the policeman took notes, the back door opened and Daddy ran in.

"Esther! What's wrong? Is everyone all right?"

The policeman with the pad stood up. "Calm down, Mr. Etienne.

Your wife just had a little scare." He told Daddy about the man and the broken car that wasn't really broken.

I began the fourth grade shortly after the "stranger incident," as Momma had called it when she and Grandma whispered together over iced tea. One day Anne and I ran the three blocks from school in pouring rain, our dresses and long blond hair clinging to our drenched bodies, to find Momma sitting at the counter drinking coffee with a man we didn't know.

"Oh, my lord," Momma declared, as we tumbled into the kitchen panting and shivering. She hopped down off the stool and ran to the bathroom to fetch some towels while Anne and I tracked water all over the brick floor, inspecting the stranger. He swiveled around on his chair as we circled him.

He wore zip-up boots underneath tight jeans and carried a gun holstered to his leather belt.

Momma held open a towel for Anne, and then unfolded one for me. I kissed her hello without taking my eyes off the man.

"Hank, these are two of my girls. Marie and Anne."

Tiny wrinkles formed at the corners of his eyes as he smiled.

"Why are you wearing a gun?" Anne asked, cocooning herself with the towel.

"I'm a police officer," he answered. "I'm going to guard your house for a while."

Guard our house from what or whom, I didn't ask. I just assumed it was the *bad guys* that Nickey kept promising to shoot and kill. The bad guys who had thrown Chess out of a car and left him to die. The bad guys Daddy feared would take more of his children.

Every afternoon Hank knocked and let himself into the kitchen. He sat on the sofa with us watching television until bedtime, smoking Camels and drinking Daddy's Cokes. Between programs he grabbed his flashlight to search outside. Sometimes after Momma and Daddy's bedroom door shut, Nanette, Claire, and I sneaked downstairs to spy on him. Most of the time he was awake, and he'd tell us to go back to bed. It was so cool having our own personal guard in the house, especially when our friends slept over and we got to show him off.

Jigger and Buzz Duhon came over every evening for cocktails. Entering the kitchen, Mrs. Duhon always called out, "It's just Jigger and

Buzz. Don't shoot!" From the den we could hear them laughing to themselves as they approached. Without fail Mr. Duhon lifted his arm to salute Hank, offering up a "Howdy."

Hank saluted right back. When the Duhons disappeared into the study, he looked at us and sent his eyeballs north.

While Hank lived with us, Momma couldn't scream or fight with Aimee. Not if she wanted to maintain her good-mother facade.

Most of the time, she kept to herself. She was pale and gaunt, her double chin and rolling belly evaporating right before us. Sometimes we had to call her three times before she looked up from her book or the pot she stirred. When we finally got her attention, she just stared right through us with a blank face. Once she slipped by Hank in the middle of the night to drive out to her sister's house in New Iberia. Aunt Lilia called Daddy saying Momma was sitting at her kitchen table drunk and crying about missing Chess.

And though she didn't scream or yell at Daddy and Aimee, she occasionally came to my bedroom when I'd been bad, as well as to Claire and Nanette's room. Because unlike Aimee, we kept quiet during our spankings.

Silent as Momma was so much of the time, her rage hovered close at hand like a stewardess walking up and down the narrow aisles, pouring coffee, doling out peanuts, handing out pillows with a forced smile, and warning us to buckle up. There was turbulence up ahead.

20 ～ California, 1992

From the time a girl first reads about Cinderella or sees a glowing bride in a beautiful white gown, she begins to fantasize about her own wedding day. And when you've reached your thirties, you've got some pretty definitive thoughts about the dress, the music, the flowers—the kind of wedding you want.

I wanted to be the belle of my own ball. To wear the most exquisite Victorian gown, covered in lace, silk, and pearls from head to toe. I wanted all my friends to see me with my handsome groom and wish they had nabbed him first. I wanted my father's eyes to mist over when he saw his darling daughter coming down a grand staircase with a twenty-foot train in tow. I wanted fabulous food, drink, and music so no one would ever want to leave my party. I wanted a pair of bride and groom cakes that would make people gasp in delight. And most of all, I wanted the man of my dreams, my own prince, to look at me and think himself the luckiest man alive.

I suppose while I was dreaming, I should have wished for the winning ticket to a fifty million dollar lottery so we could live happily ever after in luxury.

At a certain point in life, thirty perhaps, you just settle. You fear that there's nothing better around the bend, so you grab the only chance you've got and run, or stumble, with it. Then when the doubts begin to weigh more heavily than the loneliness, you tell yourself it's too late to call off the wedding. The invitations have been mailed, all your friends have paid for their nonrefundable airline tickets to Louisiana, and the attorney has drawn up the prenuptial agreement. Hell, what would everyone think? You confide in your best friend that maybe he isn't the one, perhaps he has a bit of a drinking problem, maybe he's a little too possessive, but you're thirty years old and you really want to have children. You don't worry about the corns and blisters you'll get from wearing those ill-fitting glass slippers day in and day out.

Standing at the portable bar with guitars leaning against their legs were five Mexicans outfitted in black suits with rows of silver buttons running down their pants legs and coat sleeves, white shirts and red ties knotted in a bow at the neck—the mariachi band Momma hired to play at my Victorian wedding. Were they her way of saying I should have taken the five thousand dollars she offered me to forego a fancy reception?

"Oh. Oh, shit." I left Kyle sitting at the head table and dashed over to the piano player, who was no doubt wondering what was going on. I hadn't had time to call him.

"Gilbert, there's been a change of plans. My mother hired those guys for the dinner and the dancing part. So maybe you could play for another fifteen minutes and then they'll start. Oh, and just keep the whole check. I'm really sorry about this."

He patted my arm. "Hey, don't worry about it. It's your wedding, Marie. Just go and enjoy yourself."

I wanted to crawl under my skirted wedding table and hide. I knew everyone was wondering what a mariachi band was doing at a Victorian wedding. From the ugly, lopsided wedding cakes to all the skirmishes fought throughout the week to Daddy leaning on his cane looking bored as we waited for the wedding march, my wedding scarcely resembled my lifelong fantasy. Rather a reflection of my real life.

21 ~ Louisiana, 1972

Hank guarded our house for six months before Daddy decided to cut his days back to Monday through Friday. In that time no strangers had knocked at the door. The frequent calls on my father's private telephone dwindled to the occasional wrong number. Momma was now free to misbehave on weekends again.

After one such weekend, I sat at the counter on Monday afternoon, kicking my legs back and forth as I stared at a blank sheet of paper. My classmates and I were studying phrases—their meanings and origins. The current week's expression was: "One picture is worth a thousand words." Mrs. Richardson, my fourth grade teacher, wanted us to depict happiness, pride, sadness, anger, or some other emotion. I thought of drawing my father holding up a huge fish with a grin on his face. But I decided that was stupid and too obvious. I considered drawing Nickey, crying for help in the neighbor's yard as their horny black Labrador pinned him down on the grass and dry humped him. I could show the smile on our faces as we stood by watching and laughing, yelling, "Get him, dog!" Nope, the teacher would call Momma when she saw the pink wiener poking at Nickey's ribs.

I sketched several ideas but eventually scribbled all over the drawings and ripped the sheets out of the tablet. Each time I slammed a wad of wasted paper down on the countertop, Momma glanced up briefly from dinner preparations.

The back door opened and we turned to greet Hank. He always arrived promptly at four. Turning to me, he winked as he did every day.

"Looks like you got into quite a fender-bender," he said, nodding in the direction of the carport.

I bit into my yellow No. 2 pencil and watched her reaction.

"I've been calling all day for the Cadillac people to pick up that damn car."

Hank folded his thick arms and waited. But she didn't say another word or even look over at him. Finally, he said, "Well, I'm going to go have a look around."

Turning to the door, Hank waved to the dog. "Come on, boy. You want to go outside?"

The dog ran out of the kitchen ahead of his buddy. I looked at the teeth marks in my pencil and thought about depicting *terror* for my teacher. I could draw Claire, Nanette, Nickey, Momma, and me swerving toward a magnolia tree. The smashed Fleetwood. Anne trembling, her pupils so dilated you'd think she just returned from an eye exam. Or *shame*. Claire's face when she realized we'd landed in her best friend's yard. Perhaps a little bubble that said, "Oh, no. Not here." Or *anger*. Momma's lips pursed as she slapped at her damp crotch, trying to brush off the sticky orange pulp from her wasted screwdriver.

In my mind I sketched another picture. A woman sitting in a Boston airport, all alone, slumped in a chair and bawling into her hands. But I canned that idea before I touched the lead to the paper. The teacher would just read it as disappointment—a missed connection or flight. She wouldn't read into the woman's down-turned lips and limp shoulders a decision to run away one Saturday. She wouldn't know that the woman, who would look like my mother, had driven to the airport, bought a one-way ticket to Boston, and boarded a plane. Why Boston? I didn't know. Perhaps it was the next flight available. Or maybe like me, the woman in the picture had searched the television for a lost boy. Perhaps she spotted him standing in a crowd in a broadcast from Boston. Maybe the woman, my mother, had gotten drunk and bought the ticket, thinking she could find him and persuade him to return home. Somehow, though, her drooping shoulders suggested that when she sobered up, she realized her son was still dead.

The whole story was too complicated for one picture. How would I show my father running to the telephone the next morning, grabbing the receiver and saying, "Esther? Is that you? Where are you?…Boston? Why in the hell—oh, it doesn't matter. I'm coming to get you. Don't move from there. You hear me? Stop crying. You'll be all right."

I watched my mother peel the red skin from a baby potato. Why did she want to leave us? Squirming on the stool, I clenched my pencil. Just draw something, stupid, I told myself. Anything. It doesn't matter what.

I drew a stick figure sliding a pan into an oven. Underneath I printed, "Happiness—My mother cooking my favorite meal: smothered roast with potatoes and carrots." I slid down from the stool and ran outside to join Hank.

Standing at the gate, I watched Hank toss the tennis ball across the backyard toward the playhouse. Suddenly another picture popped into my head. I could have drawn Anne, Nickey, and me on a typical Saturday morning at 9:30 following Momma's shopping cart at Walgreen's Drug Store, praying we wouldn't run into one of our friends. My mother would be a human robot. I'd sketch her mechanical arm reaching and pulling bottles off the shelves. There was no need to draw eyes. Even without looking she knew the exact position of the Smirnoff, the Jack Daniel's, and the Tanqueray. How would I capture the clinking sounds as the cart filled up? Or show the humiliation on our faces when we spotted one of the church ladies as we emerged from the liquor aisle with a cart full of booze and a mother who looked as if she could drink every drop of it?

Shortly after Easter, Hank turned in his key to our house. He shook hands with Daddy and told him to call if there were any more signs of trouble. I suppose he meant the kind of trouble that came in over his car radio. Not the kind that went on in our house but never reached the police dispatcher.

I walked into the bathroom and looked at Nanette slumped over on the toilet. "Are you all right?"

"Momma came into my room at two o'clock this morning and dragged me out of bed to clean the stupid kitchen. It took me nearly an hour and a half. I'm so tired, I don't know how I'm going to make it through school today."

"Why'd she wait till the middle of the night to decide the kitchen needed cleaning?" Nothing ever made sense. The rules shifted constantly. "She said not to worry about it last night when we finished eating. I heard her."

"I guess she changed her mind."

A few nights later, cowering under my bedcovers, I listened to my parents fight in the hall.

"You goddamn crazy woman! You're forty-three years old. Say as many Novenas as you like, but there's no way you're having any more children. No goddamn way!"

"You bastard," Momma thundered as Daddy's footsteps headed down the stairs. "I should kill myself. That'd teach you."

The foyer door opened and closed. Soon a car engine revved. I jumped out of bed and opened the blinds. Daddy's new green Eldorado peeled down the road. Once again he'd left us alone with our mother while he sought refuge at the Duhons' house.

I heard another door open and then Momma yelled, "Wake up, you goddamn bitch." I dove back into bed. Who was she screaming at now?

Penny yelled, "Get out of my room, right now!"

"Don't you dare speak to me in that tone of voice. I ought to come over there and let you have it."

Idle threat, I thought, shivering under the covers. Momma knew better than to touch Daddy's favorite. He'd kill Momma if his darling Junebug ever came down to breakfast with a black eye. Momma knew this and Penny counted on it when she shrieked, "I'm trying to sleep. Why don't you get out of here?"

I gasped and stifled a laugh. Only Daddy's Junebug could get away with sassing Momma. She was the only one who could make the whole family, especially Momma, wait on her to finish dressing whenever Daddy took us out to dinner. The one my father always handed the first baited fishing pole to, the one whose questions he answered first, the one he wasn't ever too tired to swim with.

"You little tramp. The only reason boys ask you on dates is because they want to see what's in your pants."

It was Penny's turn in the family to play the tramp, at least in Momma's eyes. The slamming of the door echoed down the hall. *Creak.* Another opened. In my mind I saw Aimee sitting up in bed, her back pressed against the headboard, her chin shaking as Momma stormed over and yanked her out of bed. She wasn't Daddy's favorite. She knew it and Momma knew it. Just like Claire, Nanette, and I weren't his favorites either.

As Momma's behavior worsened, Daddy sat in his study, night after night, drinking and ignoring her ranting and raving upstairs in our rooms. Some nights she couldn't even wait until after we'd fallen asleep to come into our rooms to spank us. Once she brought Mrs. Duhon upstairs with her and had her friend watch as she spanked Claire, Nanette, and me. When Aimee or Penny ran to him for help, he looked down at his hands, wallowing in self-pity and fear, wondering how to deal with the craziness around him. Other nights he slipped out the door, leaving us to deal with her.

On the last day of school Daddy announced that the whole family was going to Six Flags in Texas.

"What's that?" Nickey asked.

"It's an amusement park where they have rides and games and food." Daddy scratched his evening stubble as Nickey shouted, "Yea!"

"Yvette, do you think you could come also?"

She pulled the fork away from her mouth and asked why. It wasn't her "thing" to join us on family vacations.

"Well, after Six Flags I'm taking your mother to Galveston and I'll need help with the driving."

Yvette nodded and Anne blurted out, "Why's Momma going to Galveston?"

"To get some rest, Sweetheart," Daddy said. "Now eat your dinner."

22 ~

Throughout dinner I stole peeks at Momma, looking for clues in her blank face as to whether this rest was a good thing or a bad thing. She refused to look at Daddy. Her head drooped so that the gray roots in her hair were visible. She cut her pineapple slice, dipping chunks into mayonnaise and grated American cheese.

Later when Nanette, Claire and I were alone with Aimee, Claire asked why Momma was going to Galveston. Aimee got up to shut her bedroom door and then fumbled around for her cigarettes, a new habit of hers. She said Daddy was sending her to St. Mary's Hospital to get a hysterectomy. She explained how the doctors take out the part of a woman that carries the baby so she won't get pregnant anymore. Daddy had warned Momma that if she didn't go along with his plan, he'd have her declared insane. He'd expose her to all, including her family and friends. He'd tell a judge about her nightly forays into our rooms. He'd do whatever it took to stop all the craziness. I wondered if it'd really make any difference since Mrs. Duhon was a grown-up and she didn't seem to think what Momma was doing was so wrong.

"But Lafayette has hospitals," Nanette said, "why not send her to Lourdes or Lafayette General? Someplace closer to us?"

That sounded like a better idea. But then we wouldn't get to go to Six Flags. Aimee said that perhaps Daddy didn't really want all the gossips in town to know. After all, Momma hadn't even been sick as far as any of us knew.

"Will you tell us the story about Grandmother Etienne and how Grandfather sent her away when Daddy was four?" I asked. These stories had been Chess's domain but now he was gone.

"Hang on a minute." Aimee tossed her cigarette in the toilet and then checked Penny's door to make sure she wasn't listening. She was a tattletale and my father's mother was one of the many taboo subjects in my family.

"You guys must know this—you've heard it a thousand times."

"Come on, tell us again," Nanette and I whined.

"Okay. Jeez. Shortly after Daddy's fourth birthday, his father, Big Chester, and Aunt Mim told him that his mother had died. They'd always claimed her moods were just a bad case of the baby blues from having Daddy. But she really was kind of crazy—crying all the time, hearing voices, imagining that strangers were stalking her to take away her son. Pretty soon she got to be too embarrassing for Big Chester so he shipped her off to an insane asylum in St. Louis. When Daddy and his chauffeur returned from the park one afternoon, she was gone. And Aunt Mim moved in to take care of Daddy."

"Did they have a funeral like Chess's?" Claire asked.

Aimee shook her head. "Don't know, but I don't think so. I'm sure people in New Iberia knew something was up, but Daddy didn't find out she was really alive until he turned sixteen, right before he and Momma ran off to get married. His father didn't even have the decency to tell him the truth by then. I mean, to find out from some strange doctor on the telephone that your mother's been locked up for twelve years and that she's raving mad. That there's some new, experimental procedure, a lobotomy, they want to perform to help calm her down. And his father's too damn drunk to authorize it himself." Aimee sighed.

I panicked. "You think that's what Daddy's going to do with Momma? Ship her off and cut out her brains so she'll behave?"

Claire laughed nervously, and soon we were all giggling. Aimee didn't answer and I got scared. "Do you?" I asked again.

Shaking her head, Aimee said she didn't think Daddy would do that to Momma. He wasn't cold like his father. I hoped not.

"Is Yvette like Daddy's mother?" I asked. "Is that why she takes all that medicine and goes berserk sometimes?"

"It's called schizophrenia," Aimee whispered. "Daddy's got something wrong with him too. A chemical imbalance. Haven't y'all ever noticed all the pills he takes at breakfast?"

I just thought they were vitamins.

After that evening, I became vigilant, trying to determine who in my family was crazy and who wasn't. Mental illness seemed a family legacy, as inevitable as getting Momma's big upper arms. In time, I assumed and feared, strange voices would shout at me.

In the days following Daddy's announcement, I waited for Momma to get blitzed and declare that there was no way in hell she was going to be dropped off at some hospital in Galveston to have her uterus removed. But despite her somber mood, she didn't protest. Perhaps she'd given up hope that one more pregnancy would extract lasting affection from Daddy. And then there was the shame of exposure if she didn't go along.

At Six Flags, Momma sat in the shade with Yvette and smoked one cigarette after another. Later, Daddy checked us into the Seaside Motel, and then divvied up the four rooms.

"Look at your menu so that we can get out of here," Daddy said at dinner. "I want you kids in bed early so that you can tell your mother good-bye before she leaves in the morning."

"Are we coming back in two weeks to pick up Momma?" asked Anne.

"Yes, Anne, we are." He tapped a nearby waitress on the arm and told her we were ready to order drinks and dinner. Then he reached over and gave Momma's shoulder a gentle squeeze. But she shrugged, dislodging his hand, and stared at the waitress while she wrote down our orders.

My father chain-smoked his Winstons throughout dinner. He looked panicky, glancing at his watch, when Momma told Aimee we could all order dessert. It was as if he was afraid St. Mary's Hospital would say, "I'm sorry, Mr. Etienne. But you should have gone to bed earlier and arrived sooner. There's been a run on rooms. You'll have to come back another day."

The following morning I awoke to a rap on the door and my father's firm voice: "Girls, open up."

Aimee slid out of bed to let them in. Claire, Nanette, and I sat up. I could smell Daddy's spicy shaving cream and cologne. He and my mother looked like they were dressed for church—my father in the same navy suit as the night before and Momma in a new purple dress.

"Kiss your mother good-bye. We've got to go."

I climbed out of bed and waited my turn.

"Will you call us?" Aimee asked after Momma hugged her.

Momma nodded and smiled. When she crossed over to me, I threw my arms around her. She squeezed me tight and kissed my cheek. I prayed this wouldn't be the last time I'd see her. I didn't want to hear that she'd died or learn years later it was all a lie, that she'd simply been locked away like Daddy's mother.

My sisters and I stood at the door, waving until the Eldorado disappeared into the early morning fog.

Daddy put Penny in charge of meals. Anne, Nickey, and I tagged along every week to the Winn Dixie and fought over pushing one of the two baskets she filled with groceries. We begged for candy and for any new brand of cereal we'd seen advertised on television. Miss Priss always shook her head no. At the register, she counted out the twenties from the $200 Daddy gave her every Monday to buy food, slid the unused crisp bills back into her wallet, and crumpled up the receipt.

We ate foods popped out of tubes, poured from cans and jars, slid out of frozen boxes, boiled in plastic pouches, and sprung from the toaster. Daddy didn't seem to mind, and we loved it. No one missed the lengthy, messy cleanup of Momma's roast and potato dinners.

Yvette came around often to have supper with us. She puffed on an endless stream of cigarettes, but she seemed more relaxed with Momma gone. Maybe because she could engage Daddy in conversation without having Momma shoot him a dirty look that told him to move on and not get into it with Yvette, the family religious fanatic, the liberal. Free of Momma, they discussed the wholesale business, and sometimes even religion and politics—Nixon and Watergate—if Daddy was feeling frisky.

One night at dinner, my father announced that Momma's stay had been extended beyond the original two weeks. What he didn't say was that she was being *dried out*, a term I'd often heard with accompanying snickers about some of their other heavy drinking friends, when they went away mysteriously.

With Momma gone my sisters and I began experimenting. One morning Nanette called Claire and me into the bathroom. She stood naked, squeezing Crest toothpaste onto her index finger. "Want to try this too?"

"What?" Claire looked suspicious.

Nanette, who had started doing some pretty wild things, replied, "I want to see if toothpaste feels tingly down there." She stuck the Crest-coated finger between her legs. Immediately her mouth opened and her forehead creased.

"Crap!" she screamed, shaking her hands as if she had touched red coals. "It burns. Oh, God, it burns."

She lunged for the bathtub and struck at the faucet with her fist. Claire and I started giggling. Nanette moaned and slopped water between her legs, trying to flush out the toothpaste.

"I'm not trying that," I said, doubled over laughing. "That's just plain stupid."

Her next experiment came after overhearing friends talk about the incredible high you got when you sniffed fumes from an aerosol deodorant. We had cases of Arrid Extra Dry in our closets with all the other bathroom supplies Daddy brought home regularly from the wholesale.

Gathering Claire and me into our bedroom, Nanette told us to watch. She grabbed a can of Arrid Extra Dry and held a towel under the faucet. With the damp towel draped over her head, she sprayed the aerosol and inhaled. When she dropped the can and the towel, her eyes were huge and glossy. A sneaky smile spread across her face. She twirled and flittered about the room as if she were drunk. The dance lasted only a few minutes. Then she reached for the can again and held it out to us.

"Now y'all try it. It's so cool."

Claire wrinkled her nose. "Maybe later."

I shook my head. I was scared.

Nanette did it at least a couple more times that week. One day when Claire and I walked into her bedroom to see if she was ready to go for our tennis lesson, we found her with her head under a blue towel again. We heard the loud pssss of the aerosol. The room stank of deodorant. She pulled off the towel and grinned at us. Then she started running around, bouncing off the walls like a tennis-skirted orangutan in a cage, jumping on the beds, hollering nonsense, and waving the can at us.

This time even before it started to wear off she wanted more. After a couple more shots she wanted more and more. Claire grabbed the can away and Nanette's wild, dilated eyes went angry. She started chasing Claire, trying to get the can back. She looked like one of those crazy drug addicts you see in movies, screaming and begging for just one more hit. Claire took off through the bathroom into my room and back around to their room through the hallway. They were chasing each other in circles with Claire holding the can up high in the air beyond Nanette's reach. I stood back laughing.

Then Claire tossed the can to me. Nanette turned and lunged. I shoved hard at her shoulder; she lost her balance and stumbled backwards. A scary sensation told me that we'd crossed the line between fun and danger. "Stay away, you hear me?" I yelled, looking to Claire for help.

"Fuck you," Nanette hissed, clawing at my wrist. She drew blood.

"Ow! You bitch! Claire, hold her."

Claire tried to restrain her, but Nanette wrestled free and headed out the door.

"Grab her," Claire yelled. "She's going to get another can."

I chased Nanette and tackled her just as she entered my parents' bed-room. We sat on her back, pinning her on the carpet while she screamed and cussed. Penny and one of her friends came to the door.

"What are y'all doing?" Penny asked in her bossy voice.

I cupped my hand over Nanette's mouth to quiet her.

"Just playing, leave us alone," Claire replied.

"Why don't you wait in my room," Penny told her friend.

After the girl left Penny whispered, "Y'all look like a bunch of les-bians piled on each other like that."

Nanette groaned and tried to break free. Penny rolled her eyes and left us. When her door closed, we pulled Nanette to the bathroom and shook her to calm her down. She screamed, "Get your goddamn hands off me," like we'd heard Momma say so often.

Claire's open hand swung across and connected. When Nanette felt the sting on her cheek, she went really still. She started crying and say-ing she was sorry.

"It's okay," Claire said, rubbing her back. "I think you scared yourself. You sure scared the shit out of us."

We convinced her that a shower would make her feel better. Fully dressed, she stepped under the cold water. We waited in the bathroom, listening to her whimper until she sobered up and came out.

She stood there on the mat, dripping wet, looking as if she'd just gone three sets at Wimbledon and got caught in a sudden downpour. But her brown eyes were normal again.

"It's like when you get that rush, you want more and more no matter what you have to do. I would have hurt you guys just for another hit."

Claire shook her finger at Nanette like an angry mother. "If you ever touch another can of deodorant, we're going to tell Daddy. You hear me?"

Nanette nodded. Luckily she believed Claire's threat because I doubt either of us would have gone to him. He had enough problems already.

23 ~ California, 1993

One of Kyle's friends told me that when my hands and feet suddenly started going numb, I'd know I was pregnant. Four months after our honeymoon, I gleefully announced we were having a baby. Every night after dinner I sat on the carpet in our 1950s rancher in Walnut Creek, a suburb east of San Francisco, playing solitaire or cutting squares for a baby blanket, and waited for the moment I'd hold the little creature swimming around in my belly. Sprawled on the nearby futon, Kyle drank beer and watched country line dancing with the sound muted. Weekends we saw movies, tore out old paneling, worked on the baby's room, and waited.

On July 4, three weeks to my due date, Claire called to tell me Daddy was in the hospital again. Ten days earlier he'd been diagnosed with cirrhosis of the liver after his belly had suddenly swollen up, but neither he nor Momma told anyone.

In an unnaturally calm voice, Claire said, "He's got double pneumonia and…" She began crying.

I swallowed hard and waited. Kyle climbed out of bed and came around to my side. Standing before me in a torn white T-shirt, his limp penis dangling between his legs, he extended his arms to help me sit up. Hugely pregnant, I nodded, tears gathering in my eyes.

"Claire, what's going on?" She didn't answer, just a lot of background noise.

"Ma-ree," said Mr. Delahoussaye in his grandfatherly way, "your Daddy might not make it, darlin'. He just had a heart attack, and he's in a coma." I pictured my father's friend, our family accountant, with his silvery gray hair and gentle eyes.

"You think he might die?" I got goosebumps all over as Kyle squeezed my hand.

"I don't know for certain. The doctors are with him. But he's pretty weak. I know you'll want to fly out here, but you don't want to do anything that will hurt you or the baby. He might not hold out till you get here."

Not hold out? "I'm coming. I just need to make some arrangements."

"You talk it over with Kyle. But if you're coming, you better come soon."

I handed Kyle the receiver, avoiding his eyes.

"No way! You're not flying out there."

"Yes, I am."

I leaned over and pulled a pen and pad out of the nightstand drawer.

"Think about the baby, for Christ's sake. You're not getting on an airplane."

"The baby will be fine," I said, praying I was right. "I'm sorry, Kyle, but if my dad is dying, I want to be there. Hand me the telephone book."

He slammed the book on the bed and shook his head. "You better call Dr. Abel. She's never going to let you get on an airplane. The flight attendants probably won't even let you board."

I looked down at my 200-pound body and began sobbing. I looked fatter than Momma at her worst. I hadn't wanted my sisters and friends to see me until after I'd delivered.

Kyle sighed and said, "Okay, but this is my baby too. If anything happens, I'll never forgive you."

That evening we arrived in Lafayette. Nanette looked ragged when I spotted her in the airport. Kyle took my purse as she hugged me and said Daddy was dead. He'd regained consciousness just long enough to ask what happened to him and joked about wanting to go home. But before the doctor could respond, he had his second, final attack.

Momma's and Daddy's cars sat side by side under the carport as we pulled up. I knew Daddy wouldn't be in his recliner, twirling his feet, watching the news or Suzanne Somers, scantily clad, demonstrate some new exercise gadget. I recognized Anne's huge Ford truck wedged into the third spot, where my father's boats used to sit before he gave her his last one. Penny's brand-new blue BMW was parked behind Daddy's car and the Duhons' gray Lincoln. If I hadn't known better, I might have thought there was a party going on inside.

We found Momma sitting in the den in her bathrobe. She and the others stood as we entered. Walking toward me, Momma held out her arms just like when I returned home for Nickey's and Emma's funerals. We hugged, crying, our huge bellies pressed together. She leaned hard into me and I struggled to hold steady under her weight. She was smashed. I was afraid she'd send us both crashing to the hard floor with her on top of me. Finally her grasp loosened and I pulled away, freeing myself from the familiar perfume of cigarettes, vodka, and week-old hairspray.

Momma sat down and covered her knees with the hem of her robe. "Y'all sit," she said. Jigger scooted closer to her husband to make room for Kyle and me. Claire and Nanette remained at a distance, leaning against the pool table while their husbands hid out in the kitchen with their children. Luckily Aimee and her creepy husband had left just before I arrived.

Grabbing her empty glass from the end table, Momma held it up. "Patrick, another one," she said to Penny's newest boyfriend.

"Sure thing, Miss Esther," he said in a thick Southern accent, springing from his chair. "Kyle, Marie, can I get you anything while I'm up?" Penny had gotten herself a good ol' boy.

We shook our heads, and he headed for the bar, obviously familiar with the place.

"I can't believe they let you on the airplane. You're enormous!" Penny exclaimed. Buzz Duhon nodded, and everyone stared at my stomach.

Even though I knew she'd comment on my weight, it still hurt to see the pleasure she took in embarrassing me. Penny knew how sensitive I was about my size. Though things would never sit right between us after Gulf Shores, I figured for this visit she'd behave herself.

"I told the flight attendants I was in my sixth month," I mumbled. "No one hardly noticed since I held the garment bag in front of me."

Penny laughed but left it at that. Momma smiled warmly and said, "Well, you look great. Now, everybody listen up…I don't want a lot of people here after the funeral. Just the family." Heads around the room nodded. Patrick came back from the bar with Momma's drink.

Soon Claire and Nanette left to fix dinner for their children. I felt obliged to sleep at my parents' house for Momma's sake. I'd rather have had a slumber party at one of my sisters' houses.

"I suppose we should be going too," said Mrs. Duhon.

Momma shook her head and said, "Jigger, y'all stay put. Fix yourselves another drink." Patrick waved for them to sit. He'd fetch them another round.

"You know," my mother began as she lit a cigarette, "it would have been our fiftieth anniversary this year. I'd be lying if I said they were all good years, but these last few years, we were happy. We sort of made peace with each other."

"Fifty years is pretty damn remarkable," Buzz said, fingering his cigar.

"Have I ever told y'all the story of our elopement?" Momma asked, smiling at Kyle. She approved of my husband. Even told me after our wedding that she was glad I didn't marry a black man, like one of her friend's daughters had done. I laughed and reminded her that the man she was referring to wasn't actually black, he was Indian. To which she responded, "Black, Indian, it's all the same."

Everyone in the room shook their heads and waited. Momma rarely reminisced about her childhood or the early days of their marriage. Her past wasn't anything we could ever ask her about.

"Well, your father decided he wanted to get married, and I knew there was no way Pops would ever let me marry him..."

Was she showing yet? She still thinks we don't know.

"After all, I was only sixteen and Chester was seventeen. So your father figured we'd just go to Texas where you didn't need your parents' permission. We didn't have a car to get to the train station, but Chester found his friend's bicycle parked on Main Street. He got this harebrained idea to steal it. So I'm waiting in my front yard, and here comes Chester riding up on this bicycle with a big ceramic piggy bank clanging around in the front basket. We must have laughed the whole way to the train station, me riding on the handlebars, and your father panting like a fool peddling the two of us, just praying no one we knew would drive by.

"When we got to the station, your father grabbed the piggy bank and smashed it against the curb; nickels and dimes rolled out everywhere. The money he'd saved from working for his father. He bought two one-way tickets to Houston and one Coke for us to share.

"When we got to Houston, your daddy paid for the license and bought two beers afterwards to celebrate. We had just enough money left over to send telegrams to our families and friends, asking for money in lieu of wedding gifts. Your Aunt Mim was the only one who responded—she sent us $75. So we went to Galveston for a weekend and spent three days drinking and lying on the beach."

Momma smiled, studied her wrinkled, veiny hands, and ran her thumb over her wedding ring. She seemed satisfied with her funny tale, abbreviated somewhat to protect her from shame but still her legacy to us.

"Anyway, it was a wonderful weekend. I think that was the freest I have ever felt," she said, shaking her head. "But then Big Chester called your father and told him to get his rear end back home to finish school."

"Were you scared about how your parents would react to your eloping?" Penny asked.

"No. Oddly enough I didn't care. What could they do really after it was done?"

She sounded so brave talking now. But I could remember how frightened and childlike she seemed when Grandma rebuffed her pleas for compassion, when she scolded her daughter for failing at her "wifely and motherly duties."

That was one area Momma and Grandma differed, at least in my mother's estimation. Momma rarely meddled in our marriages or child-rearing unless she was in one of her angry, drunken moods. No. She just ridiculed and chastised us behind our backs to each other and to her friends. Did she know that invariably her words got back to us? How painful and shameful it felt to hear second- or third-hand your own mother trash you so?

Momma yawned and I checked my watch. It was nearly nine. Wasn't she passing out about seven o'clock these days?

"Momma, you better go to bed." Penny said. "You look tired, and Patrick and I have to go anyway."

"Okay, I guess I am. Jigger, Buzz, I'll see y'all tomorrow."

Anne, Kyle, and I helped Momma to her room. It took all three of us to get her up the stairs. We pulled down her sheets and eased her into bed. Momma asked Anne and me to lie with her a few minutes.

"Hand me your father's pillow," she said abruptly as I started to lean against the cane headboard next to Anne.

I pulled out my father's king-size feather pillow, the one he'd had forever. It was so limp with age that my fingertips touched through the fabric. I pressed it to my face and inhaled. It smelled of Daddy. A mixture of spicy aftershave, Safeguard soap, and Johnson's baby shampoo. How strange that he was dead and yet his smell lingered on his pillow. She grabbed the pillow from me and hugged it.

"Want to say prayers?" Anne asked.

When we finished with the Our Father and Hail Mary, Anne kissed Momma good night. I offered to stay with her until she fell asleep. I hadn't expected she'd say yes, but she did.

For what seemed an eternity, I lay next to her. On our backs, side-by-side, we stared at the ceiling. I kept thinking I should say something profound, but my mind was consumed with other thoughts, fears really. I felt vulnerable, being so close to her. She was so drunk. In addition to being depressed, she was probably angry. What if she goes crazy and starts beating on me? Here I am lying within reach with my precious baby nestled in my stomach. Taking the deep, even breaths I had learned in Lamaze, I told myself, She's not like that anymore. That woman no longer exists. Why would she want to hurt me? But I prayed she'd pass out soon so I could slip away.

Suddenly she sat up. I tensed but then heard the flick of her lighter and smelled the smoke of her cigarette.

"I'll be fine, Marie. Why don't you go to your room? Kyle's waiting for you," she said in a tired voice. I bolted out the door.

The next day the house was a flurry of activity. Friends, neighbors, and relatives called. The doorbell rang nonstop with flowers and food deliveries. Mr. Delahoussaye and Ben Veazey, my parents' attorney and friend, came and went several times throughout the day. My sisters and I, all getting along surprisingly well, wandered from room to room, visiting, consoling each other, and helping Momma keep the house in order.

For most of the day Kyle was my shadow. Every time I turned around he rear-ended me. We hadn't spent so much time together since our honeymoon. Even then we brought along his best man and my maid-of-honor for most of the trip to keep us company. When he finally left my side to take a nap, I sighed and wondered how my sisters endured marriage. Was it something to be *endured*? It felt that way to me. Claire was lucky; her husband was a workaholic. Immediately I headed for my father's study to hunt for memories.

I flicked on the light and felt the hair on my arms stand up from the chill. Located on the north side and shaded by a mature magnolia tree, Daddy's study was the coldest room in the house.

The seat of his leather recliner looked lonely, slightly indented and wrinkled from where my father sat for hours every day. I ran my fingers across the smooth leather arms and then sat down. What was Momma going to do with all of his collections? Hundreds of ceramic and decorative owls perched on the bookshelves and the coffee tables, their eyes following you about the room. Art books, financial books, and magazines tumbled off the tables into piles behind his chair. Silly plastic plaques with all his favorite quotes stood two and three deep on shelves. Four remote control units for the television, the stereo, and the VCR lined up like soldiers on the end table next to his chair. Juvenile bits of artwork we had given Daddy over the years littered the bookshelves. He kept nearly everything we gave him—a framed sheet of faded orange construction paper with *I love you* spelled out in glued-on pieces of eggshell that I made the year I broke my leg, an *E* that Penny carved out of a bar of Ivory soap, and the mosaic card I'd put together for Father's Day from a photo of Daddy wearing a silly straw hat, a picture of a boat, and my own drawing of a fishing pole in his hand with a giant fish on the line. Daddy's black leather journal rested near the edge of the table. I opened it and read, *I would like this book to be given to my daughter, Penny, in the event of my death.* He inscribed his collection of quotes to her, his favorite, inside the front cover. I felt a tinge of envy, but we all knew, always had, that she was his special *Junebug.* No amount of clever artwork or achievements in school and business would ever slide me into that esteemed spot.

He knew he was dying. For that I felt most angry, betrayed. Momma told Kyle and me earlier in the morning about the cirrhosis diagnosis. His condition held little promise, she said. The doctor said his heart failure was probably related to his liver disease.

It all made sense to me then. Transplant surgery, if even an option, was out because of his loathing of hospitals. Suicide was impossible. He was Catholic. And more importantly, he feared his insurance policy wouldn't pay out if he took his own life. We'd need that money to pay estate taxes to protect the wealth he'd worked hard to accumulate to take care of Momma and us. So he just sat in his recliner—he couldn't even drink at that point, Momma said—and he let his body swell up again until, hopefully, it killed him swiftly. His plan would have worked perfectly had Claire not intervened when he began hallucinating and called an ambulance. Lucky for him, his heart carried out his plan.

Would he be alive if he'd gone back to the hospital sooner? Could the doctors have slowed down his disease with medicine or performed a liver transplant? Didn't he want more time with us? Didn't he want to meet his next grandchild, my first baby?

I sat huddled in his recliner, shaking, tears streaming down my face. Why didn't he at least try to say good-bye to me in some way? We'd spoken so little in the ten months since my wedding. Daddy offered a million broken promises. In the six years I'd lived in California, not once did he visit me; it was his way of punishing me for not listening to his advice. He flew to Canada, Alaska, and Los Angeles but never to the land of the "nuts and fruits" since my arrival there. One forgotten birthday after another, endless unrecognized promotions and graduations, putdowns meant to keep us humble, and the biggest lie of all: *I love my children and I will always be there to take care of you.* Bullshit, that's what it was. Plain old bullshit.

Tuesday morning, the first day of the wake, Kyle and I joined Anne and her newest girlfriend, Kay, at the breakfast table. Kay reminded me some of Momma. She smoked, loved to cook, and doted on my sister like a '50s wife. Penny and she were about the same age, although the way Kay dressed and wore her graying hair long and straight, she seemed older. But she was easy to talk to; she had a wonderful quick sense of humor that tangoed nicely against my sister's dry wit. I hoped, as Anne did, that this relationship would be the one.

Momma was in her room, dressing. And coughing. Even though she was all the way upstairs, we could hear the results of her three-pack-a-day habit.

"She sounds real healthy," Kyle said, nodding toward the stairs.

Anne frowned. "Shame on you, Kyle. Give her a break today." In her double-breasted wool suit and starched white blouse, Anne looked like she was going to negotiate a contract rather than attend a funeral.

"Her cough does seem worse, doesn't it?" I said in Kyle's defense. She nodded in agreement and shrugged. It had turned into a protracted, retching cough that stopped her in mid-sentence, convulsed her body in violent fits, and left her red-faced and gasping for breath.

I knew what Anne was thinking. There wasn't any point in broaching the subject. Momma would say it was simply a tickle or the remnants of a little cold. Daddy had recommended once that she quit or cut back, but the tongue-lashing she gave him quelled any future heroics on his part.

We sat at the breakfast table making small talk about Anne and Kay's house-hunting adventures while we pretended not to listen for the gasps of breath that came at the conclusion of each coughing fit.

"Have you adjusted to being in Louisiana yet?" I asked Kay.

"Not really. It feels more like we're here on vacation. I think once we find a house I'll feel more at home."

"Yeah. San Francisco didn't feel like home for at least a year."

"She's already got two job offers. Can you believe it?" Anne said proudly. She reached over to rub Kay's back, and Kay returned her smile.

"That's great," Kyle said. "How about you?"

"Nothing yet. I'm hoping to snag an interview with the police department. They're not hiring right now, though." She sighed. "I wish we'd moved back earlier so I could've spent more time with Daddy. I could kill myself for waiting so long."

"You think we should be leaving soon?" Kay asked.

Anne volunteered to see if Momma was ready.

At the wake, Aimee's second husband, Byron, arrived with her son Michael, who was serving time in jail for drugs but had been entrusted to Byron for the funeral. Michael followed Byron to where Momma sat. He glanced around at my sisters and me, pausing a little longer on his estranged mother and *her* new family, who sat behind us. He stood stiff when Momma hugged him and thanked him for coming. I quickly withdrew from our own embrace feeling awkward when he didn't respond. A chilling change had come over him. Gone was that sweet, mischievous child. His beautiful blond hair had been close-cropped, and his blue eyes reflected coldness. Penny whispered that he must not have had a chance in hell locked up with all those horny men. I didn't blame him for the hate I knew he surely felt toward all of us. His own mother had cast him aside for such a loser. His idol, my brother Nickey, had abandoned him with the pull of a trigger. I wrote infrequently over the years. And his grandparents made it clear that only duty forced them to take him in.

"Hey, Byron. It's sure good to see you," Penny said in her fake, sweet voice. When had she ever been happy to see Bryon? "I know it means a lot to Momma that you came. Sit here." She tapped her red nails on the chair next to Aimee, and then met Trevis's hateful eyes with a smirk. She'd use Byron to make sure he felt unwelcome. For even though Aimee and Penny were no longer close, she hated Trevis for all the abuse Aimee had suffered by him.

Byron glanced skeptically at Aimee. She mumbled hello, and he sat beside Penny. Michael took the aisle seat.

"Boy, you're looking tanned and fit," Penny said. "You must be working out."

They both knew his tan wasn't from some fancy health club but rather from working on an oil rig. Byron smiled as Aimee and her husband stared straight ahead. Their two children, Hope and Peter, looked curiously at this strange man who had once been married to their mother.

"You still runnin' and playin' tennis and drivin' the men wild?"

Penny laughed. She asked Byron about his mother. As he recounted his mom's recent ailments, I glanced at Trevis. A vein in the side of his neck bulged. I decided to join the game, a game Momma had started when she chose all her sons-in-law to serve as pallbearers except for Trevis.

"Byron, have you met my husband, Kyle?"

"No," Byron said, playing along. "It's a pleasure to meet you. Congratulations." He nodded to my pregnant belly.

Trevis turned to me. He focused on my belly, and a grin spread across his face. A sick feeling washed over me.

I stood quickly and asked Kyle, "Will you come with me to get some water?" This family game was too dangerous.

We went into the lobby and joined Anne and Kay.

"How's Miss Esther holding up?" Kay asked.

"Pretty good," I said, turning away from her cigarette smoke. "She's talking to some man I don't recognize. Looks like a younger Dr. Guree."

"Oh, that'd be the infamous Dr. La Dousa. Bastard," Anne said. "Sorry, but I can't stand that man. He just walked past us and pretended not to notice me."

Kay nudged Anne to keep her voice down, and Kyle led me away in search of Tylenol.

The following day after the second viewing, my father's casket was moved to St. Mary's Church for the funeral service. At Momma's request, Father Latiolais gave the eulogy. It seemed an odd choice. Why not Mr. Duhon or Mr. Delahoussaye? The priest had visited with Momma and Daddy three or four times a years to solicit donations for church projects, and he and his friends used our Gulf Shores condominium at every opportunity, but he wasn't really a friend of Daddy's.

Wearing a white robe with a pine green sash, Father Latiolais stood at the altar and surveyed the audience for a moment, commanding everyone's attention with his silence. Then he began by telling of his many visits with Daddy in his study. He said he often found Chester engrossed in his financial magazines or working on a crossword puzzle. He spoke fondly of my father's quiet demeanor, saying he was a man of few words but never a harsh word spoken. He went on and on without really saying much. His eulogy could have been about anyone it was so generic. I listened to every word, waiting to hear something that truly captured the essence, the uniqueness of my father. But when he finished and invited everyone to join him in prayer, I sat there feeling empty and frustrated.

When we all piled back into the limousines to drive to the graveyard, I turned to Momma and asked, "Did Daddy take up crossword puzzles?"

She looked at me like I was nuts and said no.

"Then why did Father Latiolais say that?"

"I don't know sweetheart, maybe he got him confused with someone else." With that, she turned to the window and stared out at the traffic zooming by on Johnson Street until the car pulled away from the church. She went into that place she always goes to after funerals or heartbreak. That place where we're not wanted.

After the burial, Momma invited the family, the Duhons, the Delahoussayes, and Patrick back to the house for drinks and food. Everyone sat in the living room and kept Momma company while she got smashed. When she finally headed upstairs, the house cleared and Momma's cats were free to roam. Anne and Kay retired to their room. Kyle and I went to the kitchen to rummage through the refrigerator.

"I'm wiped out," I said, sitting down and elevating my bare feet on a chair.

"Me too." Kyle pulled Ziplock bags of sliced meats and cheeses from the bottom drawer of the refrigerator and made himself a sandwich.

Momma stumbled into the kitchen and I sat up. "Hi, y'all still up?"

She slowly made her way to the table using the counter tops and the cooking island as supports. Her eyes were slits in the puffy flesh that drooped over them. She looked more smashed than she had been earlier. She must have had a bottle tucked away in her nightstand.

Standing before us, without a bathrobe, she plopped down in a chair, panting. Kyle looked away, for you could plainly see her breasts hanging down through her sheer nylon nightgown. She might as well have been naked. I couldn't look in her eyes because I felt so ashamed for her.

"I just got off the phone with a friend of mine from grade school," she slurred, slumping over the table. "She just heard about your father and decided to call me after all these years. Poor thing, her husband ran off with a younger woman a few years ago, after more than forty years of marriage. He left her high and dry, no money, nothing. She sounded awful. At least your father always took good care of me, and I never had to suffer through that kind of humiliation. Marie, will you get me some ice water? Is there any carrot cake left?"

She picked up her fork and with great effort managed to spear a piece of the cake. As she brought the bite to her mouth, the fork and the cake fell out of her hand, hitting the brick floor.

"Here, let me get that," I said. I could just imagine her crawling around under the table and then banging her head on the way up.

"I miss your father already," she said after I'd handed her a new fork. "I don't know what I'm going to do without him." She began sobbing until her whole body shook.

I got up and put my arm around her. She mumbled something I couldn't make out with all her crying, so I said, "This must be so difficult for you. You and Daddy spent practically your whole lives together." She cried harder. Kyle didn't say a word.

Finally she composed herself and said, "Sit down. I'm fine." She took one bite of her cake, set her fork aside, and announced that she was going back to bed. After she kissed my forehead, she asked Kyle if it was all right to kiss him good night, too.

Bracing herself at the table, she started the bumpy trip back to her room. When she got to the kitchen door, she miscalculated the distance and ran smack into the door jamb.

"Are you all right, Momma?" I called after her. She mumbled a couple of cuss words, rubbed her right shoulder, backed up, and tried again. This time she made it out the door, but we heard more thuds before her own door slammed.

Oh, my. What were we going to do with her now that Daddy was gone?

24 ～ Louisiana, 1972

I don't know if from the start Daddy knew they'd do more than just remove my mother's uterus or if it was like going to the store for oven cleaner and coming out with two bags full of groceries—items you figured, hell, since I'm here, I might as well pick up also. Aimee told us that besides the hysterectomy, the doctors detoxified Momma and gave her electric shock treatments. Two weeks turned into a month. A month turned into two. After two, I tried not to keep count because I feared she wasn't ever coming home.

Since Momma wasn't home to visit our rooms after bedtime, we were free to roam about. At ten years old I abandoned Barbie, Raggedy Ann, and Nancy Drew to join Nanette and Claire, nearly thirteen and twelve, in their terrifying yet intriguing experimentation with boys, alcohol, and cigarettes. Evenings after my father fell asleep, we slid into cutoffs and halter tops and climbed down the roof to meet teenage boys from another country club Daddy had joined. We offered our new friends Easter baskets filled with magical mind-numbing potions of tiny liquor bottles—miniature replicas of our parents' grown-up fifths of Jack Daniel's, Smirnoff, Bombay, Wild Turkey, Beefeater's, and Dewar's. Figuring where Momma was she wouldn't need them, we stole her souvenirs from my father's business trips from the wet bar.

Every other weekend we drove to Galveston so that Daddy could visit Momma at the hospital. Between these trips I learned to French kiss and lie with confidence. I learned how to swallow tiny bottles of vodka without puking up my guts. I learned how empty and scary the world could feel in the morning when it felt like midgets were somersaulting inside my stomach.

In late July, our final trip to the Seaside Motel in Galveston, the manager changed the sign outside the office to read: Welcome back, Etienne Family.

My father laughed and scribbled his name on the register, when the manager said, "Your kids must really enjoy the beach."

Normally after visiting my mother on Saturday morning, Daddy disappeared behind the pink motel door looking like a tired salesman and reappeared looking like a movie star with his sleek black sunglasses, colorful swim trunks, and tanned body. Except he always wore black socks and dress shoes, even to the beach. This day as he walked past the swimming pool he looked different somehow, like maybe the door-to-door salesman had gotten canned.

"You kids get out of the water. We're going to visit your mother."

"Yea, we get to see Momma!" Nickey shrieked, tossing a handful of water into the air.

Penny and Aimee sat up in their lounge chairs and removed their sunglasses.

"Is everything all right with Momma?" Penny asked.

"She's not doing so well," he said. "The doctor suggested I bring y'all around to see if we can lift her spirits. Now hurry up."

At the hospital entrance marked *Emergency* Daddy stamped out his cigarette, and we quickly filed past him into a large waiting room. Goose bumps covered my arms. The air smelled like a Listerine and Lysol cocktail.

"Don't stare, sweetheart," my father whispered to Anne. Daddy pressed the up arrow button near the elevator. I sneaked another peek at the young man seated in a wheelchair, smoking a cigarette. His scalp was white as paper except for brown stubs of hair. He wore a strange metal crown with screws in it that attached to flat rods. The contraption disappeared into his bathrobe. He looked like Jesus minus the long hair.

We rode the elevator to the third floor.

"Mr. Etienne," said a doctor as he approached our huddle. "My word, look at all these children. Y'all can follow me"

We stopped at room 320. The doctor nodded, Daddy's cue, it seemed, to proceed. Pushing the door open, my father called out, "Esther!"

"Gather around," the doctor told us. "Esther, you see who we brought to visit you? You said you had beautiful children, but I sure didn't expect to meet such lovely faces as these."

I swallowed hard. Momma wasn't sitting up with a novel propped in her lap like I'd imagined. Her bloodshot eyes moved back and forth with either fright or surprise. She lay flat with her lips slightly parted. I offered her a smile, like the ones she'd greeted me with when I was in the hospital, but panic rose from the pit of my stomach. Matted and graying not only at the roots but inches down, her hair looked as if she hadn't washed it in years. A sheet covered her legs. She wore a hospital gown with an orange stain just below the neckline. It reminded me of the wet spot on her shorts from the screwdriver she'd spilled when she crashed into the tree.

What were they doing to her?

She whispered hello and held out her hand for Aimee. My sister took it, careful not to disturb the attached IV, and said, "Hi, Momma. It's good to see you. We miss you. We want you to come home."

Momma's skinny arm trembled slightly and then drooped. Her eyes traveled again, starting with Daddy and scanning the scared and puzzled faces around her. She paused on Nickey. The edges of her mouth came up for a moment. I wanted her to notice me and say, "Oh, my darling Marie, there you are." But she didn't.

"We've got to get you up and about, Esther," the doctor said, firmly, "so you can go home. Your children miss you."

Daddy looked at us. We nodded enthusiastically. Momma shut her eyes. Aimee still held her hand as if she wasn't sure how long she was supposed to hold it.

"We'll let you rest now, Esther," the doctor said.

Aimee dropped Momma's hand.

"Give your mother a kiss," Daddy said as we stepped back from the bed, ready to flee. One at a time, we carefully kissed her and waved good-bye.

In the hallway, Daddy pulled the doctor aside and said, "I can't take seeing her like that. I just can't handle it. I'm sorry. I can't come back here, ever again."

The doctor patted my father's shoulders. "Don't give up, Mr. Etienne. Call me tomorrow."

Daddy reached in his pocket for his handkerchief. He blew hard and then rubbed his nose as we piled into the elevator.

I wasn't sure what frightened me more—Daddy giving up on our mother or Momma lying in a hospital room looking like she wanted to die, like she might even get her wish. How could he put her in here and let them do whatever it was they did, and then just give up on her? Would he do the same to me if I got sick?

On Sunday we drove home. The next day Penny stood at the stove in her bikini scraping globs of sauce from the sides of tin cans. Her blue eyes narrowed as I grabbed a Snickers bar off the counter.

"Lunch will be ready in about half an hour." She sounded like Momma but commanded none of the respect that came with the role forced on her.

Ignoring her, I tore off the wrapper and ran upstairs to see what Nanette and Claire were doing. Seated on opposite beds they each slouched over a game of solitaire. They looked like twins in profile. Similar pug noses. Long brown hair. It was the one month of the year, August, when they were both the same age, twelve.

"Y'all think Momma's scared in that hospital by herself?" I asked. We'd come back from Galveston the day before but none of us had mentioned Momma or Daddy's breakdown.

Nanette scooped up her cards. "Probably. I had a nightmare about her dying last night."

"Y'all want to invite one of our friends over?" Claire asked, changing the subject.

Nanette and I shook our heads no.

"Want to bug Nickey?" I asked, wanting, like Claire, something to distract me from my own gloom.

Claire and Nanette curled their lips. We devised a plan. Cruel, even deviant, ideas always came to us more easily than something constructive and loving. It didn't matter the prey.

I found Nickey sitting two inches from the television with his faded T-shirt pulled over his knees. "Want to come upstairs with me for a minute?"

"No. I'm watching cartoons." Having recently lost his first upper tooth, he sprayed the screen with his spit.

"Oh, come on. We want to show you something. Nanette has some candy that she'll give you."

He studied my face to see if I was lying, and then followed me.

"She must be in the bathroom dividing up the candy. Let's go see."

"Lock the door," Nanette said as soon as I pushed Nickey into the room.

Claire jumped off the vanity and smiled at Nickey. His eyes darted back and forth between us. "I don't want any candy. Let me out of here."

"You're not going anywhere," Nanette said, unsnapping her denim shorts. "We have something to show you." She pulled the shorts past her hips and lowered her bikini underwear with *Monday* embroidered in red stitching. Nickey backed away, but Claire held him still.

"Look," Nanette said, pointing to her kinky black hair. "Want to touch it?"

Nickey shook his head. "Let me go." His chin quivered.

"Don't be chicken," Claire taunted, grabbing his hand and pressing it into Nanette's nest of hair.

He tried to wrestle his hand free but Claire and I held him there. He kicked at my shins and screamed, "Stop it! Let me…"

"Want to touch mine?" I asked, grinning.

"No! Let go of my arm."

I covered his mouth and he bit me. "Ow, you little jerk!"

Nickey's chest heaved up and down. "I'm going to tell Daddy."

Claire dropped his hand and Nanette grabbed her clothes. Tears trickling down his cheeks, Nickey held his hand to the side and stomped on Claire's toes.

"Ouch! You little brat! I ought to smack you for that."

"You're gonna be in big trouble," he warned, sobbing.

Nanette zipped her shorts. She looked scared. "Calm down, Nickey. It was just a silly joke. We really do have some candy for you."

"I don't want anything!" he screamed and ran to the door.

I threw myself against the door. "Please, don't tell Daddy. How about money? You can have my allowance."

Nickey sniffled and shook his head. "No!" He punched my arm. "Let me GO!"

That punch gave Claire an idea. "Come on Nickey," she said, lifting up her T-shirt until her training bra was visible. "Look. You can hit me in the stomach. Three times, okay?"

Nickey looked skeptically at her.

"I'm serious. As hard as you want."

Had she found the right bait? He took a couple of steps forward and curled up his fist. I held my breath as he cocked his arm back and whacked her. He punched her three times with all his might. Then he panted and squinted to survey the damage. He let out a long, shaky breath. The skin around Claire's belly button was rosy.

"You want to punch me too?" Nanette asked, stepping forward. Nickey nodded and slugged her three times. When my turn came, I squeezed my eyes shut and sucked in my stomach.

My little brother left the bathroom that morning with red knuckles and with one pocket full of quarters and the other filled with Starbursts. That evening while my father nursed his drink, my brother was in the backyard in the rain, shooting his BB gun at the dog. I didn't rat on him. I figured, fair is fair. He didn't tell on us. I wouldn't tell on him. It was sort of like one of Daddy's favorite sayings, "What goes around, comes around." And you just keep your mouth shut.

Later that evening Claire and I were sitting at the kitchen counter devouring turkey TV dinners when Aimee and her new boyfriend, Alvin, came running in. Aimee's yellow blouse clung to her chest so I could see the outline of her nipples underneath her bra. Dripping water on the brick floor, she dashed to the laundry room while Alvin stood inside the door. I stuffed some turkey into my mouth and stared at him.

He kept shifting his weight and looking from his wet boots to the laundry door and back to his boots again. Finally he looked at us and mumbled, "It's sure rainin' out there." He shook out his scraggly blond hair and shivered as if a chill had tickled his neck.

I grinned and looked at Claire; she kicked my shin. Aimee returned with her hair combed neatly back and two beach towels draped over her arm.

Alvin had graduated with Aimee in May. One night when he came to get Aimee Daddy asked him if he, like Aimee, planned on attending University of Southwestern Louisiana in the fall. He said, "No, I ain't really college material."

After he had dried his face and clothes, he stammered, "Well, I guess I'll call you tomorrow." Claire looked at me and kicked me again.

"I'll walk you to the gate."

As soon as they left the kitchen, Claire looked at me and giggled. "It's sure rainin' out there," she said, mocking his slow, hick speech.

"Golly, Mr. Etienne, I ain't got no…" I said, trying to keep one half of my mouth from moving as I spoke. The kitchen door opened and I continued, "I'm just a working boy."

Aimee walked in and glared. "He can't help the way his mouth does that." She pushed her damp hair behind her ears. "He's got a metal plate in his head. He was in a motorcycle accident, you idiots."

Aimee protected her boyfriends. The mangier and more damaged they were, the fiercer her loyalties. We snickered behind our hands, and she flipped us the bird on her way upstairs. Later, when we went to apologize, we heard Penny and her arguing from the hallway. We stood with our backs against the wall.

"I'm just asking you to charge a couple of outfits for me," Aimee pleaded. "Why can't you do that? It's not like it's your money. Momma and Daddy won't know the difference."

"I said no and I mean it," Penny said in her even, mean-spirited voice. "So quit bugging me."

"You selfish bitch!"

I couldn't understand why Penny wouldn't help her. It wasn't a matter of *thou shall not lie or steal*. I'd seen her swipe money from Momma's wallet. And Daddy rarely looked at his bills. But Penny was a hoarder. She had a closet with twice as many clothes and shoes any of the rest of us had, and she padlocked the door so that nobody, even the maid, could enter without her permission. It's as if she was always preparing herself against an invasion, a war where everything important is taken away or rationed.

The following morning Aimee ignored Claire and me as she headed to the study. I felt badly that we hadn't apologized to her for mocking her boyfriend. We heard her ask Daddy, "Can I talk to you for a minute?"

"Sure, darling." The den door shut and soon loud voices penetrated the wood paneling. Claire drained a half a glass of milk and pressed it against the wall.

I watched, anxious for my turn. But Claire rolled her eyes and removed the glass. "Doesn't work."

The inside door opened. Aimee shouted, "I'm not having an abortion. You can't make me."

I looked at Claire. I couldn't believe that my sister was going to have a baby. The door opened and she ran past us, crying.

At breakfast the next day, Daddy asked us, "Has anyone seen Aimee?" Her chair, beside Momma's, sat empty.

Six heads moved slowly back and forth.

Aimee didn't return that day or any day soon after that. Slowly everyone around me was leaving.

Mid-August Daddy announced Momma was ready to come home. Yvette agreed to be the second driver again. So we made our final trip to Galveston to pick her up. Daddy went in to fetch her, and we all waited by the curb. A nurse wheeled my willowy mother, who was all done up to look almost like Audrey Hepburn, over to us. She stood and opened her arms for Nickey, giving him a long embrace. One at a time, we greeted her with hugs and kisses. Then she looked around and asked, "Where's Aimee?"

Daddy cleared his throat and said, "She ran away with a young man named Alvin. She sent me a note saying they got married." Momma nodded as if she understood without it being said that my eighteen-year-old sister was expecting a baby.

My father banned Aimee from our house. There would be no contact between the two, just as it had been with Yvette when she decided, for those twelve months after high school, to live as a Carmelite nun, a notion my father felt was too painfully reminiscent of his own mother's existence in a mental hospital. Except for her oil portrait hanging between Chess's and Yvette's in the piano room, all traces of Aimee vanished.

Though parental love is said to be unconditional, my parents' love came packed with special clauses, certain provisions. At ten, I began to understand this about my father.

I would never know what it was like for my mother at that hospital or what her shock treatments felt like. When I saw "Francis," years later, I threw up. Knowing that someone in my family, my very own mother, could be held virtual prisoner in a hospital planted a deep fear in me: it could happen to me.

Momma rested in her bedroom for days until she gradually acclimated to being home. Once when she and Grandma were drinking coffee, I heard her say she knew that she'd beaten some of her children but couldn't remember which ones. She didn't say she felt guilty about it, only confused. She shook her head helplessly, as though the answer was right there, thinly veiled in fog, but completely out of reach.

Maybe Momma didn't remember the way she'd beaten Aimee, and maybe she didn't feel any guilt for it. But Momma must have felt something —sympathy? pity? a need to soften Aimee's shame as her own mother had never softened hers?—because months later, I saw Momma folding tiny baby outfits neatly into boxes. After she'd loaded the boxes into her car and driven away, I asked Nanette if she knew whose baby Momma was buying presents for.

"Aimee. Daddy doesn't know that Momma visits her. She lives with that guy who talked kind of funny."

"How do you know?"

"'Cause one time after Momma took me to the dentist, we stopped by the A & P. She filled the cart with diapers and baby formula and about a dozen, huge $8 roasts. When I asked why she was buying groceries for a baby, she said, 'It's for your sister. But if you dare mention it to your father, you'll be in big trouble.'"

"Really!" I felt a little angry. It wasn't like Nanette to withhold gossip.

She nodded. "Yep. And then we drove to some scary-looking trailer park. Momma honked the horn and out popped Aimee with a tiny baby in her arms."

"Did you get to hold it?" Claire asked.

She shook her head. "No way. Momma made me stay in the car with the doors locked while she unloaded the bags. I didn't even ask the baby's name because Momma was acting so funny. She just drove away, and there was Aimee waving good-bye to us."

25 ～

Aimee's absence left holes in the family structure. She had often been my link to family gossip. She had been my mother's favorite target for abuse, but now Momma used Penny to fill the void. My vigilance sharpened, because I saw that she was eating her way down the food chain.

Momma knew better than to hit Penny. She attacked just below Daddy's radar with verbal assaults to my sister's self-confidence. She sat on a kitchen stool, drinking and waiting for Penny to return from school functions to harass her about her social life, her eye makeup, her exorbitant charges to Daddy's accounts. She hurled hateful names like "selfish bitch" each time Penny strode downstairs, tardy for yet another meal. For the rest of us, though, Momma's erratic behavior changed for the better. The nights of her yanking us out of bed and spanking welts onto our legs and bottoms ended. She only yelled or punished us if we did something really bad—like when Nanette wrecked the old station wagon driving down the wrong side of a boulevard just for fun, or when I jokingly said in front of my parents' friends that they sure acted silly sometimes when they got drunk. By the time I entered junior high, the screaming came mostly from Penny as she fought off attacks by Momma or waged war with Nanette over the car they shared.

One evening we sat down to dinner—smothered pork chops and string bean casserole that Momma prepared whenever Grandma spent the night—and Daddy announced, "Guess what, Junebug."

"Tootie Breaux from the Lafayette Country Club Ball telephoned me. You've been invited to be a royal maid in next year's ball."

The ball was one of the many held throughout Louisiana every year right before Ash Wednesday. Every year they voted on a king, and a

154

queen, and a ninety-member cast: maids, attendants, dukes, dancers, maid of honor, prince, horsemen, and more.

Penny's eyes popped open as she exclaimed, "Really! Oh, can I?"

"Sure, darling," Daddy said, tucking his napkin inside his collar to protect his paisley tie. "I'm going to be your escort—a royal duke."

Momma reached for her cocktail, and I sucked in a mountain of envy. Why did Daddy's voice bubble so when it involved Penny?

Momma drained her vodka and Coke. We weren't even halfway into Lent, and she was already cheating. Daddy grabbed his drink. His abstinence from Jack Daniel's had lasted less than a week. He claimed the Catholic Church made allowances on Fridays and one could "indulge cautiously."

When I asked Yvette, the family authority on God, she just shook her head.

"Esther," Daddy said, "I've written down the number for the dressmaker. You'll have to schedule a fitting for Penny." He turned back to Penny, wrinkling his nose. "Darling, you might want to see the dermatologist again about your face and neck."

Momma stared sadistically at my sister. My mother's eyes traced from one zit to the next as if connecting the dots. I felt sorry for Penny as her face flushed. Embarrassing her daughter must have lessened Momma's own shame about her returning double chin and growing potbelly.

We'd all heard the nighttime fights behind the closed bedroom door when Daddy pushed Momma away as he slid into bed, claiming that her weight repulsed him. Nickey, who at eight still slept in my parent's room, whispered regularly about waking to Momma muffled sobs. Anytime something offended Daddy's many prejudices or his delicate stomach, he claimed he became physically ill. He quit dragging us to James Bond's movies after 007 had sex with a black woman. I'll never forget sitting next to my father in the dark theatre, hearing him groan with disgust and feeling his coat brush against my arm as he squirmed in his chair, flinching as the white and black flesh tangled. He mumbled, "Let's go," and led all six of us from the crowded theatre with half-empty tubs of popcorn.

As the ball approached, Penny visited the dermatologist for weekly injections to combat her worsening acne. One evening Daddy looked at my sister's purple scars and then scooted his chair away from the table, claiming Penny's face made him sick. He made a quick recovery, though. Just before bedtime Claire knocked on my door.

"Marie, come see what Daddy's doing."

I turned off my television and went into the hall. My father stood at the far end of the hallway in his black-tailed tux and white gloves. A green sash swept across his white vest and cummerbund. He looked like an English gentleman on a late-night rerun.

"Ready, girls?" he asked in a full-mouth grin, pushing his black glasses against his thick eyebrows.

I nodded first, even though I didn't know what I was supposed to ready for. I watched as he lifted one leg and then another straight out in front of him, hip high. His arms swung up, and then down, in time with his stiff legs just like a toy soldier in the "Nutcracker."

"What are you doing, Daddy?" I yelled, giggling.

His neck muscles flexed as he bit his lower lip like a child concentrating on balancing a book on top of his head. "Goosestepping, Sweetheartsabean," he shouted. "This is how the dukes walk around the stage. How do I look?"

"Stupid," yelled Nickey, who joined the growing audience.

"Handsome! Silly! Goofy! Funny!" my sisters and I yelled in our high-pitched voices.

Crammed into our doorways we bounced on our knees as we watched our father goosestep up and down the narrow hallway. We clapped in time with his straight-legged steps, laughing and cheering him on. Penny's door remained closed, but pretty soon Momma came upstairs to see what all the fuss was about. Our laughter was infectious. The harder we laughed, the harder Momma laughed and the higher Daddy's legs jerked up. At one point he stretched so far that his leg came down suddenly with an "Aw, shit, I think I pulled something!" I had to squeeze my legs together so I wouldn't wet my pants.

"March some more, Daddy," Nickey screamed as my father rubbed his inner thigh. "Come on, please."

Daddy said, panting, "That's enough for tonight. You want to try?"

Nickey jumped up and imitated my father to the end of the hall and then back toward us. A half-hour later Momma and Daddy yelled, "Enough already, kids. Quit stomping down the halls and get ready for bed." We were all goosestepping down the hall, trying to kick each other in the butt.

On the night of the ball the announcer called out my father's name. Daddy emerged from the parted gold curtain, kicking and grinning under the spotlight. I sat at the children's table with Nickey and my sisters, clapping along with the jazz music and laughing as he marched onto the stage. My parents' closest friends, the Duhons and Jouberts, chuckled and nudged Momma as they watched Daddy promenade around. He gooses-tepped his way from one stage mark to another, pausing before Momma's table to exchange a smile with her. "You're looking good there, Chester!" his friends hollered, as they rose to their feet, clapped and whistled. Mr. Joubert, who couldn't stand too long because of his bad knees, remained seated and drummed loudly on the table so that all the glasses and bottles danced around. Daddy's face turned as red as the rose pinned to his lapel. Running my palms over the lace of my new ball gown, I smiled at my handsome father.

Fortified with a few stiff Jack Daniel's and Cokes, my father kept perfect time. The duke that followed was a short pudgy man who barely managed to swing his shiny black shoes two feet off the ground. After the last pair of flapping tuxedo tails disappeared behind the curtain, hands fell into laps or reached across the table toward a bottle of wine or fifth of scotch. In the center of each table sat a miniature bar—buckets of ice, plastic cups, liquor of choice, and mixers.

Trumpets and horns blasted. Nearly every head in the auditorium turned. To thundering applause the dukes filed out again, one after another, kicking and swinging in a unified walk about the room. As my hands slapped together, I felt like one of the luckiest girls alive to grow up in a part of the country where grown-ups and children could pretend, if only for a night, that they were part of a magical kingdom, a world full of laughter, smiles, and beauty. And as for Grandma telling Daddy that it was all too showy and wasteful, I didn't care what she thought. She was jaded, just like Momma.

Soon the king and then other royalty glided around the room to standing ovations. I envied the queen, her maid of honor, and every girl who curtsied before my table.

The narrator announced, "Her Grace, Penny Louise from the House of Etienne."

A blaze of light met my sister at the parted curtain. Penny paused for a moment, smiling so widely that the pinks of her gums were visible. Her sapphire blue gown with its pearl-studded bodice matched perfectly her gemstone eyes. She curtsied slowly, careful not to upset the three-foot-tall headpiece of sequined magnolias rising from her decorated cap.

The light moved forward and so did she. With suspended breath I awaited my sister's approach to admire the train. I imagined the two little old ladies, as Penny had described them, bent over the pencil outline of flowers and leaves, with Dixie cups of white iridescent and green sequins, and bottles of glue. Each spangle set preciously into place by unimaginably steady fingers. Waves of applause swept her along and finally deposited her before our tables. She turned to face us, careful not to get tangled in her mantle. I rose with the others to cheer her on. Her eyes sought out Daddy first and asked, "How am I doing? Are you proud of me?"

A generous smile formed on his face, as well as on Momma's. Years later my mother would muse aloud to my best friend, saying, "You know, Penny has always been my favorite." It must have been so, although one could hardly tell.

26 ~

In 1975, desegregation in south Louisiana was in full swing. My friends and I were bussed to the north side of town, an area where our parents wouldn't even drive without their doors locked.

I begged my mother not to send me, a scrawny white girl, to Paul Breaux Elementary. I told Momma how black girls hated white girls, especially ones with long blond hair like me. "Remember the Blanchard twins," I'd say, "they were cornered in the bathroom and threatened to have their white hair cut off." But each time I offered proof of the danger, my mother shook her head and said it couldn't be that bad. But what did she know? The only time she and Daddy drove near the colored section of town was on the way to the country club for Sunday brunch.

Two days before school I decided to make one final plea. I'd offer up my future Christmas and birthday gifts in exchange for going to private school with my best friend.

I sat on the edge of the sofa beside Momma. She didn't look up from the romance novel with a young woman and a savage warrior on the cover. I stared at my chipped toenail polish. Finally she glanced up as she cleared her throat.

"I was thinking that if you let me go to Fatima, I could—"

"No. Now stop pestering me." Her eyes settled onto the top of the page. "There's nothing wrong with Paul Breaux. Your sisters went there."

"I'm scared I'm gonna get beat up, or worse." I picked at a loose thread in the cushion and pulled. Yellow foam peeked from the upholstery. Momma ignored me, didn't even tell me to quit ruining the sofa. "Suzanne's father said he'd drive me. The tuition could be my—"

"I said no. I'm trying to read." Her voice held a threat.

I wanted a reason why she wouldn't even consider it. It couldn't be the money. Daddy's business was thriving. He'd just thrown a huge 75th anniversary party, inviting two thousand friends, family, customers, and vendors. Plus he'd given me carte blanche to charge art supplies, sewing fabrics, and painting lessons anywhere in town to encourage my interest in art. Without knowing her objections, I couldn't argue against them. Perhaps that was her strategy. And maybe she just wanted to be cruel.

She turned another page. I glared at her. She wasn't even going to look at me. She'd just sit there in her polyester pantsuit and wait for her friends to arrive for happy hour. I was simply part of the drudgery she endured until the gossiping and drinking began. Each week she spent more money restocking her liquor cabinet than the entire month's tuition at Fatima would cost.

Something inside me snapped. I slammed my fist on the coffee table, rattling her glass of iced tea. She raised her chin to check the glass.

"Goddamn it! Why won't you even consider it? You don't ever listen to me. I hate you. I hate living here. When I turn eighteen I'm leaving this stupid house. You probably won't even care. You're just saying no to be mean."

My heart pounded as her eyebrows raised in a mocking way. She reached for her glass of tea as my heart pounded. *I'll show you!* I walked over to the storage cabinets lining the den walls and yanked open a wire mesh door. Grabbing the dusty books from the middle shelf, I screamed, "Ahhhhhh," flinging Daddy's old hardbacks across the room. I didn't care what she would do to me. Volume after volume, I threw as quickly as I could, not bothering to check whether Momma was coming over to jerk me off the floor and spank me. I cleaned one shelf and then the next. When I ran out of books, I looked at her, leaning back against the gold cushions with her hands cupped over her big belly, watching me intently now with her paperback set aside. At least I had her attention. Opening another door, I began again. Daddy's dozen copies of his favorite poetry book scattered under the marble table. Cookbooks took flight. Magazines landed on the pool table. I was panting and crying when I turned to look at her. But my fit hadn't pried anything loose. Her puffy, bored face still expressed no compassion.

Sobbing in complete despair, I ran to my room. Sitting in my closet curled in a tight ball, I listened for her. Surely she'd come to see if I was all right or to drag me downstairs to clean up. Maybe she'd feel so bad that she would let me go to Fatima. As I pictured myself going berserk downstairs, the look of amusement on her face when she saw that I could throw a fit as big as hers, I giggled. It had felt nice to let loose and not care. It felt like sweet freedom. But soon, sitting in my closet waiting, I realized she wasn't coming. Not even to spank me. How could she be so sure I wasn't slashing my wrists? I sobbed for two hours before crawling out of my dark corner.

At supper, I noticed the books had been picked up. She didn't say a word. Just told me to fix a plate of food. An empty feeling took hold of me, like someone had wrapped a belt around my neck and was pulling it taut. I had no clue what to do with the pain, so I told myself I didn't care that Momma didn't love me. And even though my outburst didn't win my mother over, I'd discovered the pleasure of raging. If felt wonderful to let loose and behave like a monster. For a moment I had purged myself of suffocating anger. But just like with alcohol and sex, I'd learn, the high was fleeting and always left me feeling idiotic and shameful.

Paul Breaux Elementary was almost as awful as I'd imagined and feared. I did meet some nice black kids in the Industrial Arts class I took. But after two near scuffles, one in the cafeteria and one in the girl's locker room, I devised a survival plan for the other 99 percent of the black population I hadn't befriended: No using the school bathrooms (even with friends it wasn't safe because at the first sign of trouble, they ran); no eating in the cafeteria (instead I swiped two Snickers bars from the snack bowl every morning); and no Physical Ed (My teacher gave me a C, along with the other white girls who cut class). My friends and I stayed at the back of the playground, where we could see trouble coming from all directions. On the rare days I missed the bus, I stayed home because Momma refused to drive me to *that* part of town.

Every morning after breakfast I slid off the stool and grabbed my candy bars. Kissing my mother good-bye, I'd imagine some black kid breathing on her neck, literally feeling his warm breath on her goose-pimply skin, listening to his whispered threats. She had no clue about the crazy rules we followed just to survive. Or did she?

I don't think she noticed how I ran through the door every day at three o'clock and headed straight for the bathroom. And did she notice how my hands shook while I crammed potato chips into my mouth as I fixed two grilled cheese sandwiches? I doubt it. She never said anything. Just gave me a quick hello and a blank-faced kiss as she went about dinner preparations.

27 ~ California, 1993

The strangest thing happened after Kyle and I returned home from Daddy's funeral. One night while we were sitting at the dinner table, Kyle looked at me and announced, "I've decided to quit drinking."

Stunned, I smiled. "Really? Why?"

"Seeing what it did to your father and how bad off your mother is, it just got to me. She's pretty scary. I don't want to end up like them. And, I just thought with the baby coming, it was a good time to stop."

"I think that's wonderful. I'm so proud of you."

"Don't start crying now, okay?"

As I cleaned the kitchen that evening, I thought back to when I had decided to stop drinking. While Kyle's motivation had been the fear of losing control of himself like my parents, my motivation had been the fear of being forever alone. Of not finding a husband or having children. I had watched my parents drink all my life, and it wasn't until after I stopped drinking that it occurred to me I was becoming what I hated and feared most.

On my due date I went into labor. The following evening Austin was born. The first couple of nights after my release from the hospital were hellacious. The baby's sleeping schedule was completely turned around. Days he slept. From midnight until nearly sunrise he screamed. We tried everything to calm him down—feeding, singing, rocking, and pleading. Nothing, including pacifiers, gave us more than a few minutes reprieve. Kyle insisted the problem resided with my breasts. The baby wasn't getting enough nourishment. The sugar water the hospital sent home with us would surely calm him down. I argued that if we gave him a bottle, he might not take my breast again. Exhausted and angry, I finally relented. Kyle held my baby, grinning with satisfaction while Austin sucked on the bottle of sweet water.

"See, he likes it. He stopped crying," Kyle said, not noticing that now I was the one crying. My insides turned cold as I stared at my husband. He acted as if he was the wonderful father with all the answers and I was a bad mother. Or that's how it seemed at the time. Maybe if I'd had more courage and confidence in my own maternal instincts, I would have told him to let the baby cry. Austin was a healthy nine-and-a-half-pound baby, and he wasn't going to starve any time soon.

When my milk finally did come in, Kyle prepared a feeding schedule. Every two hours, as the baby sucked on my raw, cracked nipples, he sat there timing me, twenty minutes per breast—the time he decided adequate. Why couldn't he be one of those "I'll bring home the bacon and you fry it up in the pan" kind of men?

I had fallen asleep in the living room with Austin the afternoon that Kyle brought Claire home from the airport. I woke up confused because I had been dreaming about Daddy, and then there stood Kyle ranting that it was hot in the house and wanting to know why I had left all the curtains open and hadn't turned on the fans.

"What?" I raked the loveseat to find my glasses.

"Hey, Marie," Claire said standing beside the bassinet with her suitcases. "My God, he's precious. And so big!"

She came over to give me a hug, and I asked about her flight. I heard only half of her response because Kyle was thundering through the house shutting all the curtains. After every room was darkened, Kyle began his precise alignment of the fans: two in the hallway, one at each end, and another in the living room. It was crucial, he said, to keep the air circulating during the day so the house would be cool at night. Meanwhile, Claire started fretting over the baby, claiming he was grossly overdressed and sweating. She insisted on waking him.

While my sister and my husband got the baby and the house in order, I shuffled painfully into the kitchen. I was so tired—mentally and physically. I wanted to sneak into my room and swallow a few of the pain pills that sat on the table next to my bed. But I didn't want to give Kyle any reason to stay home from work another day.

Throughout her week-long visit, Claire fixed meals, did the laundry, brought me juice and milk, showed me how to take care of the baby, watched him when I showered and napped, listened to me cry, and kept me company. She called home constantly to check on Tommy. She seemed happy to be able to help me, but I knew it was a huge sacrifice for her to leave her own family. For Kyle, though, she was an intruder in *his* house. Once when she timidly tapped on our bedroom door, entered our room, and offered to give us a night's sleep by taking Austin into her room, he practically hissed at her as she rolled the bassinet away. He said he was so angry at her interference that he had wanted to hurl the baby at her. *Hurl my baby*, he'd better not even try.

One evening he came home, slammed the screen door, and stormed into the living room, where we sat watching television. He crossed the room without returning our greetings and said, "Marie, can I see you in our bedroom for a minute?" He shot me one of his angry stares and nodded toward the hall door. I got up slowly, pressing a hand against the tender incision on my stomach, and followed him. I now walked like Harvey Korman's old man character on the "Carol Burnett Show." Kyle closed the bedroom door behind us and gaped at me, his mouth hanging wide open like he wasn't sure where to begin.

"Yes?" I asked.

"Your sister has the frickin' oven turned up to 450 degrees. It's over a hundred outside and she's cooking a roast in the oven like she's in the South in her air conditioned house."

"Is that what this is about?"

"Hell, yes." He threw his briefcase onto the bed. "I just walked home from BART because that stupid bus driver took off without me again. And now I come home and your sister has turned our house into an oven. Look, the fan isn't even turned on." I looked at the silent fan and nodded. We had failed to run the fans as we were told to do.

"I can't believe you. She's just trying to fix us a nice meal, and all you can do is complain. I wish you'd—" I stopped myself. I wasn't up to watching him pout around the house. I also sensed it was his jealously, not the heat, fueling his rage. He envied the time Claire and I spent together, our closeness, the way we laughed at the silliest memories.

I turned on the fan and suggested that Kyle change into some shorts to cool down. When I returned to the living room, Claire whispered, "What's wrong with him?"

I rolled my eyes and whispered in response, "He's just pissed that the house is hot and he missed his bus." She turned back to watch television and didn't ask, later, why Kyle was having dinner alone in our bedroom. For the rest of her trip whenever she entered the same room as Kyle, he abruptly left.

I knew she probably didn't believe it was solely his job that made him so cranky. Her silence and determination to be pleasant around him made me resent his rude behavior even more. The only comment that struck Claire so painfully that she couldn't conceal her hurt was once when I joked to Kyle that I was going to check her suitcase before she left to go home because she might try to steal our baby. After we all laughed, she excused herself, saying she wanted to take a nap. When she didn't come out at dinnertime, I went in and found her sitting on her bed, red-eyed, pretending to be reading a magazine.

"Have you been crying? Is there something wrong?"

She looked at me and brought her hand to her mouth. Her face suddenly got all screwed up. "Am I that pitiful that you and Kyle think I'm going to steal your baby?"

"What are you talking about?" Confused, I sat down beside her and touched her arm. She quoted my earlier comment about her wanting another baby so badly that she might steal Austin.

"I'm so sorry, Claire. It was a cruel, stupid thing for me to say. I didn't mean it. I know it must be so hard for you to be here. I've been whining all week about being scared that Austin is going to die because I love him too much. I didn't even think about how that must make you feel."

She drew her knees up and buried her face in her arms as she cried. When she finally looked at me with her mascara-smeared eyes, she said, "You know, Austin is the first baby I've held since Emma's death. I can't even bear to visit friends who have babies because I'm so scared I'll break down in front of them. It just tears me up inside, I miss her so much. She'd be two and a half now. Walking. Talking. I'm always wondering what she'd be like. I'm always asking God why he chose her, why my family. I get so jealous and angry sometimes."

"How can you not be angry with a God who is supposed to be loving but lets innocent babies die? It doesn't make any sense to me."

"No, it doesn't. I guess God just tests our faith to make us stronger."

I wanted to say BULLSHIT on all of that. How many tests must one pass before God finally bugs off? But if she found solace in some warped higher power, I didn't want to take that away from her. So I nodded and we both sat quietly, picking at the gray balls of lint on her blanket.

"Can I ask you something?"

As she nodded, I was certain she knew what I was wondering. She had had her tubes untied shortly after her daughter's death and had endured a painful tubal pregnancy last year.

"Do you think you and Ronnie will try again?"

She shrugged. "The doctor said there's so much scar tissue in the remaining tube that he doesn't feel I have much of a chance. Ronnie really wants me to do in vitro, but I don't really want to put all those drugs in my body."

"Yeah, I can see that."

"I'm sure Nanette told you that I asked her if she'd consider having a baby for me."

"No. Really?" I couldn't believe Claire's audacity or the fact that Nanette hadn't said anything to me.

"Yeah, but she said there'd be no way she could carry a baby and then give it away."

"That'd be really tough to do, especially for Nanette. She wouldn't even let anyone hold or touch Christopher for weeks after he was born."

"Yep. She still keeps those boys glued to her side."

"She's created her own little happy family, and she's terrified of losing them. It's amazing how powerful that love is. Austin's only ten days old, and yet he fills me up like nothing I ever got from Momma or Daddy or even Kyle."

"I know what you mean," Claire said, rubbing her eyes. My thoughts shifted.

"Do you ever get scared that it will all get to be too much, that you could somehow hurt Tommy, even without meaning to, like Momma did with us?"

Claire studied her fingernails, which she'd finally stopped chewing, and mumbled yes. The room became still. Since we were kids, we'd all sworn never to hurt our own children. Aimee had failed. Would the rest of us? Claire didn't elaborate and I didn't press the subject. Besides, I knew I should go to bed before Austin woke up hungry. I could feel the depression, my nightly visitor of late, creeping in and binding itself to my chest.

"I wish you weren't leaving tomorrow," I said, tears welling up in my eyes. "I don't know what I'm going to do without you. I don't know if I can handle Nanette and her kids right now."

My sister hugged me. I wanted so badly to tell her the entire reason I felt so sad. I had an overwhelming fear that my postnatal depression wouldn't just run its course like a summer cold. Every night when the despair began, all I could think about was my father's mother, who *they* said never quite got over her baby blues and had to be lobotomized. Had giving birth tripped that same crazy switch in my brain? Had my father's death somehow jinxed my baby's life? Would Austin be taken from me? Grow up like Daddy, thinking I'd died or abandoned him?

In addition, I felt trapped in a body turned eighty overnight, a body that might never be free of aches and pains. Why had I insisted on entertaining a steady flow of houseguests? Surely I'd be forced to mediate disputes between Kyle and Nanette, too. Then there was the guilt that every time Momma called crying I barely listened to her complaints and just wished she'd phone another one of my sisters. There was the huge disappointment of finding out that I wasn't getting any money when I read Daddy's will. For as long as Momma lived, she was to receive all the interest and income from the children's trusts, and we couldn't touch the principal. I knew that Kyle and I had grossly misjudged our living expenses, and we wouldn't really be able to live off his salary.

And more disheartening was the knowledge that six weeks, eight at best, was the most respite I'd enjoy before having to resume my wifely duties, as Claire called them. Finally it was the acknowledgement that I had married a man I didn't love and that Austin would be the one most hurt by the deceit.

28 ~ Louisiana, 1975

"Momma, Suzanne wants me to join cotillion with her," I blurted out. "It probably costs a lot of money, and you have to buy a new dress for every dance. Can I?"

Suzanne, my best friend, had followed me into the smoky study to make sure I wouldn't trick her. I'd only agreed to ask my mother for permission because I was sure her answer would be no.

"Sweetheart, that sounds wonderful," Momma answered, giving Suzanne her best June Cleaver imitation.

Suzanne showed her mouth full of metal in a smile. I felt betrayed. Private school, no. Stupid cotillion, yes. Where is the logic here?

Daddy nodded in agreement, and added, "Too bad Nanette can't take a few dance lessons since she's going to be a maid in the ball this year." He was referring to her role as one of the royal maids in the next Lafayette Ball in February. Nanette hadn't ever been invited by one of the cotillion members as far as I knew, and now at sixteen it was practically too late to join.

Reaching for her cigarette case, Momma said, "Darling, let your father know how much to write the check for. We'll go to Abdalla's this weekend to pick out a nice dress and gloves for the first dance."

I drew in a breath, casting my eyes down on the carpet. Was it a game to her? Was I a mouse in her maze?

"Thank you, Mr. and Mrs. Etienne," Suzanne said, linking her freckled arm with mine.

When we left the study I turned to Suzanne and mimicked: "Thank you, Mr. and Mrs. Etienne." Then I punched her in her bony shoulder.

Cotillion fell on the first Friday evening of each month. Suzanne and I slipped into our new formal dresses, white gloves, and high heels and giggled in the back seat of her parents' Continental. At the church auditorium we met a hundred other awkward kids to learn the fox trot, the cha-cha, the box step, and the waltz. The instructors welcomed us, and then the girls and boys lined up on opposite sides of the room. One, two, three! And the race began. Decked out in suits, ties, and Sunday shoes, the jocks raced the scrawny boys across the room to choose a partner. Every time they counted down, panic gripped me. What if no one chooses me? Do I stand off to the side and try to pretend I don't feel like a loser? Or do I hide out in the bathroom until the next song? Luckily, one kid or another always asked me to dance.

Later after punch and cookies, the instructors announced the free-dance period. We lined up against the wall again, but this time after pairing up we could dance the way we wanted. Under the bright lights, we bumped and ground our hips and shimmied our chests, trying to imitate one girl, Jami Falgout. She memorized all the latest dances on Soul Train, like the penny-nickel-dime-quarter routine where you thrust your pelvis in circles. And each time "Everybody was Kung-Foo Fighting" blared on the speakers, Jami hiked up her skirt to kick her legs and twirl. She didn't care if we laughed or applauded or if her behavior bothered the chaperones. I envied her confidence, and though I practiced at home, I couldn't copy exactly either her moves or her self-assurance.

"Now aren't you glad you joined?" Suzanne asked me after the first dance. We'd changed into shorts and were watching television with Anne. My parents had teetered through earlier on their way to bed.

"Guess so. That was hilarious when Jami's glove got stuck in her braces. Hey, I think Penny's home."

I hit the light switch, and Anne scrambled to turn off the TV. We ran to the kitchen window and opened the curtains. Suzanne and I looked like twins now with our matching short haircuts. We both had blond hair, but her eyes were blue. Whenever she slept over, we always spied on Penny and her dates.

The foyer door creaked, and we bumped heads as we stood up, plastering innocent smiles on our faces. "It's just you," I huffed.

Nickey tiptoed across the brick floor in his Mickey Mouse pajamas, his brown hair sticking straight up like a rooster's, and I rolled my eyes. Every time Anne or I had a friend sleep over, he sneaked out of my parents' room. "Be quiet and close the door," I whispered.

"He's cute," Suzanne remarked, staring at the profile of the tall guy towering over my petite eighteen-year-old sister. Penny's arms were hidden inside his navy jacket, wrapped around his waist. "She must be pretty good at that by now."

Penny sometimes had two dates a weekend since she had gotten into a sorority. They always came home drunk and horny.

"Move, she's coming," Anne said, crawling away from the window. The door opened just as the four of us were safely hidden under the kitchen table.

I capped Nickey's mouth to keep him from giggling. Penny bumped into the counter, mumbled, "Fuck," and then made her way to the sink. Suzanne bit her lip as we waited for Penny to grab a glass and turn on the faucet. She had learned from Momma and Daddy that water and aspirin taken before bed staved off cottonmouth and a hangover the next day.

She filled her glass with ice, and I held my breath. Earlier we'd wrapped a rubber band around the spray nozzle at the sink. No matter how many times we played the same gag on Penny, she never thought to check the sprayer. The minute she turned on the faucet, the spray of water shot straight out, hitting her smack in the face. Low giggles erupted as she screamed and flailed her arms. She was so drunk, as always, that by the time she finally succeeded in fighting through the water to turn the faucet off, her clothes were soaked. Anne and I exchanged frightened stares as we watched through the chair legs for her clogs to appear. But this night she just mumbled cuss words to the silly framed quotes as she fumbled her way through the kitchen and up the stairs looking like a horror-show victim with mascara dripping down her cheeks. Once the foyer door closed, we crawled out from under the table and fell over each other laughing.

Suzanne didn't drink or smoke yet in the eighth grade so I didn't either. Instead we amused ourselves with silly pranks. Besides, Nanette, the ringleader for Claire and me, had found God at the First Baptist Church in town (along with a new boyfriend, Kenny.) Claire had joined the Lionettes, her high school's pep squad, and was busy with her new friends. Suzanne didn't seem bothered by my parents' drinking and their loud voices. And I didn't care that her mother was a religious fanatic, often running into Yvette at one retreat or another.

Each day I ran from the bus stop, peed, stuffed my face, and then called Suzanne to hang out in my front yard. I told her stories of fights at my school or the newest guy I'd fallen for. She told me stories about her friends at Fatima or updated me on her cute brother and his girlfriend's latest breakup. But Suzanne's and my escapades temporarily screeched to a halt in late April when the principal at Paul Breaux telephoned my father to say I was flunking school (a fact that had escaped my parents' notice because ever since my first F, I just forged Momma's signature to avoid punishment). Daddy called me down to the study.

Standing before his recliner, I expected a terrible scolding. But he said, "Darling, I can't have one of my children failing school." He devised something motivational rather than a spanking or loss of privileges. "If you pull your grades up, and pass, your Mother and I will let you go to Fatima next year."

I glanced at Momma. How could it be that easy? "Are you serious?"

She nodded along with Daddy. I couldn't believe my luck; they didn't even mention the forged report cards. "Thank you so much," I said, stepping forward. "I swear, I'm gonna pass." As I leaned over to kiss him, all I could think of was the shriek of excitement I'd hear when I called Suzanne. Turning to Momma, I mumbled, "Thank you, too." She sat stiff with hands folded and resting on her belly, angry that she'd been outmaneuvered. I walked over and quickly kissed her too.

29 ~

For four years, Momma called Aimee every week, delivered groceries and clothes to her, and kept a picture of her grandson Michael in her wallet. But Daddy never mentioned my sister's name.

Then one night, Momma announced that Aimee had rented an apartment and was divorcing Alvin. It was strange to hear my sister's name spoken aloud, especially in Daddy's study. I set my Teen magazine down and turned toward Daddy. Casually, as if he'd never said anything to the contrary, he scratched his stubble and mumbled that it was all right for Aimee to visit us. And just like that, my sister reentered the fold.

Once a week, Aimee sat at the kitchen counter with her blond-haired boy, smoked her Marlboros, and watched Momma stuff a pork roast or stir a roux. Anne and I often tried to coax Michael away from his mother's side, but he clung to her as if he was afraid of us. He eyed the large plastic bowl of Snickers bars, but if he dared reach for a one, Aimee shot him a look and he froze. This wasn't her house anymore. She talked about her job search and her plans to take classes at USL when she could afford to pay for daycare. Every time she left, Momma slipped some folded green bills into her pocket. As she left, Aimee thanked her with downcast eyes.

Daddy didn't go out of his way to welcome Aimee back, so she visited when he was at work. But when he found a four-hundred-dollar dental bill for Michael, a charge Momma had authorized, next to his napkin at dinner one night (the designated spot where we all left our bills for Daddy to pay), he just sighed heavily and tucked it into his pocket. When an opening became available at the wholesale, he asked Momma to offer Aimee the job. And when she decided to marry beady-eyed Byron Whatley, a roughneck who called Momma Miss Esther and fished with Daddy when no one else was handy, he bought her a dress, hired a caterer and Al Hirt, and opened the house for her small wedding. He even helped them buy a house a few streets over.

Standing in the bathroom, I admired my new school uniform in the mirror, turning this way and that so that my skirt swelled and fell an inch above my knees. Claire watched and said, "Wish you were coming to Lafayette High with me this year."

"Lafayette High's too big—I'd get lost. At least at Fatima there're only two halls and the classes are small. Plus there's no black kids. Why don't you switch to Fatima?"

She rolled her dark eyes and began chewing on her thumbnail. As I applied my mascara, I watched her pout. There was something fragile and unsettled about Claire that made me feel sorry for her. I knew she was panicked because she was about to break up with her boyfriend and had-n't found another one yet.

We pulled further apart as I found myself easily accepted by Suzanne's group of friends, many of whom I had danced beside at Cotillion. Suzanne introduced me to a sophomore, Jude Thibodeaux, a curly-haired JV basketball player, and soon we began dating. He took me to all the school dances and after-game jungle juice parties.

My older sisters and I became consumed with boyfriends, parties, and school. My parents' equally busy social life left Anne, thirteen, and Nickey, eleven, at home to look after themselves. It seemed like one minute they were a couple of gawky kids—Anne the tomboy straddling a tree branch and throwing pinecones at Nickey, my little brother the gun-slinging fireman in their games—and the next minute they were get-ting into trouble like the rest of us.

"What in the hell is going on here?" I screamed, walking past the swim-ming pool to the dimly lit backyard. I had heard Nickey's laughing from the empty carport when I came home from Suzanne's house. King, the black Lab my father had recently bought, barked madly. In bare feet and T-shirts Nickey and Anne were running from the swing set to the playhouse, teas-ing the dog with my old, one-eyed Raggedy Ann doll. "It's freezing out here. Are you drunk again?" I grabbed my little sister by her arm.

She fell to the ground laughing, and Nickey threw himself down beside her. They giggled like two-year-olds. "Get up! Momma and Daddy are going to be home soon, and they'll shit if they see you like this."

I dragged Anne inside. Nickey zigzag behind us trying not to laugh but failing miserably. Up the stairs we went, and I didn't care how many bruises Anne had the next day as she bumped her knees over each step. I dumped her in the bathroom and said, "Don't move."

"Come on, you little jerk!" I said, slapping at Nickey's flailing arms. "You'll be in big trouble if they find out their precious little boy has been raiding their liquor cabinets again."

"Ow, you're hurting me!" he whined. I felt angry for having to play Mommy.

Hauling him up the stairs, I snarled, "Then get up, stupid. Pick up your legs and walk!"

When we reached the bathroom I stood his shivering body next to Anne's. "Take off your clothes and get in the shower."

"But I don't want you to see my wienie," Nickey said, breaking into hysterics.

"I could really give a damn about your wienie, you little turd. Now strip and get in the shower before I do it for you."

Anne giggled at the sight of our brother covering his private parts and stumbling into the shower. Her smile vanished when the cold water pelted her face. "I wanna go to bed!" she cried.

"Be quiet. Here. Wash your face." I handed her a washcloth. "You too, Nickey, and use the soap 'cause you stink."

"No!"

"Okay, then I'll do it." I grabbed the soap and began scrubbing his face hard. I remembered Momma sticking the Lava soap in our mouths whenever she heard us swearing, and I flinched, feeling bad for acting mean. Nickey swung his fists at my soaked shirtsleeve, and I dropped the soap. "You're gonna fall on your butt if you don't stop it. So stink if you want, I don't care."

"I'm done, can I get out now?" Anne begged. I let her out, but before she got her pajamas on, she spewed curdled pink vomit everywhere.

For the next half-hour I cleaned them and the bathroom. I felt guilty that I didn't spend much time with them anymore. Claire and Nanette had shown much more patience with me, taking me along on their adventures. But now, I did whatever I could to get away from the house.

A week later, Jude pulled into our driveway behind Daddy's boat, and I saw two tiny figures scrambling for cover behind the juniper bushes.

"Who was that?" Jude asked, scooting closer for a kiss.

"Anne and Nickey," I answered, rolling my eyes. After saying good night, I yelled toward the bushes, "I saw you two!" and then went inside to tell my parents I was home from the game.

"Hey, Sweetheartsabean," Daddy said as I entered the study.

I kissed Momma first. As I headed toward Daddy's chair, she said, "They called to invite you to be a teenage dancer in the ball this year."

"Awesome!" That would make three of us in the ball. Claire would be a royal maid and Nanette the maid of honor.

I couldn't wait to tell Nanette. I found her in front of her bedroom window hunched over Momma's old Singer machine.

"I'm going to be a dancer in the ball," I announced over the loud stitching. "Isn't that cool?"

"Oh, you're soooo lucky!" She turned toward me and rolled her eyes. "You can be maid of honor too. I hate those ridiculous spectacles. All those phony rich people telling you how beautiful you look, acting like you're their best friends. Then after the ball when you run into them at the A & P, they can't even remember your name."

"Then why didn't you just say no to Momma and Daddy?"

"I tried, but Daddy insisted, 'Butterbean, it's a wonderful opportunity to meet people'. Blah, blah, blah…" she flapped her arms like a fairy for emphasis.

I shrugged, hoping she'd shave her armpits before the big night because all that kinky hair looked gross. Later, to spite my parents, Nanette cropped her hair short like a boy right before she was scheduled to have her full-dress photographs taken.

Pairing the dance couples up for the ball wasn't like Cotillion. The boys didn't stand on the opposite side and gallop toward the girl of their desire. The instructors surveyed the room full of nervous teenagers and partnered us up in a very civilized fashion. When they pointed to me and then to my partner, I swore I'd never ask God for another thing. Chad Breaux was tall with wavy blond hair, crystal blue eyes, and had the most beautiful smile in the room.

"You must be Claire's little sister," he said, taking my hand while we waited for music to begin.

"Yes."

"I've never seen you around school."

"No. I go to Fatima." Please, hands, don't sweat.

"Well," he said, flashing a wicked smile, "it's very nice to meet you."

"You, too."

Nightly, for two weeks before the ball, Chad and I met with nine other couples and the instructors to practice our routine. It was a funny dance. We girls would begin in formal length dresses, dancing with our partners to slow music. After a couple of minutes the beat picked up, and we stopped and ripped off our outer skirts to reveal short, frilly ones beneath. Then we bumped and twirled to fast rock 'n' roll.

The evening of the Friday rehearsal ball, the boys brought a keg of beer backstage to our dressing area, and we sat around chugging while we waited to be called. By the time they gave us a three-minute warning, I could barely walk. Chad towered over me, so for the slow dance he just held me close and twirled me about. When the tempo picked up, I panicked. I'd have to stand on my own!

I ripped apart the snaps on my skirt, and tangled in the hem, nearly falling over.

"My heel is caught!" I whispered.

"Hang on," he said, stepping on the lace of my dress. "Pull!"

I ripped my heel out of the fabric. He tossed the skirt aside and we managed to bluff our way through the rest of the dance.

As we walked off the stage, he grinned at me. I smiled back, giggling.

When we stopped just behind the curtain, he bent down, squeezed my face, saying, "Little lady, you're trouble," and then planted the biggest kiss I had ever received.

"Marie…"

I looked up, and there stood Suzanne and Jude. They had arrived to bring me to a party. How in the world would I explain this to my boyfriend? I felt my face redden.

Few words were exchanged between Jude and me that evening. Even Suzanne didn't say much. She just kept shooting me looks like, what in the hell were you doing? My relationship with Jude spiraled to a close, after just two months. I was a little disappointed that I'd blown my chances of being voted a winter dance Sweetheart by Jude and his teammates, but I moved on to the next guy.

Following my breakup with Jude, a string of quick flings ensued. My first couple of years at Fatima I devoured guys like a bulldozer tearing away at a hill. Suzanne, now drinking, and I constantly got hammered with our friends. But she'd shake her head in disbelief whenever I kissed another guy in front of my current beau. Drunk, I wasn't scared to do anything. I might see a cute guy at a bar and run to kiss him. Or I might humiliate a friend by yanking up her skirt at a game. And if Suzanne wouldn't participate in my pranks, I could always count on my new buddy, Mignon, to follow my lead. She was as pliable as Play-Doh. We would have been better off without each other. I had little self-control, and she couldn't say no to a friend.

My wild impulses of Friday and Saturday night always seemed like inconsequential fun until Sunday, when I lay in bed, full of regret and shame over some indiscretion, fearful of facing the stares at school the next day. I was building a reputation as an easy girl, a thoughtless bitch. On Monday morning, I knew there would be hardly a soul who hadn't heard how that sweet kid Brett—after only one date—showed up at my house on Friday afternoon with a diamond necklace for my birthday. And how I repaid his kindness by standing him up that evening to go out with his best friend, who would surely brag that he got to second base. It didn't help that I truly felt like a heel, that I hadn't meant to get drunk and end up with someone else. It just happened.

But shame or not, I didn't change. I amused myself with tandem and overlapping relationships. If a guy proved to be too nice, he got the ax. I craved a challenge. A sure thing was way too boring, too unfamiliar. I kept telling myself that despite the bad things I did, I was still a nice girl. I could stop anytime I wanted.

30 ~ California, 1993

Let's just say that Nanette and her sons, coming to Walnut Creek on the blistered heels of Claire's visit, didn't fare much better. From the airport Kyle escorted them to the car and, according to my sister, proceeded to lay down all the house rules—no using the oven on hot days, no bothering Marie and the baby while we napped, and no commotion inside the house—even before they drove out of the parking garage. Not quite the warm welcome she had expected. By dinnertime the first evening, Nanette offered to check into a nearby cheap hotel with the boys. I begged her not to leave, assuring her that Kyle would mellow out.

"He's just scared he'll lose me and the baby," I said. "He keeps saying that we're all the family he's got." Nanette knew Kyle had lived on his own since fifteen, when his mom died of cancer. His father remarried, but died soon after, and for the last twelve years Kyle and his brother and sister hadn't spoken.

It finally came down to Kyle's eating and hiding out in our bedroom whenever he was home, and a valiant but futile effort on the boys' part to stay out of Uncle Kyle's way.

Momma called every day to ask what trouble Chris and Jack were getting into. It seemed to give her a great deal of pleasure to hear they threw rocks at our windows and stood by my bed, staring curiously at my breast as I fed the baby.

The obliging daughter in me kept feeding Momma's insatiable appetite for more tidbits on how ill-behaved her grandchildren were. It was like tossing innocent chicks to the snapping alligator so it wouldn't come after me. But I told myself that Nanette knew how much I loved her. I wish, now, that for once I had fought the urge to fulfill my role as the amusing daughter, the one Momma turned to for a laugh. What if I had suggested that Momma try to appreciate Nanette for all the comfort she provided her rather than find ways to belittle her? After all, it was Nanette who listened for hours while Momma cried and complained. She was the one who said, "No, Momma, you can't do that," when our mother admitted praying every night for death so that she could be with Daddy. It was Nanette who knew the right words when I had all but given up. Nanette had enough sense to know that a dog wasn't really what Momma wanted to keep her company at night. But despite my mother's loud protests, Penny and her boyfriend bought her a four-legged companion. Buying a puppy and showing up for happy hour were Penny's contributions.

Nanette and her boys departed after a grueling two-week stint, and much to my surprise, Penny telephoned me one Saturday and asked if Kyle and I were up to one more visit toward the end of September. Momma really wanted to see the baby. She asked for the name of a nice hotel, insisting they didn't want to inconvenience us. I assumed the real reasons were the scathing reports on our hospitality from Claire and Nanette and their desire to booze it up in private.

With a brief reprieve from visitors, Kyle went back to his ten-hour work-days. He'd only come home early before, it seemed, to torment himself.

I cherished my time alone with the baby. After his first feeding I'd put Austin in my bed, and we'd sleep on and off until noon. When we were awake, I read to him. Dangling spidery fingers above his head, I recited Mary Howitt's "The Spider and the Fly," using a sly, gentle voice to imitate the spider. Austin tolerated about a half hour of my reading before he started squealing. Then I picked him up and rocked him, singing an off-key, jumbled medley of my favorite songs from the '70s.

Every day I spent with Austin I loved him more. I couldn't wait for him to wake from his naps so that I could cuddle him. It was the most wonderful feeling in the world, this innocent rapture, something I had not known before becoming a mother.

The day Momma and Penny flew in, Austin and I stayed around the house in case they got lost driving over from San Francisco and needed directions. At four o'clock the telephone rang, and I ran to the kitchen to pick it up.

"Ma-ree!" Penny yelled excitedly into the phone. "We're here!"

"Ask her if she wants to come to the hotel for dinner tonight instead of going out," I heard Momma shout in the background.

"Did you hear that?" Penny asked, chuckling.

They definitely had enjoyed a few cocktails on the flight over. "Yeah, that's fine. What time?"

"Give us an hour to get settled in."

I rummaged through my closet. With twenty pounds left from the fifty I'd gained during pregnancy, my only option seemed a faded pink floral dress I had bought a couple years back for my birthday. I wasn't about to wear one of the baggy maternity sets that Kyle had been begging me to get rid of. I managed to button the dress, barely.

On the drive over to the hotel I kept telling the baby that his grandmother had come all the way from Louisiana just to see him. I couldn't believe she had made the trip. After begging and pleading with my parents for seven years, Momma finally had come alone. I knew she hated flying. Simply walking from her bedroom to the kitchen exhausted her. This is a big deal for your grandmother, I told Austin. This is a big deal for me.

When we reached the hotel room, I could smell the cigarette smoke from the hallway. My heart raced as if it were a job interview awaiting me. I smiled down at Austin, smoothed my dress, and knocked.

Penny appeared at the door, gave me a quick, loose hug, and then peeked into the baby carrier. Her eyes sparkled. "Oh Marie, he's darling!"

"Let her come in! I want to see my grandson," Momma called from inside the room.

"Wow, are y'all moving here?" I teased, looking through the haze of smoke at three large, overstuffed suitcases that sat opposite Momma on one of the beds. It was easy enough to identify the two bags belonging to Penny. A mess of expensive matching lacy underwear and bras crammed in with running shorts and T-shirts exploded from one, and the other bag spilled sandals, clogs, tennis shoes, pumps, a Walkman, and a curling iron onto the bedspread. The third bag, no doubt Momma's, was zipped up and probably contained an adequate number of neatly folded pantsuits.

Momma rose from the bed. Something about her looked different. The heavy brown eyeglass frames were the same. What was it? I set the carrier and the diaper bag down. She squeezed me long and hard. It felt really good to be in her arms. When we pulled apart, she looked down at Austin and smiled.

"He's beautiful, sweetheart."

I gently removed the baby from the carrier and proudly placed him in her arms. She sat down on the edge of the bed and studied her grandson. He stared up at her, squirming as she ran her hand over his fuzzy pink scalp.

Momma snickered. "Look, he's got thin hair just like his Aunt Penny." She combed his long, wispy, blond strands with her fingers.

Penny rolled her eyes. I tried not to look at her thin, layered blond hair. She went to such efforts to make it look fuller. Bleaching it. Curling it and then teasing it until it stuck out in all directions like Phyllis Diller's hairdo. Going over to the credenza, Penny grabbed an open pack of Virginia Slims and a blue Bic lighter from the clutter. It looked like they had stocked up for a party: two six-packs of Diet Coke, a gallon jug of vodka, a carton of cigarettes, a nearly full bucket of ice, and an economy pack of lighters. All for a four-day visit.

"How were the flight and the drive over?" I asked.

"Oh, fine," Penny answered. "Momma was a bit nervous on the plane, so she had a few cocktails. Of course, I joined her so she wouldn't feel alone."

"That's a bunch of crap. You were slamming them back faster than me," Momma said. They giggled like a couple of high school pals, until Momma erupted in one of her coughing fits. Her whole body started shaking, and I was frightened she'd drop the baby. She tried to cover her mouth with her free hand.

"You want me to hold him for a minute?" I asked. She nodded and I took him from her. As she hacked away, I glanced at Penny, wondering how in the world she could still smoke.

When we sat down at the table in the nearly empty hotel restaurant, I realized what was different.

"Momma! You let your hair go gray. And it's shorter. You look so much like Aunt Lilia now."

"Your father always insisted I color it, so I did. But now I don't have to bother anymore."

As she opened her menu and studied the offerings I wondered how much of who she was had been dictated by other people (Daddy and her parents, in particular). Would Kyle or marriage chip away at my independent spirit until I didn't recognize myself anymore?

The waitress came and started her spiel, but Momma cut her off right in the middle of the fish special to order a Bloody Mary. Penny asked for a Chardonnay, and I ordered mineral water.

While we waited for our drinks, Momma complained about how hungry she was. But when the waitress reappeared, she ordered only a bowl of French onion soup and a piece of cheesecake, telling the woman to wrap the cake, that she'd take it up to the room for later.

"I thought you were starving? Will soup be enough?" I asked, trying to decide between salmon and pasta.

"Plenty darling," she answered, looking down at Austin sleeping in the carrier.

Penny ordered a chef's salad, and I ordered the salmon. I was famished and didn't have a nice buzz that a perfectly reasonable dinner might squelch.

"Nanette told me that you put your new Dalmatian puppy to sleep."

Momma nodded. "Damn dog, he was crazy from the start. And hyper as hell. I told *them*," she sneered at Penny for a second, "that I didn't want another pet to have to take care of, but no, they insisted I needed company."

"It's too bad they had to kill him. Seems like they could have just found him a home with a bunch of kids and a big yard," I said, feeling ashamed at the callous way my family treated animals.

"No, he was a mess. Every day I'd wake up and the damn thing had crapped all over the kitchen floor. I'd spend an hour cleaning up after the mutt." Momma went on about how the dog just howled and moaned and messed all over the place. When she finished with her dog woes, I asked Penny if she and her boyfriend were discussing marriage.

"They better not be," Momma interjected, shaking her head. "Penny treats Patrick so poorly that it'd be a shame for him to get stuck with her."

Penny jabbed Momma and they both started laughing. I couldn't believe that this was the same mother and daughter duo who had usually chosen opposite ends of the dinner table. Nanette told me of the dramatic change in their relationship—a mutual dependency really—but I hadn't been able to envision it.

Sitting with them at dinner, Penny digging her spoon into Momma's onion soup, insisting that Momma try her wine, made a believer of me. I suppose I was jealous; I felt like an intruder in their little tête-a-tête. In amazement I listened to Penny tease Momma about everything from her drinking to her incontinence. I remembered too well being yanked out of the shower and slapped across my face for "humiliating" her in front of her friends by mentioning her drinking.

During dinner Momma said Yvette was going into the hospital the next day for tests. The doctor wanted to remove some bumps from her vocal cords. Momma felt really bad she wasn't available to go with her to the hospital.

"Is she going to be okay?" I asked, trying to remember how old Yvette was. Forty-seven or forty-eight, I figured.

"I hope so," Momma said. A solemn look spread across her face as she reached over to fidget with the salt shaker, slowly turning it in circles. "The doctor thinks so. But she won't be able to use her voice for a couple of weeks."

"That'll surely kill her," Penny said, puffing on a cigarette. Momma and I pretended to ignore her ugly remark.

Seated at the kitchen table, Kyle was just about to unwrap a piping hot Swanson's turkey TV dinner when I walked into the house.

"Hey, how was it?"

"Fine," I said setting down the baby carrier and sitting. "They were pretty tired after the flight, and Austin was fussy."

"You seem bummed out. Is everything all right?" He leaned over to kiss me.

"I'm okay. It's just so depressing seeing them act ridiculous when they're drunk."

"You didn't leave your mother alone with Austin, did you?"

I rolled my eyes and said of course not. I told him they had seemed so eager for Austin and me to leave after dinner. As though they had a little party planned and I wasn't invited. He frowned when I told him about the bottle of vodka and Cokes in their room.

"I felt like a third wheel. Like their whole trip to meet Austin is just an excuse for a party weekend together."

"I'm sure they were just tired. That's a lot of traveling for your mother."

The next afternoon, Kyle and I drove over to the Doubletree Hotel to pick up Momma and Penny and found them waiting out front. I got out of the Honda to let Momma sit in front with Kyle but she insisted on sharing the backseat with Penny and Austin. I could tell immediately that she was soused. Besides reeking of vodka, she sounded as if she had a mouthful of novocaine.

Penny, who seemed only slightly less anesthetized than Momma, leaned over the baby and cooed, "Hi sweetheart." She tickled his cheek with her long, polished nails and Momma shot her a disapproving look.

"Leave that child alone. What are you trying to do, wake him?" Penny arched her eyebrows playfully as Momma gave her a little shove, knocking the carrier with her thigh. Austin's arms flew up into the air. They both giggled. "See?" Momma whispered as I watched to see if he'd awaken.

In the French restaurant we were seated in a large booth near the front podium. Sliding the baby carrier over to the wall, I prayed there wouldn't be too much noise. Penny proceeded to tell us how she and Jigger Duhon had taken Momma shopping for their trip. Momma had bought four new outfits because she was afraid her old clothes wouldn't pass muster in Walnut Creek.

Kyle and I laughed as Penny told us how nervous Momma was, trying on racks of dresses and slacks, making sure that everything matched perfectly, and fretting over whether she needed new shoes and a fancier purse. Momma confessed that she ended up buying two new purses because she couldn't make up her mind. I was shocked and flattered that she had gone to the trouble.

Kyle and I devoured our dinners while Penny and Momma barely nibbled at theirs. Obviously more interested in drinking, they asked the waitress to pack their dinners to take back to the hotel. Momma insisted that Kyle and I order dessert. When my chocolate mousse arrived Momma practically gurgled and asked the waitress to throw a couple of those in doggy bags, too.

Just before she paid the bill, Austin woke up. At first he looked around curiously. Having an alert, potentially noisy baby at the table made my mother nervous. Three times the waitress passed our table and Momma held up her credit card, saying, "Miss, excuse me. Miss…" Everyone at the table starting fiddling with their napkins and glasses as Austin became restless, kicking his feet and waving his arms about. Each time I offered his pacifier he refused it. By the time we got to my car, the baby was wailing, full-throttle.

Momma insisted again that I sit up front, and she and Penny would sit in the back with the baby. The entire ride to their hotel, five minutes that seemed endless, Momma kept telling me that he was hungry while Kyle asked why I hadn't expressed a bottle of breast milk. Instead of just letting Austin cry, Momma kept trying to quiet him and calm him down by repeatedly shoving the pacifier into his mouth. He'd suck for a minute and then pop it out and cry harder.

"Oh shoot, he popped it out again!" Momma slurred, grabbing the pacifier and aiming it at his mouth but hitting his nose.

"Here, I'll hold his hands still while you hold it in so he can't push it out," Penny told Momma.

"He'll calm down in a minute," I said, panicking, "maybe he doesn't want the pacifier right now."

They ignored me, shoving the plastic plug into Austin's mouth, holding it in until he was flailing his arms and his face was red with anger. Kyle and I kept begging each other silently, with fearful eyes, to say something to make them stop torturing our son, but neither of us did.

I wanted to scream, "Take your fucking hands off my son. You're scaring him and me." I wanted to scream at Kyle to stop the car, and tell Momma and Penny to get out and walk back to their hotel. I wanted to scream at the top of my lungs until my throat was so raw that no sound emerged. I wanted to protect my son, but I had no voice. I was a coward. Maybe, given the chance, my mother and sister would have stopped and even apologized had they known how upset I was. As angry as I was with them, I was angrier with myself. I loved my son more than anything. Yet where was the courage to stand up for him? Had I truly loved him, more than myself, then my shame at being ridiculed later wouldn't have stopped me from protecting him.

When we arrived at the hotel, Momma wished us good luck with the baby and good night. I gave her a perfunctory kiss and watched her stagger toward the automatic doors. She looked so pathetic, so weak as the doorman caught her by the elbow just before she stumbled.

I climbed into the back seat with Austin and whispered that we'd be home soon, that everything was going to be okay. Holding his tiny hands in mine, rubbing his fuzzy warm head, I bent over and tenderly kissed his wet face.

Kyle pulled away from the hotel and stared back at me. "Why didn't you say anything?"

Why didn't you? You're just as weak as I am and that's why I can't love you. Fighting back tears, I looked up and said, "I tried, but I couldn't. I didn't want to start a big fight and ruin their trip." I unhooked the baby from his car seat and rocked him in my arms.

"You're unreal. And your family. Your mother practically fell on her face when she got out of the car. They were stone drunk."

"Big news. They were smashed when we picked them up."

The next morning Momma called to say that Penny had found a salon on Main Street. They wanted to know if I cared to join them for a massage and manicure—Momma's treat. I told her I'd check with Kyle and call her back. When I asked Kyle if he minded watching Austin for a couple of hours so that I could go with them to the salon, his face immediately turned sullen and he started toward the kitchen.

"Well?" I said following him.

He stopped and leaned against the oven. "You want to get a massage. No way. I don't want you lying on a table in just a towel with some strange guy touching your body. That's disgusting. They're probably a bunch of perverts at those places."

"You know, you're probably the most paranoid, possessive guy in the world. How do you know the masseuse won't be a woman? I could request a woman."

"No. Why do you want someone else touching you anyway? You hardly even want me to touch you, much less make love to you."

I was wondering how a salon visit with my mother and sister had turned into an argument about our waning sex life. It was true that I pulled away or stiffened whenever he touched me. But he always seemed to get the *urge* when I was right in the middle of cooking or just when we had gotten Austin down for a nap. In the afternoons and evenings when I had a couple hour's break from the baby, all I wanted to do was relax—sew or work in the yard or read the newspaper. I didn't want another person tugging on me.

Whenever Kyle touched me I went cold inside. All he wanted and needed was reassurance that I loved him, that I was committed to our marriage. But sex felt dirty and animalistic, as though my body had now found a pure purpose in motherhood and fucking degraded it. Sometimes when I refused him, Kyle suggested that perhaps I was turning into a lesbian like my younger sister. I supposed he needed some way to explain my constant rejection that only I knew wasn't meant to be cruel or jilting. Some nights he begged me over and over again until I cried. I quickly discovered that shedding tears or screaming at him were the most effective way to keep him at bay. Was that how Momma learned to get her way?

Kyle finally agreed to let me join my sister and mother if I promised to get only a facial. Which I did. I picked Penny and Momma up at the hotel, and we had a quick lunch. They looked pretty wretched—baggy, red eyes and shaky hands. I was thankful it had been three years since my last bout of the champagne flu.

Waiting for our names to be called, Momma mentioned that she had spoken with Claire and learned that Yvette's operation went well. They had scraped her vocal cords and removed all the benign growths. She couldn't speak for a couple of weeks so she carried a pad and pen everywhere. Momma also informed me that Aimee was divorcing Trevis. He had moved back to Tennessee, and my mother hoped that would be the end of him. She said Aimee was returning to USL to get her masters in—"God only knows what."

That evening Kyle and I pulled up to their hotel at six sharp. Even on vacation, Momma was a stickler for punctuality. I spotted them sitting in the lobby polishing off a couple of drinks.

"Hi, darling," Momma said as I approached. She stood up and we kissed hello. The combination of her sweet perfume and vodka made me nauseous. Some people argue that vodka doesn't smell, but I can smell any booze, clear or dark, anywhere, even under the disguise of Listerine. And I can usually divine in an instant who's drunk and who's not. It's my special radar.

"Hey, Ma-ree," Penny said in that high-pitched, I'm-loose-as-a-goose-and-ready-to-party voice she slips into after her first cocktail.

I opened the front passenger door and waved Momma over. "Here, Momma, you sit in the front seat so you'll have more room. It's a pretty drive to the restaurant and you can see better."

She insisted that she was perfectly comfortable in the back with the baby and Penny. Kyle flashed me an uneasy glance as I slipped into the seat next to him. But this time, I'd sworn to myself earlier, I would stop them before they got out of hand.

We drove quietly along 680 South, and I pointed out Mt. Diablo. Along the way Momma told me, verbatim, how she had spoken with Claire that morning and that Yvette was doing fine. They scraped Yvette's vocal cords, and the doctor expected to release her in the morning.

"That's good," I said. "I bet you're relieved." One more dinner to get through and then she and Penny would be leaving in the morning and taking their craziness with them.

31 ~ Louisiana, 1978

Dr. La Dousa warned Daddy, recently diagnosed with diabetes, that merely taking insulin wasn't enough. If he didn't stop drinking and smoking, he might lose his eyesight, or worse, his feet. The idea of being crippled sent my father into a weeklong depression. Momma feared he wouldn't be strong enough to stop drinking or live with a "deformed" body. And without him, who would provide for her, and set things right when disaster struck?

Panicking, Momma offered to quit drinking with him.

I was cynical. How could she just stop cold? What kind of mother would she be if she wasn't drinking? Perhaps sobriety would finally bring about a loving mother/daughter relationship. Or make her more vigilant, impeding my own drinking and carousing.

Despite our doubts, they both did it, but we watched to see how long it would last.

Momma showed surprising determination. But Daddy, from day one, complained incessantly. He moaned about his pathetic luck. He said now he had nothing, nothing at all to live for. I stared at him, wondering where that left me in his eyes. My father, unknowingly, began his quick descent from the pedestal on which I'd placed him while my mother took a step up from the tar pits.

Momma looked the other way when he sneaked a drink or two. She was so determined, so hopeful. She just guzzled her tea and coffee and Tab all day and evening. Who would have ever thought she'd be the strong one? I was proud of her.

It wasn't easy. When cocktail hour became tea time, their friends completely abandoned them, even the Duhons and the Jouberts. I heard Momma whisper to Grandma on the telephone that she didn't understand why her friends never returned her phone calls anymore. If I hadn't been scared she'd slap me, I'd have told her she was better off without them. That their fickle friends only looked for people they could get drunk with without feeling shameful. That was, after all, how I chose my pals.

As Daddy bellyached about his abstinence, I awaited my high school boyfriend Dwayne's return from his senior class trip. In the week he'd been gone, I started panicking about being pregnant. I swore to myself that if I got my period he wasn't touching me again. Claire, his classmate, had driven home a day early from Florida and, after much badgering, she tattled on him.

"That bastard," I cried. "He swore if I let him screw me that he'd be faithful. He just used me."

"Y'all are having sex, already?" she asked.

I nodded, ashamed. I was only sixteen—Momma's age when she got pregnant with Yvette.

"Maybe they just kissed and nothing else," she said. "But they were going after it pretty heavy. I'm sorry."

I plopped down on the bed next to her and she rubbed my back as I cried.

The next evening, borrowing one of Penny's famous tactics, I made Dwayne wait half an hour when he came to pick me up. I walked in the kitchen and pretended not to notice that his mop of red hair was styled differently. He kissed me without looking in my eyes. "Hey, babe, it's great to see you."

Offering a blank stare, I asked, "What happened to your face? You look like a molting snake." I wanted to hurt him, and I knew he was sensitive about his complexion.

"Thanks a lot. This sunburn really hurts. Are you okay?"

"Yeah, are you?"

Seated at a table, Dwayne grabbed a tortilla chip from the bowl and began breaking it into little pieces. "Marie, I've got something to tell you. First, I want to say that I really love you, and that it's so nice to be back here with you—"

"Yes?" I interrupted, twirling the skinny straw around in my frozen sangria.

"One night I got really drunk. We made a bonfire right there on the beach. It was really cool. One thing sort of led to another, and before I knew it..." he took a quick sip of his margarita.

Half listening, I wondered how I should react. I couldn't scream in the middle of LaFondas. Slap him so hard that his green eyes popped out of his sunburnt, freckled face? Throw bean dip on him?

"Marie," he continued, "It was nothing, really. I promise it won't ever happen again. We were both drunk, and she was sad because she just had her wallet stolen, and you weren't there, and I was...."

He sounded like a character in Momma's romance novels. I wanted to stab his hand with my fork. "I'm going to the bathroom," I said quietly. I grabbed my purse and gave him that hard look I'd seen my mother use a hundred times.

Avoiding the hall to the bathroom, I pushed past the mob in the bar and left. It took me half an hour to walk home, but with every step I grinned at the thought of how angry he'd be when it dawned on him that I'd left. How long would it take him to figure it out?

His blue mustang was waiting in the driveway.

"Marie, stop," he called, following me to the gate. Was he crying? *Maybe he is really sorry.* "You have every right to be angry."

"You're damn right. You lied to me. I can't talk to you right now, so go home."

Dwayne groveled all week. When I felt I'd punished him enough, I warned him there'd be no more second chances. And luckily, I got my period.

"Hey, Babe," he greeted me after one of his baseball games. I jumped up to embrace him but tripped over the bleachers. He caught my arm, and steadied me, shooting my friend Mignon a sideways look. "You two been drinking again?"

"Yep, but she's the drunk one, not me," Mignon said, rolling her big brown eyes.

"I'll drive," Dwayne announced, grabbing my keys.

Mignon slid across the leather seat of my newly inherited Cadillac. Daddy had recently bought Momma a smaller Fleetwood, so Momma gave her old car to me. Now Claire, Nanette, and I all had our own used Cadillacs. Mine was brick red, and enormous. Dwayne loved it; it had an 8-track, and he said it was made for parking.

We went to the local pizzeria and pub, where they seldom carded us. I led Dwayne and Mignon to a table near the stage. The cavernous place began filling up just as the waitress brought us a second pitcher of beer. I watched The Catahoulas, four gorgeous guys in a new Cajun group, set up for their first song. I had a huge crush on the accordion player. But a wink or a smile from the lead singer, or the other two guys playing their fiddle and guitar would have also made my evening.

By the time we dropped Mignon at home, we were both drunk and Dwayne was horny. It didn't matter to him if he stunk worse than a dead horse. He always wanted sex. Despite my pleading to end an occasional evening with just a kiss, nothing deterred him.

"In the boat?" I asked in disbelief, looking at the CrisCraft in the carport. "I don't think so. That's my dad's precious boat. He'd kill us. Why not in the car if we have to?"

"Come on, it'll be fun," he said, pulling on my arm.

"No, Dwayne. How about the backyard? We haven't done it there in awhile." The last time we screwed near the playhouse, we both got eaten up by mosquitoes, and King barked over us while Dwayne took forever. Why did I put up with it? I knew each act of sex granted me one more stay of the inevitable breakup.

He pulled me toward the boat, and I jerked my hands away. "Okay, already."

We climbed into the cabin and Dwayne undressed me. I lay against the damp vinyl seats as he began kissing my neck. "I love you, Marie," he said as he started pumping.

Yeah, yeah, whatever. It must be a hundred goddamn degrees in here. Every time I moved, I had to peel myself off the plastic. With my eyes squeezed shut and my sweaty skin making that embarrassing farting noise against the vinyl, I prayed he wouldn't think I was really passing gas, as Daddy would say. What if Penny or Nanette came home and saw the boat rocking? What if we rocked the boat so much the chocks slipped out from under the tires and the trailer rolled into the road? It would be humiliating to get hit by a car while fucking in my dad's boat.

Dwayne slowed down and pulled almost all the way out, held it a moment, and then eased back in. "Do you like it like this?" he asked, moving so slowly in and out.

"That feels good, I guess." It did. Pretty soon I prayed he'd never stop. "Dwayne, Dwayne…" All of a sudden I felt myself blacking out. I squeezed his arms hard. His drenched body stiffened, and he collapsed on top of me.

We lay completely still for what seemed like hours. Then he rolled over onto his side and smiled. "Did you like that?"

"I think I had my first orgasm." I suddenly felt very sleepy. "We better get—"

"Shu, did you hear that?"

The gate had opened. Someone was walking toward the boat. The footsteps stopped. A light from a flashlight moved overhead at the cabin door. I heard a throat clear.

It was Daddy.

I could feel Dwayne's heart beating against my arm. Daddy cleared his throat a second time. He tapped the end of his metal flashlight against the boat. Then the footsteps resumed. The gate slammed shut. I started shaking all over.

"Do you think he knew we were in here?" Dwayne asked.

"I don't know. How am I going to go inside? I am never doing this again."

We huddled in the hot cabin for an hour, gathering our nerve to peer out. Dwayne pushed his Mustang down the street before he started the engine. And I crept to the backdoor asking God to be merciful, not to have Daddy standing on the other end.

I tiptoed into the dark kitchen. Only the hum of the ice-maker and a tap, tap at the sink. The foyer door hinges creaked. I ran to the stairs without looking into the huge mirror on the opposite wall. Ever since Dwayne and I had started having sex, I feared that Chess or his ghost would be waiting for me at the bottom of the stairs. I took two steps at a time, my heart thumping like crazy. I didn't want Chess to *get* me, hurt me somehow, like one of his story villains. I knew my brother was dead. But I also thought that perhaps he'd do whatever he could to make sure I didn't ruin my life like he had his.

32 ~

Momma and Daddy had used violence to try to keep Aimee from getting into trouble with boys. With Penny, my mother resorted to name-calling. By the time Nanette, Claire, and I hit adolescence, they simply gave up. Growing his wholesale business and struggling with his diabetes consumed Daddy. Momma concentrated on changing her life. She started exercising. First sit-ups and then jumping-jacks. Soon she ordered a stationary bicycle. When her pants drooped, she bought new clothes. She joined the health club. Hired a trainer. Every few months she shopped for newer, smaller-sized dresses and pantsuits until her weight fell to 98 pounds. At seventeen, I wore the same size as my mother although my breasts were now larger than hers.

She became involved in charity work, baking dozens of cookies for a nursing home and helping with their bingo games. On Fridays she volunteered as a pink lady at Lafayette General. She brought home new friends—my favorite a divorced lady who wore stylish suits even though she didn't work. They sipped tea and smiled at Daddy as he passed through the den with his ice bucket.

Our house suddenly became a greenhouse. Momma filled nearly every counter and table with plants. Succulents, ivies, cactus. She also bought three puppies. Three humping, snorting, sneezing, shitting, and dragging-their-butts-all-over-the-floor Pekinese puppies. Sable, the much-in-demand red and white female, was the worst pest of the trio, defiantly crapping right next to the paper set out for them. Yet Momma doted on them.

My heart filled with envy. I hoped one day she'd catch me watching her, and say, "Let's sit down, darling, and have a chat. Tell me about you and Dwayne."

One afternoon I presented her with a handmade card.

"I made this for you," I said, leaning against the kitchen cabinets. Momma took out the card and looked at the lopsided vase of red roses.

"I painted those with watercolors," I said, feeling hopeful.

She opened the card. I waited for her to gush at the mushy Mother's Day poem I'd copied from one of her magazines. Even though she didn't really fit the mold of the mother described, I hoped she'd be touched. She closed the card, and reached for an open pack of cigarettes. "That's nice, darling. Go ask your father if he wants baked or stuffed potatoes tonight with the steaks."

Humiliated, I nodded. She set the card on the greasy counter, and I swore I'd never go out of my way to give her anything again. Sobriety, it seemed, wasn't going to be the bridge I'd longed for between mother and daughter.

Momma darted from one appointment to another, high as Everest on caffeine and diet pills, subsisting on a bird's portion of food. Her weight-loss obsession derailed briefly during the wedding preparation for Nanette's marriage to Boyce Maynor, an Air Force second lieutenant. Neither the First Baptist Church nor Kenny had managed to fully convert my sister. Though she hadn't resumed drinking or smoking, she was marrying a man who did both. For the shindig, Momma ordered new draperies for the piano room and had all the antique furniture reupholstered. She ordered flowers and candles to fill the house and yard. Daddy rented live swans for the swimming pool. Nanette chose elaborate bride and groom cakes. Toby's Restaurant was catering crab cakes, peeled shrimp, fried catfish bites, crawfish pies, marinated crab claws, boudin, spicy meatballs, cheese and fruit plates, and caviar. Several bars would be fully stocked and staffed. Friends and cousins we hadn't seen in years were invited. Even Grandma would leave her house for the wedding.

On the wedding night, I walked into Nanette's room. She peeked through the window slats at the arriving guests.

"God, you look like Cinderella."

"Thanks. Dwayne must really like that dress on you." She eyed the low swooping neckline I had chosen.

"Yeah, well, he's not complaining. Are you about ready? Daddy looks like he's anxious to hit the bar."

"Just about." She fumbled with her veil. "I can't believe we're going to Illinois tomorrow and we're going to be living far away from each other."

I nodded, trying not to cry so my makeup wouldn't run. The door opened.

"Hey, Daddy sent me to see if you're ready." Claire wore a long lilac dress. Nanette had chosen her as her maid of honor. I had been left out of the wedding party because Nanette wanted to keep it small and we had had a fight right around her nineteenth birthday, when she announced her engagement.

Even though I didn't like Boyce, a fast-talking lady's man, I was happy for Nanette—she was escaping. I was going to miss her.

Nanette touched my arm and asked, "You think if we had a big group hug we'd wreck my dress?"

I shook my head and pulled Claire over. We held on tight, and giggled.

As the band played the wedding march, Dwayne and I held hands. A hundred heads turned to watch Nanette and Daddy descend the stairs. Daddy had tears in his eyes. Momma, too, as she wiped beneath her glasses.

Dwayne squeezed my hand and whispered, "One day that's going to be you coming down the stairs, and I'm going to be so proud."

"That would be great," I said. But I wasn't so sure.

At sixteen, I wasn't certain about much. But one thing was clear: I was tired of proving my love to Dwayne. One Friday night I walked into work, where the remedy to my paralysis stood grinning behind the front register in a new uniform: Chad Breaux, my dance partner from the Lafayette Ball. We flirted all evening. At closing time he invited me to see his new garage apartment. I knew this would decide my fate with Dwayne. Did it matter that Chad still had the same girlfriend? No. Did he care that I was dating his former classmate? Apparently not. Perhaps they just added to the excitement. From the moment we entered his apartment, we both knew what was going to happen. I just didn't expect him to be so boastful, so soon after.

On Sunday night my telephone buzzed. I rolled over, blinking at the clock. Midnight. Damn, did Claire lock herself out again?

"Marie, it's Dwayne. Come down here!"

He knew. I swallowed, stammering, "What are you doing here?"

"Just open the door. I need to talk to you."

Chad, that bastard. He promised he wouldn't say a word.

What should I say? I looked at the pile of stuffed animals that now lay where Anne used to sleep before she took over Nanette's room. I could deny it. Would he believe me? No, I thought, pulling on a sweater. I was in for it. I ran down the stairs.

"Dwayne, why aren't you at school?"

He just glared at me. I smelled beer and sweat. "Why did you do it?" He yanked me out of the house. "Tell me!" he demanded, shaking me. "Tell me that I'm not the laughingstock of the whole goddamn fraternity right now."

"I'm sorry, Dwayne. Ow! You're hurting me." He took his hands off and held them up in the air.

"Chad Breaux, for Christ's sake!" I shuddered as he grabbed the Ping-Pong table and shoved it into the French doors. The glass shattered. Frozen in fear, I waited, sure he was going to hit me. But he stared at the broken glass, then started crying.

I startled when I heard the back door squeak open. Daddy poked his head out and whispered, "Marie, is everything all right?"

"Yes, Dwayne and I are just talking," I said, trying to sound normal. "I'll be up in a few minutes."

"All right, but don't go on too late. You have school tomorrow." He glanced at Dwayne, and then at the askew Ping-Pong table before ducking back inside.

Dwayne paced back and forth. "Do you know how humiliating this is? I found out through my roommate, who heard it from one of Chad's friends. It's all over the fraternity house. Can you imagine how I feel?" He searched my face.

"I'm really sorry, I didn't mean to hurt you. It just kinda happened."

"Oh, you're sorry. Sorry, shit. And what does that mean…it just *kinda* happened. You just *kinda* fucked him? You know what's even worse than imagining that bastard on top of you? It's that my parents fucking know. I blew the transmission on that piece of crap car, and I had to call them to pick me up on Johnston Street. So of course my dad wanted to know what I was doing driving around Lafayette when I'm supposed to be sleeping in my dorm in Baton Rouge. I don't even know how I'm going to get back to school tomorrow," he said, looking defeated as he began crying again. "I can't believe you did this to me. To us."

I tried to hug him but he shoved me away. Who in the hell was he to act so self-righteous? Hadn't he screwed that girl in Florida because she'd lost her wallet? As we both stood silent, I shivered, my bare feet pressing against the cold cement. Should I beg him for forgiveness? Should I tell him to leave? Why didn't he realize that screwing Chad was my way of saying I wanted to break up?

Our relationship still hung in limbo when he finally drove off. I felt weary, so weary, like I'd climbed aboard a moving carousel that just spun faster and faster until I'd either die of fatigue trying to hold on or break every bone in my body trying to dismount.

33 ～ California, 1993

After Momma's visit to meet Austin, she mailed me a check for $10,000. She and her attorney, Ben Veazey, had begun doing some estate planning, and this gift to all her daughters was the first step. She would keep the other changes to her will a secret from most of us for some time. Her nightly phone calls resumed. Every evening as Kyle and I sat in the living room watching television, I waited for the dreaded call. Kyle smiled sympathetically as I ran to answer the phone before it woke the baby, cussing her under my breath. It made me furious that she bothered me at night when I was exhausted from a full day of taking care of Austin and the house. Why didn't she talk honestly in the mornings about her loneliness and her desire to die when I called, trying to offer help and condolence, before she had a chance to uncork the sherry bottle? Perhaps I am a cold daughter, but it seems a waste of time to have a conversation that won't be remembered or appreciated the next day.

Some nights she was so tanked I could barely understand her. I just sat listening to her cry as I wrote out my grocery list or cleaned out my purse, saying "I'm so sorry, Momma…I wish I knew what to say to you…I wish there was something I could do for you…"

Nanette, Claire, and Anne called me occasionally to talk about Momma's depression. A couple of times Nanette suggested that perhaps Momma would be better off if she died because what did she have to live for anyway? She wasn't taking care of herself. Eventually all the drinking and smoking was going to catch up with her like it had with Daddy. Those words, as cold as they sounded when spoken aloud, had often crossed my mind. Especially when Momma called during one of my favorite sitcoms.

Kyle and I finally decided how to spend the $10,000. Updating the kitchen. New counter tops, freshly painted cabinets, new hardware, and new lighting. Kyle promised that he could complete the job himself in two weekends if I didn't pester him like I had with other renovations. Three weeks later the kitchen was still a mess. We had one working drawer and no counter tops. Everything conspired against Kyle to keep him from completing the job—a nasty, weeklong head cold, unforeseen water damage under the sink, and work problems that prompted him to complain and sulk instead of hammer and saw.

One Friday evening when we were eating takeout, I asked if he thought the kitchen would be finished by Thanksgiving.

He slammed his fork down and glared at me.

"What?" I shouted back.

"You just can't let me have five minutes rest without bugging me, can you? Why can't we have one weekend of peace?"

Perhaps that's what my father meant when he often warned my sisters and me that we'd never get married because we were too spoiled. We expected too much. I expected that two weeks meant two weeks, plus or minus a few days.

I hadn't intended to pick a fight with him, especially since I had wanted him to get up early the next morning to work on the kitchen. But I was upset with him because he strolled into the house at nine o'clock that evening, announcing that one of his friends from work had invited us over for dinner on Saturday and he told him we'd bring dessert. So on top of watching the baby the next day while Kyle supposedly worked on the kitchen, I needed to come up with a dessert.

I said that I found it hard to feel peaceful when I doubted we'd ever have counter tops again. Finally, after a few more barbs back and forth, I left Kyle sitting at the dinner table and went to bed in the guest room with Austin. The next morning, I awoke to noise coming from the kitchen. I thought, he must be working on the counters!

I walked out to see. To my disbelief, he was standing over the kitchen table unloading several plastic grocery bags.

"What are you doing? I just went shopping yesterday."

"I thought I'd make some French toast this morning and then bake an apple pie to take to dinner tonight."

He unloaded a bag of Granny Smith apples and a large bag of flour. "We already have flour in the pantry," I said. "And how exactly are you going to work on the counters today *and* bake an apple pie?"

He grabbed a Sharps nonalcoholic beer from a new twelve-pack and sighed. "You know, you always pick a fight when we're supposed to get together with my friends."

The thought of socializing with one of his work buddies, hearing Kyle and his friend brag about how important they were to their company while we pretended things were just hunky-dory, was too depressing. There was no way I could pull it off. I went to the bedroom and grabbed the phone book from the bottom shelf of the nightstand. Kyle's friend wasn't home, so I spoke with his wife.

In the kitchen, Kyle was still unloading groceries. Standing at the doorway, I said, "I just called your buddy and told his wife that we were having a huge fight and that we wouldn't be much company tonight. So now you don't have to make the apple pie."

His face drained to a pasty white. He stood there with his lips slightly parted. His silence made me nervous. Suddenly he slammed the refrigerator door so hard, the jars rattled. "You're joking, right? You didn't call them and tell them that we're fighting?"

"Yep." I was trying to sound cocky.

He ran his fingers through his hair and squeezed his eyes shut. Then he let out a horrible scream and grabbed the metal teakettle. I froze in the doorway. Was he going to throw it at me? *Now you've done it, Marie. He's finally going to snap and let you have what you deserve.* No, he hurled it across the room at the wall.

"Why do you do this to me? Do you want everyone at work to know our marriage is totally screwed up?"

He covered his face, crying, his body heaving. I walked over to him and touched his hand. "Leave me alone!" He twisted away and ran toward the back door. I hated myself.

After an hour in the garage, Kyle came inside and dressed. He wouldn't even meet my gaze. Grabbing his briefcase on the way out of the bedroom, he took off for his office. At ten o'clock that evening there was still no sign of him. I started picturing him slumped over his desk, blood puddled around his chair. I kept wondering how I was going to explain to Austin about his father's suicide. Perhaps I would just tell him and everyone else it was an aneurysm. But at ten-thirty, the motion-sensitive lights on the patio flipped on. I went to the kitchen. Standing on the front steps, on the other side of the kitchen door, staring through the dusty window into the house, was Kyle.

I opened the door and asked him where he had been.

"The office," he said, his chin starting to quiver.

"I'm really sorry, Kyle." I stepped closer to hug him, but the stench of cigarettes and beer stopped me dead.

"You've been drinking and smoking, you sonofabitch. Is that your way of getting back at me?" I wanted to slap the pathetic look right off his face. He whined that he had smoked only a couple of cigarettes and drunk one beer, and he didn't even want them after he bought them.

"Where are they?" I demanded. He pointed over to a brown paper bag. I reached down and grabbed it. "You are not going to start drinking and smoking in this house again. I'm not putting up with that crap anymore. You can just get the fuck out of here right now if that's what you're planning and leave Austin and me alone. I'm sick and tired of all your shit. Sick of your complaining and sulking and blaming me for all your unhappiness."

He trailed behind me as I headed straight for the garbage can and threw the beer and cigarettes away. Slamming the trash lid shut, not looking at him, I started back to the kitchen.

"Please stop for a minute. Can't we talk?"

"There's nothing to talk about. I wish you'd just move. If you want to talk about something, how about our getting a divorce?" I couldn't believe I had finally said it.

"Why are you being so mean to me? Do you hate me so much that you'll say anything to get rid of me?"

I told him I didn't hate him but that I was fed up. That I was tired of being pestered all the time about sex. Tired of his sulking when he didn't get it. Tired of having to spread my legs to get some peace and quiet. Tired of being told that I was abnormal when most new mothers aren't interested in sex.

He bellyached that all he had ever wanted was a family and I was trying to take that away from him. That I was a cold, selfish person who had used him to get a house and a baby and now I didn't need him any more.

I said we'd both used each other because we both wanted to get married and have children. He knew as well as I we were a total mismatch. We argued and complained till nearly one in the morning. Finally, I told him I was going to bed because Austin was going to be up in a little bit and I was the one who would have to feed him.

After I climbed into bed and turned out the light, I heard him in the hallway. The bathroom door opened and closed. Then silence. He was probably going to stare at the silent television or wander around the

house. I hated when he did that after a fight. It made me scared to close
my eyes. I kept imagining him coming into the bedroom to do something
to me. I wasn't sure what, exactly. He never hit me or even threatened
to. He never yanked me out of bed like Momma. But I felt vulnerable
knowing someone was awake and angry in my house. I lay awake half the
night, at times pounding my pillow with exhaustion, crying, wishing I
could fall asleep. One time he came in and stood there just staring at me.
Pretending to be asleep, I listened to him walk over to his side of the bed,
sit for a minute on top of the covers, and then sigh before leaving the
room again.

The next day Kyle worked on the kitchen, and I took Austin for a
walk down to look at some new houses being built on a former llama
farm. Kyle said he wouldn't want one of these enormous homes because
they had no character. I would have grabbed one in an instant. Big closets. A master bath. Plumbing that actually worked. I'd just douse the
house with the kind of character that department and furniture stores
sold, I teased him the first time we snooped around.

I picked a two-story house at the end of the court and lifted the
stroller into the front doorway. Austin was snug sleeping under one of the
quilts I'd made for him. The workers had begun nailing sheets of drywall
into place. Weeks earlier it had all been only a flat plot of dirt. Quickly
the empty space among the mature oaks gave way to a slab of cement and
a lumber skeleton. A few days later, the roof was in place. The spitting,
matted llamas and the old barns were a faint memory.

Before they had covered the exterior of the structure with mesh and
stucco, the house still felt open, like a part of the surrounding beauty.
Now, with the drywall hung, the house had closed itself off from the outside world. Isolated itself. Made itself impervious to outside forces—
wind, rain, animals. Soon it would provide shelter, security, and comfort
only for the people who held the coveted key. People were like that
sometimes, I thought, settling down on the cold cement floor.

I removed a notebook from the bottom of the stroller and read the
words I'd scribbled on my last entry.

He said he wished I had never gotten pregnant. Marrying me was
clearly a mistake. That I didn't love him as much as he loved me. He
said he feared I'd be as selfish with my love toward Austin as I was with
him. I told him to go to hell, but now I wonder if he is right.

That evening after Austin went to sleep, Kyle came into the living room where I was reading the paper and asked if we could talk. Reluctantly I folded the Chronicle and pushed it aside.

Sitting on the futon together, he started off by telling me how he truly loved me and all he wanted from me was a little respect and to know I loved him. I told him he had to earn respect by keeping his word and that I didn't think I loved him anymore.

"You're so fucking cold, you know that?" He studied me like he was trying to look inside my head for some clue as to why I was programmed to be so mean.

"Yeah, maybe," I said, shrugging.

We went back and forth like a game of volleyball, serving up old transgressions and rallying hurtful accusations. When we got around to his inevitable complaint, I told him that I'd had all the sex I wanted when I was single and dating, that all I wanted from him was to be left alone. Impossible, he said. He had strong needs, and I knew that when I married him. Well, then, I told him, why can't you just go boink your secretary like other normal, unhappily married men? He said that was disgusting. Then he said that most women complained they didn't get enough foreplay, but I was always telling him to be quick about it. I told him that good foreplay started in the morning when a man dragged his butt out of bed to make an honest attempt to complete all the projects he had begun around the house, when a man came home from work on time with enough energy to have a pleasant conversation with his wife, and when a man, freely and without complaint, helped with the laundry and baby. When a man offered as much as or more than he took.

For hours we argued in circles, resolving nothing. As always, we managed to wear each other down, leaving emotional nicks and bruises. Desperate for a peaceful night's sleep, I finally said, "Let's forget about the whole idea of divorce. I'm sorry I called your friend and embarrassed you. Can we go to bed now?"

Side by side we brushed and flossed our teeth. He waited by the bathroom door while I changed into my nightgown. Then I followed him to our bedroom, and we climbed into bed.

"Can I hold you?" he whispered, sliding closer to me. I nodded, lying perfectly still hoping that simply holding me would be enough for him. But as always, his hands slowly worked their way inside my gown. "Can I do it? I'll try to be fast," he whispered. I nodded, screaming quietly inside my head as I rolled onto my back and pulled up my gown. I closed my eyes and flinched. I held onto his T-shirt until he was done and then squirmed out from under him. "That was nice, thank you. I love you." I hated it when he was pitiful.

"I love you, too," I mumbled, rolling over to face the opposite wall, wondering how much more of him, of this lie, I could tolerate. How could I know that my disaffection for Kyle had little to do with him? How many times in my life had I told someone—my mother, my husband, my boyfriends—those three empty, meaningless words? *I love you.*

34 ～ Louisiana, 1978

The broken glass had been swept up by the time I woke the next morning. My parents never asked why Dwayne shoved the table into the French doors. Daddy simply phoned Aimee's husband and asked him to stop by after work to replace the windowpane. And just as I'd found a way to forgive Dwayne, he forgave me. Or so he claimed. I atoned for my misdeed with sex. He wanted it more often and in different, scary ways. We didn't make love anymore. It felt impersonal, yet personal, like punishment. He took longer and longer each time, it seemed, and he always mumbled while he pumped that I didn't know how to love him like he loved me. When he'd finally finish and roll over to stare at the wall of some friend's house, I'd be thinking, I hate you. I hate you so much. I hate myself.

I could smell her cigarette before she tapped on the door.
"Come in," I yelled.
Momma smiled faintly, her face gaunt from dieting, as she set down her ashtray. I stood in my bra and panties, waiting for her to help me lift the dress. I felt embarrassed. My mother hadn't seen me unclothed in years.
Together we lifted the heavy, sequined pink ball gown, and she raised it over my head. After I slid my arms through the puffed sleeves, she pulled the back together to zip it up. I sucked in my stomach; I was so afraid it wouldn't fit. She tugged and pulled, finally exclaiming, "There! Can you breathe?"
"A little." The dressmakers tailored the dresses to fit like a second skin. How could they expect growing teenagers not to gain a pound for a whole year? They warned us about the difficulties of letting out the sides and reminded us we would have to wear them more than once throughout the year. That weekend I was going to the Southern Governors Ball. "Can I take it off now?" I asked, taking minuscule breaths.

Saturday morning busloads of queens and maids from assorted krewes around Louisiana took over the New Orleans Hilton. The queen of the Lafayette Ball invited me to a party in her hotel room. Usually, the queen and her maid-of-honor didn't socialize with the mere maids, but Ebbie wasn't as stuck-up as some.

I knocked on the door and Ebbie jerked it open. She pulled me in, checking the hallway for signs of lurking chaperones before she closed it again.

The room was smoky and filled with girls with heavily painted, smiling faces and perfectly coiffured up-dos. "Want a hit?" Ebbie asked, grabbing a joint from another girl and shoving it at my nose.

"Sure." I had smoked pot once with my friend Mignon. It had made me feel so paranoid I'd sworn I'd never do it again. I took the joint and sucked on it the way Mignon had shown me. When I couldn't hold it any longer, the smoke exploded out of my mouth in a series of painful coughs.

"God, that burns!" My eyes watered.

"Here, have a beer." Ebbie's maid-of-honor handed me a can.

I chugged the beer to quiet my cough. Grass and alcohol. I soon realized I should have eaten something before I joined the party.

The pot came around several times, and soon I was as giddy as the others. Everything anyone said was hilarious. I couldn't stop laughing. Nor could I keep my thoughts straight. I wasn't sure if I had actually heard someone say what I thought I'd heard; I didn't know if I was repeating myself or even speaking aloud. And I prayed the beer wouldn't give me gas. I didn't want to fart in front of these girls.

"Is anyone hungry?" Ebbie yelled above the laughter and chattering.

"Yes!" we all screamed. We pored over the room service menu and pointed to everything from the nachos to the BLTs to the spring rolls.

When Ebbie called down to order the food, she was laughing so much she had trouble talking on the phone.

"Ask them to bring up ten glasses and a pitcher of water and some sodas," one girl shouted to her.

It occurred to me then that the waiters would be coming to the room and it was obvious what we'd been doing.

"It's pretty smoky in here," I told the others. Gasps, squeals, giggles— and a frantic rush, all of us running around waving our arms trying to fan the smoke out the window.

It didn't do much good. When the two black waiters arrived, they gawked at what they saw before them. A dozen white girls stoned out of their minds, trying to put on a straight and proper appearance while enveloped in clouds of marijuana smoke. The older man rolled his cart in first, laughing and shaking his head as he surveyed the room.

"You girls having a good time?" he asked. "What you burning in here? You can smell it all the way down the hall." We all lost our fake composure and began giggling. "Jimmie, bring yours over here, boy," he ordered the younger man, who acted like he was afraid of us. "They ain't gonna bite you now."

"Who gets this?" the old man asked holding out the black folder. Ebbie reached for it and signed the check. "Why, thank you, Ma'am," he said. "You girls be good now." He chuckled to himself as they left the room.

Within minutes we'd eaten everything but the parsley, and the queen was licking her fingers. When the phone rang, we jumped.

"Shit, we've got five minutes to be dressed and in the lobby," Ebbie shrieked after she hung up. Instantly the party dispersed.

"God, I feel awful," I moaned to one of the maids as we stood balancing our towering headpieces. My six-foot white checkerboard with pink plumes and sequins swayed as I waited to hear our names announced. My head hurt, there was no room in my dress for my bloated stomach, and my neck was stiff from holding up the headpiece. When the man called out our club I was elated. At last I could move. Slowly our krewe proceeded down the aisle of the auditorium, smiling and waving as the audience whistled and applauded.

Other krewes followed until the entire stage was filled with fake royalty. We stood still again, waiting, as a well-dressed man took his place at the podium. The rhinestone choker around my neck felt like it was plotting with my dress to suffocate me. The stage lights were hot and got hotter. Barely able to breathe, I prayed the man would be brief.

"Does this place have air conditioning?" I whispered. The Princess of Norway just lifted her shoulders and shook her head slightly.

The man finished his speech and Ebbie mumbled, "Thank God!" I tried not to giggle. But another man took the stage.

I tapped the security guard standing below me on the floor. "Excuse me, but do we have to stand up here for the entire presentation? It's really hot."

"Y'all don't come down until after all the speeches. It's gonna be a while."

I shifted my weight, trying to find some relief from the pain. I couldn't stand much longer, sweating and itching underneath my dress and all the layers of slips.

"Sir, could we at least get a stool?"

"We don't have any stools, Miss, you're just going to have to wait." He didn't bother to try to conceal his agitation.

Queasiness rippled through my stomach. I tried to breathe as deeply as possible but after all that food and beer, I could hardly fill my lungs.

I tapped him on the shoulder again. "Excuse me, but I need to get down."

"No, miss..." was all I heard before the room went black.

"Missy, can you hear me? Back up, I think she's coming to. Can you hear me?" the man asked as he moved something across my nose.

"What is that?" I cried, shoving his hand away. "What happened?"

"You fainted. Luckily the security guard caught you before you hit the floor," the paramedic answered.

I looked around and realized we were in the middle of the hotel lobby. I glanced down and saw my gown puddled around my waist. "My dress! I'm naked!"

I grabbed for the sleeves as the man helped cover me.

"We had to take your dress off so that you could get some air. Now, don't try to get up yet," he warned. "I need to check you over. Are you on any sort of medication?"

"Uh, I'm not sure..." I stammered as one of the chaperones looked on.

"Her heart is racing," the paramedic said to one of the chaperones.

"We've got one more!" another voice called out.

I turned and giggled when I saw Ebbie draped across a security guard's arms as he made his way past the concierge's desk. Soon the girls began dropping like drunken flies trapped in a greenhouse.

Upon my return home, I made my obligatory Sunday night call to Dwayne. I skimmed through my ball program, half-listening as he gave me a play-by-play account of his weekend—the fraternity's Friday night social, tennis on Saturday, and six hours on Sunday of studying in the library. To avoid a confrontation, I pretended that I had indeed missed him.

"Well, I'm exhausted. We'd better hang up now," he said after we'd made tentative plans for the following weekend.

"All right," I said, feeling deflated by our conversation. "Dwayne, I don't want to start a fight, but perhaps we'd be happier if we dated around. Maybe we're not meant to be together." Where had the nerve come from? I wondered. I had fantasized about breaking up with him the entire drive back to Lafayette.

He was quiet for a few moments. I closed the program I had been riffling through and squeezed my eyes shut. I wanted to take back my words, but much to my surprise, he said okay. By Wednesday I received a letter saying he couldn't continue like this and that he would miss me, but he needed to break up. I wasn't the same girl he had fallen in love with.

Free of Dwayne, I went wild, drinking and smoking pot with friends from school and work. I slept with anyone that showed interest, whether we had just met or dated a couple of times. Long-term relationships, commitments—no thanks! No more jealousy and no more controlling boyfriends. I was free at last. Free until it all caught up with me.

35 ~

"I've been throwing up all day," I whispered into the phone as I fiddled with my senior class ring, "I think I'm pregnant."

I chose Becky, one of my co-workers from Pizza Inn, as my sole confidant because a month earlier she called me with the same news. Four days before her parents took her to get an abortion, we talked about running away to Houston, finding waitress jobs, and raising her baby together. I had $1,000 in savings and offered to use it to get us started. That's how much I wanted to leave Lafayette.

It's probably lucky for her baby and us that she somehow knew better than to take me up on my offer. Besides, she wanted to be the first in her family to graduate from college.

Now that a baby was in my belly, I just wanted it out. To pretend it never existed.

"Are you serious?" Becky asked.

"No, I'm lying," I said. "Do you have any of those pills the doctor gave you?"

"Yeah, you want me to bring them over?"

"Please. I'm so scared my parents are going to catch on. Daddy just brought me a Coke to settle my stomach. Of course he was too chicken shit to ask if I've gotten myself knocked up."

I couldn't believe I was really pregnant. I hadn't paid much attention to my monthly cycles since breaking up with Dwayne. But who was the father? I was sleeping with two guys from Pizza Inn. How pathetic, I thought. I'm seventeen, pregnant, and I don't even know whom to blame. As if the fault lies elsewhere.

"Marie," Becky said, poking her head inside the door. Curled up in bed, I felt too rotten to do anything else. I waved her in, and she crossed the room wearing her red, white, and blue waitress uniform.

"Here you go." She fished an amber vial from her front pocket and wrinkled her nose. "Boy, you look like shit."

I took the bottle of anti-vomiting pills and rolled my eyes. "How many do I take?"

"One. Every four hours." She sat down beside me on the bed. "Are you going to tell your parents?"

"No way!" I couldn't face the shame or disappointment on Daddy's face. Claire and I didn't share secrets anymore. Nanette was off living happily ever after with Boyce. And I had no idea whether Momma would be sympathetic or outraged. Most of what went on in her head remained a mystery.

I popped a pill into my mouth and shook my head. "I just want to get an abortion as soon as possible. What was the name of that place?"

"Delta Women's Clinic. You want me to get the number and address for you?"

I nodded. "Do you think you could come with me? I don't know who else to ask."

"Sure."

Suddenly I was overwhelmed by nausea again. Clamping my hand to my mouth and kicking off the covers, I mumbled, "Excuse me" and ran to the bathroom.

When I returned Becky patted my shoulder. "It sucks, doesn't it?"

"Yeah." I started crying. "I know you wanted to keep your baby, but who knows what this one would turn out like with all the crap I've been drinking and smoking."

"It's okay. You better call soon. They're open on Saturdays."

"How much did it cost?"

"A hundred and seventy-five."

"Yikes."

Becky nodded. I knew her parents sometimes struggled just to pay her tuition at USL.

"Hey, on the way up here your dad showed me his new Dalmatian puppies. How many dogs do you have now?"

"Six. He bought those dumb puppies to go with his red Suburban. You know, *firemen's* dogs." Becky laughed. I wondered if she resented my family's money. It sure didn't bring us any more happiness than her parents' circumstances brought them. Probably less. "I give the dogs a week, two tops, before he gets rid of them."

"That's a shame."

I nodded. We were all dispensable—dogs, maids, children. If Daddy found out that I was pregnant, he would shun me like he had Aimee.

The next morning before school, I took a pregnancy test. When the little pink plus sign appeared, I dropped the test into the bathroom sink and pounded my fists into the pleats of my uniform. That afternoon I made an appointment for the abortion.

I slept over at Becky's house on Friday night so we could wake up early to pick up her boyfriend. He was coming with us to Baton Rouge to help with the driving after my appointment.

"Mornin', Tupper," Becky and I said as he climbed into my car.

"Hey, girls." He grinned his toothy smile, his thick brown mustache stretching out to his dimples. Sliding into the middle of the back seat, he reached over to kiss Becky and then gave my shoulder a little squeeze.

"I've been so worried about everything," I confessed. "I kept thinking I would forget my checkbook or something."

"Checkbook?" Becky stared at me. "You know you have to pay with cash, don't you?"

"Cash? What do you mean? I deposited the money into my checking account to pay the clinic by check."

"They don't take checks."

"How do you know that?" I looked at her to see if she was just giving me a hard time. But she was combing her black hair behind her ears with her fingers like she did when she was nervous.

"There's a big sign at the check-in counter."

"Shit." I eased my foot off the pedal. "I've only got about fifteen dollars in cash. Do y'all have any money?"

"No," said Becky.

"Nope," said Tupper, raising his eyebrows.

"Hold on." I made a quick U-turn into Albertson's parking lot.

"You're gonna get us killed!" Tupper yelled.

"No, I'm not." I pulled to the front of the grocery store. "I've got an hour to get money and get to my appointment. What if I'm close to the twelve-week cutoff point?"

I raced to the nearest open checkout counter. "Excuse me," I said to the heavy-set black lady, "but I need to cash a check for $175."

"I'm sorry m'am, we can't do that. We only take checks for the amount of purchase."

"Please, you've just got to. I have a receipt from the deposit I made yesterday into my checking account." I pulled my wallet out of my purse while she shook her head.

I ignored her and fished the deposit slip out of my wallet anyway. She looked at it and then started reciting the store policy again.

"Can you call a manager? I swear it's a good check. It's an emergency."

She paged the manager and explained my request to him. He'd started to give me the same spiel when I said, "I know all that. Can't you make an exception? Please."

"No, we can't. Maybe you'll find a bank in Baton Rouge that is open. Some are starting to open on Saturdays." I ran out of the store thinking he was an idiot. No banks were open at seven o'clock in the morning.

"Did they cash it?" Becky asked when I got back into the car.

"No. They're assholes. The clinic is just going to have to take my check. I'll pretend like I didn't know."

A crowd was standing in front of the clinic entrance. They were holding signs:

ABORTION IS MURDER.
DON'T KILL GOD'S CHILDREN.

"Shit, protestors," I mumbled.

"They weren't here when I came," Becky said, as if I might be blaming her.

"Why me? This day is going totally wrong." Climbing out of the car, I pushed my way past the protesters. They started yelling at me.

"We can help you. Don't make this big mistake."

"Don't kill your baby!"

Becky followed behind me, practically stepping on the heels of my tennis shoes.

"Excuse me, excuse me," I pleaded, trying not to make eye contact with any of the zealots.

Once inside I rang the bell. The window slid open and a chubby pink face appeared before me. "I'm Marie Etienne and I have an 8:00 appointment."

"Are you here for an abortion?" the pink face asked. She looked to be in a snit. Maybe she had gas.

I wanted to yell, Do you have to shout it so everyone in the whole place knows my business? "Yes," I whispered.

"Fill this out and return it with your payment of $175."

A few minutes later I handed her the completed forms and a check made out to Delta Women's Clinic. She looked at the clipboard, shook her head, and removed the yellow check, setting it down on the counter.

"We don't accept checks. You see the sign right in front of you?"

"I didn't know about your policy. No one told me that when I made the appointment. Please, can you make an exception?"

"Look, I'd like to help, but our—"

"Please, I've got to do this today. There's no way I can come back another day. Please, take the check. It's good, I swear on the Bible."

"All right, leave it here with your paperwork, and I'll see what I can do."

Becky, Tupper, and I sat together and waited for my name to be called. Discreetly I looked around the room to see who else was getting an abortion. It was strange to see such a wide range of ages among the women. There were a couple of young girls like me, but most of the others looked as though they were in their twenties and thirties. There were couples sitting together holding hands. There was one scraggly family that had four other children running around the waiting room, hitting each other, and tugging on their mother's purse, begging for chewing gum. I wondered if the kids knew what their mother was about to do. How would one explain to children that they were killing a sibling?

I prayed no one I recognized would walk in.

Each time the door swung open and a nurse appeared, I hoped it was my turn. I was scared the woman behind the glass door would call me back and tell me that they wouldn't take my check.

"Good luck," Becky whispered when my name was finally called.

I followed the nurse to a desk, and she told me to have a seat. She ran through the routine with me. First I'd receive some counseling about my options. Then there'd be an exam, a shot, and, finally, the procedure. I nodded as she talked and in answer to one of her questions, said I hadn't the vaguest notion when I'd had my last period.

After the exam, I heard her tell the doctor that I was approximately ten weeks along. Two and a half months. I couldn't believe it. The baby was a quarter of the way developed. I didn't want to know that.

When they put my legs in the stirrups, I was groggy from the shot but fully conscious. They turned on the suction machine, and my whole body jerked. It sounded like a huge vacuum cleaner. When the doctor touched me between my legs, I jumped again.

"Lie still," he muttered.

"I'm sorry."

"This will be just a little uncomfortable." I felt the machine touch me.

I must have jerked again because he stopped. "Be still, or I won't be able to perform the procedure."

I tried to lie still, balling my hands into fists like I did at the dentist's office. It hurt—a lot. I couldn't help it. It felt like he was yanking out my insides. I moaned.

"You're acting like a silly child." He stopped again for a moment and stared at me. "I'm warning you to quiet down. You're going to scare the other women. Do you understand?"

I nodded and blinked back tears. He was going to tell me to get up and go away. "Yes. I'll stop." I tried to think of something to distract myself. A recent movie? Nothing came to mind. Panicking, I grabbed hold of the first thing that popped into my head: "Friends, Romans, countrymen, lend me your ears." The overscheduled doctor lowered his head again and resumed the procedure as I silently recited Marc Antony's address to the Romans that I'd had to memorize recently for English class.

"Miss Etienne, can you hear me?" I opened my eyes and saw a nurse standing next to the cot. I must have passed out. I started to sit up but my head felt light. "How do you feel?"

I let my head fall back to the pillow. "A little dizzy. Is he done?"

"Yes, you can go home now. You should expect a little bleeding for a day or two. Call your doctor if it persists or if it's really heavy. Here's some Tylenol to take if the cramping gets too bad." I kept blinking as she rattled off her lines.

When I walked into the lobby, Becky and Tupper stood up and met me at the front door. "That was horrible," I said, handing Tupper the car keys.

It wasn't until later that I realized the protestors had gone. I lay across the backseat and said I was going to sleep for awhile. Closing my eyes, I told myself that getting rid of the baby had been my best option. I didn't want to be trapped in a crummy marriage like Momma and Aimee had been. I wanted to go to college, to have a career, and, most of all, to move out of Lafayette as soon as possible. I couldn't have done that with a baby, and I was too selfish to carry a baby just to give it up for adoption.

Hours later, it seemed, though really only forty-five minutes since I'd lost track of Becky and Tupper's conversation, the car shuddered and stopped.

"Shit," Tupper cussed.

"What's happening?" I asked, easing myself up.

"This piece of shit just stalled again. Now I can't get it to move." I looked out the window. We were on the shoulder of the highway. "When I press on the gas, it doesn't do anything. It's not catching or something." He looked at Becky helplessly.

"Do you know anything about cars?" I asked.

"No."

"What else is gonna go wrong?" I wanted to scream. "My father will kill me. We're not supposed to take his cars out of town or on the highway. How in the hell am I going to explain this?" I looked at the front window. We were less than a hundred yards from the exit to Lafayette. "Can't we just get the car to move a little farther?"

"Yeah, right!" Tupper said. "I told you it won't move. Listen." He turned the key to demonstrate the lifeless clicking sound. "See?"

"You're going to have to call someone to tow it," Becky said.

I called Daddy. What else was I to do?

"Daddy, it's Marie. My car stalled on the highway just before the exit to Lafayette. I was giving my friends Becky and Tupper a ride home, and the car just died," I rambled. "I think it needs to be towed."

A diplomatic silence followed and then he asked, "Are you all right?"

"We're fine."

"Stay there and I'll call someone to come get you right away."

When the tow-truck driver dropped me off, I went right to my room, speaking to no one. I climbed in bed and slept until Momma called me down for dinner.

"Are you feeling okay?" Momma asked as I sat at the counter. "You look pale."

"I'm fine, I'm just tired. Becky and I stayed up late last night talking."

"Well, come serve yourself," she said, glancing at Daddy as he pulled out his chair.

Did they know? I wondered, filling my plate with a fried pork chop, mashed potatoes, green beans, and two crescent rolls. I was so famished that my hands trembled as I carried my food to the counter. I ate quickly. I didn't want to get a lecture from Daddy about taking the car on the highway without his permission. Luckily, he didn't say a word. He just smiled as I thanked Momma and excused myself from dinner.

A few days later I walked into the kitchen to scrounge for a snack. Daddy set the mail on the table, saying, "Hello, Sweetheartsabean."

He bent down so I could kiss his cheek and then I reached over to sift through the stack of bills and letters. I came to one addressed to me. American Bank? What was this for? I ripped open the envelope and read. "Insufficient funds! They didn't, they wouldn't have returned my check." Without thinking, I'd said it aloud.

"What's wrong, darling?" Daddy asked, loosening his tie with three quick tugs.

"Um, I made a deposit a couple of weeks ago and then wrote a check for the same amount and the bank is saying that I didn't have enough money."

"Can I see that?"

"Uh, okay." I handed him the letter. It didn't say who the check was written to.

"It's all right. They still honored the check, you're just overdrawn by ninety-eight cents. They want you to make a deposit."

"But you don't understand, I had to beg the people to take my check and I had enough money, I swear I did. I'm so embarrassed. When will this stupid thing ever end?" I asked, standing at the frayed edges of hysteria.

"It's fine, Sweetheart. Here." He took out his wallet. "You take this and deposit it into your account and that'll leave you with a little extra. Don't cry now." He handed me fifty dollars for a ninety-eight cent overdraft.

"Thank you." He patted me on the back and left the kitchen. Though relieved, I thought it strange he didn't ask why I had written a check for such a large amount. Maybe he knew. Maybe he didn't want to know. Perhaps he and Momma were just relieved I'd taken care of the messy business on my own. When I went to the see our family gynecologist for my post-abortion checkup, the doctor gave me a prescription for birth control pills and advised me to use them. It was the best advice I got.

36 ~

My letter of acceptance arrived from USL just as I knew it would despite my C average.

I made the announcement at dinner, hoping to glean some enthusiasm from my family's reaction. Daddy beamed, saying, "That's wonderful, Sweetheartsabean." Momma and the others mumbled congratulations, too. I tried to act pleased, but I think they all knew I wasn't exactly excited about it. I had begged, cried, and raged, and still Daddy wouldn't consider letting me go away even as far as Baton Rouge.

Ever since Chess's death, which had brought the evil world too close to home, Daddy fixated on keeping us nearby, "keeping a lookout for my children." He'd made it clear that if any of us chose to go somewhere other than the *University of Slow Learners*, which offered Remedial English and Math for freshman like myself, we were on our own. We'd have to pay for everything: tuition, housing, books, food—everything. Since none of us were really scholarship material, that kept us in Lafayette under his watchful eye. Only Yvette had been allowed to go away to Loyola in New Orleans, but that was long ago, before Chess's death.

Knowing how Daddy felt, I had tried several escape routes. Pleading and anger didn't work. But my mortuary school plan almost succeeded.

Early in my senior year, my English teacher said he'd wanted to be a mortician. He'd even gone through the one-year program. But there was a problem he just couldn't overcome. He was lousy at putting makeup on the corpses. The men and women he worked on looked worse after he'd finished with them.

When I heard him say the closest school for mortuary science was in Houston, I decided to tell Momma and Daddy I really wanted to be a mortician. I even went to observe an embalming at Blanchard's funeral home to convince them of my sincerity. Eventually Daddy said yes. I could go away for just that one year but then I had to move back home.

Even a year looked good at that point, but not good enough. I never even managed to complete the application. For months I tried to force myself to finish it and send it in, but the thought of working with dead people was just too much for me to handle. Daddy had wagered and won, agreeing to send me to Houston only because he knew I wouldn't actually do it. Finally, I bagged the idea and resigned myself to staying in Lafayette until I finished my undergraduate degree. Then I'd move away. Somewhere far from home, that was for sure.

Daddy didn't ask what I was going to study, so I volunteered the information. "I'm going to take Accounting 101 and the four other classes suggested for first semester accounting majors."

He looked up from his plate and smiled again. "You might want to take a typing class. It could come in handy if you don't get married and you need to get a job as a secretary or bookkeeper. You know, I was a pretty fast typist during my days in the Army. That desk job kept me from having to go overseas."

I bent the neck of my fork back and forth as I stared at Daddy, at his tie thrown over his shoulder to avoid staining. I imagined him sitting in his pressed army uniform, a cigarette burning in a nearby ashtray, as he quickly typed, "We regret to inform you that your son…" With each precise key stroke he's thinking: Thank God that's not me coming home in a body bag. At least I'm alive.

His low expectations felt like tablespoons full of arsenic contaminating my well of dreams, spoon after spoon. With swelling anger, I wished I'd followed through with mortuary school.

I looked at Momma's plate of cottage cheese and fruit. Her arms were freckled and skinny, Ethiopian skinny. Her striped blouse hung flatly over her chest. A strand of gray pearls decorated her stiff neck. I glanced at her shrunken face. Daddy seemed to be the only person in our family who hadn't noticed that Momma was slowly dieting herself to her grave.

The last bitter exchange between my parents erupted shortly after Daddy's diagnosis of diabetes. He'd yelled that Momma ought to go out and find herself a *real* man. We all knew the insulin he injected left him impotent. It was one side effect that bothered her more than him, or so it seemed. He now had the perfect excuse to avoid intimacy with our mother.

She shakily reached for her Tab and Daddy for his glass of Jack

Daniel's and Diet Coke (the *Diet* in deference to diabetes). This could be me in forty years. I knew I'd made the right decision to abort my baby when I considered how Momma's life had turned out. I swore I wouldn't make the same mistakes.

Momma finished her cottage cheese and then pushed away from the table. She fixed a plate of food for Anne and took it to her. Something was up in our house, but only Momma and Anne knew exactly.

"What's wrong with Anne?" I had asked Momma the day before. "She's in her room crying."

"She's having a little trouble at school with one of her friends," Momma replied, stuffing a piece of garlic into a little slit she had cut in the roast. "Sarah's parents don't want them hanging around together anymore."

"Why? They're practically inseparable." Now that Anne had her driver's license, she was all the time driving over to Sarah's house.

Momma shrugged. She stabbed the meat again and again, each cut an inch away from the other, and then pulled apart the flesh to sprinkle in her premixed spices—salt, black pepper, and cayenne pepper. She refused to say any more, and I was late for work.

I ran to the stairs and nearly collided into Daddy.

"Hey, Sweetheartsabean, where are you going so fast?"

"Oh, hi. I'm working tonight."

"Can I talk to you a minute?" I nodded and tried to look innocent. Was he going to lecture me about staying out all night again without calling? "Have you heard anything about Anne?" he whispered.

I almost smiled with relief as I shook my head. "She was crying yesterday and she stayed home today. What's going on?" He obviously wasn't getting any further with Momma than I had.

"I'm not sure," he said. "The principal is talking about expelling her. They're accusing her of having some sort of funny relationship with another girl, her friend Sarah. Her parents found some peculiar notes that the two have been writing to each other. Do you think there's anything to this business of her, uh, you know, liking girls?"

Poor Daddy looked sick.

"I don't know," I said, "I could ask her." How in the world was I going to ask my sister if she was a lesbian?

"Well, I don't want to upset her any more, but maybe if you do find anything out you could tell me. I just don't want her to get kicked out of school. Thanks, Sweetheart." He kissed me on the forehead, then disappeared into his study. Sending his daughter on a spy mission—that was Daddy's way of "keeping a lookout for his children."

Momma returned from upstairs with an empty glass, a soup bowl, and an armful of dirty clothes. As she trudged to the sink, I tried to figure out a way to broach the subject with Anne. I'd already rejected a million different scenarios. It wasn't a topic I felt comfortable with, and I didn't want to hurt my little sister's feelings by saying something insensitive. Not like Penny who used to taunt all of us with accusations of acting like a lesbo with our *little* friends, when she wanted to be cruel.

Luckily, by week's end, Momma saved Daddy and me the trouble. She and Anne devised a plan. All I knew was that when Anne finally came out to face the world and the Christian academy she and Nickey attended, she agreed not to have any contact with Sarah. It wasn't until many years later that Anne would tell me that Momma said there was nothing wrong with girls liking girls. That if she and Sarah were meant to be, it'd have to wait until they both finished school. This was the advice given by a woman who had often mentioned how she loved and admired a certain nun in her high school. My mother had spent her afternoons reading every book in the library just to be near the sister. She read so much that at fifteen she earned a full scholarship to Loyola. But then she met my father and all that changed.

Soon after, Sarah left for boarding school. The door that had opened with her, though, would lead Anne on a long search to find her own happiness.

37 ~ California, 1993

For a week after our big fight, Kyle and I both made an effort to be kinder. I cooked a chicken and sausage gumbo, his favorite, without complaining about how tiring it was to make the roux, clean the chicken, and chop up all the onions, garlic, and bell peppers while keeping Austin happy for a whole afternoon. He managed to come home by seven every evening and made considerable progress on the kitchen the next weekend. I tried to read the newspaper while the baby slept in the afternoon so that I wouldn't have my face buried in it while Kyle watched television alone. In return, he asked about my friends from the New Mom's group and pretended to be interested in our outings. But after a couple of weeks of being on our best behavior, we both slipped back into our old ways. He'd call at eight and say he'd just gotten out of a long meeting, and I'd stiffen or pull away every time he got near me.

A week before Thanksgiving, sitting in bed watching television, I looked over at him and said, "My mom could really use something to look forward to with the holidays approaching. You know, the first year without my father. I thought Austin and I could go out a week before Christmas and you could join us on Christmas Eve and stay for another week."

He flicked off the television. "I guess that's okay. But that's a long time for me not to see Austin. And are you sure you want to spend that much time with your family?"

"I think it'll be nice. I want to see my sisters and nephews and show off Austin to all my friends."

"You're not going to, like, leave him with your mother and go off gallivanting, are you?"

"You sure have a lot of faith in me."

It was settled then. A few more weeks of playing the agreeable little wife, and then I would be away from him, for a week anyway.

When I told Momma I was coming, she insisted on paying the airfare. So I decided that since she was being so generous, the least I could do was fly out even earlier. Eventually I got up the nerve to tell Kyle that I was actually leaving a week *and a half* before Christmas. But I made sure to purchase the nonrefundable tickets before I told him.

Momma greeted me at the kitchen door with a big hug and a kiss. "Let me see him!" I turned Austin around in my arms and she smiled, tracing his right cheek with the backs of her fingers. "Boy, have you grown. What are you feeding him?"

"Me, all of me it seems. This kid is constantly nursing. You want to hold him?"

"No, I better not. I think I'm coming down with the flu."

Nanette said, "We'll get your bags from the van, Marie. You stay and visit with Momma." My sister ushered out her reluctant boys, Chris and Jack. They wanted to stay and pet their nephew.

I accepted my mother's offer to make me a sandwich. "Baloney, lots of mustard, no mayonnaise?" she asked as she opened the refrigerator.

She might not recall which of her nine children she had beaten, but when it came to feeding us, Momma's memory was impeccable. She knew who liked mayonnaise and who didn't, who drank decaf versus regular, that I liked white meat and Nanette liked dark, that Anne liked the pink sweetener and Yvette the blue.

When Nanette and the boys had carried in the last of my bags, they joined Momma and me at the table. I devoured my sandwich on good old white bread, and Chris and Jack raided the pantry for chips and cookies.

I started to ask Momma something when she suddenly heaved forward, her face red and strained. We waited in silence for her to finish coughing. The fit eventually stopped and her face relaxed.

"Well, darlings, if you don't mind, I'm going to go to bed." She stood and picked up her glass of water. "Oh, Marie, the keys for my car are right up there near the telephone, and the tank is full. I only need it on Wednesday for my hair appointment." She kissed the tops of our heads, wished us good night, and slowly began shuffling toward the door. Then she stopped and turned back.

"Be sure and keep your bedroom door closed so the cats don't go in your room. You don't want them in there with the baby. And Nanette, lock up before you go."

After Austin and I were settled into our room, I called Kyle to let him know we had arrived safely. When we hung up, I opened the door because Momma had the heater running full blast and the room was stuffy.

Laying Austin in the middle of the bed, I changed his diaper and clothes. "You're tired, aren't you? It's been a big day for you. Flying on two airplanes. Seeing grandma and Aunt Nanette and your cousins tonight. Can you believe it's just you and me, my little Uggaboo?" I blew a loud, wet kiss on his stomach. He smiled and wiggled, waving his arms in the air.

Propping the pillows against the headboard, I made myself comfortable and then picked him up. While he nursed I sucked in a deep breath and slowly exhaled. I could feel the muscles in my shoulders and neck finally starting to relax. I was a free woman, for ten whole days. Two thousand miles away from Kyle and all my worries.

I set Austin down and covered him with his special quilt I had brought with us. With a full tummy, he sucked away on his pacifier. His face looked so calm and beautiful. I gazed down at him, wondering if he dreamed yet. And if he did, what he dreamed about. I hoped they were good ones.

What could be better than this? A sleeping baby and no husband to nag me. I could stay up late, watch both the news and the Late Show if I wanted. I set the television volume setting to one and scanned the channels.

"Marie!"

Momma stood at the door in her robe. Instantly I hit the power button on the remote and drew my hands into my lap. "Did I wake you with the television?" I asked anxiously, feeling as if I'd been caught doing something illicit.

"No. But your door is open. You have to keep it closed. Those stupid cats will come in, and you don't want them in the crib with the baby."

"You're right. I'm sorry."

"Good night, sweetheart."

"Good night, Momma."

She turned, pulling the door closed behind her. I sat there frozen for a few minutes before I got up the courage to turn on the television again. I could hear Momma coughing in her bathroom.

The next morning Austin and I slept in. As I dressed that morning, I heard Mr. Delahoussaye's familiar voice coming from the kitchen. I hastily finished my makeup and changed the baby because I wanted to go downstairs and catch him before he left. I hadn't talked with him since my father's funeral five months earlier.

"Well, look who it is—Ma-ree!" he called as I walked into the kitchen.

"Hi, Mr. Delahoussaye. You want to meet Austin."

Mr. Delahoussaye stood up, hugged and kissed me hello, and then exclaimed, "My, he's a handsome fellow. You look just like your daddy. Can I hold him?"

"Sure," I said handing Austin over.

He squeezed Austin's fat cheeks, tossed him in the air a couple of times, and then he was done. "You wanna go back to your mommy, Handsome?" He put the baby back in my arms, saying, "I was just about to show your mother some sketches of your father's tombstone. Would you care to see them?"

"Sure." I glanced at Momma to see if there was any sign of hesitation in her face. She smiled and asked if I wanted something to drink. I declined, noticing that there were two glasses of sherry and a white folder on the kitchen table.

We sat down and Mr. Delahoussaye moved his glass out of the way to open the folder. He placed a drawing between Momma and me.

I stared at the pencil sketch of a large rectangular slab of carved stone. Stenciled in black ink were the names Chester B. Etienne and Esther L. Etienne.

"Why's Momma's name on it?" I asked, not looking her way. Superstitious, I surely didn't want my name sitting over some empty grave until I was stiff as a paddle.

"Your mother wanted their names to be together on one tombstone, so we'll just carve her dates in at a later time." He pulled a second sheet from the folder and said, "Here's what the back will look like. The names of all the children—from Yvette on down. Y'all need to look at the spelling and the middle names to make sure it's all correct. Once it's up, there's not much you can do if it ain't right." He laughed and Momma grinned.

Momma took a big sip of her drink. Smiling, Mr. Delahoussaye followed suit with a small taste. I think he was embarrassed, because he said he and Momma only occasionally started the morning off with a little sherry. That Momma was a bad influence on him.

We visited a while longer and then he took the stack of mail

Momma had left by the telephone for him. She didn't even bother opening her mail; he just gave her back the personal items like letters and announcements.

That afternoon we sat together in the living room while I nursed Austin on the sofa and Momma reclined in her chair, watching her favorite soap opera.

"I can't believe Luke and Laura are still on this show," I said. "They were fighting and making up when I was in high school." Momma smiled, but her eyes didn't veer away from the screen. She lit one cigarette after another and got up only during the commercial breaks to refill her drink, the eternal vodka and Diet Coke.

When the soap was over, she turned to me. "You know, your father would have a fit if he saw you sitting in the middle of the living room nursing a baby. He'd be so embarrassed."

"Does it bother you?" I hadn't even thought to ask if it was all right.

"No, I'm fine with it. I just can imagine the look on his face if he were to walk in here right now." She finished her drink and then said casually, "I always envied women who breast fed."

"Why didn't you try it?" I asked, unsure how safe these waters were to tread.

She shook her head. "Mom said no. That breast-feeding was too time-consuming and your father needed me more. That Chester was my first concern."

"Really. That's weird. But I guess it would have been a lot to nurse nine children and take care of everything else."

Momma's face hardened and she retorted, "I *didn't* mean that I wanted to nurse all nine of you. I just wanted to be able try it, at least once. To see what all the fuss was about." She grabbed her drink and left me there shaking. The waters were safe enough, I just didn't know how to navigate them.

That night I had the newspaper and magazines spread out before me, the television on, a piece of pecan pie sitting on the night stand when Austin woke up crying. He had been sleeping fitfully all evening. I picked him up from the crib and tried rocking him to calm him down. Our room felt like a toaster oven.

"Sweetie, what's wrong? Why are you so upset?" His crying got louder and louder until it was a full-fledged wailing. "Shu, Austin, please stop crying. You're going to wake your grandmother." I'd heard her coughing and retching in her bathroom several times that evening.

I paced the narrow aisle between the crib and my bed, bouncing Austin in my arms, singing "Puff the Magic Dragon," verse after verse, trying to placate him. Suddenly, without warning, the door swung wide open. Momma stood there in her sheer baby blue gown, swaying, fury on her face.

"Marie, I told you to keep your door shut! I can't find the damn cats anywhere, they must be in here."

"I, uh, I haven't seen them. It was just hot in here, so I opened the door for a minute. I'm sorry."

She approached the other side of the bed, bumped her thigh on the corner of the desk, and mumbled, "Goddamnbed." She was tanked. I guessed she and the Duhons had really tied one on while I was out having dinner with Nanette. I held Austin to my chest. He cried, wiggling to get free. Momma dropped onto the floor and tore back the covers.

"Come here, you goddamn cat," she said, crawling around, trying to squeeze her head and shoulders underneath the bed. Standing with my back against the window, I watched her, afraid she'd bump her head on the frame and then blame it on me, giving her an excuse to beat the crap out of me. Or worse, she'd have a heart attack and everyone would say it was my fault.

She made another swooping motion and I heard the cat hiss. "Got you. Prissy, don't you bite me, you stupid cat."

Momma scooted back and eased her head out from under the bed. She held Prissy by his left hind leg. He tried to scratch her. I stood frozen, not sure if I should go over and help her to get up. But she managed to stand without losing her grip on the cat. She carried him, twisting and nipping at her arm, and threw him into the hallway. "Now go away." She turned back into the room. "Herman, where are you?"

Austin was whimpering. "Shu, sweetie," I whispered, "it's okay." She headed back to the bed, coughing and breathing hard. "Momma? You want me to crawl down there and get the other one?"

"No, I'll get him," she spat back at me. "Herman, you come out of there!" She paused by the side of the bed, holding her stomach and panting, trying to catch her breath.

I looked down and saw a gray and black striped tail sticking out from under the baby's crib. "He's here, Momma," I screamed, unsure of what to do. I didn't want her coming over to my side of the room, so I stomped my foot next to his tail to scare him, and Herman darted out and toward the door.

"Get the door!" Momma yelled, holding onto the bed.

I ran to the door, praying I wouldn't frighten the cat and send him back under the bed. Thank God he waited there for me to let him out. "He's gone!"

Momma started to pull herself up, but her left hand slipped off the mattress and, wham, she was back on the floor. The thud startled Austin and he cried louder.

"No, no, Austin, don't cry, it's okay," I said, watching Momma struggle to pull herself up. When she was standing, she rubbed her hip and then looked over at Austin.

"Give him to me!" she said in a thick slur.

"What?" My heart pounded. I remembered seeing her standing over Nickey's crib just weeks after they came home from the hospital, spanking him, cussing and swearing about what a bad baby he was.

"Let me have him." She walked around to the foot of the bed where I stood with Austin drawn tight against my chest. *God, she's so drunk, what if she drops him? What's she going to do to him? What if she explodes and starts hitting him? Stupid Marie. Stupid. Why'd you leave the door open again?*

My arms shook uncontrollably as I held Austin out to her. I offered my precious son to quiet the angry monster. She grabbed him from me. What are you going to do if she slaps him or tries to force him to shut up? I asked myself. She cradled him and carried him to the rocking chair in the corner of my room. Plopping down, her face softened. She cooed, "There, there, Little Fellow, what's wrong, you can't sleep tonight? Don't cry now." He wailed until his whole body twitched and his head jerked with sobs. She rocked him back and forth for a moment, then shrugged.

"You better take him. He doesn't seem to like me." I grabbed him and she stood up. "I hope he doesn't keep you up all night." She kissed me on the forehead and left the room, coughing.

I locked the door behind her and scrambled to feed Austin. Eventually he relaxed and fell asleep. Sitting on the edge of my bed watching him, I swore up and down that the absolute next time, I wouldn't hand him over to my drunk, mad mother, no matter what. I would protect him. Tears rolled down my face, because I realized that I was just as afraid of Momma as she was of her mother. She couldn't tell Grandma that she'd decide whether or not to breast feed her own babies. That she'd decide what constituted being a good wife. And I probably would never be able to tell her no, that she was too drunk to hold my child.

I thought about the dreams I had where I was paralyzed with fear. I couldn't remember a time when I ever tried to pull away from Momma. I always stood perfectly still. Obedient. Frightened. Hoping it would end soon.

I rubbed my eyes until the blackness behind my lids gave way to stars. Then I slipped into bed and tried to convince myself that she wasn't coming back, that it was safe to go to sleep.

38 ~ Louisiana, 1983

One afternoon in my sophomore year of college, I sat on my bed studying for spring finals, wondering how, in one week I could possibly read Homer—*The Odyssey*, prepare for my algebra, statistics, and finance exams, write a paper on Isadora Duncan, and work three night shifts at the club. Mignon and I had jobs now as cocktail waitresses at a ritzy private club.

It was impossible. I picked at my nails and read the black scribbling on the boxes lining the walls of my bedroom. I was moving out of my parents' house after finals. Daddy had bought and furnished a two-bedroom townhouse for Penny and me to share. An odd roommate pairing since we barely interacted outside of the dinner table. But Momma told Daddy she was tired of our coming home at all hours, never calling. He suggested investing in a development just a few streets over. That way he could keep an eye on us and Momma wouldn't be waiting up, sorting laundry at 4 A.M. when we tiptoed into the house smelling like a distillery, eyes dilated from cocaine, and hair as disarrayed as our clothes.

Momma had tried ignoring us. She pretended, as we did, that everything was dandy. But we were the kind of daughters she never intended to raise. Who wants to look into a mirror image of herself to see where she has failed? No, it's too easy to rebuke oneself. You let go of all rules and what's left? Drunk, wasted, lying faces to greet you in the early morning.

I read and reread the first line of Homer. None of the words stuck in my cloudy mind. If I flunked out, I'd be stuck in Lafayette forever. I was nearly in tears when my telephone buzzed.

Daddy wanted me to come down to the study. He didn't sound angry so I figured he hadn't yet received the huge bill from the dinner and drinks I'd charged for my friends.

I trudged into the study and found my parents in their recliners watching the news. In the old days, when Momma was still drinking, the room would have been filled with the Duhons and Jouberts, all talking, arguing, and laughing.

"Hey, darling, you've been chosen as queen of the Lafayette Ball next year," Daddy said. "Mrs. Breaux just called."

"Really?" After all the stunts I'd pulled, I was surprised my name wasn't laughed out of the nominating room. "I can't believe it," I exclaimed, shaking my fists in the air. I could just imagine those blue-haired ladies saying, *Absolutely not! Chester's a fine man, but some of those girls of his…* No doubt other girls were considered. But it probably came down to who in this current oil recession could afford to spend $6,000 on a ball dress. Momma smiled and laughed as I did a little jig around the sofa. Ever since Anne had been maid-of-honor the year before, I'd prayed I'd be chosen queen. The possibility seemed so remote.

"I'm proud of you. You'll make a beautiful queen," Daddy said. "Sit down and visit."

"I'd love to, but I've got finals this week. I've got a ton of work to do." I suddenly felt hopeful I'd be able to pass. Queens could do anything, after all.

As the ball approached, Momma took me shopping for clothes. She grabbed a sales lady and asked her where the formal white gowns were. My mother was eager to make our purchases and return home to fix Daddy's lunch before she left again to volunteer at the hospital.

"My daughter is going to be the queen of a ball in February, and she needs three formal dresses, a couple of luncheon suits, and a couple of cocktail dresses. And shoes and bags to match," Momma said as the sales lady escorted us to the evening wear salon.

I pulled dresses from the racks, then Momma sat outside and waited for the modeling to begin. In less than an hour, we had assembled an entire queen's wardrobe.

As we waited for the saleslady to ring us up, I said, "I think I'll wear the ivory lace dress for my picture in the newspaper."

"Yes, that would look nice. Do you think any one would notice if I wore the same dresses from last year?"

"No, I doubt it." I couldn't figure out why, with all their money, Momma had begun buying her shoes at Payless and only bought nice clothes if they were marked down at least fifty percent. She took this martyrdom too far.

"You know what, darling," Momma whispered, "I've got a diamond solitaire necklace and some earrings to match that you can borrow for the photographs and the ball. They were your father's mother's diamonds."

"I'll take care of them, I swear."

"You better. You're not too old to spank." She smiled, but I felt my shoulders pull away from her. I turned to watch the lady wrap white tissue around my evening handbags and slips before carefully setting them into a bag.

As we drove past Girard Park, Momma said, "I was thinking…instead of throwing a queen's reception at the house for the maids and dukes and such, what if your father and I just gave you our charge card and you bought something more practical like a fur coat. You'll need a nice coat for the ball, and a party seems like such a waste of money. A mink will last you much longer."

I turned my head as I carefully steered her Cadillac onto St. College Road. Didn't she care that people might take it as an affront if we didn't host the traditional queen's reception? Was it really a matter of practicality or was she ashamed of me? Ashamed of the way my sisters and brother all got sloppy drunk at weddings, reunions, and parties? It would be exciting to have a reception where everyone made a big fuss over me. Her face offered no clues as to her motives. Perhaps a fur coat would be nice. Maybe she doesn't want to spend an entire evening with a bunch of drunk people.

I shrugged. "Sure, I'll take a mink coat."

Momma opened a pack of cigarettes and nodded. "Watch the road, now. You better not wreck my car."

A black and white portrait of me, Queen of the Lafayette Ball, officially announced my participation in the 1983 ball. For weeks the daily society section of The Daily Advertiser ran portraits of all the young girls and older men participating in various Mardi Gras Ball krewes. Momma and I bought a hairpiece from a wig shop on Jefferson Street to fit inside my crown. Underneath the king's and my photographs were write-ups about our academic histories, hobbies, and future aspirations or current jobs. I wrote that I wanted to go to law school after I finished at USL. Seeing that proclamation, in print for everyone in town to read, felt a little daunting, as if setting myself up for one huge embarrassment. I listed golf, tennis, and sewing as hobbies. My king's write-up doubled the length of mine. He listed the name of his wife, his children, and his school and business affiliations. I was surprised he didn't go back as far as Boy Scouts when I read the list of oil-related and fraternal organizations and hobbies.

Just like a real bride, as queen I registered silver goblets at a local boutique. I chose the cheapest pattern on the recommendation of the saleslady. She warned that I'd receive fewer gifts if I selected the pricey goblet. I figured she'd heard some gossip. My reputation, I feared, preceded me like an elongated shadow, cast from behind and visible to everyone. I was so angry later when I went back to the store and saw what another krewe's queen had chosen. Even my maid-of-honor had the confidence to choose an expensive goblet.

Krewe and family friends sent bouquets of flowers and gifts. Each day I tore open white boxes to remove shiny wine goblets from beds of tissue. The Monday before the ball I received a huge bouquet of flowers from my king. His card read, "Looking forward to our reign together."

My king was an unbearable snob. Within the social hierarchy of Lafayette, he perched himself at the top of the order. He was the kind of man who talked without looking at your eyes. His attention focused on other conversations just within earshot. At rehearsals he huddled with the men and had to practically be dragged over to stand beside me. At one of the luncheons, my maid-of-honor said she'd received an invitation to the king's party. Was our invitation lost in the mail? Perhaps he didn't feel it necessary to invite his queen and her parents to his party. My father was well liked by the krewe members so I naturally fell back on the assumption that it was my reputation that had made us outcasts. I wouldn't have minded so much being snubbed if I wasn't scheduled to tend bar that night at the club for his party.

On Thursday evening, two nights before the big ball, a black limousine arrived to bring me to the krewe cocktail party. I stood left of my king in a receiving line, pretending not to care that I'd been so overtly excluded from his party, as an endless stream of acquaintances and strangers wound their way up the staircase to congratulate us. I smiled as many said what a beautiful queen I made and nodded when they asked if being queen was exciting. Those brief but superficial exchanges frightened me. Did they know how unworthy I felt masquerading as royalty? Me, a girl who had already slept with a couple of the krewe members, married men who had children about my age.

Mid-evening the receiving line disbanded, and we were free to chase down the waiters offering hors d'oeuvres and drinks. Momma and Daddy approached, sighing in unison.

"You look like a queen." Daddy was a bit unsteady as he kissed my cheek.

"Darling, you don't mind if we leave now," Momma said, taking my hand into her thin hands. "I've been up since 4:30 doing laundry, and I'm pooped."

I shook my head.

Momma smiled and said, "The diamonds look nice on you."

My hand clasped the one-carat solitaire that rested below my collar-bone, and I nodded. I checked it and the matching earrings often to make sure they hadn't fallen off.

"I want you to keep them. They look perfect on you."

"Seriously?"

I turned to Daddy. His eyebrows wrinkled like they always did when Momma gave away pieces of his family's jewelry or antiques without con-sulting him first. But he didn't rescind Momma's offer so I stammered, "Thank you."

The Saturday evening of the ball a waiter knocked on my dressing room door and delivered champagne, compliments of my cohorts at the club where I worked. By the time "The Sarge," Tootie Breaux, poked her red head into the door to tell her volunteers to "Get those girls up and ready," my face glowed a natural-looking pink, my nervousness having receded.

The horn section led the orchestra into a lively number. As the music quieted, the announcer's voice sang out, "Ladies and Gentleman, we present Her Majesty, the thirty-fifth Queen...Marie Claudia Etienne."

As *Etienne* echoed slightly in the auditorium, the curtain parted and the sound of people clapping, hollering, and whistling drowned out the orchestra. I smiled broadly as we had been instructed to do. The muscles around my mouth quivered as I forced my lips apart. "Show some teeth," Tootie had yelled over and over at the rehearsals.

I stepped forward and squinted under the warm spotlights. My heart pounded as I approached the first mark. Without my glasses, the audi-ence of black suits and assorted colored dresses blurred like Christmas lights seen through a hazy window. As I turned to face the first group of tables of standing ball guests, I smiled wider. My mouth felt so dry that I wished I had caked even more Vaseline on my teeth.

Just as I had practiced, I slid my right foot back and waved my scepter from the tip of one shoulder past my huge sequin-studded collar. A young boy in a black tux quickly ran out and straightened my glittering mantle.

He ducked back behind the curtain as I waved my scepter a second time.

I walked to the next mark and slowly turned to the crowd. Men, women, and children rose and clapped. A little girl reached out to touch the gold and crystal beads on my skirt before her mother whisked her away. I lost my composure and giggled at the little girl's eagerness and thought about what my own attendant had said when I asked her if she wanted to be a maid when she grew up.

"No. I want to be the queen. Just like you." I had hugged her.

"You're gorgeous, little lady," one man screamed. His hands came together so loud that they sounded like boards slamming against each other.

I swept the jewel-studded scepter across the crowd of well-wishers and then posed briefly with the stem resting in my left glove, as we were taught. When I arrived at the station in front of my parents and friends, Daddy blew me a kiss and Momma offered a huge smile.

"Way to go, Marie," Candice screeched in her hell-raising voice. Daddy turned toward my new best friend and took a gander at her generous bust, as she threw back her long blond hair, winked, and nodded to tell me that I was doing fine by her estimation.

Penny's eyes twinkled as she waved to me with her perfect red nails. She and her blond date made a perfect couple.

Claire and her fiancé, Ronnie, stood clapping next to Anne and Nickey. I looked at the huge grin on Claire's face. I wished Nanette weren't off in California so she could be there to see me. I looked beyond my family and friends at the crowd of familiar and unfamiliar faces. It was unbelievable that they were all cheering for me.

When my walk was complete, my king descended from the throne and met me on the lower stage. Hand in hand we walked, curtsied, and waved our scepters to the audience. I set my pace to his unhurried steps. By the time we reached the stairs leading to the throne, I was ready to sit down and let someone else parade around.

From our throne on the upper stage, the king and I watched my maid-of-honor take the spotlight. Her black velvet dress was gorgeous. She met her royal knight for their walk. Like a caricature of a prince, he wore a fake goatee and his long jacket was decorated with silver sequins and rickrack.

The maids in their exquisite ball dresses promenaded around the room until they were met by their dukes. The soloist began performing "That's Life," and the audience grew restless. Young kids crawled under tables to collect doubloons and necklaces thrown earlier by the floatriders. Adults meandered about the packed room, visiting and shaking hands.

After the king and I performed our royal dance, we received the audience. The sound of chairs screeching against the floor and heels clicking filled the auditorium. A line wrapped around the stage. The buzz of conversations surrounded us. One gray-haired woman said she was a friend of Daddy's from New Iberia and had been a maid-in-waiting the year he was king of their children's ball. She said that at fifteen my father was quite a handsome fellow. A real catch. Then she said something about Momma I couldn't make out before her husband nudged her along.

My parents inched their way toward me. Penny and my friend Candice filed in right behind them in the line. Daddy patted my gloved hands. "You did a fine job, Sweetheartsabean. Fine job." His favorite and highest compliment to his children.

"Thanks, Daddy." He wore the same tuxedo that he had donned ten years before when he was Penny's duke and we'd watched him goosestep up and down the hall. He looked older now. Tired.

"You were lovely, darling." Momma bent over to kiss my cheek. I could feel the soft warmth of her skin as we touched. She smelled like a potpourri of baby powder, perfume, cigarettes, and hairspray.

When the receiving line thinned down to a few friends of the king, the faceless voice of the announcer summoned the king and queen for the final royal dance. Soon the pageantry part of the evening ended. It was time to peel off the layers of scratchy tulle slips, my dress, collar, and mantle to enjoy an evening of carousing.

I don't remember leaving the auditorium that night. Somehow my date, a high school friend, managed to put me to bed. I woke up with cottonmouth, my head throbbing, my formal twisted and wrinkled around me. Memories of my big night laid waste, regrettably, to an overabundance of alcohol.

A few weeks later I went downtown to see the Mardi Gras parade. The City of Lafayette queen waved her scepter at the crowds of people filling the sidewalks and doorways. Children sat on their parents' shoulders, begging the masked float riders to "Throw me something, Mister!"

I watched the queen soak up the excitement of all the hoopla and relived my own.

Throughout the year I modeled my dress for various conventions and balls, surprised and relieved each time my gown zipped. The culmination of my reign was the Washington Mardi Gras ball where I spent a week touring the nation's capital with thirty other queens from all over Louisiana. Miss Fig Festival queen, one of the prettiest of the southern girls, also turned out to be the funniest. We sat beside each other on tour buses and at luncheons exchanging tales of our experiences as queen. Together we poked fun at a girl chosen as The Queen of the queens, an old-New-Orleans-money goddess, for her air of superiority and for puffing out her bosom whenever a man walked within thirty yards of her. We agreed that poor Miss Gumbo Festival queen had the ugliest crown of all. Huge ruby rhinestones spelled out GUMBO on her head. The first runner-up in our game of ridicule went to Miss Shrimp and Petroleum Festival. Her crown was shaped like an oil derrick. Niceties gushed out of her mouth like the river of taupe rhinestones cascading from the top of her crown.

Why were we so spiteful? What prompts two girls, pretty in their own right, to be so mean? So critical of girls whose main faults were that they were too nice or too rich? Envy? Insecurity? Shame? Desire? But for what?

39 ~ Louisiana, 1993

My visit wasn't turning out to be quite the escape from Kyle I had looked forward to. I realized I was just in another kind of prison. At breakfast time I found Momma in the kitchen, standing over the sink, hastily blowing out her cigarette smoke as a coughing fit seized her. Red-faced and watery-eyed, she panted to catch her breath. Holding Austin aside, I leaned in to kiss her cheek good morning.

"You're quite the popular one today. Nanette's called twice already and Anne and Claire once." Is that a hint of contempt in her voice? I hoped one of my sisters was calling with a dinner invitation. "I'm going to get a glass of milk and then take a bath."

"Would you like me to watch the baby while you bathe?"

"Oh, no thanks. I'll just set him in his car seat next to the tub like I always do. I like his company." There was no way in hell I would leave her alone with Austin.

I called Anne and pounced on her dinner invitation, saying I'd love to see their new house. They had invited Momma as well, but she refused.

From the curb I spotted Anne's short police officer haircut, her thin frame bent over a half-planted flowerbed, and I honked the horn as I parked. She waved, went into the house, and emerged with Kay.

After greeting me, Anne knelt by the baby carrier I'd put on the sidewalk and tickled Austin's neck.

Kay peered over her shoulders, smiling. She nudged my sister. "What I'd give to see you pregnant." Anne rolled her eyes and ushered us inside.

Once inside the foyer, I immediately spied many of our family antiques in their dining and living rooms. One of the downsides to living in California was not being around when Momma gave away furniture. She'd apparently been doing a lot of this since my father's death.

"See the pretty Christmas tree," I said to Austin as I unfastened the straps.

We stood in their living room and admired the chubby Monterey pine flocked in fake white snow with its tallest branch scraping against the ceiling. "Looks like you two have quite a task ahead of yourselves." I nodded to the stack of boxes labeled "Christmas decorations."

Anne laughed. "That's Kay's department. I climb the ladder and she directs."

We toured the rest of the house admiring Kay's knack for decorating. It was strange to think of Anne in such surroundings—lace doilies on every table, knickknacks in every corner, embroidered pillows on all the chairs and sofas, and lacey curtains throughout the house.

"Wait till you see the backyard," Anne boasted. "This is my domain." She pointed to the lush green lawn and the sparkling swimming pool. We stepped onto the patio.

"Looks like you have your own private paradise." I started to lean against a nearby table and then stepped back.

"What's Daddy's marble table doing here?" I looked down to a lion cast in black iron.

"Momma said I could have it after Daddy died. Someone's coming next week to give me an estimate for refinishing it." She smiled and ran her fingers across one of the stained panels.

"Really?" I felt myself becoming anxious. "Momma promised me that table."

"That's odd. She never mentioned it had been promised to you." She glanced at Kay and remarked offhandedly, "Well, I'll keep it for the first ten years, and then you can have it for the next ten. We'll take turns."

"Sure," I mumbled, thinking, Yeah, right. Just smile like it's no big deal. I shifted Austin and walked toward the garden. First thing tomorrow I'd talk to Momma. I wanted something of my father's besides his Sony stereo and his paint brushes.

Pretending to admire the statues and the fountain left by previous owners, I hid my anger behind that "just make nice" ol' southern way.

Inside, Anne and I sat on opposite antique settees while Kay basted the chicken. The unsettled business had inserted a wedge into the evening, despite our best attempts to pretend otherwise.

"So how's it going staying at Momma's house?" Anne asked, holding Austin in her lap and teasing him with a rattle.

"It's okay. She flipped out last night because the cats got into my room. She pulled Prissy out from under the bed, scratching and hissing."

"Your mother or the cat?" Kay asked, entering the room with two glasses of water.

"Shame on you, hon," Anne said, trying not to laugh.

"Do y'all go over there much?" I asked, watching Kay slide in beside Anne.

"No, not since we bought this house and I put both our names on the deed. I guess you heard she was going to lend me the money, but only on the condition that I left Kay's name off the title. I told her, 'No thanks' and we took out a bank loan instead."

I shook my head, saying I hadn't known. Momma and I never talked about anything significant.

"It really hurt my feelings." Anne shifted Austin in her lap.

Lighting a cigarette, Kay added, "Your mother was probably insulted that Anne picked me over her."

"That really wasn't my intention. I just worried if something were to happen to me, Momma would sell our house and everything else, just as she did when the others died. And then she'd have thrown Kay out into the street like a stray. I want Kay to know she'll always have a home."

Kay's eyes filled with tears. She whispered, "Thank you, sweetheart," squeezing Anne's arm.

It turned my stomach a little to see Anne and her girlfriend get mushy. Was it envy? My sister loved and trusted this woman so much that she was willing to share everything she had. No prenuptial agreement like the one I had had Kyle sign.

"You know what? This is going to sound ridiculous, because I'm a grown woman, but it scares the crap out of me to be in the house alone with her. I know I must be paranoid, but I'm so afraid she's going to come after me like she did when we were kids."

My sister and her girlfriend sat silent for a moment. I watched their wordless exchange, wondering what it meant.

"Come on, what's up? What are those looks about?"

"It's probably nothing, really, but you know that Dalmation puppy that Penny and Patrick bought for Momma?" Anne paused for a moment, glancing again at Kay.

"Yeah, what?"

"Momma told everyone the vet said Blacky was inbred and that he went crazy on her, so they had to put him to sleep. But when Kay and I were staying with her, Kay was about to go into the kitchen one night when she heard Momma cussing at the dog because he evidently peed on the floor. Kay peeked in from the foyer door and saw Momma corner the puppy near the telephone. She trapped him and started kicking him. Kicking him in the stomach and legs, one hard kick after another. Then she stepped on his stomach, pinned him down while he yelped and told him he was a goddamn mutt, that she wished he would die." Anne's shoulders began trembling. I felt my legs shaking. "Kay said she just kept kicking him in the head, over and over, looking like she was enjoying it."

"Holy fuck. Did she kill him right there?"

"No, but she must have kicked him around so much that she finally scrambled his brains. He could barely function—he crapped all over the place and whimpered for days."

"It wasn't a one-shot deal, either," Kay added. "I saw her do it two other times after she got drunk and thought no one was looking. One night I was coming down the stairs and I heard her in the kitchen. So I sneaked over to the door and saw that she had him corned by the stove. Just as she lifted her leg to kick him, I called out, 'Hey, Miss Esther, is Blacky sick again tonight?' I tell you she nearly fell on her butt she turned around so fast. Talk about the ugliest look I ever got. She just sneered and stumbled out of the kitchen. But she knew I caught her. She knows I know what really happened."

"Do you remember the night before Chess died how she yelled to him that she wished he were dead?" Anne shook her head. She always slept through the fights and spankings. "She seems to always get her wish, doesn't she?"

The three of us sat for a moment, only Austin babbled unaware. I asked myself, over and over, what could have happened in my mother's life, her childhood, that turned her into such a sadistic monster? What desecrated her humanity? I could just imagine the dog's terror. I didn't blame my sister or Kay for not saving the puppy. Only occasionally did Nanette or Chess try to help one of Momma's victims.

"God, do you think she's gonna hurt Austin and me? I know I'm acting like a baby, but..." I broke into sobs.

"You're not a baby." Anne handed Austin to Kay to join me on the other settee. Throwing her arms around me, she said, "You're more than welcome to stay here with us. It might just look a little weird if you up and move out on her. I'm not sure you want to piss her off. But you've got Austin to protect."

I sniffled and nodded. "Why can't I just stand up to her? It feels like I'm four years old again. I know she's older and out of shape, but she's got the strength of a fucking bear when she's drunk. I freeze when she gets that mean look on her face and her voice goes all hard and hateful."

"You don't have to explain it to me," Anne said. "All I can tell you is to keep your door locked."

40 ~ Louisiana, 1983

Between parading around as a queen and attending college full-time, I was promoted to head bartender at the private club and then demoted back to waitress. The official explanation: I seemed to be having difficulty juggling work, school, and my social life. The real reason: I was getting drunk too often behind the bar, alienating coworkers by my choice of friends, and showing up late for work. In a bitter argument with the manager over playing favorites, I quit the club. Lucky for me one of the women at Daddy's wholesale business (a woman he complained wore pants so tight he could make out all her privates) was pregnant. My father gave her a bonus to leave early. Mr. Delahoussaye, the controller, took me under his wing into his bookkeeping department. He became my mentor. I tried hard to please him by learning quickly and performing well.

Working with Penny compounded an already difficult living arrangement. Mornings, whenever she found me idly soaking in the tub, she'd start yelling for me to get out. Cornered in the bathtub, I'd try to explain that it was unreasonable for her to expect me to hop out the moment she returned from her jog, whatever time that happened to be. But I always gave in because I was scared of her. She ate my food, smoked my cigarettes, and drank my beer but hoarded expensive wine upstairs in her closet. Though her clothes were strictly off-limits, she viewed my wardrobe as an extension of her own. And worst of all, she was not just a slutty drunk, flaunting her tiny figure and enhanced bust in front of my dates: she was a vicious, nasty drunk. And inconsiderate! Once I came home to find she'd lent my bed to one of her married girl friends so that this woman could have sex on my new satin sheets with a guy she picked up at a bar. Yuck. The roommate situation was not working out the way my parents had hoped.

After my complaints appeared to go unheard, once again I threatened to move away—Houston, Dallas, anywhere but Lafayette, anyplace but Karen Drive with Penny. In a panic Daddy bought another townhouse ten doors down. And Nanette and Boyce, her Air Force husband, grabbed a carrot Daddy dangled in front of them—their very own New Orleans-style townhouse and a huge salary for Boyce at the wholesale if he quit the Air Force and moved back to Louisiana. It was a much gentler way of handing over the baton, the family business, than how his father had done it—telling Chester Junior that he either quit the Army and return to pharmacy school or that he and Momma (struggling new parents) were on their own, forever. We girls were ticked off that Daddy chose Boyce, with no business experience, to take over the family business. Had I planned on sticking around after earning my bachelor's, I would have argued with his reasoning: Nickey was too unstable with all his drinking and carrying-on, eighteen at the time, and we girls couldn't run a $30 million business.

It was lucky for Daddy that he had enough money to buy his way, and our way, out of trouble. He tried to keep his children closer to home, with the scribbling of a check. Trouble is, though, sometimes you just don't learn how to really grow up unless you're allowed to feel a few bumps and bruises.

Soon Penny moved her stash of wine a few doors away to her own townhouse. My best friend, Candice, and I threw a party to celebrate Penny's departure.

Mr. Delahoussaye, a gentle, silver-haired Cajun with worn-down teeth, had begun working for Daddy two days after I was born. He told me how Daddy had brought me into the office to show off his brand-new baby girl. Mr. Delahoussaye was full of stories. He saw the positive side to every situation. Whenever I entered his office on the verge of tears, he'd motion for me to close the door, and then he sat quietly while I cried or explained my predicament. He never threw back that conservative, old-fashioned bull I got from Daddy. He always talked proudly about his own children, even if recounting a divorce.

Mr. Delahoussaye showed me how to use the ten-key so I could add the invoices faster. Even when I was second fastest in the office, I kept working on speed. After I keypunched invoices and tallied them, Yvette checked them over. That was the part I hated. She was always pretty nice if I was having a good keypunching day. But if the salesmen or I made a lot of errors either keying them in or coding them, she lost it, yelling and screaming. Sometimes she ran shrieking through the warehouse, and even outside, with Mr. Delahoussaye chasing after her trying to calm her down. Chasing Yvette down the block or into the street, letting her throw her tantrum, even beat on his chest in fury was part of Mr. Delahoussaye's job as he saw it. With his calming voice, he'd tell her to settle down, assure her that everything was going to be fine. In the two months since I'd arrived, she'd already had two such outbursts.

One of the girls in the surgical division told me how it worked: when the time between Yvette's outbursts got shorter, it meant she was getting close to a total meltdown. Then she'd be out of the office for a week or two. A paid vacation of sorts. My family's craziness didn't quit in our homes. It just followed us to work each day.

It was month-end, heavy keypunching time. I finished two thick stacks of invoices and walked them over to Yvette.

"Hey, how's it going?" I asked, standing at the door to her tiny office, a small box on the perimeter of the dark warehouse.

Puffing away on a cigarette, she sat at her desk, surrounded by a mess of paperwork. "Okay," she said, blinking rapidly.

"Well, great. Here's a couple of stacks for you."

She took them from me, staring back at my smiling face. I always tried to be friendly but quick with her. She made me so nervous. Like skateboarding next to an active volcano.

"Guess you haven't heard, have you?" she asked, lighting a new cigarette off the other one.

"Heard what?"

"About Nickey."

"No, what?" I felt a surge of fear.

"He got drunk last night and shot up the house. Nearly killed Momma and Daddy. Lucky he was so wasted he couldn't aim worth a damn."

"You're joking?" I knew by her frown that she wasn't.

"He's in jail until Daddy can have him transferred back to the chemical dependency hospital. Don't know why he did it. Momma says he wanted Daddy to buy him an automatic rifle. Daddy wouldn't. Maybe he was angry about that."

"Well, hell, it's a good thing Daddy finally said no to that spoiled brat."

Yvette cocked her head as if to say, Who are you to talk?

A week into Nickey's six-week rehab program, Nanette arrived from California. Boyce sent her on ahead to get their new townhouse ready.

Nanette and I sat on the sidewalk in front of Baskin Robbins, eating butter pecan ice cream cones. "So what exactly happened between you and Candice?" Nanette asked, referring to my fall-out with my friend.

"We both started going out with these guys from New Iberia—"

"The guys y'all went to New Orleans with."

"Yeah. Anyway, I heard from a mutual friend that Candice was making fun of me behind my back. Plus now that she's landed that rich guy, Dicky, she doesn't need me anymore."

"Well, that's crummy." Nanette smashed a mosquito on her thigh. The blood reminded me of my last date with Boo, a guy Candice and Dicky had set me up with. Boo got rip-roaring drunk, as always, and slipped on one of Candice's fancy Persian rugs. He fell against an armoire and split open his eyebrow. Dicky took him to the emergency room. But even that hadn't stopped him.

I woke in the middle of the night feeling my legs being nudged apart, and I closed my eyes, wanting him to hurry up. Then I felt something wet and warm hit my neck. I opened my eyes to see drops of blood leaking from his bandage.

"Stop! You're bleeding. Get off me."

He chuckled and pumped harder.

"Boo, please, it's not funny!" I whined, turning my head from the droplets.

He ignored me and continued until he finished, rolled off, and passed out. I lay there, speckled with blood, crying. The next morning, when I showed Candice and Dicky the blood spots all over my nightgown and face, they thought it was hilarious. Candice was more concerned about her stained sheets and headboard than how creepy it must have felt to have some horny guy bleeding all over me.

I shook the image from my head. "So, are you excited to see Boyce tomorrow?"

"Sure am! Hey, look over there." She pointed to the Winn Dixie parking lot across the street. We watched a security officer, sitting in his car, drag a stranded shopping cart from the middle of the lot over to the front of the store. One after another he pulled up next to a cart, grabbed hold of the handle, and slowly drove them to the corral.

"Must be a busy night for him." We watched the man while we finished our cones. I thought how nice it would be if I could tell Nanette the whole truth about Candice and me. How hurt I felt when she and Dicky told other friends that Boo claimed I always faked orgasms. I never had orgasms with Boo. I was probably moaning with pain, pain after hours of his screwing me again and again. Screwing me until I swelled so much down there that the next day I couldn't even wear jeans.

"Are you okay?" Nanette asked.

"Yeah, why?"

"Oh, your face had a really sour look for a minute there."

"I'm fine. I was thinking about Nickey. You ready?" I felt too ashamed to tell her what a slut I felt like for letting Boo treat me that way. Ashamed for picking guys like Boo in the first place. Popular, macho, good ol' southern boys who dumped you if you dared complain or bucked their way of doing things. Plus, I didn't want to get the lecture that it wouldn't kill me for once to actually date a boring, *nice* guy.

As we walked to my new Honda, I heard the shopping carts clanging together across the street. An odd memory flashed in my mind. "Remember how you found your pet hamster dead and you tried giving it mouth-to-mouth resuscitation?"

Nanette laughed. "You and Claire gave me the hardest time about that. But boy, I loved that hamster."

"You think Nickey feels like he's in a cage? No way to escape. This is the third hospital in less than two years."

Nanette's shoulders drooped. Was she remembering how cruel we'd been to him? Teasing him. Excluding him. Making him do perverted things? No wonder, I thought, he's so screwed up when you throw us into the equation with Momma and Daddy.

The next day I was keypunching invoices when Daddy whispered that he'd like to see me in his office. I followed him, wondering what I had done wrong.

"Close the door, Sweetheart," he said gravely. "Boyce called your sister this morning and told her he's not coming. He wants a divorce and isn't going to work for the business. Just like that," Daddy said, his chin quivering. "That son-of-a-bitch did that, to your sister, to your mother, to me. She's devastated."

"God! Why?"

"Just said he wasn't happy and couldn't live like they had anymore. What in the hell is that supposed to mean? He's married, he's got a responsibility to her. Not happy? Well, happy or not, who gives a damn?" Daddy pounded his fist on the desk, toppling three of his plaques.

"I'm sorry. I know you must be disappointed."

He nodded. "Your sister is really upset. She's at the house now, crying. I thought after work maybe you could see if you can help her."

I looked at my watch after every invoice I keypunched, made twenty trips to the bathroom just to kill time, and finally five o'clock struck. When I got to the house, Momma, who was cooking in the kitchen, pointed upstairs.

I tapped on her old bedroom door. "Nanette, can I come in?" There was no answer. I went in anyway. "I'm so sorry," I said, crossing to the bed. She rolled over and I pulled her into my arms. Her whole body shook as we both cried. "Have you spoken to him again?"

"Yeah. I told him we should just forget the whole deal with moving here, that I'd fly back, and we'd just pretend that none of this happened. But he said no, he doesn't want to be married to me anymore. He won't even give it another try. He won't even talk about it. What is so awful about me that he can't even stay married to me? Has to trick me into moving back here just so he can dump me? God, am I that horrible a person?"

"No, Nanette, he's the horrible person. How could he just drop a bomb like this over the phone? How could he just throw five years of marriage away without a decent explanation? It's not fair. You don't deserve this. God, I love you so much."

"Can I join y'all?" Claire was at the door. Nanette nodded and Claire hopped onto the bed with us. "You poor thing. Momma told me what happened." The three of us huddled together, sobbing. I wished that Boyce would die.

"Daddy's so mad and hurt," Nanette said, grabbing a Kleenex. "He even called Boyce back and cussed him out. Told him he was a spineless bastard and that he should get his ass back here and tell us all in person. That if he were here right now, he'd smash his face in."

"What's Boyce planning on doing?" Claire asked, rubbing Nanette's arm.

"He says he's going to stay in the Air Force. See if he can transfer to Germany. I would go to Germany in a second, but he doesn't want me to."

A week later Boyce finally showed up. He cried when he saw Momma and Daddy and Nanette and begged them not to hate him, to understand that he just didn't see any other way, apologizing over and over for being such a despicable man.

Eventually Nanette moved into the new house she'd been planning to share with Boyce. Claire became her roommate. For Momma, it was the blow that sent her over the edge. Nickey's drinking and drug problems, her sweet daughter dumped like day-old garbage, her husband's chronic drinking despite his diabetes, her other daughters' constant problems, and all her daily struggles. It was more than she could stand. She started drinking again, just figured no one was looking. She thought no one noticed her slurred speech, the smell of booze on her breath, or sensed her annoyance if you stayed in the kitchen while she cooked, keeping her from her cocktail. She fell face first off the wagon. Hit the pavement and said the hell with trying to get back on. To hell with being a better person, to hell with all the pain, and to hell with feeling anything at all. I think she simply said to herself, I'm going to get drunk and stay drunk. Soon she drank openly, her cold eyes daring anyone to cross her.

Nickey remained at the CDU facility with all his new friends, playing cards, smoking cigarettes, watching movies, and drinking Cokes. And like vultures circling overhead, waiting for the wounded animal to succumb, the Duhons and the Jouberts returned to my parents' house, swooping down and devouring the flesh of Momma's lost resolve. Every afternoon they arrived for happy hour, picking up exactly where they had left off years earlier, drinking and commiserating with Momma and Daddy in their self-pity and anger. And Momma's thin, frail body swelled once again from the good life she and Daddy and their friends poured into themselves. One by one all her plants shriveled and died. And she quit her charity work.

As Nanette coped with her big changes, we spent a lot of time together. Daddy hired her to work in the warehouse running the call desk. After work we often played racquetball or cooked dinner or on weekends went camping or sewed together. At work we were always running into the warehouse laughing hysterically at a shared joke as the stockboys pretended to ignore us. We laughed so hard we'd have to cross our legs so we wouldn't pee in our pants. Penny was a great source of amusement. She constantly scolded us for infractions like taking too long a break. We were to set a good example for the other workers, a rule that didn't apply to her and her two-hour lunches.

Nanette and I spent a lot of time eating ice cream, sharing our dreams, exchanging stories. She always seemed so amazed that I wanted to spend time with her because she claimed to be such a fuddy-duddy compared to my wild friends. But I liked a change of pace. The others were too intense. With her I could be myself. Or the most myself anyone ever saw.

Just before Nickey's last week in the hospital, Daddy called Yvette, Penny, Nanette, and me into his office. "Girls, the doctors think it would be very helpful for Nickey if the whole family attends a week-long therapy session. They say it's important for your brother."

"That's a wonderful idea," Yvette blurted out. "We could really use some family therapy. Plus Nickey will need all our support to deal with his alcoholism and drug addiction."

Penny rolled her eyes. She didn't waste civility on Yvette and that AA *crap* she peddled. "Well, I can't possibly attend. I'm too busy here. Everyone at the office is going to be pissed off if we all decide to take the entire week off."

Daddy shrugged and looked at Nanette and me. "How about you two?"

"Sure," we both said. Anything for a paid week off.

41 ~ Louisiana, 1993

The image of Momma stomping on the puppy's stomach and head stayed in my mind as I drove home from Anne's. I shuddered at the pleasure she must have gotten from torturing the poor dog.

The thought of going back to her place, lying in my bedroom, and waiting for my turn was too frightening. Instead of turning off on Brentwood or Doucet or even St. College, any of the streets that would have taken me to her house, I kept driving until I was parked in front of Nanette's house.

"Hey, Marie," Sam greeted me at the front door. I could see his boys in their underwear bouncing on the sofa.

"Is Nanette here?" I bit my lip to avoid bawling right there on the step.

"Sure, she's sewing in our room. Go on back. Can I watch Austin for you?"

I nodded and handed my brother-in-law the carrier. Chris and Jack screamed, "Yeah, we get to play with Austin? Watch this, Aunt Marie…"

Ignoring my nephews, I walked quickly past the table full of dirty dinner plates into my sister's bedroom. Nanette heard the door open and turned around with a scowl on her face, ready to plead for just a few more minutes.

"What's wrong?" she asked, turning from her sewing machine. She shoved aside a pile of laundry and patted the bedspread. I plopped down beside her. The stories of Blacky's abuse, the cat rampage the previous night, and Momma and Penny's horrible visit to Walnut Creek all tumbled out between sobs. By the time I was finished, we were both shaking.

"I think I'll call Kyle tomorrow and tell him I'm coming home. To not bother flying out."

Nanette shook her head. "No, you can't leave. Just stay here."

"There's not enough room here for all of us." Her house was a pigsty. Kyle would flip out.

"How about if the boys and I come over to spend a couple nights with you at Momma's? We could pretend it was the kids' idea. Surely between the two of us we can take her down if she gets out of hand," Nanette teased, pounding a clenched fist into the palm of her other hand. "Come on, stay until after Christmas at least. Please. I've been so looking forward to spending time with you."

"Will Sam mind if y'all are gone for a couple of nights?"

She rolled her eyes. "Yeah right. It'd just kill him to have the house all to himself to watch television and drink beer."

I looked at Nanette and sighed. "Remember in the old house when Momma and Daddy would start fighting. Sometimes Claire and I would sneak out of The Darkroom to climb into bed with you. The three of us in your tiny twin bed…tickling each other with those goose feathers."

In my mind I could see the three of us, our legs intertwined, plucking feathers from the paisley comforter, tickling each other's necks until we fell asleep. It was the bond with Nanette and Claire, I'm certain, that first assured me that life indeed held hope.

Nanette hugged me, saying, "I love you."

"I love you, too."

When I rolled into Momma's driveway late that evening, the house was dark. Only the carport lights awaited my arrival. I saw no sign of her as I crept into the house.

Several times during the night I awoke to the sounds of Momma coughing and retching in her bathroom. It got so bad that once I considered tiptoeing into her room to check on her. The image of her crouched over a toilet didn't pose much of a threat. Besides, surely I could outrun her. But the moment I started to slide from bed, I heard the toilet flush. I told myself that she was all right.

The next morning Momma's eyelids hung heavy, and she walked slowly. Twice she hurried to the bathroom, and I heard her hacking and retching as her bowels emptied violently into the toilet.

The second time she staggered out of the bathroom, I asked if she'd like me to heat some soup for her. She shook her head, saying she couldn't keep anything down. She took a large bottle of Tylenol from the pantry and struggled with the safety cap until I offered to open it.

"How many would you like?"

She whispered, "Two." I handed her the caplets and watched her shaky hands deliver the medicine to her mouth. She looked like ninety instead of sixty-four. How could I possibly fear this person who is so frail?

"Darling, would you mind taking me to my hair appointment at ten? I don't think I can drive myself."

When we returned home, Momma went straight to bed, exhausted from having her hair trimmed and curled. I decided to call Anne to let her know how I really felt about Daddy's marble table.

My sister said she was sorry but added that she also really wanted the table. We hung up, and I went into my room, crying. Minutes later the phone rang.

"Marie."

"Yes?"

"You can have the table. Just arrange for someone to come and pick it up."

"Are you sure?"

"Yes. I don't want a stupid table to come between us. All right?"

"Thank you."

Anne hung up and I wiped my nose on my sleeve. I knew I could have been the bigger person and told her to keep the old table. But I really wanted it. And besides, she had gotten Daddy's pool table and his last boat. We were a family that kept tabs on what each other got. Because despite knowing that we were more fortunate than many, we were all hungry and wanted *more*, as if another table or car would fill our voids.

Claire invited me to join her and her son, Tommy, to go out for boiled crawfish. I hesitated for a moment, remembering my sister's impatience in restaurants with young children, especially babies, but I told myself that maybe this time she wouldn't be so uptight. "Maybe this time" equals huge mistake, always! If it weren't for a chronic case of refusing to admit the truth, I would have known that by then. We headed to the Boiling Point off Highway 90 at five o'clock to avoid waiting an hour for a table and finding the steaming red critters sold out. Within ten minutes of sitting down in the half-full restaurant with one hyper toddler and a squealing baby, I realized that once again I had ignored my instincts, had done something I knew was foolish, and would now suffer the consequences.

Every time Austin made a peep, Claire looked right then left to see if anyone was staring at us. She constantly shushed Tommy, telling him he was disturbing the other families with his loud voice. I tried assuring her that no one could hear us over the jukebox and the noise from the large group of scruffy oil-field guys. But Claire kept tapping her fingers on the table, mumbling, "Where's that darn waitress…I wish she'd bring our food…Do you think I should go ask the manager?" When the platters of steaming crawfish finally arrived, it was all business—pinch, break, peel, dip, and pop those tiny morsels into her mouth, breaking her motion only to say, "Tommy, hurry up and eat your fried shrimp."

Driving home, my neck muscles ached. I didn't bother telling Claire about Momma and the dog, I just wanted to say good night to her, put the baby to bed, and wait in my room for Nanette and her boys to return from the symphony.

When I turned into Momma's driveway, I saw Penny's car. "Looks like Penny is back from New Orleans. Are y'all coming in?" I asked, hoping she'd say no.

Tommy screamed, "Please, Mommy." He adored Aunt Penny.

The back door was locked so I tried my key. The door opened only an inch; the chain had been latched. "That's odd." I rang the bell.

We stood outside shivering in the cold.

After a couple of minutes, Claire pushed the button again. Still no one came. "This is ridiculous," she said, and pulled out her cell phone. She dialed twice, no answer.

My heart started racing. What if Momma's flu was worse?

After one more try, Claire finally reached Momma. Soon my mother and her happy-hour sidekicks stood at the door. "Hey, Claire, hey, Ma-ree," Penny said gaily, "You remember Patrick, don't you?"

We shook hands, and he greeted Claire and Tommy. Just as I was about to ask what had taken them so long, Penny announced they were going to a Christmas party and she'd see us on Christmas Eve.

"Be sure to call if you need anything," Penny told Momma, giving her a hug and a kiss good-bye. "And try to get some rest." Then she tugged on Patrick's sweater and told him to come on, they were already late. She couldn't have seemed more eager to leave.

Patrick's eyes rolled and he said, "Got to go, Miss Esther. The boss has spoken. See y'all later." He kissed Momma's cheek and waved good-bye.

As soon as they were out the gate, the cheerful look on Momma's face faded and she started coughing. "Well, darlings, I'm going to bed. I'm tired."

Even though my mother was a dog killer and an unsafe bet left alone with Austin, it still hurt to see how quickly her mood changed. That old "maybe this time" optimism—that for once, maybe she'd be as delighted to see us as she'd obviously been to see Penny—was just wishful thinking.

Claire and Tommy left soon after. Around ten I heard Nanette, Chris, and Jack. I threw my robe on and went to greet them. The boys looked handsome in their white turtleneck shirts and navy blue suits. Nanette carried in their bags as they told me all about the concert over snacks in the kitchen. I told Nanette how Momma had chained us out of the house earlier.

"That's weird. You think they were having a little *menage à trois?*" Her thinking was as warped as mine.

"What's a *menage à trois?*" Jack asked his mother as cookie crumbs spilled from his mouth.

"Nothing sweetie. Just a meeting."

"That's a disgusting thought," I whispered. "Whatever they were doing, Penny sure seemed eager to leave when we interrupted them."

When the children fell asleep, Nanette and I sat up talking.

"She sounds awful," Nanette said when we heard Momma coughing.

"Yeah, some nights she's up five or six times. Sometimes I worry that she's dying, with all that vomiting, diarrhea, and coughing."

"She hasn't called me about Daddy this week," Nanette whispered.

"Every time I try to ask how she's doing, she just says she's fine, that of course she misses Daddy, but she's fine. I hoped we'd have some good talks, but I get the feeling she just wants to be left alone."

Momma never left her bedroom again. Her coughing fits and upset stomach worsened until she had barely enough energy to make it to the toilet. She kept a tall glass of water, I thought, next to her bed. When I offered to refill it with fresh ice water, she shook her head violently and said, "Leave it alone. It's fine."

I figured she'd given up on the Diet Coke and was drinking her vodka straight now. Nanette and I offered to get her milk shakes and juice, but she refused, saying it just made her stomach feel worse. Aimee brought over homemade vegetable soup that sat untouched in the refrigerator. Twice I called Penny to tell her Momma appeared to be worse.

"Can you come over and talk to her?" I asked. "Maybe suggest she cut down on her smoking and drinking until she feels better."

"We're pretty busy right now at the store. I'm working double shifts up until Christmas Eve. But I'll try to stop by."

She didn't, though, not until Christmas Eve night.

In the meantime, Nanette called my parents' doctor, Dr. La Dousa, the man whose name appeared on thirty-plus vials of medicine scattered throughout the house. She asked him if he would come over to see Momma. He said no, that if she really needed a doctor, she'd have to go to his office, that he didn't have the proper equipment to make house calls. But Momma insisted it was just the flu and she'd be better soon. Finally, to get Nanette to quit calling him, Dr. La Dousa phoned in a prescription for some antibiotics. We had the prescription filled, but Momma took only a couple of the pills. After that, the amber vial sat undisturbed on her nightstand.

Kyle arrived Christmas Eve. He had no idea what he was in for. Neither did the rest of us.

42 ~ Louisiana, 1984

On Monday morning, I pulled into the lot of the chemical dependency hospital where Nickey was confined. We had so many secrets and
sensitive subjects that I couldn't imagine having an open dialog. Momma
and Daddy and all my sisters stood in the lobby. All except for Penny.
She'd decided at the last minute to fly to Arizona to a tennis camp,
despite her supposedly grueling work schedule.

Other families also waited, their glances shifting, their hands restless
and twisting, just like mine.

At 8:30, a pudgy, balding man came into the lobby and smiled at us.
He was Henry, Nickey's therapist. Daddy apologized for Penny's absence
without elaborating.

Henry's brow furrowed; an awkward silence followed. "Well, that's
unfortunate," he finally said, waving us to follow him into a meeting
room.

"I wonder when the first coffee break will be," Yvette said. Momma
gave her one of her shut-the-fuck-up looks. A few minutes later Henry
returned with Nickey trailing behind.

Nickey waved hello and plopped down in a chair like a large puppy. I
smiled at him and thought how handsome he was. His shiny, dark hair;
perfect olive skin; rascally, brown eyes; and full lips. Even though
scrawny, he was a girl magnet. There was a certain vulnerability about
him. I watched his hands. Jittery as usual, picking at a callus. He looked
around the room, cracking a smile, shifting his glance before anyone
could make eye contact. I felt so sorry for him. Here he was locked up
again, and his big sisters were staring at him.

"Where's Penny?" he asked, glancing at his doctor.

"She couldn't make it, son." Daddy didn't mention that she was prac-
ticing her backhand.

"Yeah, right," Nickey said. The smirk he had walked in with melted off his face, replaced with hurt.

Henry leaned against the door as if he thought we might try to escape. "All right, I want to just say a few words before we go into the next room to meet the other families." He went into a whole spiel about how we were there to help Nickey. That our presence offered hope and support for Nickey and for us. That we should feel safe and able to be completely honest about our feelings. That everything said this week was confidential. He ended his speech by saying how important it was that we were as clear-headed as possible, so drinking or drug usage either here or at home were prohibited for the entire week. We all agreed.

Henry escorted us to a larger room to join four other families. This room felt sterile and cold. Metal folding chairs formed a circle around a solitary chair set right in the middle. Henry took the middle chair. The other four families looked like ordinary people you'd find cheering at a baseball game. After all the introductions were made, he asked one of the detox kids to sit in the middle of the circle. Then he joined the rest of us on the perimeter.

A teenage girl took center stage. She looked everywhere but at her parents and brother.

"Okay, Caroline, tell us about your addictions," Henry said.

She combed her blond hair behind her ears and mumbled, "Alcohol, pot, coke, sex."

Sex? It hadn't occurred to me that sex could be an addiction. I watched the girl and tried to imagine myself in her place. A room full of family and strangers judging me, all given the go-ahead to say whatever they wanted about me.

Henry nodded and looked at the girl's mother. The woman seemed like the kind of mother who had hosted hundreds of Girl Scout meetings.

"Tell us what it's like living with Caroline."

She glanced at her husband, and he looked down. She described the scrapes and bruises on her daughter's body after she'd come home from a three-day binge with her friends. How she'd heard from another mother at Caroline's school that her daughter was swapping sex for drugs. Caroline chewed on her lip and traded smiles with Nickey.

Family therapy felt like a circus. The featured act: screwed-up children ranging in age from twelve to eighteen. Henry, the ringleader, led one child after another into the circle to be addressed first by their families and then by the entire audience. Anything was permitted. "What are you doing to yourself?" "Why are you so mad at us?" "Do you *really* want to die?" "When did this all start?" "Where's this going to end?" "How can I help you?" "What do you want from me?" "What's it like being in jail?" "Do you know how much we fear for your safety, our safety?" "Do you even *like* us?"

It was so strange to hear the other families' bizarre tales. You'd never run into these people at the A&P and think, 'Oh, yeah, she's the one with the daughter who's so addicted to sex that she offers her body to drug addicts, black men, white men, and women.' Or, 'he's got a son who'll snort anything, even the nutmeg from his mother's kitchen, just to get high.' No, these people all looked pretty normal. Just as we did, I guess, from a distance. Learning that we were not the only screwed-up family on the block liberated the shame from me.

When Nickey took the stage, his eyes jumped from face to face. I flashed him a reassuring smile.

"Okay, Nickey, you can begin," Henry said, pacing.

"I'm Nickey. I've been drinking and taking drugs since I was eleven." He paused, rubbing his right index finger, the stiff one that didn't bend because he'd cut to the bone once, playing with a hunting knife.

"Can you be a little more specific?" asked Henry.

Nickey cleared his throat, looked directly at his counselor, and mumbled, "I'm an alcoholic."

"All right. Mrs. Etienne, would you like to begin? Perhaps you could tell Nickey how his behavior has affected you personally and what you're hoping he will get out of this program." Momma nodded. Henry pulled up a chair to sit behind our family. Not being able to see him made me nervous.

"Well, it breaks my heart to see him so unhappy. But it's been somewhat of a relief having him in here, where I know he's safe and I don't have to lay awake all night wondering if he's coming home. I've spent so many nights listening for the phone, fearing the call that tells me he's been in an accident." Momma rubbed the tears as they trickled down her face. Daddy stared at Nickey, who was grinning.

"What's so funny, Nickey?" Henry asked impatiently.

"Nothing."

"Well, then why don't you wipe that smirk off your face, son?" Daddy said. Nickey looked away, toward the door. Was he wondering if he could make it through the door before his counselor tackled him?

"Okay, Nickey, I want you to look at your mother. Try to feel the pain she's sharing with us." He turned to her, but I could tell by the distance in his eyes that he'd already escaped through his own back door.

Momma continued. "I just don't know what your father and I have done so wrong that made you hate us so much. Can you tell me? What is it you need from us? Or want? I really do want to help you. What haven't we given you?"

Nickey opened his mouth to speak but Henry shook his head. The kids weren't allowed to talk yet, which seemed stupid to me because how were they going to remember everything they wanted to say?

When Momma finished, Henry thanked her and asked Yvette if she'd like to say something next.

Yvette nodded and began. "Well, as I see it, the crux of Nickey's problem is Momma's and Daddy's drinking. My parents," she said, turning around to Henry, "are alcoholics…"

Alcoholics! Holy shit! Momma and Daddy sat frozen in their seats, stone-faced. As Yvette went on, Nanette gave me a little nudge and I glanced at her. What if we really opened up here? Told what it was like living in their house? Would Momma and Daddy find a way to punish us? Take away our allowances, our townhouses? Beat the crap out of us?

Yvette's speech turned to the subject of her own struggles with alcohol and mental illness. How she was never really accepted by the family. Daddy began squirming in his seat as if someone were sticking needles in his ass. I wanted to shake Yvette and say, "Shut up. This isn't about you. Get back to Momma and Daddy."

We were supposed to be free to ask Nickey anything, to reveal anything about our family, or to address our parents and siblings on any matter. But it's no mystery why victims stand behind two-way mirrors when pointing out their attackers. Otherwise, the intimidation factor sets in. Nanette mentioned feeling guilty for picking on Nickey so much when he was little. Anne said she was angry that Nickey had turned on her when she started being with girls, that he and his friends tormented her, vandalizing her car and caking dog shit on her head while she slept. Claire said she was angry at the way he treated Momma and Daddy after they had given him so much, and I remained loyal to my parents. I said that even though things weren't perfect growing up, you just had to make up your mind to do whatever it takes to get on with life.

But no one mentioned the physical abuse, Momma's suicide attempts, Chess's death, the late-night fighting, the ridicule, the ugly name-calling, the threats from Momma, or the neglect we'd suffered. No one mentioned how Nickey had slept in the midst of the turmoil, in my parents' bedroom, until he was fifteen. God only knows what he saw and felt in there. How Momma had already begun beating him before the stump of his severed umbilical cord had dried up and fallen off. We tap danced around the big issues and when prodded by Henry or other families to be more specific, to say how we really felt or what we'd experienced, we offered sanitized and benign revelations. Any time we came close to divulging anything meaningful, the presence of Momma and Daddy, just a chair or two away, was too stifling. I'd deluded myself into believing that if we did this therapy, the skeletons would finally, painlessly dance around the room, show themselves, and be put to rest for good, ending decades of silence, denial, and hurt.

"We'll break for lunch now," Henry announced after we'd finished with Nickey.

Nickey bolted from the room. I stepped into the hall to wait for Nanette and Claire. A headache the size of Texas burrowed from one temple to the other. As families moved past me, I watched Nickey push and elbow Caroline. All the kids seemed so comfortable and playful together. They chain smoked, gulped colas, laughed. Nickey hadn't been that much at ease with us in years, if ever. Everything we said he construed as condescending or hurtful. I was envious of his friends because they probably knew my brother better than I ever had. I imagined them razzing Nickey, saying, "Well, your family's pretty fuckin' hopeless. Next…"

One of the other mothers stopped Momma in the hall to say something to her. Momma nodded, wiping away a tear as the woman stroked her hand, and offered words I couldn't make out. Daddy approached and asked, "Ready, Esther?" He probably wished he'd flown off to Arizona with Penny to bat a few balls around.

On Friday afternoon, it was the fathers' turns to sit in the middle of the circle with their children. Caroline's father sat upright, describing the terrible disappointment of seeing his bright daughter turn into trash, someone he didn't even want to touch. I could feel her shame as she stared at the scuffed floor.

Daddy and Nickey went next. They sat facing each other. At first Nickey couldn't even look at Daddy. Each time he tried, he laughed nervously and quickly turned away.

"Chester and Nickey, I want you to face each other and hold hands," Henry ordered.

Daddy's enormous hands held Nickey's firmly. Tethered together, could they feel each other's apprehension? Daddy shifted in his chair. He was uncomfortable being the center of attention. Henry nodded for my father to begin.

"Son, your mother and I have tried everything we could think of to help you. Perhaps we've given you too much. But your recent behavior is completely unacceptable. You shot up our house, Little Fellow. You pointed a gun at your mother and me. You could've killed us chasing us around, firing like a crazy person."

Stifling a smile, Nickey looked sideways at Caroline. She shook her head.

Daddy cleared his throat and shifted his knees. "Maybe this tough-love stuff they're promoting is the answer. Because you know what, son, I'm tired. I've raised nine children and I've worked hard. I don't have the energy for your pranks and foolishness anymore. I want to live in peace and quiet." His voice sounded angry and hard as he said how he didn't want Nickey and his friends carrying on drinking all night long under his roof, raiding his liquor cabinet, stealing from his mother's purse. He wanted respect, respect for his property, respect for Momma, and respect for himself. But most of all, he wanted to live in peace and quiet. That seemed his mantra these days.

A vein in Nickey's neck stood out, purple and angry. He tried to pull away, but Daddy tightened his grasp. Nickey glared at him and spat, "That's right. It's all about what you want. You want me to be seen, not heard. Well, what about what I need, huh?"

"Son, I don't know how to help you. No matter what I do, we end up back here. You need help, I see that now, but you've got to take some responsibility for your life. It's your mess, not mine. I'll help as much as I can, but you're wearing me down."

Was that how he and Momma viewed our lives: A mess too big now to be swept into a corner?

"I love you, Little Fellow, I sure don't want to lose another son, nor does your mother. It's killing us to watch you ruin your life like this." Daddy started crying and kept mumbling over and over, "I love you, son, I love you."

I looked around the circle. A couple of the other fathers folded their hands to their chests, their heads hung low, their shoulders shaking. One man rubbed his knees, looking off to the side. Most of the mothers sobbed, hugging themselves or holding hands with their children. The

whole time Daddy wept and squeezed Nickey's hands, Nickey kept looking away, his chin quivering. He struggled still, fighting off the tears that
he didn't dare share with us. When Henry nodded at Daddy that they
were done, Daddy stood up and paused. Before Nickey could pull away,
Daddy drew him into an embrace. They held each other tight, their bodies shaking, and Nickey finally buried his face in Daddy's suit jacket and
cried like he hadn't done since he was young. Nanette took my hand, and
I reached for Momma. All your could hear in the room were sobs and
sniffles.

On Saturday morning a graduation ceremony was held for the
patients and their families. Henry, looking older in his suit and tie, stood
at the podium, and addressed the crowded room.

"This part of the therapy is over, but it is far from over for these five
children. Look at these children, your children, your brothers and sisters.
If they don't continue their work and get the support they need from you,
I guarantee you, they will be dead within a year. I mean dead as in forever, because they are all on a collision course and they've been lucky to
have survived this far. When they get out of here next week, whether
they go to a halfway house or reenter your homes, I am entrusting them
to you. Help them."

Dead within a year, I repeated to myself. That can't be so. He's just
trying to scare the kids and families.

Over the next few days, while Nickey finished out his stint at the hospital, Momma and Daddy discussed his future. They wanted to send him
to a halfway house, but Nickey refused. He begged to come home, threatened to run away. But they didn't want him in their house anymore.

Conceding on the halfway house issue, Daddy found an apartment
near the USL campus. Nickey agreed to go to college after he got his high
school equivalency. Upon his release they handed him a set of keys to a
newly furnished apartment. Momma stocked his pantry and refrigerator
with supplies that ranged from Coca Cola to filet mignon. Daddy had the
Schwinn dealer drop off a bike. Everything their son needed, or so they
told themselves, they placed within his reach. "You'll be close to school,
you'll have you own place, and you can come visit us anytime you like,"
they assured him as they kissed him good-bye.

43 ~

The Jack Daniel's that filled Daddy's belly definitely started to pickle his brain. Every evening he told the same stories, verbatim. Sitting on the opposite sofa nibbling pistachios, I waited for him to apologize for his redundancy, but he never did. Sometimes I thought it was a game with him. Perhaps he wanted to see if I was listening. Perhaps he had a bet with Momma to see how many times I'd sit through, "You know darling, the business is changing. Mom and Pop stores are giving way to the deep discounters. It's getting tough…" Perhaps I was just paranoid. But it was sad to watch him go to seed that way.

Often during my visits, Nickey popped in for five minutes. He sat next to me, answered Daddy's how's-the-weather questions, got up, grabbed a Coke from the fridge, lit a cigarette, sat down again, fidgeted with his fingernails, stood, fidgeted with Daddy's owl collection, and on until it seemed as if he would explode. Instead he'd leave.

This restlessness unnerved my parents. They treated Nickey like an unwelcomed visitor. Every day he arrived with a glimmer of hope, but it quickly vanished. Hope then pain. Hope then pain. He was as delusional as I was that one day things might be different. Hadn't any of the three clinics he'd been to counseled Nickey not to have unreal expectations?

One Friday afternoon Nickey came by even more hyped-up than usual. He'd started dating a girl he was crazy about. Bouncing around the study, he cracked jokes, fussed with the ashtrays, and teased me about my new perm. Daddy cleared his throat and said in his I-mean-it voice, "Little Fellow, if you can't behave when you are at our house, I will have to ask you to leave. And you won't be invited to visit. Now either sit quietly or go. Your mother and I want some peace and quiet."

"See you later," Nickey mumbled, looking down at the worn green carpeting.

I followed him into the living room. "Hey, wait a minute," I called. "Don't let him upset you. He's just an asshole."

Flipping his long brown hair out of his eyes, he shrugged me off.

"What a *huge* loss it would be to be banned from this house," I teased, making him smile. "Gosh, we'd have to find some other lushes to visit just to amuse ourselves."

Nickey's eyes rolled, and he said, "Yeah, well, I've got to go." Not sure of how to talk to him, I always seemed to carry the sarcasm too far.

I touched his shoulder and he pulled away.

After he left, I went to visit Momma in the kitchen. She stood at the electric burners, with her allies: the last of the three snorting Pekingese (the other two had drowned in the swimming pool), a tall glass of vodka and Diet Coke, and a cigarette.

"Hi, what are you cooking?"

"Meatloaf. Want to stay for dinner?" she teased. She knew I couldn't stand ground beef and body parts in anything—hamburgers, meatloaf, rice dressing, goulash, whatever.

"Yeah, right. I'll see you Sunday afternoon after the Avery Island party, probably." I paused and she looked up.

"Wait a minute, I want to give you a little something." That was exactly what I'd been hoping she'd say. She ran her hands under the water for a minute and then dried them on the striped towel that hung above the sink. I watched her walk over to her purse, thinking, how does her body do it, going up and down, two hundred to one hundred, one hundred to two hundred in just a few years? She pulled two twenties from a thick wad of bills. "Here you are, sweetheart."

Momma always rewarded those who paid her a visit. It might be money, some piece of crystal or furniture she didn't want anymore, an offer to charge dinner or clothes on Daddy's account, or some other token. Did she believe that otherwise there wouldn't be any reason for us to visit?

Driving home I wondered what would happen if we walked into their house one day and it was stripped. Nothing but bare walls and empty cabinets and two lonely people who had run out of bribes for their children. Would Daddy finally get the peace and quiet he wanted?

I left my parent's house $40 richer but feeling depressed. Nothing a 32-ounce frozen margarita from the drive-through Daiquiri Factory and a weekend of water skiing, champagne, and cocaine couldn't obliterate.

Blaring Helen Reddy's "Greatest Hits," I drove out to Avery Island to meet Candice, Dicky, and their friends at the Moss House. Since Candice wasn't one to apologize, and, after all, it was I who cried and yelled during our last fight, I had finally called and invited her to lunch, pretending there'd been no lapse in our friendship. Soon we were best pals again.

The guard waved me through the gate. I continued past the Jungle Gardens until I reached the exquisite old house. All around, sprawling live oaks draped in swags of Spanish moss crowned the rolling hills. The Moss house, available to the families of the Island, reminded me of a finely appointed sorority house with its fourteen bedrooms and its huge dining room. Approaching the front steps, I heard Candice's favorite B-52s blasting through the walls. Shirtless and sunburned, Dicky answered the door.

"Hey, Ma-ree. There's a keg out back, and Candice's somewhere around here," he said, flashing his shit-eating grin.

I smiled, trying to slip past him before he mentioned his redhead sidekick. But he stopped me with a hard pinch on my rear-end, saying, "Better grab a room before you have to shack up with Boo for the weekend."

Candice appeared from around the corner decked out in denim with a strand of lapis beads about her neck. "Hi, sweetie! I thought I heard the door."

"Your pervert boyfriend just pinched my ass."

She punched his broad shoulder. "Dicky, you'd better keep your hands to yourself. You hear me?"

He laughed. We all knew no amount of scolding could reign him in. During the last party he donned one of Candice's skimpy see-through nighties and ran around, hooting and hollering like a wild man. Dicky was fun as long as you weren't the object of his amusement.

Lucky for me Boo was eyeing some blond bimbo and barely acknowledged me later when we ran into each other. He just grunted hello and continued past me. I waited in line to serve myself a plate of smothered quail and rice.

In the library, after dinner, I joined a conversation about the economy. Louisiana and other oil-dependent states were in the midst of a recession. The slumping oil industry threatened to take nearly everyone down with them. The big joke in town was: last one out, turn off the lights. I mentioned that my finance professor had thought the stock market would never exceed the 1300 mark because of the fear of the number thirteen. Triskaidekaphobia. I talked about the way the Dow had crossed the threshold and retreated. I suggested perhaps investors should look at companies such as Goodyear. If people couldn't buy new cars, maybe they'd put their money into fixing their old ones. And that was about as far as half a semester in banking and investments carried me.

For the rest of the weekend, whenever I wasn't swimming in the Island's Blue Hole or out chugging beer on water skis at Cypermort Point, I could hear Candice teasing and taunting me: *EF Hutton. When she talks, we listen. What's your latest stock tip? Ms. EF Hutton?* I should have just kept my mouth shut. It wasn't smart to hand people like Candice an arrow, pleading, Now don't use that on me. I might as well have had a bullseye tattooed on my forehead. By Sunday afternoon I was ready to go home, curl up with a six-pack and a blanket, and watch television for hours. Alone. My own version of peace and quiet.

The winter of 1985 brought celebration and change. Claire and her boyfriend, Ronnie, married. Nickey celebrated six months of sobriety. Aimee dumped her twelve-year-old son Michael and his pets at my parents' door to run off to Tennessee with some fat, hairy rough-neck. Nanette began dating Sam, a gem of a guy from New Iberia. And in December, Nanette and I both graduated from USL.

After five and a half years, I finally received a B.S. in Business Administration with a major in Finance. Best of all, though, Daddy presented me with a bankbook bearing my name on the cover. The balance read $23,591.00. He had accumulated the dividends from the stock I owned in the family business. Now I understood how Penny had bought herself a brand-new car when she finished college. Daddy swore the others to secrecy, Nanette confessed. My father didn't know it, but he'd just helped me realize my lifelong dream—to run away.

There was an old woman, and what do you think?
She lived upon nothing but victuals and drink:
Victuals and drink were the chief of her diet,
And yet this old woman could never keep quiet.
                                        —Mother Goose

44 ∼ Louisiana, 1993

I felt guilty we weren't doing more. Ashamed really. A part of me secretly wished she'd succeed. Hoped she'd die without much more fuss and that it wouldn't appear obvious to Kyle and the others that we should have intervened.

From the moment my visit began, I sensed what she was doing. But I didn't have the courage to say, "Stop treating me like a fool. If you're killing yourself by not eating, refusing to put anything into your body but vodka and cigarettes, at least have the decency to admit it." That was how Grandma had killed herself. She was in her eighties when she died, a respectable age, I figured, to say "To hell with living. I've had enough."

"Don't you want to tell us good-bye?" I longed to ask. "Won't you let us say all the sappy things you'd ordinarily shrug off?" But I was scared of her response and her anger.

Nanette, the only one of us with courage, finally asked Momma if she were indeed trying to kill herself. I watched as Momma laughed, limply shaking her head so the loose fat under her chin wiggled.

"No, sweetheart, it's just the flu," she droned. But when Nanette persisted, begging her to see a doctor, my mother's face tightened. Her hard eyes radiated a familiar warning. Withdrawing from her bedside, we both nodded obediently as she insisted, "It will pass, now let me rest."

By noon on Christmas all six of my sisters and their families had arrived as well as the Delahoussayes. Kyle and I rummaged through our suitcases, trying to find something to wrap for Aimee's children because she had unexpectedly presented us with a gift for Austin.

A chaotic energy swelled through the house. Nanette's rowdy boys buzzed about showing everyone their new Power Ranger watches, pestering the adults to verify the time. Yvette paced the brick floors, troubling the strands of Santa Fe beads that hung around her neck, worrying that Tony's catering had forgotten our Christmas dinner. It was the first holiday where all four burners and the two ovens sat cold and the cast-iron pots were hidden. The first time our Christmas stockings were not hung and bulging with boxes of perfume, panty hose, chocolates, and small white envelopes.

Momma looked like an apple doll—her taunt, ruddy plumpness now shriveling and softening. Her dark eyes drooped. My sisters and I reluctantly took turns going in her room to check on her.

"Y'all want to start opening gifts?" Anne asked in her crowd-controlling voice, trying to pretend it was Christmas as usual while Momma hacked away in the next room and Daddy's old leather recliner sat vacant.

"I guess," Yvette said. She winced as we heard another coughing fit.

"Should we, maybe, insist on calling her doctor?" Nanette asked.

Penny, leaning against the table, shrugged and whispered something to Claire that wasn't meant for the rest of us. I glanced at Kyle's blue eyes and was relieved I couldn't read his thoughts. Aimee and her two children sat rigid under Daddy's prized marlin. My timid sister delayed her vote to cast in with the majority. Nanette's eye settled on me, beseeching me, her closest sister, for support. I managed only a cowardly tilt of my head.

Anne set down her coffee mug and responded to Nanette's suggestion, "No, absolutely not. Momma doesn't want that."

Standing beside the antique desk, Sam turned up his hands and gave Nanette a consoling look. "You tried," his sympathetic smile said. The circles under Nanette's eyes seemed to darken, and I felt like a heel. I just wanted a peaceful Christmas; I didn't want to be pulled into an argument, especially not with Penny.

Everyone found an empty cushion or a spot on the floor, and we began handing out gifts. It was easy to identify Anne's presents. Kay had topped the Florentine wrapping with hand-tied gold ribbons. As Kyle and I amassed a pile of gifts, the doorbell rang. Our food had arrived; Yvette could stop worrying. Soon she'd be finished with her obligation to the family. She could depart before we upset her nerves with some offensive remark, perhaps some unchristian comment. Her only remaining concern, and admittedly mine as well, was whether Momma had remembered to write out our $400 Christmas checks, and if not, would she be able to do so.

The caterers began setting up the dinner with several large aluminum containers of stuffed turkey, oyster dressings, dirty rice, spicy eggplant and crab casserole, baked sweet potatoes, green bean casserole, pumpkin pie, mincemeat pie, pecan pie, and all the trimmings. The house instantly smelled like Christmas. It may not have felt like a holiday, but at least we had the food and gifts to prove it was.

Kyle handed me a large package, and the fine lines around his narrowed eyes deepened as he whispered, "This sure feels weird. Your mother sounds like she's dying in there."

"I know," I said. He hadn't yet learned to ignore those sharp splinters under the fingernail. "Here, just open your gift." I handed Kyle his first gift, a calendar I had made for him—a different picture of Austin or Austin and me for every month. I tore open my box and peeled back the tissue to find an oversized beige sweater. It wasn't hard to imagine him trudging into Nordstrom's and grabbing the first XL he found on sale. I slid the sweater back into the box and tucked my bitterness in with it. Mumbling thanks, I watched Kyle unwrap the calendar.

Cocking his blond head, he flipped through the pages without saying a word. "It's for your office," I said proudly.

He stared at the collage I'd pasted together for May. The theme was Mother's Day. I had cropped several pictures of me holding Austin, selecting photos that hid my slight double chin and ones where I'd remembered to remove my glasses that he hated.

"They're going to think I'm a little obsessed with my baby and my wife," he said, flipping back to January.

I looked at him and wanted to lash out, "Well, aren't you?" But I shrugged and swallowed my disappointment.

"Hey, Kyle, let me see," Nanette said, peering over his shoulder, her brown eyes intent on the photo of Austin sitting under a 'Happy New Year' banner. She pushed her dark curls behind her ears and said, "Let's take Momma's in to her." She knew I'd made her the same kind of calendar.

I stood up and grabbed the two gifts I had brought for Momma. Nanette followed me to her room where we found Mrs. Delahoussaye sitting beside her. Momma's two cats, Herman and Prissy, slept on Daddy's feather pillow that my mother had kept beside her. They awoke from their cat-dreams, yawning at the next round of intruders. Centered above the headboard, two inches from Momma's matted gray hair, hung a gold cross.

"I brought in your gifts," I said.

Momma smiled faintly. "Can you open them for me?" Her voice sounded as if she'd swallowed sandpaper.

I nodded and sat carefully on the edge of the bed. Nanette helped me rip off the ribbon and green paper. Holding the calendar up, I slowly began turning the pages. Her eyes blinked like traffic metering lights signaling me to go quickly: turn the page, turn the page, turn the page. On April I paused and anxiously watched her face distort as a coughing fit took hold of her. When she settled back against the headboard, I exchanged a frightened look with Nanette. Despite feeling ridiculous, I continued on with my presentation. To stop would have meant accepting defeat, so I flipped through the photographs hoping for one "Oh, that's a nice picture, darling."

"Thank you," she whispered at the end. Gathering my last shred of hope at pleasing her, I picked up the other, larger box and ripped off the paper. As I held up the crimson velour bathrobe, her pasty face suddenly tightened with pain. She cried out loudly enough to be heard, I was sure, in the den. The cats stirred again and meowed at her.

Momma gasped. "Marie, help me to the bathroom."

I tossed the robe aside, panicking in the unfamiliar role of assisting my mother. Nanette pulled away the covers while I grabbed Momma by her arm. Her limp body trembled as I eased her out of bed.

"Hurry up!" she fussed like a scared little girl.

"Okay, here we go," I said, recoiling slightly from her sour breath. I prayed she wouldn't have an accident in front of Mrs. Delahoussaye. I just needed to get through this stupid holiday without any screaming, I thought, slowing my steps to match hers. Leading her past the double vanity, I let go of her arm when she was standing next to the toilet.

"Wait, you've got to help me!" she cried, fumbling with her gown.

"Sorry." I slid my hands under her armpits and felt her sharp black stubble. Tucking the sheer fabric under her chin, she struggled to peel off her adult diaper. I feared we'd both topple so I spread my feet, waiting for further orders. She looked innocent and harmless in her toddler-like pull-ups. My feelings toward her softened as she tugged at the elastic material. When she finally managed to pull the diaper over her sagging belly, she plopped down on the toilet seat.

I started to leave to give her some privacy, and she whimpered, "Don't leave me. Stay here."

"Okay, Momma," I said, biting my lip. Two nights ago I thought she'd harm my baby and me. Now she appeared even less threatening than a preschool bully napping on a cot with his thumb stuck in his mouth. Clutching her gown to her breasts, she grunted. Her eyes squeezed shut, and she reached over to grab my arm. As her gown fell between her legs, I gathered the fabric and held it up to prevent it from falling into the bowl. Never before had I been so intimate with my mother. The roles had definitely reversed since I was a kid sitting on the toilet with my full-leg cast and Momma hovering nearby. She strained and coughed while I focused on the stained green carpeting. Her bowels produced nothing. Finally, she told me to take her back to bed.

"Momma, please can we call the doctor?" Nanette asked, sniffling. "I'm really scared. I don't want you to die. We just lost Daddy, and I don't want to lose you." Momma shook her head adamantly.

I hated myself for having wished she'd just die. It seemed now that I might just get my wish. Maybe this time she'd change. Maybe I'd be worse off if she were gone. Forever parentless, no grandparents to offer my son. I felt tears well up as I read the undeniable charge on Mrs. Delahoussaye's face: How can you girls do this to your own mother? Looking down in shame, I began crying.

Momma patted Nanette's hand and said, "Sweetheart, I just need a little rest. If I'm not better tomorrow, call Dr. La Dousa. Maybe you could fix me a plate later. Now y'all get out so I can sleep."

When we entered the living room, all three sobbing, we were met by a room full of terrified stares. Each daughter, I'm certain, silently weighing the options—obey Momma or behave like a courageous adult, either choice promising unpleasant consequences. Claire and Penny shoved their unopened boxes aside and left the room. The thin fabric of Claire's warm-up suit crinkled as her thighs swished together and her pigeon-toed feet hurried off to the bar. The gift exchange suddenly seemed inappropriate. The sound of paper ripping and kids squealing quickly faded. Anne checked on Momma and returned saying that she had ordered us to eat while the food was hot.

The Delahoussayes, followed by the grandchildren, carried their plates of food to the formal dining room and scattered about the table. I slid in between Kyle and the baby's highchair. No one had thought to create a centerpiece or even stick candles in the polished candelabra.

The sound of Momma's hacking cough resounded through the quiet and found its way into the dining room. The murmur of conversation paused. Yvette, now seated in Daddy's chair, far away from the youngest child, shook her head when Mr. Delahoussaye glanced her way. His eyebrows drifted up as he shrugged.

"I can't eat a thing," Claire said, entering the room with a glass of red wine.

I turned to see whom she was talking to and saw Penny nodding vigorously in agreement. She sighed, leaning against one of the china cabinets.

Nanette entered the room and cleared her throat. "I've called an ambulance for Momma," she announced. "They're on their way."

Penny's and Claire's mouths dropped open. But before they could speak, Anne stole the floor. "What?" she asked, setting down her fork midway into a bite. "Did you ask her first?"

"Of course not. She would have said no." Nanette's voice rose an octave and cracked. "But I'm not going to sit around and let her die in there." She started crying and Sam got up from the table to put his arm around his wife.

Anne shot Kay a private look and mumbled for everyone's benefit, "She's gonna be pissed. She didn't want to go to the hospital."

"I don't care," Nanette said.

Penny rolled her eyes at Claire, intimating that, as usual, she thought Nanette was a twit. Her red nails had ceased their tap dance on her wineglass. I looked at Nanette and smiled, wishing I had her courage.

Anne smashed her paper napkin into her food and headed out of the room.

When the doorbell rang, I whispered to Kyle, "Stay here with Austin," and followed Nanette and Claire to the front door. A young paramedic stood under the gas lamp in the warm, humid Louisiana sunshine (even the weather wasn't celebrating Christmas properly), sweating in his blue uniform as if it were July in Maui. Another man waited at the curb. I waved to the nosey neighbor standing on his sidewalk and prayed he wouldn't come over.

"M'am, did y'all call for an ambulance?"

"Yes, she's in bed. She doesn't know that we've called you, so we'll go in first," Nanette said. I followed and a few others came behind.

"Momma, I called an ambulance to take you to the hospital," Nanette said. "You're very sick and I'm worried about you."

Momma turned her head and scanned her daughters with heavy-lidded eyes. Looking back at Nanette, she whispered, "An ambulance, oh." There was no resistance, no anger.

Penny decided she should ride with Momma to the hospital and we should wait for a call. An hour later she called with the room number and said she was running home for a while but would meet us there later. Dr. La Dousa had examined Momma, and she was resting.

Leaving the children, the husbands, and Kay behind, Claire, Anne, and I went to Our Lady of Lourdes Hospital. Pulling into the parking lot, Claire mused that she sure hadn't expected to be back at Lourdes so soon. It hadn't been six months since Daddy had died there.

We peeked into Momma's room. She was lying there with her eyes shut and her blue-veined hands folded on her stomach. She must have sensed us because her eyes popped open and she waved us in. We approached cautiously. She looked much the same as she had at home except she had two tiny plastic tubes inserted into her nose.

"Are you mad at us?" Claire asked, taking Momma's hand into hers.

"No, darling," she said softly. "I'm glad to be here."

Claire's shoulders relaxed and she said, "Good. We love you, and we don't want anything to happen to you."

Yvette lumbered over clutching her huge vinyl purse and a steaming Styrofoam cup. "Has the doctor found anything yet?" she asked, blinking in that rapid, nervous way of hers. She fired off questions. My jaw muscles tightened as I felt Momma's irritation mount.

"I suppose he'll run more tests," Momma said, her voice edged in exasperation.

Undeterred Yvette blinked and uttered, "Well, what—"

"Isn't this a wonderful place to spend Christmas?" I said, derailing my sister. "I bet they have delicious turkey soup and cranberry Jello for their patients today."

Momma smiled at me, and I felt pleased with myself. She glanced down at the buttons on her bed rail while Yvette gulped down her coffee. Our eyes wandered about the room. Anne said the television was a nice size, and we all agreed. I wracked my brains trying to think of something else cheerful to say when suddenly, Momma cried out. Shrieked. Her entire body stiffened and jerked as though it had just taken a bolt of lightning. Her arms flew into the air, and her face screwed up. Then her tongue stuck out of her mouth, as if it was choking her. Gasping for breath, making a *hhuuuh* sound, her body jerking, her face twitching, she plucked at her chest with clawing fingers. When the strained skin of her face turned purple, we started screaming. I backed up into a corner of the room, yelling, "What's wrong with her? Someone help her! Momma, don't die!" Claire called out the door for someone to come quick.

I kept screaming and crying. Anne shouted for a doctor over Claire's shoulder and then came to me. Grabbing my arms, she yelled, "Shut up, Marie. You're going to scare her. Calm down, damn it."

Hospital staff quickly assembled around the bed. A doctor, who didn't look much older than Michael, told a nurse to get us out of the room immediately while another nurse, fussing at us to quiet down, put an oxygen mask on Momma.

Dr. La Dousa arrived forty-five minutes later. After he checked on Momma, he asked us to describe what we had witnessed. Yvette, Claire, Anne, and I started beating on our chests and waving our arms in the air to mimic Momma's attack. We described her twitching purple face. I told him she hadn't eaten in days. She had only drunk alcohol. She had been vomiting and going to the bathroom all week. He said it sounded like a seizure. They would do a whole series of blood tests and scans.

When we were allowed back in Momma's room, she asked, "What happened to me?"

Claire took Momma's hand. We went through the rendition we had given Dr. La Dousa.

"Really?" Momma laughed at our performance. When our arms settled by our sides, her face quieted. Turning toward Anne, she again asked, "What happened to me?"

Several times we described the episode for her. Each time she laughed. Then, as if someone had hit an erase button in her head, she'd ask again.

Penny arrived. She had changed from her jogging shorts to a pair of designer jeans so tight that only someone who spent two hours a day with a fitness trainer could squeeze into them. I pulled my sweater down to cover my flabby ass and tried to ignore the generous smile Momma offered my sister. A mixture of perfume, Listerine, and booze wafted through the air as she bent over to kiss Momma. "I hear you gave everyone a scare," Penny chided. "I just talked to Dr. La Dousa. He's moving you to ICU."

"ICU? Why?" Yvette demanded from across the room.

"So she can get some rest," Penny said. "They don't want her having too many visitors."

"Where's my money?" Momma asked Penny abruptly.

We looked at Penny. She smiled. "It's here in the drawer. I'll make sure it gets moved with you. Are you planning on going somewhere?"

"No, but let me see it," Momma demanded.

Penny opened the drawer of the nightstand and pulled out several bills.

"What's the money for?" I asked.

Penny shrugged, saying only that Momma had insisted earlier that she not leave her alone without some cash. She demanded ten dollars—one five and five ones.

We watched a Lawrence Welk rerun while we waited for Momma to be transferred to ICU. Periodically, she lifted up her oxygen mask and asked one of us again about her ten dollars. We assured her it was still there. Was the money cab fare in case she decided to spring herself?

At nine o'clock two nurses transferred Momma to a new room. Nanette, Aimee, and Mr. Delahoussaye finally arrived. Dr. La Dousa met with us briefly, explaining that preliminary tests showed an electrolyte imbalance and high levels of toxins in Momma's blood. Toxins, well, duh, I wanted to say. I pictured the vials and vials of pills that lined her medicine cabinet, her nightstand, the kitchen cabinets and drawers, and her bathroom vanity.

"Y'all want to stay here tonight to keep an eye on things?" I whispered to Nanette and Claire when Penny and Mr. Delahoussaye announced they were heading home. Besides being concerned for my mother, I saw a rare opportunity to sit up all night visiting with my sisters.

"Maybe I'll hang out for a while," Aimee said meekly as the others left.

We claimed four chairs along the back wall of the waiting room. Directly ahead of us stood a metal table with an industrial-sized coffeepot, cups, and condiments, two bathrooms, and two payphones. An older black couple sat to our right. They smiled at us and then resumed flipping through their magazines. Seated in the far corner, a solitary man rested his head against the wall, his flannel-sleeved arms folded across his chest. I felt sad for him, spending Christmas night this way—alone in a chilly, quiet hospital waiting room.

"This'll be one Christmas I'll never forget," I said. My sisters nodded in agreement as they squirmed in the uncomfortable chairs.

Claire sipped her Diet Coke and asked, "So what did Kyle say when you told him you weren't coming home tonight?"

"He was fine. I said I'd be home in the morning to feed Austin before my breasts exploded. Who's watching Hope and Peter?" I asked Aimee, now that Trevis and she were divorcing.

"A neighbor." Aimee fidgeted with her purse strap, saying, "She's gonna call if there is any trouble,"

"Trouble with the kids?" Nanette asked.

"No, with Trevis." Aimee hesitated. "Damn," she stammered, covering her mouth as her chin began to quiver.

"What's going on with Trevis?" I whispered.

Aimee looked down at her lap, her shoulders moving up and down. Sniffling, she told us the story as she had just learned it.

"What?" Claire asked, looking at Aimee as if she had just spoken in Pig Latin.

"Yeah, it's true. Peter slipped this afternoon, said how Papa made Hope sit on his lap again at the park and touched her underwear."

"What a bastard," Nanette spat.

"Hope said it had happened before, on the day of Daddy's funeral. Can you believe it, of all the nerve, he did it in our bedroom when we came home from the cemetery?"

I could believe it, and I didn't think his timing was coincidental. I remembered how at Daddy's wake Penny and I had slobbered attention on Byron, Aimee's second husband, to make Trevis feel excluded from the family. Trevis was the only son-in-law not asked to be a pall bearer. As my sister's soft cries filled the silence among us, I pictured Trevis, sitting in Daddy's study the prior Christmas, and Hope, shyly hovering about her mother. My niece's mini-skirt was short, inappropriately short, it seemed, for a girl approaching eight. I watched Trevis's constant surveillance of his daughter. He studied her legs and perky bottom as she rubbed against her mother's jeans like a cat. I knew then that Hope was in danger but prayed she wouldn't be this young before he pounced.

As Aimee cried, I wondered if Trevis had said to himself as he slid his grimy hands under his own daughter's skirt, *Take this, Miss Esther, and your high-and-mighty daughters.* I felt ashamed that if by emasculating this man we caused an innocent girl harm. Did he take his daughter's innocence as a way of proving to himself that he was indeed a man? I shuddered, remembering his hateful stare. The way he glared at my hugely pregnant belly at my father's funeral. There was not a trace of humanity, only raw anger in those cold brown eyes. An anger I had so often seen in

Momma's own eyes.

"How are we going to survive all this craziness?" I mumbled, trying not to cry. Trevis corrupted his own daughter, no doubt filled her with his own shame and hatred. What a fucking legacy. And what will be our legacy to our own children?

Claire and I looked down at our hands while Nanette embraced Aimee, telling her to let it out. Nanette, the family consoler. It was a role I avoided. So often I had seen contempt in Momma's face when Nanette comforted my father. I could imagine her thinking, "You fool! Where is your armor? Don't you realize there are people wielding swords inches from your throat?" I could comfort Austin, my baby, because he hadn't yet rejected my hugs or laughed at my assurances.

I touched Aimee's shoulder. "I hope you never, ever see that jerk again."

She shook her head, her thin, straight brown hair flopping against her wet cheeks. "I'm not. When he called this evening, I told him I knew what he did to Hope and that he wasn't ever going to see his kids again. It was one thing to beat the crap out of me, but I wasn't going to let him touch my children. He didn't even try to deny it. He just said, 'Okay. Bye.'"

"I never could figure out what you saw in that creep," Claire blurted out. I had to stifle a laugh at her honesty. Nanette glanced sideways at me, like, "Yeah, I was wondering the same thing."

Aimee shrugged. She began the story of their strange courtship. It seemed wholly plausible, as she told of their all-night talks, that one could exchange comfort and companionship for a few disturbing quirks. Hadn't I made a similar trade-off with Kyle? He with me?

"For the longest time," Aimee said, "I'd just lie in bed and pray I'd die in my sleep. Each time he beat me or forced me to have sex, I begged God to put me out of my misery."

"Why didn't you leave?" I asked, thinking how often I wished Kyle would try to hit me so I'd have a good reason to leave him. It hadn't occurred to me yet that forcing sex on a partner was a sufficient reason to break up.

"I didn't have any money or even a birth certificate for Hope. I sneaked her out of the hospital because we couldn't pay the bill. And Trevis kept threatening to turn me in if I tried to leave him." She went on to tell how she convinced him to move back to Lafayette after Daddy sent her a check from the sale of the family business. But after a few months without his mother, Trevis headed home to Tennessee.

"Once I got accustomed to sleeping through the night without some wacko waking me up, slapping my head, and saying, 'Get up, I can't sleep,' I couldn't go back to living like that for anything in the world. I screwed up with Michael, but things *are* going to be different for Hope and Peter."

"How is Michael?" Claire asked.

Michael was still in jail for breaking probation.

Aimee shook her head and rolled her bloodshot eyes. In other words, don't ask. Claire nodded.

"At least he's still alive," I said. "He made it past nineteen." Aimee cocked her head. I told her that I used to baby-sit Michael before I moved away. Twice he told me that if his life hadn't improved by his nineteenth birthday, he'd kill himself. He'd shoot himself just like his Uncle Nickey. As soon as I said this and saw the tears in Aimee's eyes, I wished I'd kept quiet. I knew that she already felt guilty.

"It is weird how only the women in our family have survived," Nanette said, moistening her cracked lips, "and that we're all pretty strong, considering."

"Yeah, for a bunch of wimps," I said. Nanette punched my arm and the conversation rolled along, twisting and turning at familiar landmarks, cycling from present to past to future, sometimes speeding along with all four of us talking at once. Four women sitting against a wall in a hospital room, trembling together, laughing together, fighting back tears together. Traveling through memories, noting discrepancies and missing pieces.

"Was that really Chess's body in our freezer?" I whispered to Aimee.

"Where'd you get an idea like that?" she asked as Nanette and Claire leaned in to hear her response.

"Rumors. Plus, I think you told us that."

"I'm not sure. I've heard so many different stories. But I think it was tissue and blood samples they were sending to a lab in Houston for analysis. For a while I thought it was his organs for donations. But that doesn't seem plausible. I guess we'll never know."

"Do you know why he was murdered?" Nanette asked. "Or who did it?"

"I don't know who for certain but one theory I heard from the maid seemed to make sense. Remember how Chess got into that bad car accident—"

"—And he had to drive around with chains holding the broken passenger door in place until he saved up enough money to fix his car," I interrupted.

"Yeah, well, the cops found marijuana. And not just a joint. They took him to jail and called Daddy. Suddenly Chess is free, and the charges are dropped. I think word got out, and his suppliers figured he turned into a narc. Sooner or later he'd give out names. They decided to shut him up. I think that's who he met out on the old highway. After a couple of drinks they still weren't reassured Chess wasn't going to double-cross them so they slipped something into his drink, gave him a lift in their car, and then when he started getting groggy, they tossed him out."

"God, it's creepy to think that those murderers are still out there. How do people get to be like that?" I asked. "Maybe Daddy didn't do Chess such a favor by bailing him out. Maybe he'd have been better off left in jail to serve his time. I don't mean to sound cruel, and I know seeing your own son in jail would be torture..." I looked at Aimee and she nodded.

"...but sometimes if you try to protect your kids too much, they never learn, and they end up worse off for it. No survival skills, like Nickey. Maybe that's the difference between the boys in our family and the girls. How many times were we girls left to bail ourselves out of our own trouble? And we have. Pretty much."

"How was Daddy to know that helping Chess would kill him?" Nanette asked.

"I think you're right," Aimee told Nanette, "and look how Momma's scare tactics backfired on me? She didn't want me getting pregnant like she did so she kept calling me a tramp. I was so shy. I wasn't even screwing around yet. But finally I had had enough and decided what the hell, I've already been condemned."

"Can you believe we're talking about them like this?" Nanette whispered. "Momma might be in that room dying right now." We all looked around to see if anyone was watching or listening.

"I don't know," I whispered back. "I feel safe saying this stuff, knowing she can't come get us."

"Yeah," Aimee said eagerly. And, like someone snipped the knot off a balloon, more stories rushed out of her and took us with them on their flight.

"Daddy must have shit in his pants," Nanette said, after Aimee told us how she had once called Brother Alfred from school to break up a fight between our parents.

When Aimee finished talking, Claire shook her head and said, "It's funny, I can't remember anything about my childhood. I guess I've blocked it all out." She grabbed a Cosmopolitan from a stack of magazines.

"You're lucky," Aimee said. "I remember more than I want to."

We sat for a moment, silent, until Nanette broke the spell. "Well," she said, "should we go in and check on Momma?"

We crept past the ICU desk and found Momma staring at the ceiling.

"What are you still doing here?" she whispered, smiling. I wondered if she could tell what we'd been talking about by the looks on our faces.

"We're keeping an all-night vigil," Nanette said, bending over the bed to kiss her. We took turns kissing her forehead before she started coughing. When her fit was over, she struggled to catch her breath. "I'm tired, darlings. Go home."

But we could say no to her now. We said we'd be staying. She closed her eyes, and we left her to return to the waiting room.

In the morning I went home to nurse Austin, eat, and rest. When I walked into the kitchen, I found Kyle holding the baby in his lap, feeding him a bottle of formula.

"Oh, darn," I said, walking over to kiss Kyle and Austin hello. "I was going to nurse him. My breasts are about to burst."

"Sorry, but he was hungry and crying. I wasn't sure when you'd be home."

"I suppose I should start weaning him. I'll probably be coming and going a lot for the next few days." The thought of giving up my special bond with Austin depressed me. He was just five months old. If Momma had taken care of herself, I wouldn't have to be visiting her in the hospital while Kyle got to hold and feed my baby.

Kyle grabbed my ass and squeezed. "We sure missed you last night."

I moved his hand away and forced a smile. I wanted to tell him to keep his hands to himself, but I didn't want to start a fight. Instead I sat down at the table to admire my son.

"So, how's your mother?"

"She was running a fever this morning. They're not sure what's wrong."

"Oh," he said, pausing to frown. I figured he was choosing the right words to caution me about getting my hopes up about Momma. "What do you want to do today? I'm going bananas here. The milk lady woke us up at seven, and then the gardener rang the doorbell. Those stupid cats have been meowing like crazy at your mother's bedroom door. The phone hasn't stopped ringing. Your Aunt Lilia called twice. She really wants you to call her back." He wiped the drool off Austin's chin and looked at me as if he'd just thought of something unpleasant. "You're not planning on staying here longer with Austin after I leave, are you?"

"I don't know, Kyle. I don't know what's going to happen." I told him I was going to lie down. My head was throbbing. I felt like I'd been snorting cocaine.

That afternoon I found Yvette in the ICU waiting room.

"Hi, Marie. Have you seen her?" Yvette asked a little too loud before I had even reached her chair. She seemed jacked up, like a kid overindulged on chocolate and soda. I always feared she was one disappointment away from surrendering to a fifth of vodka or carton of Winstons.

"No, I just got here. Have you?"

She shook her head and said that Penny, Claire, and Aimee were in there. That explained why she was sitting in the waiting room drinking coffee instead of visiting Momma.

"Dr. La Dousa wants to meet with us at five."

"Okay. Is something wrong?"

"How should I know? I'm just the oldest daughter. That obviously doesn't carry any weight around here." She walked over to the coffeepot. She looked like Daddy, solemn, tall, and lean, hunched over the table, quickly stirring in one blue packet of sweetener at a time.

At five o'clock, Dr. La Dousa gathered my sisters, Mr. Delahoussaye, and me for a meeting in one of the consultation rooms. He said that Momma's breathing had become labored and she had a dangerously high fever. He wanted our permission to hook her up to a ventilator for a couple of days until he could bring her fever down.

"That sounds pretty serious," Yvette said. Her skeptical gaze shifted back and forth between the doctor and Penny.

"Your mother is weak, and I want her to be able to fight the fever," the doctor explained. He avoided our eyes and kept rubbing his square jaw with his hand. "She'll be more comfortable if she doesn't have to struggle so much with her breathing."

"Momma isn't going to be very happy about that," Anne said. "She's got a living will that says no life support." The doctor didn't look at Anne but turned to Penny instead. Penny and Mr. Delahoussaye were co-executors of Momma's living will.

"This isn't life support," Penny said impatiently. "It's just to help Momma breathe more easily for a couple of days."

"At what point does the living will come into effect?" Yvette asked.

"Yvette," Penny said, "we're trying to save Momma here. We're not talking about whether or not to terminate her. That isn't even relevant at this point."

"Yes, I understand that," Yvette persisted, glaring at Penny. "I was just wondering when it would be relevant."

Mr. Delahoussaye reached over, patted Yvette on the shoulder, and said, "Yvette, your mother is only sixty-four. She's got a long life ahead of her. Let's help her to fight this fever and get her home."

Yvette slid her hands into her blue jean pockets. "Whatever y'all want."

The doctor rose from his chair after the rest of us gave our consent. "All right, then, give me an hour or so, and I'll let you know when you can see her again." He paused at the door and said, "Penny, can I see you for a moment?"

She followed him out of the room and I caught Nanette's eye. "What's that about?" I asked with that unspoken look she knew well. She shrugged and looked at Anne for a clue.

"He's as arrogant and rude as he was when Daddy died," Anne said.

"He's just trying to help Momma," Claire said.

A few minutes later Penny returned. In a very condescending tone she said, "Now, I need to talk to you about this. Dr. La Dousa is trying to keep us all apprised of Momma's condition, but he doesn't want a barrage of calls at his office, and he doesn't want to be attacked in the parking lot by second-guessers. He asked me to pick one or two representatives from the family, and he'll communicate only with them."

"Was he referring to me?" Anne asked. She squared her shoulders to Penny's. "'Cause I didn't attack him in the parking lot. I simply asked him why it took him so long to respond to his page last night. And then I asked how Momma was doing."

"Well, he said that you accosted him when he got out of his car, that you wouldn't let him pass, but let's—"

"What a fucking wimp," exclaimed Anne. "I did no such thing. How dare he!"

Mr. Delahoussaye stood up and put his arm around Anne. "Come on, girls. We're all here to help your mother. Let's not fight."

Anne jerked away and put on her don't-fuck-with-me look.

"Anyway," Penny said, avoiding Anne's icy-blue stare, "I'd like to volunteer to be one of the representatives. Anyone else?"

I'm heading back to California as soon as possible, I thought. This is going to get ugly.

"I would," Claire offered immediately, raising her hand like a schoolgirl.

"All right, unless there are any objections, it'll be Claire and me."

Nanette looked at me. I looked at Aimee and Yvette. Aimee looked down at her hands while Yvette glanced over at Anne. Mr. Delahoussaye said, "Penny and I will keep you girls abreast of her condition, and we won't make any decisions without your consent."

Our one chance to overthrow Penny and Claire passed so quickly that no one recognized it until it was too late.

We sat in the ICU waiting room until the doctor reappeared to say he'd inserted a tube through Momma's nose to hook her up to a ventilator.

"I must warn you, girls, she was rather anxious and uncooperative," said Dr. La Dousa. "She was really fighting me. I had to sedate her and strap her down by the ankles and wrists."

My sisters and I looked at each other and drew in nervous breaths.

"She'll calm down soon enough. Good night." He hit the elevator button and left us to deal with her.

"Momma," Claire whispered from the doorway, inching her way toward the bed rail. We trailed behind like poltroons. "I know you're probably angry with us, but we're only doing what the doctor feels is necessary."

We formed a circle around the bed and tried not to stare at the tube stuck in her nose or the respirator expanding and compressing noisily nearby.

Like an ensnared wild animal, Momma glared at us. Her dark eyes darted back and forth from Claire to Anne, Penny to me, Nanette to Yvette, Mr. Delahoussaye to Aimee. She tugged at her wrists while the muscles in her neck distended. Anger hung in the air so thick you could lather in it. Her head moved from side to side, and her unblinking eyes bulged out at us.

In a feigned, upbeat voice, Penny said, "I know you're a little upset, but this is only temporary. Just until you get stronger." She smiled and gently stroked Momma's arm. Momma jerked her hand, pulling the restraints taut. Penny winced and stepped back, scared, no doubt, that Momma was going to rip through the white straps and grab her by her skinny, jeweled neck.

Momma's stare fixed on Penny. The room was quiet except for the steady noise of the compression machine.

"Well, I have to go to work tonight," Penny said, forcing a smile. "I'll stop by later." With more bravery than I had in me, she slowly reached across the bed rail and patted Momma's shoulder before she turned to leave.

Penny hadn't wavered a minute in authorizing the doctor to do this to Momma. Now she fled while we stood there deflecting her hateful stares.

A minute later Aimee took Penny's lead and said she had to go. Within minutes, the rest of us mumbled excuses and left. Penny and Aimee waited for us in the hall.

"She looked like she wants to kill us," I said, shivering. "You think she's having a flashback of when she was in the looney bin and they restrained her?"

"That hadn't occurred to me," Penny answered. "Maybe that's why she's so angry. Boy, I couldn't wait to get out of there."

Yvette cleared her throat. "I think that you'd better call Dr. La Dousa and make sure he knows Momma's history. Especially the shock treatments. If she's reliving all that...."

I searched my sisters' faces for assurance that every thing would work out, that we'd made the right decision. But they offered no comfort. Saying good night, I hurried home to Kyle's safe, though suffocating, arms.

45 ~

First they inserted a tube into her nose and then into her throat to help her breathe. Unable to speak, she scribbled notes on a yellow-lined tablet. *Why are you doing this to me? Is this a dream? I promise to be good if you take the straps off. Who's taking care of my cats?*

Feeding tubes soon replaced Jell-O and juice. Spiking fevers and high levels of unidentifiable toxins required blood transfusions and kidney dialysis. IV drips and heart and blood pressure monitors appeared and kept time with the other bedside machines. Unresponsiveness and despondency led to alcohol drips to perk her up. Agitation was soothed with sedation. And each time her kidneys failed, she swelled up like a hot, yellowish boudin link. It was horrifying to witness.

Within the first two weeks her strength waned. Holding a pen became too difficult. Restraints were no longer necessary. As she lay there, moving further and further away from us, I wondered if she was reliving her own past. One of the nurses said he often found her lying awake nights with tears trickling down her cheeks. Free of tranquilizers and alcohol, could she finally feel the deaths of her sons, her husband, her parents? Did she remember whipping us each night?

Was she scared every time she heard the code blue alarm go off for one of the other patients that she'd be next? Scared she'd go to hell? Maybe she hoped that her confinement and suffering were God's way of making her atone for her sins. Maybe she prayed, as I did, that she would be allowed to reunite with Daddy, Nickey, and Chess when she did take her last breath.

Many nights I woke up shaking and crying, relieved to find it was just a nightmare, that my mother hadn't escaped from the hospital with tubes hanging from her bloody nose and arms. She really wasn't standing at my bed, yelling, "Get out of bed and hand me your baby."

For four months we watched her life steadily decline. As tubes multiplied, so did the dissension among the sisters and Dr. La Dousa. Nanette, Yvette, Anne, and I wished we had never called for an ambulance, and we prayed for God to intervene. Penny, Claire, and Dr. La Dousa couldn't see the cruelty in the unending heroics. Aimee withdrew from the conflict and visited only when she felt certain she'd find Momma alone. Occasionally our visits were met with a forgiving smile if she had managed to sleep.

Sometimes Anne sat by Momma's hospital bed for hours, asking for a yes or no, a blink, a simple squeeze or a wiggle of her toes—anything—if she wanted her daughters to fight for her right to die. But she never answered. Perhaps she feared what lay ahead, or perhaps, in some warped way, she didn't want to disappoint Penny, who kept cheering her on to better health.

I traveled back and forth as I often as I could to see her. One April morning as I packed to catch yet another flight back to California, the telephone rang. I dropped the bag of baby bottles and ran to the kitchen.

"Hi, this is one of the nurses taking care of your mother. I haven't been able to reach your sisters Claire or Penny. I need a signature from a family member to authorize a procedure Dr. La Dousa has requested. Can you come by to sign?"

I wanted to tell the meek voice on the phone, NO. Just leave her alone. But I knew I'd catch hell from Penny.

When I got to the ICU, the nurse at the desk briefly explained the procedure while I scribbled my name on the authorization form beside the doctor's arrogant signature. I barely listened. I didn't need to know where the new tube was going and why. It was just one more useless, misery-making measure. Balancing Austin on my hip, I handed the form back to the nurse.

"May I bring my baby in to show her for just a second?"

She nodded.

A huge smile spread across Momma's face when she saw Austin in my arms. Her taut skin was as yellow as the smelly water left too long in a vase holding weary flowers.

"Hi, Momma, look who wanted to say hello." I walked closer to the bed, hoping that the sight of her wouldn't frighten Austin. He babbled and waved his arms, probably thinking he'd like to play with all those interesting buttons and tubes. "Isn't he big?"

Momma slowly moved her head. Her eyes drank him up.

"See, Momma, if you get better and go home, Austin and I could come stay with you for a while to help you out." She looked up at me and mouthed something I didn't understand. "What?" She tried again, but I couldn't make out her words. "Can you try one more time but slower?"

Slowly and deliberately her dry, white-crusted lips moved. But still she couldn't shape the words distinctly. Shaking my head, I apologized. "I still don't know what you're trying to tell me. My plane leaves in an hour. I've got to go."

She nodded and opened her mouth briefly as if to try again. I think the look of panic on my face—a fear of both missing my plane and hearing her urgent message—derailed her attempt. She simply smiled, and the muscles in her jaw relaxed. I held Austin aside and bent over the railing to kiss her damp, burning forehead. As I waved good-bye, she mouthed the words *I love you.*

"I love you too, Momma." I carried Austin out of the room. An hour later as we flew over Lafayette, past the golf course at the country club where I'd learned how to do a one-and-a half somersault on the high board, tears rolled down my cheeks. I wondered why I had panicked when Momma tried desperately to tell me something. What was it—perhaps an apology for all the hurt and neglect—that I feared? Would her words have unleashed a tidal wave of emotions or forced me finally to forgive her?

Two days after I returned to Walnut Creek, I was on my way to a fabric store in Berkeley when a Jeep ahead of me on the freeway stopped suddenly. I screeched to a halt to avoid it. Throwing my right arm out in front of Austin's car seat, I prayed the driver behind me would stop in time. Cars veered to the left shoulder and the right lanes to avoid each other. I rolled down my window and tried to determine the cause of the stall. We crept along for ten yards until I saw it in the road. A deer. A beautiful toffee-colored doe struggling to stand up in one of the left lanes. Her hind legs and the white of her stomach were covered in blood. She must have come down from the hills to graze and tried to cross the highway.

Each time the doe managed to stand up, she'd frantically dart out in front of another car and get hit again. "Come on girl, you can do it," I whispered. "Get to the side of the road." She kept trying to straighten her legs, but they either buckled under her and she fell or she lurched forward into another car. Drivers swerved to avoid her, but they couldn't predict where she'd go. She was struck again and again and kept managing to get back up. I inched my way to her. As she stood up on her shaky legs and stared at me through my side window, I put my foot on the brake. Her eyes were sad and defeated. She looked as if she was begging for help. "Get to the side of the road," I mumbled to her and accelerated past. Let her die, I told God, tears streaming down my face. Don't make her suffer any longer.

Annie called to tell me something one of Momma's favorite nurses had told her after a visit. Momma had had a rough night because of her fever. At one point when he was checking her temperature, Momma asked if she was getting any better. He considered lying but decided to be honest. "No, Miss Esther, I'm sorry to say you're not. Nothing the doctor is trying seems to be working." Momma stared at him for a moment and then started crying. She said she wanted to die and asked why they were doing this to her. He told Anne if he were sick, Dr. La Dousa would be the last person on Earth he'd let treat him.

Yvette sent me a copy of a letter she had mailed to Penny. She questioned Penny's behavior, her motives in prolonging Momma's suffering, and called her actions "reprehensible and scandalous." She said her failure to include us in the decision-making process denied us, as our mother's daughters, a part of our birthright. Her final words held more compassion than I felt toward my sister: "Penny, I really feel sorry for you. God help you."

When I returned home from Berkeley that afternoon, I wrote a letter for Claire to read to my mother. In it I told Momma I'd understand if she couldn't fight anymore.

I didn't want her to keep suffering just because some of us couldn't face losing her. Claire never had the chance to read my letter to Momma.

46 ~

"Marie, it's Penny." I looked at the clock. 6:45 A.M. "Momma's not doing so well. Her kidneys have shut down again, and Dr. La Dousa wants to put her back on dialysis."

"You can't be serious."

"Hold on!" she snapped. "I'm not going to sign the authorization. I'm just telling you in case you want to fly out. They're going to start disconnecting the machines today." She began to cry. I wondered if all the pressure Penny had been getting from the family had finally gotten to her. "I think we've done all we can."

"Thank you, Penny," I said gently. "I know how hard this is for you, but I think it's what Momma—"

"Just get here as soon as possible," she said, cutting me off. "And don't mention this to any of your friends in Lafayette because we don't want any interference. Only the attending nurses and Dr. La Dousa will know what we're doing."

We hung up. Kyle sat up and held me while I sobbed. One of my friends agreed to watch Austin for us during the day while Kyle was at work. He drove me to the airport to catch the first available flight. I kept wondering if I'd make it in time to say good-bye. How long it would take for her to die? Was she aware of what was happening? Would it be scary to stand by her bed and watch her take her last breath? Would it be hours, days, or weeks? I hoped, for her sake, as well as my own, that it would be quick and easy.

I arrived in Lafayette late that evening. Claire met me at the airport. Her voice was hoarse when she said hello.

"She's still alive, but it won't be long," Claire said in response to my look. "Dr. La Dousa turned down the oxygen concentration going through the respirator, and he removed some sort of patch he'd put over her heart. She's unconscious and looks pretty awful. You better prepare yourself for the worst."

Claire bit her lip and we both started crying.

Heading to the hospital to meet the others, we drove down St. Mary's Street in a soft drizzle, the windshield wipers moving slowly back and forth. The night streets were quiet. The street lamps highlighted puddles on the asphalt. The azaleas were starting to bloom. Soon all of Lafayette would be awash in pink, purple, and white. I thought how odd it was that the people in the houses along the way were tucking their children into bed, and there I was going to watch my mother die.

When we passed the nurses' desk in the ICU, a nurse stood up. He said, "You must be Miss Esther's daughter from California. I think your mother has been hanging on all day waiting for you."

I smiled and nodded. When I got to Momma's door, Nanette asked Claire, "Did you prepare her?" She looked as if she hadn't washed her hair in days, and I felt a sudden irritation at her trying to protect me.

"Nanette, don't worry, I'm not expecting her to look good," I said, pushing my way through the door.

Momma did look awful. But not frightening. She looked like someone whose body was slowly shutting down. The skin on her arms was yellowish-brown and swollen taut again. Worse than on my previous visit. Her stomach was distended, as if someone had tucked a pillow underneath the bed sheet.

"Hi, Momma," I whispered. Her eyes opened suddenly and I jumped back. I looked at Aimee but she shook her head.

"It's just an involuntary reaction," said the nurse standing near the door. She pointed to the ventilator set low. "There's so little oxygen going to her brain, I don't think she's aware of anything."

I moved closer. Her cloudy, bulging eyes blinked, shifted around without focusing, and then closed. A purple vein over her right eyelid protruded through her ruddy skin. The feeding tube had been removed from her nose.

"Momma, it's Marie. I wanted to say good-bye to you and tell you that I love you." I rubbed her hot arm and wondered if she could sense our presence. Was her spirit floating overhead like you read about in books? "Daddy and Nickey and Chess are waiting for you to join them in heaven. You'll see them soon, and you'll finally be at peace." I leaned over and kissed her forehead.

"Momma, go to Daddy," Nanette said, sniffling. "Don't fight anymore. You just let yourself go and be with Daddy."

The heart monitor hovered at around seventy. "Where's Penny?" I asked Yvette. She shrugged and said she had left about an hour earlier.

I wanted to offer Momma some prayers in case she could still hear us and was scared about what lay ahead, but despite my years of attending catechism, I only knew the first half of Our Father. I looked around the room for the prayer cards Father Latiolais had been leaving during his visits and saw them on the stand next to the bed. Some of the get-well cards taped to the wall near the door also had prayers in them. I took what I needed, carried my little collection back to my spot near Momma's bed, and began reading to her. As I read, her eyes opened and closed. The number on her heart monitor slowly dropped from seventy to sixty-five to fifty. After I'd finished, Yvette suggested we join hands and recite the Our Father and Hail Mary. We chanted prayers around our dying mother until a nurse came in and whispered, "It's going to be soon. You should probably call your other sister."

We all looked at Claire, figuring she would know, if anyone, where Penny was. She offered to try calling her at home. A couple minutes later she returned from the nurses' station saying that Penny was neither at home nor at Patrick's house. It occurred to me that she might have gone to feed Momma's cats, so I volunteered to try Momma's number. Penny answered on the first ring. I told her the nurses said Momma would be going soon and she'd better come quickly.

Flanked by Patrick, she arrived fifteen minutes later. Momma's heart-beat was hovering between thirty and forty. Penny came to my side of the bed; she smelled of alcohol. I knew she had spent the last hour of Momma's life fortifying herself at the liquor cabinet.

She bent over the bed rail. "I'm here, Momma."

The heart monitor number bounced back to fifty. I panicked. She'd better not decide to hang on for Penny's sake. "You're so close," I told Momma, "don't stop now."

"Try to relax, Momma," Claire said as tears ran down her cheeks. "Go meet Daddy. When you see Emma, please give her a big hug and a kiss for me. Tell her I love her." Those were the same instructions she had given Daddy when he died. Momma's lips clamped tightly together. Her arms jerked and rose off the bed.

Patrick cleared his throat. "I don't think you girls should just *stand* around and watch your mother die. It'll probably be very upsetting. She might go into convulsions or something."

I mumbled that I wasn't going anywhere, that I could handle whatever happened. Everyone else just ignored him and watched Momma's struggle. He shook his head and left the room. Momma fought for air. The heart monitor fell below thirty, and the alarm started beeping. A nurse flipped off the alarm button. Momma continued to gasp. She looked like she was trying to hold her breath. When she relaxed and released some air, Nanette said, "That's it, Momma, let yourself go." Momma's bulging eyes opened wide. Her arms lifted off the bed and dropped again. Gradually the frightened look on her face eased into serenity. Her chest continued to move up and down, but she stopped struggling.

"I hope you have a peaceful journey," Yvette whispered. I watched Momma's eyes, wondering if she could see us through the cloudy lenses.

"I love you Momma," Aimee whispered. The rest of us told her the same thing.

The nurse tapped Penny on the shoulder. "Excuse me, but your mother is dead," she whispered. "She died a couple of minutes ago."

Puzzled, I looked at the nurse and said, "But she's still breathing."

"That's the ventilator. It takes a while after they die for the air to leave their lungs."

Momma's chest continued to move up and down. Her mouth made gurgling sounds as saliva bubbled from her tranquil lips. I couldn't believe she was dead. We hadn't even recognized the moment when it happened. I wiped the remnants of tears from my face. Momma was finally at peace. I felt calm for the first time in months. Our fight was over.

"Shall we say one final Our Father?" Nanette asked.

We all nodded and reached for each other's hands again. I took Penny's hand and watched with amazement as she reached for Yvette's. Linked that way around the bed we softly prayed "…thy Kingdom come, thy will be done, on earth as it is in heaven…"

Sitting in the hospital parking lot in Claire's car after we'd all dispersed, I sighed and said, "I feel like I've been run over by a whole fleet of Mack trucks. Except for childbirth, I've never been so drained in my life."

She sniffled and nodded. "Me too. You hungry? 'Cause I'm starved."

"Yeah. Is Taco Bell still open late?"

She slipped the key into the ignition and then turned to me.

"I have to tell you something. Apologize really, for something I've carried around with me for forever." She paused, and I knew exactly what was going to follow. "Do you remember when we were little, you must have been four, maybe five, and I got mad and started banging your head into the brick wall at the old house."

I nodded.

"I've always hated myself for doing that to you. I think about that often, how I really hurt you. It was like it wasn't even me at the time."

She started crying. I scooted closer and put my arm around her. Should I tell her my part of the story, I wondered, feeling ashamed. I knew I had to so we could both forgive each other and ourselves.

"You might hate me for this, but I got you back. You probably never even realized it."

She blinked and set her weary brown eyes on me as I told her how I'd heard Momma in the hallway that night. How I'd thrown a puzzle across the room to make noise, figuring Momma would likely spank her first. And she had.

"But I hated myself the moment she yanked you out of bed and started hitting you. So don't be too hard on yourself. I could be pretty mean myself. I'm so sorry."

She shook her head and then we both giggled. It felt incredible to purge myself of that little secret.

Shortly after Daddy's funeral, Momma told Mrs. Duhon that she wanted to be buried in the blue dress she wore to my wedding. She asked for a simple service at the funeral home chapel, rather than a big production in a fancy church.

Yvette contacted Father Latiolais and asked him to perform the mass. Claire, Mr. Delahoussaye, and I went to the funeral home to complete the paperwork and deliver Momma's dress. We brought the only recent photograph we could find, taken back in December. She was standing at the kitchen sink holding Austin. I asked Mr. Blanchard to crop Austin's face from the picture because I was superstitious about having him appear on a death announcement.

Penny was the first to suggest that we gather at Momma's house the next morning to divide the jewelry, silver, crystal, and china, leaving the art and furniture for after the funeral so that the house wouldn't be noticeably empty when people came over to pay their respects. Yvette said there was nothing she wanted, though she asked that we set aside any photographs we found of her or of Daddy's mother, for whom she'd been named.

Penny had the keys to Momma's file cabinet. The keys that held the secrets of those mysterious gray drawers I had watched Momma safeguard since I was a toddler. She unlocked the top drawer and removed several velvet boxes in assorted colors. The black ones, I knew, were from Paul's

Jewelry Store in the Oil Center. Penny carried the boxes to the dining room table. We established one ground rule—sets were to be kept together to preserve their value. We sat down and Penny opened the boxes. No one moved. Then I reached into the box that held Momma's white pearl and diamond necklace and matching earrings.

"Who wants these?"

"I would really like to have them," Nanette spoke up. "If no one minds."

Next I removed Momma and Daddy's gold-plated watches from a white cardboard box. No one expressed any interest so I said I'd like them for sentimental reasons. They were the only watches I had ever seen my parents wear.

I removed Momma's cocktail ring with the large round emerald and smaller rubies, sapphires, and diamonds. "How about this?" I felt a little like a novice auctioneer without the gavel and cards. No one said anything. I looked at Aimee. I figured even if she wanted something she'd be too shy to speak up. "Aimee, would you?"

"I guess. If that's all right with everyone else." The others nodded. I passed the ring to her.

"Does anyone mind if I take Daddy's college ring?" asked Anne. No one objected.

The distribution went along in a civilized manner, while Nanette's son Christopher played "chopsticks" over and over on the grand piano. Much to my surprise, there was no fighting. Penny chose a pair of pearl studs. I took a gold rope chain. Anne asked for Daddy's gold hammered cufflinks. Claire just sat there, scraping determinedly at an unidentifiable blob of food that had fossilized on the arm of her chair. It looked like all the muscles in her face were being pulled toward the vertical axis. I couldn't tell what was bothering her—perhaps the spectacle of her greedy sisters combing through Momma's belongings?

"You don't want anything, Claire?" Penny asked.

Claire shook her head no, tapping her fingernails on the table. Suddenly, she stood up and yelled at Chris over the sound of his "Chopsticks." "Stop banging on the keys! You'll damage the piano." The piano, everyone knew, now belonged to Claire. She made Momma swear she'd leave it to her. Chris stopped and stared at her, while I went on with the "auction."

"Daddy sure liked these tacky beads and earring sets." I pointed to a strand of smooth, round purple stones that Daddy ordered from a catalog. I held an earring up to my ears. "Lovely, aren't they?" They were supposed to look like grapes, but they didn't. Penny was the only one who smiled.

"What are we going to do with all this crap?" asked Anne. "I thought there'd be nicer pieces in these boxes. I wonder what happened to it all?"

Penny shrugged. "She's been giving pieces away to all of us over the years. I guess this is what's left."

"What about Momma's wedding and engagement rings?"

"Oh, I decided to keep those, if y'all don't mind. They're very special to me. Besides, I'll probably never get married so I'd like to have hers." Penny smiled and looked away.

You bitch, I thought, staring at her. You weren't even going to say anything about keeping her wedding ring. You probably knew when you took it off of Momma's fingers at the hospital that you'd never give it back. No telling what else you stole from her file cabinet. That's probably what you were doing the night Momma died. Drinking a glass of wine and ransacking her house before the rest of us had a chance.

I picked up a teardrop-shaped silver locket. "I'd like this. My initials are the same as Aunt Mim's."

"Maybe we could call Yvette and see if she wants any of these other bead and earring sets," Nanette suggested.

"Yeah, they're more her taste," said Penny.

"Oh, in case y'all are wondering," I said, "Claire and I found Momma's gray pearl necklace and earrings on her dresser. We took them to the funeral home. I thought after the funeral we could give them to Mrs. Duhon to thank her for everything."

We all nodded and worked our way down. Much to my disappointment there wasn't much of interest inside. No shocking revelations. No adoption certificates that would explain the vast differences in my sisters, brothers, and me. No souvenir suicide notes of Momma's telling us why she kept trying to kill herself. No journals or steamy letters from secret lovers. No adorable memorabilia of us like first hair clippings.

There was a gun (the one Nickey had used to kill himself), two boxes of bullets, a box of silver flatware that Anne asked for, twenty-plus years of canceled checks and statements for Momma's personal account, Daddy's wallet, several albums of family photographs, and nine folders, each marked with a child's name, containing our Baptismal and Holy First Communion certificates and our report cards.

While the others flipped through the photo albums, I read my report cards. Even in first grade I had not been a model student. I noticed Claire holding Daddy's wallet.

"Where's all the money that was in here?" she asked Penny because my father always kept a hefty amount of emergency funds on hand.

"I used some of it for stuff like cat food and to pay the gardener," Penny answered nonchalantly.

Claire shook her head. "I saw this wallet when Daddy went to the hospital. There must have been two thousand dollars in here. You spent all that on cat food and the gardener? No way."

"There wasn't two thousand in there. It was more like four hundred. Maybe Momma spent some of it after Daddy died." Claire stared at Penny for a moment. I was all set for a good fight when Claire just threw the wallet back into the drawer. Collecting her pile of goodies, Penny said, "Shall we close up the drawers and go separate the china and silver now?"

I trailed behind the others with Claire. I was surprised she had openly questioned Penny about the wallet. She had been so loyal to her for the past four months. Touching Claire on the shoulder, I asked, "Are you okay? You seem really upset about something. Do you think we're horrible for going through Momma's stuff so soon after her death?"

She leaned against the wall. "It's not that, really. I'm just so depressed. I still can't believe she's gone." She began to cry.

"I know. I feel like she's still at the hospital and I need to go visit her. I think after the funeral it'll sink in. Then it'll hit me that she's not coming back."

"I know I'm being selfish," Claire said, "but I wish she were still alive. At least then there was hope. Now there's nothing."

"Yeah, but you know she's better off this way."

Claire sniffled.

"It's going to be weird to sell this place," I said. "I can't imagine someone else living here."

"I wouldn't bother worrying about that," Claire said. She wiped her nose on the cuff of her sweater.

"What do you mean?"

"Nothing. Let's just wait and see what happens." She walked away. Something was up. I didn't know what it was. But I was remembering that Penny had squelched my suggestion that we get together to have a cleaning party to prepare the house for market.

47 ~

Throughout her four-month stay in intensive care, Momma had refused visitors, except for family, the Duhons, Mr. Delahoussaye, and Father Latiolais. She didn't want friends seeing her without dentures and with tubes stuck in just about every orifice. She didn't want tongues wagging all over town about how awful Miss Esther looked. It's just as well she never knew that word spread regardless. From the nursing staff, my longtime friend Suzanne seemed to know more, at any given moment, about Momma's condition than we did. Wanting to give Momma a send-off that wouldn't cause her shame and might dispel the rumors, Claire and I asked the funeral director, Mr. Blanchard, to try to improve the appearance of her bloated body.

They managed to reduce the swelling in Momma's stomach and arms considerably. In fact, they went a little too far. Mr. Blanchard warned my sisters and me on the morning of the wake not to be alarmed if we touched our mother's abdomen. They had to insert a piece of cardboard under her dress because her midsection had caved in. I pictured some pale man jabbing a huge needle into Momma's stomach, sucking all the fat and fluid out of her. How he must have panicked when he noticed her whole stomach had collapsed. When I went to her coffin to pray, I looked for the obvious outline of the cardboard, but they had concealed it under her blue dress. Momma would be happy about that.

Kyle and the baby flew into Lafayette the evening after the first wake. Standing at the airport windows, I watched a helicopter land in the distance and studied my reflection in the window. I received several compliments on my new navy blue dress from my friends. Under the circumstances my appearance should not have mattered, but it did. I figured I'd see a lot of old friends and relatives and didn't want them pitying me both for losing my mother and looking terrible. So I splurged. Penny must have done the same thing. Nanette elbowed me when our sister walked into the room wearing a long, slender black skirt with a slit that ran to her mid-thigh. Sleek pumps and an iridescent charcoal gray blouse perfectly matched her heavy eye shadow. The others sisters looked subdued in their conservative black clothes. I felt a twinge of shame that appearances meant so much to my family and me.

A voice announced on the loudspeaker the approach of the Continental Airline flight from Houston. I whispered thanks to God for delivering Austin safely to me. Spotting Kyle's weary face among a second wave of deplaning passengers, I watched him stroll down the gangway with the baby in his arms. They were a matched set with their deep blue eyes and hair as white as a lampshade. I grinned and waved until Austin noticed me.

"Hey, sweetie," I cooed, taking the baby from Kyle. "It's so good to see you." I kissed Austin's warm cheek, and he squealed. Bouncing him in my arms, I moved to let the other passengers through.

"Don't I get a kiss?" Kyle whined, holding the overflowing diaper bag tucked under his left arm.

I reached up and kissed his pouty lips. "Are you hungry? Because guess what I found in Momma's oven this morning." Before he could respond, I exclaimed, "A huge container of eggplant casserole left over from Christmas."

Kyle made a sour face, and I laughed. "Can you believe no one smelled it for four months? I guess the housekeeper doesn't do ovens!"

"You're certainly in a better mood than I expected," he said, glancing down at my cleavage and then around the room to make sure no man was ogling my breasts. "So how come you're all dressed up? Is that a new outfit?"

"Yeah," I said, "I didn't want to wear the same fat clothes I wore to my father's funeral." I motioned for us to head toward the baggage claim. Combing my fingers through Austin's wispy hair, I asked, "Do you like it?"

He nodded and pulled me into him, kissing me harder than before. I pushed him away with "It's hardly the time or place for sucking face." That was my way of telling him not to have any false expectations for the next few days.

Later after Austin fell asleep, Kyle and I sat in the living room talking about Momma's final hours at the hospital. I told him how well my sisters and I were getting along. When I mentioned that we had already divided up the jewelry, silver, and china, he rolled his eyes and said, "You girls are despicable. You sure don't seem very upset by your mother's death. I thought you'd be a mess, crying and carrying on about how you're going to miss her."

I looked down at my fresh-painted pink fingernails, feeling small and ashamed. Was it wrong for me to feel relieved? "I am upset that she's gone. And it's a bummer knowing that I don't have a father or a mother anymore. But I also feel like I've been mourning for months. I just want to get through the funeral, and then I'll cry later."

"Whatever," he said, reaching for the remote control.

My sisters had already split up into their safe, comfortable groups in the Camellia Room when Kyle and I arrived. Shivering, I pulled my suit jacket closed. Funeral homes made me feel like I was standing next to the frozen food section in the supermarket. How does Mr. Blanchard manage to eliminate any trace of odor? The air was as odorless as distilled water was tasteless. Shouldn't there be some trace of a medicinal stench?

Penny stood flanked by Patrick at the podium reading the sympathy cards. We said hello and then walked across the room to where Yvette talked with Father Latiolais who had insisted on performing the service despite our hints that we'd prefer a different priest. Perhaps someone who wouldn't have been too busy to look in on his newly widowed parishioner other than during fundraising.

"Hey, Yvette. Father, do you remember my husband, Kyle?"

While they shook hands and Kyle hugged Yvette, I reached inside my coat pocket and took out the folded piece of paper. Handing it to the priest, I said, "Here's a few suggestions for the eulogy like you asked for. I hope it isn't too late."

He smiled at me and shook his balding head, unfolding the paper.

As he read the list, I turned to Yvette, who, as the eldest, was going to say a special prayer with her own eulogy. "Are you ready to give yours?"

Yvette nodded. "I'm going to say how Mama was such a devoted wife to Daddy and mention all the cooking she did for the family." She turned toward the door to see if the new arrivals were friends she'd need to attend to.

My short list didn't take the priest more than a moment to read, even though I had lain awake for hours after Kyle trudged off to bed. I couldn't come up with any appropriate remembrances. Neither could my other sisters, it seemed. I asked them to call me if they wanted to add to the three items I'd thought of: How Momma insisted on driving me to the airport after I moved to California and would return home for a visit. How she sat with me, holding my hand, until my flight arrived. That we usually talked more in those few minutes than we did throughout my entire visit. How Momma insisted I keep her diamond earrings and neck-lace I wore to the Lafayette Ball, saying they looked lovely on me. And how generous Momma had been to all her children.

My sisters promised to think of more. But I heard from no one. The morning of the funeral everyone claimed they couldn't think of anything else. Penny said that whatever I wrote would surely sound fine. Nanette said we were a miserable bunch, and Claire agreed. Anne and Aimee seemed distant so I didn't press them. In the end, I added one item to our list: that it had meant a lot to me when she came out to California to see my baby.

Father Latiolais folded up the list, and Yvette excused herself to go talk to Aunt Lilia. Kyle and I smiled at the priest, a man I scarcely knew. All three of us gazed about the room until I said to Kyle, "Hey, you want to walk over to the casket?"

Kyle frowned as if to say, now why on Earth would I want to do such a thing? Both his parents had been cremated, and he didn't really under-stand all these drawn-out Catholic death rituals. But I insisted, and we left the priest to fend for himself.

I expected a bigger turnout of mourners. About one hundred attend-ed. Where were all the people from the balls and the Rotary Club? Our neighbors from the old house on Canterbury Street? Dr. Guree? The Pink Ladies from Lafayette General? I had expected a mayoral-sized crowd of people because when we were growing up, our house was always teeming with activity. Aunt Lilia, Uncle Joel, and two of their sons drove in from Houston. Momma's and Daddy's close drinking buddies huddled in cir-cles around the room. Only a handful of New Iberia friends made the drive over. They talked with their Lafayette friends whom they probably hadn't seen since the last funeral. Momma's hairdresser, the housekeep-er, and the butcher stood off to the side, fiddling with their keys and purs-es or rereading their memorial program, looking anxious for the service to begin. I wondered if Momma had requested her funeral mass to be held in the adjacent chapel because she feared a small turnout. Even Daddy had managed to fill nearly all of St. Mary's Church.

Soon Mr. Blanchard whisked through the room, asking everyone except for the immediate family to leave. It was time for the final good-bye to our mother. By nightfall, Momma would be several feet under freshly turned soil, and I'd never lay eyes on her again except in my nightmares.

I knelt before Momma, praying she had found herself in a happier place. I asked her forgiveness for the past four months and whispered, "Good-bye, I love you," four words I must have said to her a million times and not always meant. I kissed her forehead and backed away. Anne went next. She knelt down and made the sign of the cross. The cuff of her gray wool slacks flopped over to the side like a Great Dane's ear. She bowed her head (had I remembered to bow?) and whispered a prayer, tears rolling down her face. As my little sister kissed Momma and turned away, tears welled in my eyes.

When we'd all said our farewells, Mr. Blanchard nodded to Father Latiolais. He stood poised in the back of the room in his robe, holding his black Bible to his chest. Linking hands, my six sisters and I watched the priest approach the casket. He opened his book and read a few words. Then he asked us to join him in the Our Father.

Mr. Blanchard escorted my sisters and me out of the room and to the first pew of the adjacent chapel. The organist played "Green, Green Grass of Home" as Father Latiolais walked up the aisle. Kyle, Ronnie, Sam, and the other pallbearers followed, carrying the casket to the altar. I stood between Penny and Nanette and sobbed at the sight of the closed coffin. The business surrounding Momma's funeral had ended, and suddenly Momma's death felt real. I was parentless now.

Silence followed the organist's final note. Father Latiolais cleared his throat and raised his arms to the congregation. His robe spread like a bird's wings, and in a low, dramatic rumble he said, "Dear family and friends, we have come together today in loving memory of Esther Etienne. On behalf of the family, I'd like to express appreciation for your presence here and the love that you have shown Esther throughout the years."

I dried my eyes and watched the two altar boys. What a depressing way for them to spend a weekend. I imagined them tearing off their robes and running out to meet their friends at the video arcade after the service. When the priest finished his introduction, he asked everyone to sit. Yvette went to the podium. As she slid on her glasses and opened her Bible, I thought it was a shame she couldn't be a priest for her beloved Catholic church. She was so eloquent in reading and interpreting God's words. It was what she loved most.

As she returned to her seat, Father Latiolais began the eulogy. "Esther was a quiet woman. She was content reading in the study with her husband or playing solitaire. She was a devoted wife and mother..."

I glanced at Nanette, wondering, Where does he get his material from? Momma played solitaire about as often as Daddy worked crossword puzzles. Engrossed in the eulogy, Nanette failed to notice my bewilderment.

"Her children wanted for nothing," the priest said. "Esther gave them everything—jewelry, beautiful clothes..."

I looked at Penny's wrinkled forehead. "Where's he going with this?" I whispered, and she shrugged.

"Esther made sure that as debutantes, her daughters went to cotillions and had their proper coming-out..."

"Debutantes!" Penny spat. "What's he talking about?"

"I didn't tell him to say that," I said. I was the only one of my sisters who had gone to cotillion, but I hadn't included that in my suggestions. Was he trying to make us look like a bunch of fools? We never pretended to be highfalutin' debutantes. That's not what the Lafayette Balls were about for us. It wasn't like some grand device of Daddy's to formally introduce us into society. We were just having a good time. Playing dress-up.

"Their mother made sure they participated in the Mardi Gras balls. One daughter shared a story with me about her mother giving her a beautiful pair of diamond earrings and a necklace. She also remembered holding hands with her mother in the airport each time she flew back to California. But Esther's generosity knew no limits..."

So much for my notes.

"I can remember how she'd call me each spring and ask what dates I wanted to reserve for my personal use of their family's condominium. You see, Esther and Chester had a beautiful condominium..."

Penny raised an eyebrow. I laughed uneasily.

"...right on the beach of Gulf Shores, Alabama..."

"She insisted that I be her guest as often as I wished. I'd say, 'No, Miss Esther, let your children and friends have the first pick.' But she'd say no. She insisted that I choose a few weeks or weekends for myself first because she knew how much I enjoyed myself there. I loved that condo in Gulf Shores..."

"What a wacko," I said to Nanette, who was trying not to laugh. Penny smirked.

To keep myself from bursting into laughter, I looked down at the kneeler on the pew and tried to think of Momma lying in the closed coffin. But it didn't work. I lost it when I heard Father Latiolais say, "I will really miss spending evenings on the beach watching the sun set..." Next to me I felt Penny shaking as well.

Nanette elbowed me and told me to stop. I covered my mouth. A vision popped into my head: the old priest sitting on the beach and several altar boys prancing around, splashing in the warm ocean in their little Speedos. I bit my lower lip to suppress the giggles. Would I burn in hell for entertaining such thoughts in the house of God?

"To say that she was generous is an understatement," the priest continued. "She gave to all those around her. Use of that condo was a very, very special gift I will always remember and miss. I remember once...."

As Penny, Nanette, and I struggled to maintain our composure, Father Latiolais went on for five more minutes about the condo and Momma's generosity. Kyle poked me in the back several times and said people were staring at us. Shaking his head and holding his fist to his heart as if the memories sent shooting pains down to his very soul, Father Latiolais bellowed, "Gulf Shores, Alabama!" Mrs. Duhon gasped and I nearly peed.

Finally his eulogy ended. I felt like a complete idiot for allowing that man to make such a mockery of Momma and us. After mass I rushed out of the aisle, my eyes glued to the dull carpeting, past my friends, my mother's relatives, and my parents' long-time friends. I wished I could head straight to the airport and fly home that very moment.

Penny and Mrs. Duhon jumped in the first limousine. I followed on their heels. I couldn't wait to hear what they had to say about the service. I climbed into the back seat with Nanette and Aimee trailing right behind.

"The others can take the second car," Penny told the uniformed driver. "We're ready to go." He nodded and closed the door.

As the driver pulled away from the funeral home, we traded glances. I couldn't wait any longer. "Can you believe what that man said? I could hardly keep from rolling on the floor laughing."

"Girls, your mother would be so upset if she had heard that ceremony," said Mrs. Duhon. "That was awful. Coming-out parties! Your parents never put on airs like that. I bet she's rolling over in her coffin this very minute."

"I almost died when he called us debutantes," Aimee said. "I was never in any of those balls. I feel so ridiculous."

"Well, what about the condo?" Nanette exclaimed. "He just went on and on."

Penny wiped away a smear of mascara and said, "I hope the people sitting behind us thought I was crying and not laughing. I couldn't control myself."

Mrs. Duhon straightened the hem of her dress and slowly shook her head. "Father Latiolais is some piece of work. Standing up there and ranting about the damn condo. I bet he just wanted everyone to know he was out a vacation spot and needed another benefactor."

How would I face my friends at the burial? I flinched at the knowledge that Suzanne, one of the biggest gossips in Lafayette, had heard every stupid word the priest said. She was probably on her cell phone at that very moment starting the relay.

It is said that often people die as they have lived. In my mother's case, that was certainly true. She lived and died in shame.

48 ~

Just before the graveside service, Ben Veazey, our family attorney, approached me. His pasty white fingers, long and skinny like his body, touched my shoulder as Kyle, Anne, Claire, Nanette, and I banded together.

"Ma-ree, can you and your sisters come to my office tomorrow for the reading of your mother's will?"

Anne said she'd have to check her work schedule, but the rest of us agreed. He gave a solemn nod and then scurried over to Penny and Aimee. A few minutes later he headed toward Yvette and Mr. Delahoussaye. What can be so urgent? I wondered as I ran my hand down the smooth granite of my parents' gravestone.

Four plots. Soon to be all filled. Chess's and Nickey's graves bookended my parents'. What about graves for us, the girls? Daddy must have figured we'd just fend for ourselves.

Mr. Veazey's secretary led me into his office. Mr. Delahoussaye had already arrived and was talking with Anne. The empty holes in my sister's earlobes seemed at odds with the stiff blue uniform and gun she wore. I slid in beside her and smiled hello to Yvette when she took the chair next to Mr. Delahoussaye. Aimee, Claire, and Penny arrived next, seating themselves at the far right end of the attorney's desk.

When Nanette got there, Mr. Veazey began the meeting.

"I'll pass around a copy of your mother's will. You'll notice that there are two documents attached. Codicils One and Two. Please read through these first, and we'll begin there."

Yvette removed her copy and passed the stack to Anne. Curious to find out what a codicil was, I took a copy and handed the rest to Aimee. Silence and anticipation moved through the room.

In bold black letters, the first title read: Second Codicil to Last Will and Testament. I read the page once and then reread section B-1. It couldn't be. Why would...

Yvette's chair screeched against the floor, and I looked up to see her standing, panting, glaring across the table at Penny. The ribbed hem of Yvette's pullover shirt had crept up, and everyone could see the elastic of her underwear sticking out of her knit pants. She turned, staring at Mr. Veazey, and screamed, "This is unbelievable." His face didn't even twitch. He didn't speak or look away. She turned again to Penny. "You get the goddamn house, after all you've done. You selfish bitch. God damn you!"

A smile spread across Penny's face. Yvette's clenched her fists.

"Yvette," Claire called out, "for someone who professes to be such a good Christian, you sure aren't talking and behaving like one."

Yvette jerked around to face Claire. Now you've done it! I thought. Claire's warmup jacket rustled as she uncrossed her arms and laid her hands in her lap, readying herself for Yvette's attack.

Expelling a quick breath, Yvette began waving her fists in the air. Her hem shot up further. She shrieked, "Goddammit! I know you'll all just dismiss me as your crazy sister, but I have a right. I have a right, god-dammit!"

Seemingly unfazed, Penny continued smiling broadly enough to show the front teeth she'd had capped.

"You-you jerkass!" Yvette yelled, startling even Mr. Veazey who had seemed so unmovable. His eyes opened wide, but his hands rested calmly on his desk as she grabbed her papers and purse, storming out of the office.

For a few moments, not a word was spoken. Then, as if nothing had happened, Mr. Veazey glanced over at Mr. Delahoussaye and calmly said, "If you will turn to page three..."

"Excuse me, Mr. Veazey," Nanette said in a shaky voice, "but before you go on, I'd like to know why my mother did this?"

With his hands still flat on the desk (as if by removing them he risked being blown away into outer space), he looked at Nanette. "I don't know, dear. She just decided in November that she wished to change her will, leaving the house to your sister. You will see that she intended to compensate each of you with $50,000 if Penny elected to accept this legacy."

Nanette's mouth quivered. While she was on the verge of tears, I wanted to ring Penny's scrawny, complicitious neck. "But it doesn't seem fair. We each get only $50,000 while Penny gets the entire house? It's got to be worth $400,000. Momma and Daddy always showed their love through what they gave us." Turning toward Penny, she asked, "Does that mean that she loved you more than the rest of us? We all knew you were Daddy's favorite. He always gave you more. But this! It just really, really hurts that Momma would play favorites, too." Nanette started to cry.

Penny said, ever so sweetly, as if she had practiced her rebuttal, "Nanette, I don't think she meant it that way. I think she wanted it to remain in the family and thought that I should have it because I'm the only one who doesn't already have a house." Even from the grave Momma managed to remind us of her wavering love.

I looked at the date at the bottom of the Codicil. November 5, 1993. Just a month and a half before Momma went into the hospital. How convenient for Penny. I looked at Claire. She had known about the house. I could tell. She didn't show the slightest trace of anger or surprise as she fiddled with the solitaire in her wedding ring. I remembered her saying we didn't need to worry about getting the house ready to sell.

Penny sighed and spoke gently. "I really want everything after this point to be split evenly. I think we've already begun by equitably dividing up the silver and jewelry."

I didn't try to conceal the anger in my eyes or my voice. "If it was Momma's wish for you to have the house, so be it. But I'd like her car. Mr. Veazey, do you think that's possible?"

"I'm not sure how we could do that, Marie." He eyed Mr. Delahoussaye. "But perhaps, if there isn't any opposition, I could work something out."

"That's fine with me," Penny said.

"Me, too," Nanette added. Mr. Veazey said he'd work on it and let me know.

"Now, the second Codicil establishes your sister, Penny, and Mr. Delahoussaye as co-executors of the succession," said Mr. Veazey. Suddenly it all made sense to me. The big change in affection, Momma and Penny becoming pals. Penny never gave a damn about Momma before Daddy died. But when she saw an opening, she took it. She wedged herself right between Momma and the rest of us by becoming her constant drinking buddy, her travel companion, and her dining partner. We had let her assume those roles. We might as well have said, "Go ahead, Penny. You carry the burden of Momma's grief and take your rewards as you see fit."

Stunned by the will, numbness colliding with anger, I wanted to head straight for the airport and not see anyone from my family for a long time. I wanted to hide out in my own little rancher with Austin and not talk to a soul. Just wait for my share of the stocks and bonds to come through, roughly one million dollars for each daughter, and pretend like none of this happened.

But at the end of the meeting, like a mutt with a tail-wagging desire to please, I offered to phone Yvette and to ask her to join us the next morning to divide the household furnishings. That evening after we had put Austin to bed, Kyle nudged me off the sofa, saying, "Go on, get it over with." I sighed and went to the kitchen to phone Yvette. Why had I offered to call her? I hoped to hear her monotone voice on the answering machine. But on the second ring she picked up. I quickly explained why I was calling.

"Are you serious?" she asked. "I don't want anything from that house."

"Okay. I'll tell them—"

"So what'd you think of my behavior?" she asked, sounding pleased with herself. "I guess y'all got a big laugh out of it."

"No. Strangely enough, the meeting continued on as if nothing had happened. You know, it's natural for you to be angry. I'm mad too. But I wish you could just speak your mind and then sit back down. Yell at Penny or Claire all you want but stay so that you'll know what we're discussing and so you can give some feedback and suggestions." I paused, fearing she'd scream at me for lecturing her like a child, but her reaction was mild.

"Yes, I guess you're right. I just got so angry that I wanted to smack Penny. Knock that smart-ass grin right off her damn face."

"I know. She's a cold bitch." I looked at my watch, eager to be off the phone. "Anyway, is there anything you'd like us to set aside for you?"

"I suppose the painting of me in the living room. I hate to leave it there for her to throw darts at." She laughed. I rolled my eyes. "And maybe the small television in the kitchen. Hell, forget about the television. I don't really need it. Just the painting. And one more thing,"

"Yes."

"Don't you think that Claire isn't spending enough time with her son? From what I hear, she's always at work or at the gym. He's always in daycare or with babysitters. He isn't the most friendly kid in the—"

"Yvette, Claire's doing the best she can. I think Claire spends as much quality time with Tommy as she's able to."

"You sound tired."

"I am. We're leaving tomorrow, and I've still got a lot of packing to do. I'll ask Nanette or Anne to drop the painting off at your house."

I set the phone down. One of Momma's cats came by and rubbed up against my leg. "Go away, Herman," I snarled. I wanted to hurl him across the room to make myself feel better. Instead, I sucked in a mountain of air and squeezed my eyes shut. How dare Yvette criticize anyone else's parenting? She couldn't keep a pet longer than a week. I'd like to see her deal with endless hours of dirty diapers, projectile vomiting, and washing bottles. She'd have the baby packed and sitting on the hospital steps with a sign that said "Return to sender" the first day.

Thinking about the first fifty thousand dollars I'd soon receive, I wondered what would happen if I just cashed the check, grabbed Austin, stole off somewhere like Montana under a new name. No more family. No more husband. No more fighting with my sisters. They could fight over everything else. I'd have peace and quiet.

I went back into the living room and sat down beside Kyle.

"Are you all right?" he asked. I rolled my eyes and sighed. He flipped off the television and put his arm around me. "I heard you raise your voice in there. What'd she say that pissed you off so?"

"She just started in on Claire and how she's neglecting Billy. It's like no one can leave anyone else alone. We're always running around talking behind each other's backs and ridiculing each other. That's one thing I'm not going to miss about my parents. I don't want to hear their criticism of how we're raising Austin."

"That's the dumbest thing I've ever heard. What difference does it make what they think or say? I'd give anything to see my mother or father again."

I tucked my feet under me, shifting against his shoulder. I didn't know how to respond other than to say it did matter. I wanted their approval. I wanted everyone's approval. But if I couldn't have my parents' love and approval, then they might as well be dead. Was I cold-hearted? Or finally tired of being hurt?

"You ready for bed?" asked Kyle.

We lay in bed that evening, and I buried my face in Kyle's cotton T-shirt. The familiar laundry soap smelled comforting. Holding me tight as I cried, he probably figured I was crying about Momma, but I wasn't. I cried for myself. For the overwhelming panic I felt at not knowing exactly where I fit in and how I would survive the emptiness that engulfed me.

49 ~ California, 1994

At home again in Walnut Creek, I tried to settle back into a routine with Austin. But staying home all day gave me too much time to think. I found myself getting upset over all the infighting among my sisters over my parents' furniture or Momma's Cadillac. Claire had initially claimed she didn't want anything but the piano. Suddenly she decided that the antique dining room set and the living room furniture were perfect for the huge house she and Ronnie were building. Unpleasant memories of Momma kept popping into my head, and my patience with Austin dwindled. He had seemed so easy before Momma's death, but after, it felt as if he was constantly doing things to irritate me. Like throwing his plate of food onto the floor or screaming to get out of his bouncy chair while I gave myself a hurried bath.

The morning Austin kicked his way free while I was changing a soiled diaper and smeared shit on my bedroom floor, I nearly slapped his bottom. I lifted my hand to strike, but caught myself, and instead hit the metal frame of the bed. Cussing and whimpering because my knuckles stung, I realized how easily I nearly hit my child, and I panicked. Is this how Momma started? Am I going to be a monster like her? But it's different, I love Austin.

I finished diapering Austin and set him in his highchair so I could call my friend Alice. Talking with her always lifted my spirits.

"You're not going to believe what happened to me this morning," Alice whispered into the phone. "I was in San Francisco for a meeting, and the wind was blowing like crazy. I was on the corner of Market Street and Montgomery when I felt a breeze on my legs. I looked down and I'm standing there in only my jacket and pantyhose. I didn't even have underwear on."

"What?"

"Yeah, my wraparound skirt completely blew off. Luckily it caught on a MUNI sign post, so I grabbed it and ran into a side entrance of a building and tied it back on."

I laughed so hard that I startled Austin. He dropped the blocks he had been clapping together and his blue eyes stared up at me. "Did anyone see you?"

"I don't think so. But I was so busy dressing that I didn't have time to look around. Can you imagine? What if it had blown all the way down Market? Can't you just see me, running..."

We made up scenarios for a couple more minutes before she needed to get back to work.

That afternoon a letter from Aimee came in the mail. I ripped open the manila envelop to find a sheaf of copies of pages torn from a spiral notebook—the torn holes showed on the left side. A note from my sister said she thought I'd be interested in Momma's journal found tucked away in her closet.

The handwriting was Momma's familiar chicken scratch. I sat down at the kitchen table and began reading.

April 18, 1966

Drove home from Dr. Muncy's office at 6:55 P.M. Phoned Mother who was much relieved to hear my room at the "hotel" had been cancelled. Even sent Chester a kiss she was so relieved. Used unusually endearing terms of affection toward me. Is leaving early in the morning for N.O. for her monthly checkup on cancer.

Momma wanted so much for her mother just to love her. Do children ever outgrow that need? I wondered.

Called Mrs. Duhon to thank her for the lovely flowers and to tell her I was sorry to have missed seeing her but not at the "hotel" where she tried to visit me. Invited her to have coffee tomorrow and also Irma Dooley. Irma says she'll return the favor by having me for coffee with Clara Abshire, my neighbor, since we have not been speaking for three years. Just called Chess in to find out why. Chess remembered I complained about their outhouse when they were building.

7:30 P.M. Doc Guree called to see if it would be convenient for him to drop by. Answer—yes. Aimee, Penny, and I are working on a puzzle in living room. Chester reading. Chess studying in his room. Yvette studying in her room in between working on her puzzle. Aimee and Penny are begging Anne to sleep with them. No luck. Anne's "no" getting more emphatic. Nanette, Claire, and Marie in some bedroom watching TV with Mrs. Credeur. They will be asleep by 8:30. Next week I have to put them back on schedule if possible.

8:30 P.M. Doc arrives. Doc and I drink two pots of Sanka. Tasted as bad as it sounds. Chester had a few cocktails. I'm sure they were as good as they looked.

She must have had to keep a journal for her psychiatrist after her first suicide attempt, I figured.

10:30 P.M. Doc had three calls so he decided he'd better take off. Very pleasant visit. Say good night and crawl into bed with Nanette. Not ready to sleep with Chester yet. Feel tired enough to sleep without RX, so will turn off light and see what happens. (Doc does not approve of my rooms in the new house we're building. He says I'm closing myself off from people. He must mean Chester because there will certainly be enough children up there.) 11:00 P.M. Anne has just crawled in with me and Nanette. Aimee and Penny just kissed me good night.

12:00 P.M. Decided to take two tsp green RX. Am getting more awake every minute. Questions starting to pop like popcorn.

What questions? I wondered. Why are they so frightening?

Tuesday 5:00 A.M. Awake. Mad and anxious.

6:00 A.M. Called Dr. Muncy. Sleeping.

7:00 A.M. Called Dr. Muncy. Gone.

9:00 P.M. Chester had couple cocktails. I played piano. Mrs. Credeur refereed the dinner discussion. Brother Alfred called. He is concerned about Chess.

They were right to be concerned.

What are mice for? (Chester) Caring??

A rodent? How funny. She always called him a 'spineless bastard' when they fought. What was he so afraid of? Afraid to love, to care?

Wednesday 7:00 A.M. Took RX last night about 9:30. Chester kissed me good night and mentioned casually "I love you." Doctor, if I thought you were still sleeping it would give me great pleasure to wake you up to let you know that I slept from 10:00 P.M. to 7:00 A.M. Those pills may not be so bad after all. Think I had almost forgotten what it feels like to be a human being.

4:45 P.M. I wish the feeling had lasted longer!

Apparently it didn't!

Her journal mentioned Grandma's crawfish bisque. It was odd how such a cold woman could make the most comforting, delicious soup. An ability and fondness for cooking was one of the few things Momma and her mother had in common.

Depression and irritation in full swing but will exert every effort not to show. (Succeeded). Chester came in about 6:00 while I was sleeping.

Batman in progress. Children all glued to TV. After this, Lost in Space. Must either make comments regularly or smile because if I do not, Chester is asking if something is the matter. Luckily Mother and Chester do not live in the house together with me all day.

She would hate living with Kyle then, I thought.

Thursday 7:15 A.M. On third mug of coffee while writing this. Doctor, do not believe that you can ever understand me unless you would meet and know my children a little first hand. They are of average intelligence, but—

What? I was only four years old. How can she know already that I'm just average?

—their sweetness is above average (most times). Have spoiled Nanette a little more than the others so she is not always so sweet. Will have to discipline a little.

And I bet you did!

Two of Chester's famous jabs:

"I met Esther sitting under a table at Deare's, drink in hand, saying, 'Kiss me!'"

and "I married Esther to find out what went on in her mind because she talked so little. I soon found out nothing went on and that's why she didn't talk."

Daddy could be so cruel when he wanted.

Friday 7:00 A.M. Just awakened. Thursday afternoon sexual relations improved considerably. If they continue in this vein, you can be the next Godfather. After leaving your office, Chester and I went to Toby's for dinner. Had two Old Fashions, one dozen Oysters Rockefeller and coffee. Behaved. Went on to the show to see "My Fair Lady." Chester and I agreed we enjoyed the evening thoroughly and would get out more often if babysitters can be lined up as we do not leave Yvette at night by herself with all the children.

pg. 58. 1—Applies; 2—Does not.

Pg. 59. 3—Why do I, knowing how much more fortunate I am than most people, have this depression?

Why do I also feel this way? Is it part of our legacy?

I read through the journal pages twice and then called Nanette.

"Pretty weird, isn't it?" Nanette said. "I think she had just gotten out of the mental hospital."

"Yeah, that's what the *hotel* was. It just left me with the saddest feeling. She must have lived in her own little hell with Daddy and Grandma always watching over her. Like she couldn't express an honest emotion or just be blue if she wished. Scared that Daddy would send her back to the hospital for more shock therapy." I could truly empathize with her hatred of their constant surveillance. Her every emotion scrutinized. But to give Daddy some credit, I knew how much I hated seeing Kyle depressed. As if his sadness would lasso me in and pull me down with him.

The line was silent for a minute, then Nanette said, "Did you catch the part where she said I was getting a little too spoiled? I bet I got a few beatings right about then, just to set me straight!"

"I'm sure." We giggled. "You think they would have been happier if they'd married other people?"

"Maybe. They seemed to fuel each other's misery. Perhaps if they had each married someone with a more normal childhood, they wouldn't have drunk and fought so much."

"Do you realize that at the time Momma wrote that journal she must have been pregnant with Nickey? He was born in December and she wrote it in April. No wonder he had so many problems. All the drugs Momma must have been given. Plus the alcohol."

Nanette sighed. "I didn't think of that. Have you heard from Claire?"

"No. And I don't plan on calling her again." Claire and I were fighting over Momma's Cadillac. She refused to sign over her portion of the car to me even though I pointed out that she had been living rent free in one of Daddy's houses for the past seven years. Our last phone call had turned into an ugly name-calling, screaming match.

"Well, I've got to run," Nanette said, sounding dispirited. Momma's journal had managed to trample both our spirits.

Kyle came home that evening elated about a new project at work. He was heading a huge general ledger conversion, and it meant greater exposure for him to the higher-ups. I showed him Momma's journal. He skimmed the first page and put it down, saying he couldn't read her handwriting. Feeling hurt, I wondered, if it was too much to ask for him to show a little interest in the things that concerned me? I wanted him to feel as awful as I did.

That evening as I was bathing Austin, the telephone rang. Kyle stood at the bathroom door with his hand cupped over the receiver. "It's Claire. Do you want me to tell her you're busy?"

"No, I'll talk to her. Will you finish Austin?"

He nodded.

"Marie, I wanted to call and tell you that I signed all the papers today for Momma's car. It's yours," Claire said.

"You didn't have to. I'm quite happy to pay you your share."

"No. I don't know what got into me. I *want* you to have the car," she said emphatically. So much for Ronnie and his concern over who is getting what. "I hope you can forgive me. I didn't mean to create a rift between us. You mean too much to me."

"I'm sorry, too, about what I said. You caught me off guard. I've been so depressed. I thought that on top of losing Momma and Daddy, I had lost you, too. Over a stupid car."

"Let's just forget about it."

After we hung up, I went into Austin's room where Kyle was dressing him. I reached down and ran my hand over my son's hair. It felt so fluffy and soft after a bath.

"So everything is now hunky-dory between you and your sister?" Kyle asked, slipping a green sleeper onto Austin.

"Yeah." I shrugged. "We both apologized, and I get the car."

He zipped Austin's sleeper and sat him up on the bed. Then turning toward me, he said, "Why is it you can forgive your sisters so easily every time they do something to you, but you're still harboring grudges against me from our wedding? Why don't I get the same level of compassion?"

Where in the hell did this come from?

"Kyle, can we discuss this after Austin goes to sleep?"

"No. You always promise we'll talk later, but then you're too tired or you want to read the newspaper or watch television. You never have any time for me. I'm not as important as your sisters or your friends or all the money and crap you're dying to get your hands on."

Why can't you leave me alone? I wanted to scream. Why can't everyone just leave me the hell alone? I'm tired of fighting. I'm tired of giving, giving, giving. In a hateful tone, I said, "I'm going to fix a bottle for Austin and then put him to bed. We'll talk after that."

I knew there was a perfectly good reason that I couldn't ever forgive him, but it eluded me. Slamming the cabinet and microwave doors, I wanted to let Kyle know that I was pissed and to watch out. Just like Momma used to do before she came up to our rooms.

Kyle and I argued until nearly two in the morning. He was lonely and unhappy. He felt invisible in our marriage. He didn't understand why I acted so cold toward him. I told him I hadn't much left over after Austin. I felt like I was going to explode or die of suffocation. That I needed him to fulfill himself, independent of me, until I figured out why I was so miserable. He said no. That he couldn't live like roommates. I suggested that we divorce, that he move out. Absolutely not, he replied. He suggested that I move out and he keep Austin. I said absolutely not. Austin was my whole life. We waltzed around to familiar tunes until we were exhausted and finally chose sleep over divorce. A couple of months later I was pregnant with our second son.

The dove says, Coo, coo, what shall I do?
I can scarcely maintain two.
Pooh, pooh, says the wren, I have ten,
And keep them all like gentlemen.
                                   —Mother Goose

50 ~ California, 1995

Kyle nudged me, but I didn't open my eyes.

"Marie!" Penny called out. "We're waiting."

I closed the refrigerator door and followed her to the dining room.

Momma still looked sick. Her legs stuck out immodestly from her soiled hospital gown. An IV dangled from her wrist. I paused at the door. Penny nudged me along. Maybe she'll die again, I prayed. I smiled at Daddy as he turned toward me. He didn't seem to recognize me.

Taking the seat farthest from my parents, I nervously apologized for being late. Momma started coughing and suddenly a tube sprouted from her trachea.

"Do you want your money back?" I asked when her fit stopped. That was what my sisters and I were all afraid of. Momma jerked her head around, facing me. Daddy looked over, scowling, and slowly nodded. "But I've spent some of it on my house. I bought a swing set for my boys." Ashamed, I looked down at the table. The others had begun spending their inheritance too.

"I'm not giving mine back," Penny announced. "You can have the house, but I'm keeping the stocks and bonds."

She's going to make them mad at all of us. My legs trembled. Daddy slammed his fist on the table, and the crystal salt and pepper shakers fell over. Tiny white and black grains scattered across the polished walnut. Claire said she couldn't give her money back because she and Ronnie had used it to build a lovely new house. Aimee said they could have it all, and so did Anne. Yvette said they'd get it back only over her dead body, and Momma laughed. Nanette asked if she could keep just a little.

Suddenly, I was sitting on a bleacher next to Nanette in the L. J. Alleman gymnasium. Sixth and seventh grade girls played basketball. Momma, dressed and younger looking, sat between two friends, smoking one of her Virginia Slims. She held Nickey, an infant, on her lap.

"Nitwits, every last one of them," Momma told the lady to her right, casting a hateful glance at Nanette and me. "They'll never amount to anything."

"That's not true, Momma," I stammered. She exhaled a cloud of smoke and poked her finger in my arm, as if daring me to dispute her.

I woke up and felt Kyle nudging me. The baby was hungry. Through the monitor on the nightstand I could hear him crying. I peeled off the covers and trudged down the hall. It was only a dream, I assured myself, just like all the other ones. Not until Zack, my three-month-old baby boy, was nursing contentedly did I finally convince myself that Momma and Daddy were still dead and that dead people couldn't come alive and hurt me.

"Do you want some water?" Kyle whispered from the door. He was standing there squinting, wearing only a white T-shirt with a gaping hole under the right armpit.

I smiled at him gratefully and said, "Yes, thanks."

After he brought me a glass of ice water and climbed back into bed, I thought about the dream. I often dreamt of Momma and Daddy return-ing to life. They always came back angrier or sicker or more threatening in some way. Never was I happy to see them. Their presence scared me. I felt so guilty each time I woke up and found myself relieved that it had only been a dream, and then I thought I must be one of the most despi-cable people in the world for wanting my parents dead.

My grief for Momma had been delayed, it seemed, by all the arguing. We held several family meetings during the year following her death. I attended one when I picked up Momma's car and even ended up fighting with Claire and Nanette. Penny tried to stay above the fray—why squab-ble over the furniture when you've gotten the whole house? Mr. Delahoussaye warned us to use caution because we couldn't take back the hurtful things we said to each other. Anne and Aimee just kept their mouths shut. Yvette declined to attend the meetings at all.

I switched Zackary to my left breast. He rested his tiny hand on my chest and nursed sleepily. I thought about Penny and wondered what she was doing at that very moment.

Just a few months earlier Mr. Veazey notified us all that Penny was taking her full executor fee for attending a few meetings. I fumed for a whole day. I was big and fat and pregnant and mad at the whole world. I waited until Austin was sleeping, and then I dialed Penny's house.

"Hello, this is Penny. I'm unable to come to the phone..."

"This is your sister Marie," I said calmly. "I just received the final papers for Momma's succession, and I am appalled by your greed. I can't believe that after all you have gotten, you're taking your full executor fee—$48,000. Doesn't it matter at all to you that time after time you've screwed your own sisters? You make me sick. You've always been a greedy bitch. You locked your closets, you stole from Momma's purse, and I know you stole that $2,000 from Daddy's wallet. I hope all this money makes you happy. But I doubt it will. You'll be just as rich and miserable as Momma and Daddy. Well, take it all. I know your birthday is this week, so here's my wish for you. I hope you sit all alone, drinking champagne out of the silver goblets you stole from the rest of us but didn't think we noticed, and I hope you're miserable. You're a drunk, just like them. Now you have everything, their house, their money, their bed. Good riddance to you. I hope I never see you again."

After I hung up, my temples throbbed with pain. I wanted to kick in every cabinet door in the kitchen. Instead, I dug my nails into my palms and fell on the floor crying, rocking myself like a baby. Penny would never speak to me again after that message. I felt relieved and sad. Even though I hated her for how she'd treated us during Momma's illness, she had been there for me during difficult times, and now she'd never be there for me again.

When I told Kyle that Penny was taking her fee, that she was making nearly $80,000 that year off my parents' deaths, he shrugged. I told him about the message I'd left. He said, "Just as well. I haven't spoken with my sister in over fifteen years, and I don't miss her."

I contemplated divorce often when I had only one child. It felt reassuring knowing that at any point I could leave Kyle and take Austin with me. But once I had the second baby, everything seemed harder. I felt outnumbered and besieged by constant demands, physical and mental. Simply packing up the boys and leaving their father no longer seemed like an option. Whenever I mentioned divorce, Kyle threatened to tell our friends and the judge about my explosive temper. How I threw myself on the floor like a two-year-old or put my fist through the wall when I didn't get my way. He'd say that without him to lash out at, I'd go after the boys. He'd tell the court they weren't safe with me. So I felt trapped.

It wasn't that my children were bad. I knew Austin didn't topple his plate of macaroni and cheese on purpose and Zack didn't spew vomit in my face just to vex me. But some days, it felt like everyone from the cranky gay checker at Safeway to my boys wanted to make my life hell. Mornings—especially after I dropped Austin off at preschool—were generally okay. But afternoons were another matter. Getting Austin to take a nap seemed impossible. He refused to stay in his room. If I planned it perfectly, I could get the baby down first and then lie with Austin until he fell asleep. Then I'd sneak out of his room to enjoy a brief respite before beginning dinner. But some days no amount of singing or holding him would work. Shaking with anger, scared because the idea of spanking Austin was beginning to seem reasonable, I'd pack them both into Momma's Cadillac and drive straight to the freeway. Heading either north toward Sacramento or south to San Jose, I glanced from time to time into the rearview mirror, watching their lids blink in unison until they slowly closed. My neck muscles finally relaxed, and I drove for hours enjoying the peace and quiet.

Being constantly on the alert when the boys were in a room together drained me. I might be changing Zack on the living room floor, and Austin would decide to hurl the remote control across the room at Zack's head. Or he'd tip the bassinet over while running through the living room. He constantly tried to feed the baby things like nuts or grapes.

All I did was yell. "Austin, leave him alone…Austin, please get away from the baby…Goddammit! Austin, get away from him right now."

I'd throw the head of lettuce I was washing onto the floor or turn off the stove and run into the family room yelling, "Do you really want to hurt your brother? Why don't you ever listen to me?" as I pounded my fists on my thighs.

Austin's face would go completely blank, and his mouth would open. The Brio train he had threatened to hit Zack with would fall from his dimpled hands. He'd begin to wail and drop to the floor sobbing, calling

out, "Mommy, Mommy..." I had just pelted him again with my angry
words. Words or hands, it didn't matter. After each episode, I scooped
him into my lap and begged his forgiveness. I sobbed and said that
Mommy didn't mean to hurt him. I begged him to please listen to me
when I said stop so I wouldn't have to scream. I swore to myself I'd never
yell again. But I did.

The anger and hopelessness that bubbled up in me was like my mother's rage and despair. I began hating myself.

Nights when Kyle came trudging in from work after nine, complain-
ing about his grueling day, heading straight for the television with his
Sharps beer, I stuffed my anger. I knew he'd never agree to a divorce, and
I was too worn out to leave him.

One night when Zack was six months old, I woke from a terrifying
dream to find Kyle's hand sneaking its way up my gown.

"Kyle, not now," I whined. "I'm exhausted. I just had a horrible
dream."

I squeezed my eyes shut and tried to replay it. I was in some secret
apartment. There was a knock at the door. A group of knife-wielding
men and women forced their way in. I ran for the sliding doors, but they
surrounded me and I froze. One woman stabbed my neck. One after
another they jabbed at me. *Die, Marie. Die,* I told myself. Finally, I was
dead. Suddenly I stood in the hallway and the blood was gone. I ran to
the elevator and pounded on the call button. The mob of suits cornered
me. Their knives sank into me time and time again. I felt my body succumb to death, and there was a moment of peace. Then I woke, and this
time I was on the street. Over and over they killed me.

Kyle moaned. "It'll just take a minute, I promise."

That's what they all say before they fuck you. How many guys have I
had between my legs? Promising me that they'll be quick, that they'll
love me, that I'll enjoy it once they get started. Sticking in the knife. Or
yanking my panties down to spank me—Momma—time after time after
time. Never just letting me sleep in peace.

I let Kyle move my protesting hand away from my panties. He yanked
them down. I succumbed. I lay there with my eyes closed. I prayed that
God would help me to find strength.

A week later. 8:30, I checked my watch. Twenty minutes to feed and
dress Austin, to pack his lunch, and get him and the baby into the car.

You can nurse Zack after Austin's in school, I told myself, determined to be on time for the morning bell. I didn't want to receive another dirty look from Miss Charlotte, Austin's teacher.

I dressed Austin and sat him down in front of a bowl of Cheerios. "Come on sweetie, eat now. We're running late. We don't have much time." I left him at the table and went to wake the baby.

Setting Zack into his car seat on the kitchen floor, I slipped the pacifier in between his lips. "There you go, Uggaboo." He sucked happily.

When Austin finished his cereal, I plucked him from the chair. Smelling his foul diaper, I hurried to the laundry room to change him for the third time that morning and then carried him to the car. It still felt strange seeing Momma's Cadillac with the Louisiana license plate in my garage.

"I'm going to leave you here for a moment while I go get your brother. Okay, Austinrooney?"

He reached for a nearby toy hammer, and I ran inside to grab the baby. Just as I picked up his car seat, Zack's face turned crimson red. I heard the explosion. A wet, runny poop. He'd had diarrhea for days, and all the doctor could do was tell me to keep him hydrated. I knew that if I didn't change his diaper, he'd have a bloody rash by the time we got home.

Damn it, I mumbled, unbuckling Zack and carrying him into the laundry room. I laid him on the towel littered with dirty diaper bundles. We'll be late. I pulled some wipes from the box and imagined the nasty stares in store for me. For Christ's sake, it's only preschool. Doesn't she understand that I'm trying my best?

After changing the diaper, I looked at my watch. Three minutes past the bell. I sighed heavily. I couldn't face that teacher today. Blinking away tears, I bit my bottom lip. *Why, why me, goddammit? Why can't something go the right way for once?*

It wasn't just the dirty diapers. It was dreading Kyle's return that evening from a business trip in New York. Again, it was knowing that with two children, both in diapers and waking up during the night, I couldn't simply pack them up and leave my husband. Even if he let me take the kids, which he said he wouldn't, I couldn't manage, physically or emotionally. My life seemed like a prison, with little hope of parole, let alone escape.

I snapped up the baby's pants and buckled him into his car seat. Crying, I clenched my fists. What was I going to do with both boys at home all day again? I needed some quiet time to prepare myself for being pleasant when Kyle returned. The constant vigilance over an active toddler and a baby exhausted me. I simply couldn't spend another morning at the park, making small talk with other mothers, acting as if my life is hunky-dory so as to not scare them away.

You're not the first woman to raise two small children, I told myself, kicking the box of diaper wipes across the carpet. If other people can manage, why can't you? The box struck the toy bin. Zack's pacifier popped out of his mouth, and his arms flew up in the air. At the same time I slammed my fists into the nearby bi-fold doors. Why can't I cope like a normal person? Anger welled up, and I wanted to really hurt something. Smash it. Rip it to pieces. I wanted to make something feel as bad as I felt. My chest heaved as I fled to the kitchen and looked around at the cabinets and counter tops. Not Kyle's espresso machine. The vase would break into a thousand pieces, and I'd spend the entire day sweeping up shards of glass. I saw the dining chair next to the window and the stupid uneven curtains I'd sewn when we bought the house. Grabbing the chair, I lifted it high into the air, knocking the fixture above so that the light flickered. I slammed the chair down hard on the white linoleum floor. With one crash the chair snapped apart. I looked down at my clenched hands and realized all that remained was the curved piece from the back. I gasped and fell to my knees, crying above the baby's cry from the other room. Pounding my fists on the floor, I knew that Austin was probably getting frightened about being in the car alone. I knew that before long, I would be out of walls to punch and chairs to break, and the kids would be next.

I stared at the four splintered chair legs strewn about the room. One of them had ripped an inch-long hole in the floor. *Kyle's going to have a fit. There's no hiding this outburst.*

51 ~

Standing at our old gas stove, I listened for Kyle's car. The heat blowing down from the wall register failed to drive away my chill. My thoughts, swirling about my head like falling leaves in a hurricane, settled again on Zack and Austin. I glanced down at the torn linoleum and cringed. Hadn't I learned anything from my own childhood? I always swore I'd be different, I wouldn't abuse my kids like Momma did. But was raging in their presence any better?

Kyle would be home any minute. As I waited to hear the grind of the garage door, I pictured myself removing the largest knife from the wooden block and jabbing it over and over into my belly. Brief pain, but then nothing. No more unhappiness. No more guilt. Only peace. As quickly as the fantasy entered my head, another vision—Austin finding me on the floor, begging Mommy to wake up, crying at the sight of blood oozing out of my stomach—slammed into my mind. Quit indulging your own self-pity. You can't dump your pain off on those boys like that, I told myself.

At 6:30 Kyle opened the screen door and shuffled into the kitchen. Before he had time to walk over and kiss me, I pointed down to the torn linoleum. Austin sprang up from the laundry room floor where he was stacking boxes of diaper wipes to kick over, a game that made him laugh hysterically. He ran to greet his dad. With arms wrapped around Kyle's slacks, he said, "Mommy break floor."

Kyle dropped his suit bag onto a chair and slid his brief case across the table until it banged on the nearby wall. He reached down and picked up his son. Kyle's blue eyes darkened. It felt as if it were them against me.

"It was a shitty day," I said, sniffling. "Austin didn't get to go to school. Sometimes I feel like I'm going to lose it with them. Hurt them or something. I think I need some help."

His hands trembled as he said, "You've got a cleaning lady twice a week. Austin's in daycare half the time. How much more help do you need?" He thinks I'm talking about getting more domestic help. What about someone to fix me? Standing there in his suit, not a trace of baby vomit on his tie or jacket, he looked and sounded like my father when my mother complained. I hated him.

"I don't know," I mumbled, looking down at my maternity shorts. Six months after giving birth I still couldn't fit into my regular clothes. My life felt out of control. I wanted some assurance that everything would be fine. But Kyle silently stared down at the gash. I reached for Austin, telling him that he could watch television until dinner. As I searched the living room for the remote control, my husband carried his bag off to our bedroom.

A few minutes later he returned to the kitchen. I noticed his left hand tucked inside his pocket. He leaned against the screen door watching me as I stirred the frozen peas into the gooey risotto. It made me nervous when Kyle stared at me and didn't say a word. I figured he was about to spin off into one of his depressions because he had come home once again to find me angry and out of control.

"Kyle, what is it?"

"Nothing." His eyes moved from me to the tear in the linoleum.

"Bullshit. I can see it in your face. Tell me."

He pulled his hand out of his pocket and held up an unopened condom. "I found this in the top drawer. Aren't they usually kept in the medicine cabinet?"

I squinted, half expecting him to smile. But he was serious.

"What in the fuck are you accusing me of? I just told you how scared I am that I'm about to do something terrible to the kids or myself and all you can think about is whether I'm screwing…who?…the gardener. Look at the fucking floor. Look at my big fat belly. Does it look to you like I'm having a party here while you're out of town? Are you crazy? Are you so fucking out of your mind that you think I want anyone touching me? Don't you get it? Hasn't it sunken in yet that I just want to be left alone? I don't want you or anyone else trying to fuck me?"

Kyle winced as I started pounding my fists against my chest, again and again, faster and harder. Even though Austin was probably watching me from the other room, I couldn't stop. I hated myself for scaring my son, but hurting myself felt like the only way to drive out my misery.

"Stop it. Calm down, Marie."

With my fists held mid-air, I paused and gasped for breath. Panic-stricken, Kyle scurried around the kitchen, slamming the door and drawing the curtains so that, God forbid, the neighbors wouldn't see his wife losing her mind. Part of me wanted to laugh at him, and the other part of me wanted to cry. Was this what Daddy and his father did when their wives lost control of themselves? Did Momma and grandmother feel driven to such lunacy by their own crippled husbands? My arms fell to my sides, and I felt my legs start to shake. He looked so innocent I felt riddled with shame for my tantrum. He just couldn't help himself. His insecurities ran as deep as mine. Was he really trying to be mean? No. He just couldn't see past his own engulfing needs. Neither could I.

This is nuts! I told myself. You can't live like this. So what if you find some strange comfort in this tired, familiar routine. Does beating on yourself, scaring every person around you, really lessen your misery? Can't I get people to listen to me some other way?

In my steadiest voice, I said, "I know what you're accusing me of, and I'm not even going to dignify it with a response."

"Don't be mad," he begged, stepping toward me. I put my hands out to warn him to stay back. He withdrew and pouted for a moment. "It's just that I figured maybe there was someone else, that that's why you never want to make love to me. I'm sorry."

"Dinner's ready. Go get Austin while I check on Zack."

I walked over to cover the rice pot and then lowered the blue flame. Surprised by my lack of reaction, Kyle left the kitchen.

I opened the door to the baby's room. He slept contentedly despite having kicked off his blankets and dropped his pacifier. Leaning over the crib railing, I gently touched the soft wisps of blond hair on his head. He was so beautiful. Both my boys were. I couldn't believe how angelic their faces looked when they slept.

I looked at the purple speckles on Zack' forehead between his eyebrows. "Angel kisses" is what one of the delivery room nurses called them after Austin was born with similar markings. Another nurse laughed and called them "storkbites." Dr. Abel pushed her red eyeglasses up on her shiny nose and said they were capillaries, simply clusters of capillaries close to the surface of the skin. She said the marks would fade over time, often leaving only a trace. Perhaps these *angel kisses* were reminders of both the miracle and the pain of birth. I had hoped that the discomfort of squeezing their way into the world would be the greatest pain Austin or Zack would have to endure. But this day I left one sitting in the car wondering if he'd been forgotten while frightening the other with my wrath. Some days I screamed so loud that Austin ran cowering behind the futon, horror replacing the purity on his face. I had only swatted at his diaper once, so far, but sometimes I wanted to beat his tiny body into submission.

I ran my hands over my arms, wondering if invisible clusters of bruises lay beneath my skin. Undoubtedly they covered my entire body, never having been given a chance to heal or fade. I had grown accustomed to the pain just like I had become accustomed to the chaos in my life. I'd allowed myself to be used by guys like Dr. Schmidt, Dwayne, and Boo. I found a man who thrived on chaos as I did, and together we lived from crisis to crisis. It would be difficult to wean myself from this familiar way of living, but I had to.

Pulling the fuzzy lilac blanket up to Zack's waist, I felt my shoulders slowly relax. The anger slipped away, temporarily receding.

52 ～ California, 1998

Three years passed since that morning I slammed the kitchen chair against the floor. Kyle and I sought help from three different marriage counselors. Finally, when Zack turned two, Kyle agreed to move out. We'd share the children jointly.

Leaning against the headboard, I listened to the escalation of laughter at the end of the hall. The chimes outside my bedroom window, usually still in August, danced and collided in the cool evening breeze. Energy sparked both inside and outside the house.

I sighed with exhaustion and slid off the mattress.

My appearance at the doorway of the playroom sent the foursome, Austin and Zack, five and three, and their young friends, Jenny and Ryan, shrieking and heading for the closet. They fell all over themselves and each other in fitful giggles until I cleared my throat and stood, with my hands on my hips and a righteous look of annoyance on my face, and pointed to the door. Scurrying past me to return to their bedding, they left in their wake the fruity odor of toothpaste and a stale smell of chlorine.

"Now I mean it…" I scanned the four sets of eyes peeking out from their blankets. "Go to sleep, or I'm going to call your parents to come pick you up. Do you want me to do that?" I, least of all, wanted to have to call my neighbors and admit that I couldn't manage a simple sleepover.

Jenny and Ryan kicked their legs under their sleeping bags and shook their heads no, trying not to giggle at my whiny, pleading voice. Austin and Zack with their straight white hair fanning over their pillow lay motionless on their twin mattresses. Their large pupils crowded out the blue in their excited eyes.

I exhaled loudly and left the room, knowing full well I hadn't dampened their spirit. In two minutes or less I'd hear another outbreak of laughter.

I walked down the hall, glancing through the picture window at the huge eucalyptus trees off in the distance. Usually the striking silhouette of branches and foliage against the evening sky seemed like a reward after our lengthy bedtime ritual. But this day I felt depleted. Too much playing the perfect hostess to the neighbors and their kids.

I sat on the edge of my bed and waited. Maybe this time they won't get up. Ha. The SF Chronicle sat on the nearby pillow next to the thick white envelope from the divorce lawyer. The clock blinked: 9:36. An hour past their normal bedtime, leaving me just one hour for myself. Closing my eyes, I waited.

At the sound of feet padding in the hallway and stifled chuckles I sprang from the bed, my heart racing. How dare they defy me again?

I ran down the hall past the stairs, grabbing Austin's arm as he tried to duck back into his room. Jenny and her brother stood opposite us at the guestroom door, their hands cupped over their mouths, their skinny sunburned legs crossed.

"Come on, Jenny," Zack's squeaky voice called from somewhere unseen, not knowing I had returned.

My grip on Austin's arm tightened, and I jerked him forward.

"I told you kids to go to sleep. Now I'm tired. I just want to read my newspaper and go to sleep."

Jenny snickered. Her dark eyes twinkled with innocence. She was the ringleader, I figured, coaxing them from their bedding for another game of hide-and-seek. I filled with rage at her innocence. It didn't matter that Jenny was four.

"If only you kids would listen," I said, striking Austin's bottom. He tried to pull away, and my hand hit again. He kicked my shin and I moaned, slapping his fanny once more. Zack peered out from the playroom, and his mouth fell open in fright. They watched as Austin kicked at my legs, tears welling in his angry eyes.

Stop, Marie, I thought. They understand that you're serious. I panted, and then said, "Okay, truce. You stop kicking me, and I won't spank you anymore."

Scared and humiliated in front of his friends, Austin twisted to free himself and aimed another kick at my legs.

"Quit, I said."

I turned to the others and, warned, "Get in bed right now, and I don't want to hear a peep out of you."

They scrambled, and this time, they'd remain quiet. But for insurance

I added, "If I hear a single word from you two, I'm calling your dad." A lie, of course. I was already panicked about what they'd tell their parents. Maybe they'd forget about it by breakfast. Or keep quiet out of guilt, blaming themselves, their bad behavior for my outburst. That's what I had always done.

I ushered Austin down the hall, shushing him as he screamed for me to let go of him. I needed to apologize and set things right between us.

"Stop crying, sweetheart. I'm sorry." But sorry wasn't going to work this time. I had singled him out when the mischief wasn't solely his doing. He was hurt and angry at the injustice. When we reached my room, I tried to hug and console him, but he punched me in the arm.

"You little shit," I spat, picking him up and lifting him onto the bed. "Don't you dare hit me again." He lunged forward and I pinned his shoulders. When I had him overpowered, he stuck out his tongue. I wanted to knock the devilish look right off his face but instead chose a lesser punishment. I turned him over and began slapping his bottom, mumbling, "I told you I was sorry. Why can't you calm down? Is this how you show your thanks for all I've done tonight? I wasn't even up to having your friends spend the night, but I said yes anyway."

My hand came down hard several times, in quick succession, and then I missed his shorts and struck his stiff arched back. I heard the sting and he screamed out. I pulled away, cringing both for Austin and for his friends. *What is Marie doing to him? Are we next?* I knew the terror that they were feeling.

Clutching his backside, Austin sobbed.

"God, I'm sorry. I'm so sorry."

I tried to embrace him as he rolled over, but he knocked away my hands.

"I hate you. I hate you so much. Why do you always pick on me? Why not Zack or Jenny? They were doing it too."

How could I admit that I chose him because I knew I could get away with it? If I struck another child surely there'd be repercussions. With my own there'd also be consequences, but I figured I could mitigate those over time with good behavior.

"Please Austin, let me see if your back is okay."

He sat on the edge of the bed trembling, wailing, and I gently lifted his T-shirt. A big red welt right above his elastic waistband. I had left a perfect imprint of my hand. I gasped at the raised skin. They were seeing their father tomorrow. What would he say if Austin showed him this mark? Would Kyle have enough ammunition to seek full custody as he'd threatened when I asked him to leave? Part of me wanted Austin to tattle, to find the voice I never had. The other part of me, the dominant and fearful side, wanted his loyalty and silence.

"Austin, I swear I didn't mean to hurt you. I'm so sorry. Mommy did a terrible thing. I shouldn't have spanked you. You don't deserve this. Ever."

We both sat on my bed, tears running down our cheeks. How could I do this to my son? I pictured myself sitting in my therapist's office, next to the window where the apple tree would be in full bloom for yet another season, my head bent in shame as I replayed the entire episode. Her eyes would narrow with disappointment. Maybe I shouldn't even tell her, just swear to myself that this time would be the absolute last time. But what was the point in seeking help if I wasn't going to be honest?

I looked at Austin, his perfect posture. He was only five, and already I'd spanked his bottom on five different occasions. Five times in five years. From a single swat to this.

Softly I said, "I want you to know how truly sorry I am. I know I've scared you. I've embarrassed you in front of your friends. And I've hurt you. For all of that I'm so sorry." He looked up, hugging his arms to his heaving chest, searching my face to make sure the ogre had really gone back into its dark cave.

"This wasn't about you being bad because you're not. You're a good boy. Mommy just doesn't know how to control her temper yet and to set limits. It's okay to be angry with me right now, because there's no excuse for how I've behaved. You might even hate me. When I was a little girl and my mother spanked me, I hated her. But I don't want you or your brother to hate me. That's why I'm working so hard to be different. That's why I go to talk to that lady, Ms. Jennifer. I'll learn. I promise you that. It's okay for you to tell Daddy tomorrow that I've hurt you."

Austin sniffled and said, "I miss Ma-teke."

"I do too."

After Kyle had moved out, despite my many doubts, I bought the boys a Labrador puppy at their urging. The hyper puppy turned out to be too much for me. After discovering chewed off sprinkler heads and gnawed bender-boards, I panicked. I feared he'd uproot my entire new landscaping. I couldn't afford to sink more money into repairs. So I called the breeder, and hysterical with shame and fear, I asked her to please take him back. I said I was scared I was going to hurt the puppy.

Austin loved the chocolate Lab and took her return the hardest. The entire experience, reminiscent of all the unlucky dogs that found their way into my family, so many of them mistreated, had only one positive note: I had said, Enough, before I hurt the dog. Of course that doesn't negate the hurt done to Austin, but it felt like a tiny step toward humanity. And wasn't it humanity, benevolence toward each other, that I was seeking?

"Can we get another dog?"

"No, sweetie. I can't handle a pet right now."

Austin nodded as if I'd given the correct answer. He withdrew an arm from his chest, carefully setting his hand down between us, open and tentative, waiting. Was he saying I was forgiven? I searched his face to make sure I hadn't misread the overture. He looked so beautiful and innocent I wished for a moment I were dead. Dead and far away from my children so they'd never be hurt by me again. But I knew that would just be the cowardly way out. Lightly I took his warm hand and held it in mine. We sat quietly, looking at the empty wall ahead where I'd recently removed Kyle's and my wedding photograph.

For hours that night as Austin lay sleeping in the bed next to me, too upset to return to his room with his brother and friends, I thought about the evening. Why hadn't I just separated them after the first warning? Why hadn't I simply said no to the boys' request to let their friends sleep over if I was so tired? I needed to stop being lazy and listen to my instincts. God (or someone) gave me that little voice for a reason. I told myself that after this incident—seeing my handprint on Austin's backside—I would never lay another hand on either of them. And I haven't.

But I couldn't just stop there. No more kicking in cabinets when bad or disappointing news arrived. No more screaming at the top of my voice when the kids failed to do as I asked after the tenth warning. It wasn't enough to tell myself that I had had it worse and that whatever they got from me wasn't half as bad as I had received. Sooner or later I'd be caught. They would tell Kyle or he'd notice a mark. Or they'd refuse to return to my house on Sunday afternoon. I couldn't risk losing my boys. I needed them as much as they needed me.

I learned soon after this episode that simply feeling bad and ashamed would not invite change. I am *not* by nature wholly altruistic. I do *not* do something unless it somehow serves me. Often the paths I have chosen are to prevent me from getting hurt, to make me feel happier, or to further my own agendas. Perhaps I am cynical. But I do believe it is my own grief or the possibility of it, not my victim's, that primarily dictates and changes my behavior. But if in improving myself my children benefit, then they are dually served.

The cock doth crow
To let you know:
If you be wise
'Tis time to rise.
—Mother Goose

Epilogue ~

I replayed the dive in my mind —a back one and a half with a half twist—and felt again the exhilaration of flying through the air. At my coach's urging, I'd finally taken the dive up to the three-meter board and succeeded in putting it in. Twice. The third and fourth time I smacked my face and arms. But I'd done it. And I would do it again. She can flip and twist like the Tasmanian Devil, I whispered aloud to no one else in my car. Oh, yes, she can. Okay, maybe like a thirty-eight-year-old Taz Devil, but so what? I pulled up to my house feeling like life couldn't be more wonderful. The boys were with their dad for the weekend after several long good-bye hugs. My muscles felt pleasantly fatigued after two hours of diving. And now I'd change out of my wet swimsuit for dinner and a movie. A date with myself. A great way to end a good, but hectic, week.

I walked down to my mailbox and pulled out a stack of letters. Fanning the envelopes in my tanned hands, I plucked the blue card out first. I didn't recognize the compact handwriting so I turned it over to read the return label. My heart quickened. After all these months I hadn't expect Aunt Lilia to write back.

8 April 2000

Sorry about taking so long to answer your letter. As to your questions about abuse from my mom and dad to your mother, that is completely unfounded—Pops was too gentle a person. He never raised a hand to me. The only times I saw Pops abusive to my mom was after drinking but never to us children. Mom could not even fuss at us around Pops—he was just too sensitive...

I paused, almost laughed at her contradictions.

"Hey, Marie," my neighbor said as he noticed me sitting on the edge of my driveway. "Boys off with their dad this weekend?" He walked across his lawn with gardening shears in one hand and a Frisbee in the other.

"Yep." I set the letter aside and watched him toss the chewed-up blue disc for his dog, Jessie, our street's canine speed bump. "You guys doing basketball this weekend?"

"What else!"

I smiled and then grabbed the letter.

Mom was a "Sargent" but not at all an abusive person. She slapped me once because I talked back and switched my legs because I threw your mother's books outside...

She went on to describe Momma switching Chess for getting into mischief. In retrospect, Lilia said, perhaps Chess should have just been sent to his room. Expectations had been handed down from mother to daughter, for raising perfect children.

...As to your mother's temper, we all lose our temper at times. With nine children besides the ones she lost, that is really something to deal with. Not always did she have a maid. Their early married years were very hard years—not much money. Your grandfather, Big Chester, would not contribute to their support. Mom did as much as she could— took care of Yvette, gave them food all the time. Your dad was never much help with the children. That was the way most men were. I can see if your mother became angry in evenings but I'm sure it was only on occasions...

She doesn't mean to sound cold, I thought, and clearly Momma never confided in her.

...Hope this helps you understand. You asked if your parents were in love. Yes. They adored each other. Your mother at 16 having a child, your dad still young, both immature—starting so young. Your dad grew up with servants doing for him, no family life, no mother at home. Your dad just didn't know about family life. He and your mother had a lot of

growing up to do. They both worked hard and left their children o.k.
financially. I agree their drinking was terrible.
Do your sisters have similar remembrances?
Or have I let my imagination run wild? I waved good-bye to my
neighbor and then took the mail inside. Aunt Lilia's letter would sit on
my desk for weeks because I didn't know how to respond.

I've spent years trying to figure out why my mother was so cruel. Was
it the drinking? Her mental instability? Depression? Some horrible viola-
tion that stole her humanity? To differentiate myself from her, I felt I
needed to know the source of the rage that drove her from room to room,
night after night, to beat her children. Daddy's coldness toward her? The
shame and loneliness of her marriage? Something in her childhood?

Aunt Lilia's letter didn't provide the key to understanding my mother and her rage. Perhaps many small afflictions constantly tortured
Momma. I'll never know.

Like Kyle and me, my parents found each other, two damaged people
searching for someone who spoke a similar language, and someone who
understood the *rules* of warped families. Together they raised children.
They did all they could do, I suppose. But surely within their community there were role models. I find myself constantly watching other parents interact with their children.

At thirty-eight I might be brave enough to spring from a board and
try dives that leave bruises all over my body, but I'm still afraid of dark
rooms, family ghosts, and noises in the hallway. I can fly halfway around
the world alone with my boys, but I can't fall asleep unless I'm lying on
my back and facing the door. Even though I know Momma is dead, part
of me remains vigilant. I startle easily, fly out of my chair at work when
someone enters my office too quietly. I still become overwhelmed and
anxious by some of life's everyday challenges.

Yet I feel fortunate in my sisters and brothers. They helped me make
it. They graced my childhood with laughter and love. They are the concerned voices on the other end of the phone when I call, crying, to ask,
"Do you have a minute?"

For my sons, I want more than what my parents wanted for me. I don't
want my children to be afraid to go to sleep at night or to express their
feelings. Momma decided early on to forsake our love and act out her
own shame and hatred. What incredible strength it took her to frighten
seven girls, two boys, and a husband into submission. I want to focus my
energies into loving my children.

Often, I have stumbled. At least once every few months I am tempted to rage and tear my children's innocence into threads. But I don't. I keep in mind a science experiment I once did with my boys: Cover a mixing bowl with clear plastic wrap and sprinkle salt over the drum. Stand close and scream, and the salt will dance. Stand close, and instead of screaming, sing, and the granules will dance again. Fear or love, that's the choice.

Author's Note

Writing Storkbites began as a cathartic endeavor—I needed a constructive means of dealing with, and diffusing, all the anger, hurt, and confusion that surfaced after my parents' sudden deaths in 1993 and 1994. This, coupled with the stress of my own divorce and the struggles I faced as a single parent, forced me to seek help and solace from many sources: therapists, family, friends, self-help books, and finally, writing. Deconstructing my past and acknowledging the abuse and neglect helped me to gain a better perspective on my current behavior. The result was Storkbites, a book I greatly hoped would help others.

Although I used letters, journals, photographs, and legal documents in writing Storkbites, my memoir is based primarily from memory— mine, and those belonging to my sisters, other family members, and friends. Where there were discrepancies, my memories shaped the story. Recalled conversations are not verbatim transcripts of my life but rather reflect the sentiment of the people involved. In some instances relating to my early childhood, I used facts and treasured family lore as a skeleton on which I fleshed out events I perceived as emotionally true.

Events that I learned of second hand and didn't actually witness, yet placed me in the room, were changed in later editions.

In a few cases, I embellished to create greater drama. At my mother's funeral, for example, where the priest goes on and on about our family's vacation condominium in Gulf Shores, I ratcheted up his ridiculous behavior for literary emphasis. The abuse scenes, however, were at times toned down to the benefit of the abuser, to make her or him appear less of a monster, and to protect the privacy of my siblings and sons.

Names and some personal details, including occupations were changed. Identifying details were purposely blurred to protect the privacy of family and friends. Although the facts were true, I changed the doctors' names to avoid lawsuits. My mother's siblings and their families were condensed into one family. My parents' West Bayou Parkway house was originally an amalgamation of the Woodvale and Oakleaf houses (for no other reason than it just seemed easier). And finally, in some cases, I compressed events.

Marie Etienne
Walnut Creek
September 18, 2007

Born in Louisiana, Marie Etienne currently
lives in Northern California with her two
sons. She is a competitive springboard diver,
a freelance writer, and a member of the
Squaw Valley Community of Writers.